SYNOPSES AND LISTS: TEXTUAL PRACTICES IN THE PRE-MODERN WORLD

Synopses and Lists

Textual Practices in the Pre-Modern World

Edited by
Teresa Bernheimer and Ronny Vollandt

UNIVERSITY OF CAMBRIDGE
Faculty of Asian and Middle Eastern Studies

OpenBook Publishers

https://www.openbookpublishers.com

Any digital material and resources associated with this volume will be available at https://doi.org/10.11647/OBP.0375#resources

Semitic Languages and Cultures 22.

ISSN (print): 2632-6906
ISSN (digital): 2632-6914
ISBN Paperback: 978-1-80511-118-4
ISBN Hardback: 978-1-80064-916-3
ISBN Digital (PDF): 978-1-80511-148-1
DOI: 10.11647/OBP.0375

The Munich Research Centre for Jewish-Arabic Cultures kindly supported the publication of this volume.

Cover image: A fragment of a numbered and tabulated list of 22 biblical and rabbinic passages relating to the Sabbath, each referenced by means of a short lemma (T-S D1.76 from the Cambridge Genizah Collection). Courtesy of the Syndics of Cambridge University Library.
Cover design: Jeevanjot Kaur Nagpal

The fonts used in this volume are Charis SIL, SBL Hebrew, SBL Greek, Scheherazade New, Estrangelo Edessa, and Serto Antioch Bible.

CONTENTS

Contributors.......... viii

Teresa Bernheimer and Ronny Vollandt

Introduction.......... xii

Enrique Jiménez

Quotations from Lexical Lists and Other Texts in Later Mesopotamian Commentaries 1

Lennart Lehmhaus

A Rabbinic Epistemic Genre: Creating Knowledge through Lists and Catalogues.......... 23

Liv Ingeborg Lied

The Unruly Books of Abdisho of Nisibis: Book Lists, Canon Discourse, and the Quest for Lost Writings.......... 62

Peter Tarras

A List in Three Versions: Revisiting al-Kindī's *On Definitions* 104

Matthew P. Monger

A Syriac List of the Names of the Wives of the Patriarchs in BL Add 14620 141

Teresa Bernheimer

Revisiting Lists in Early Islamic Historiography 172

Martin Wallraff

A List in Three Dimensions: The Case of Eusebius's Canon Tables of the Gospels 191

Rebecca Ullrich

Lists of the Songs of Ascents (Pss 120–134) in the Cairo Genizah: Their Form and Its Implications 215

Maroussia Bednarkiewicz

Regularity and Variation in Islamic Chains of Transmission 247

Marilena Maniaci

Chapter Lists in Giant and Beneventan Bibles: Some Preliminary Remarks 282

CONTRIBUTORS

Maroussia Bednarkiewicz is research fellow at the Cluster of Excellence for Machine Learning and the Institute for Oriental Studies at the University of Tübingen. She wrote her Ph.D. dissertation on the early history of the Islamic call to prayer and works currently on the evolution of *ḥadīth* chains of transmission. Her current project aims at developing algorithms for the study of *ḥadīth* and classical Arabic texts.

Teresa Bernheimer (D.Phil Oxford 2007) is postdoctoral fellow at LMU Munich on the project *Beyond Conflict and Coexistence: The Entangled History of Jewish-Arab Relations*, funded by the German Federal Ministry of Education and Research (BMBF). She is a historian of the Middle East with a particular interest in the formation of Islam in the context of late antiquity and beyond, on which she has published several books and articles. From 2019 to 2022, she was spokesperson of the CAS LMU research group *Textual Practices in the Pre-Modern World: Texts and Ideas between Aksum, Constantinople, and Baghdad*, together with Ronny Vollandt.

Enrique Jiménez has held a chair in Ancient Near Eastern Literatures at LMU since 2018 and is the winner of a 2017 Sofja Kovalevskaja Award. He specialises in literature and scholarly texts from ancient Mesopotamia, in particular from the first millennium BCE. He is PI of the *Electronic Babylonian Literature* project (http://www.ebl.lmu.de/).

Lennart Lehmhaus, Ph.D. MLU Halle-Wittenberg, is Akademischer Rat (senior lecturer/assistant professor) at the Institute of Jewish Studies of the University of Tübingen. His research interests include rabbinic literature (Talmud/Midrash), Jews in late antiquity, comparative history of premodern medicine, sciences and knowledge in Judaism and beyond, ethics, literary theory, and diachronic dynamics of religious motifs and concepts.

Liv Ingeborg Lied is Professor of the Study of Religion at MF Norwegian School of Theology, Religion and Society in Oslo, Norway. She is the author of several books and articles. Her most recent monograph is *Invisible Manuscripts: Textual Scholarship and the Survival of 2 Baruch* (Mohr Siebeck, 2021).

Marilena Maniaci serves as Full Professor of Palaeography at the University of Cassino and Southern Lazio. Her research is concentrated on the history of medieval manuscript books and their scientific analysis, incorporating innovative methods and technologies. She has authored five monographs and over 130 articles, while also taking on the role of editor for several essay collections in close conjunction with both Italian and foreign scholars.

Matthew Monger is Associate Professor of Near Eastern Languages and Literatures at MF Norwegian School of Theology, Religion and Society in Oslo, Norway. His research interests are the languages and texts of the Ancient Near East, including Akkadian, Hebrew, Syriac/Aramaic, Ethiopic, and Arabic, and the intersections of texts in these languages. He is currently working on a book that investigates the names given to the wives of the pre-Abrahamic patriarchs in Antiquity and traces their reception history throughout a wide range of texts and manuscripts in Antiquity and the Middle Ages.

Peter Tarras is currently research fellow in the ERC project *MAJLIS* (Ludwig-Maximilians-Universität, Munich). Previously, Peter has worked for the Arabic and Latin Glossary (Julius-Maximilians-Universität, Würzburg). His areas of interest include intellectual history in the Near and Middle East, the Bible in Arabic, book history, manuscript studies, and provenance research. Peter is also interested in the communication of research to a broader audience and has recently launched his own blog, Membra Dispersa Sinaitica, which is dedicated to the the dispersed manuscript heritage of St Catherine's Monastery.

Rebecca Ullrich is postdoctoral research fellow at the Institute for Jewish Studies at the Freie Universität Berlin in the project *Materialized Holiness: Torah scrolls as a codicological, theological, and sociological phenomenon of Jewish scribal culture in the Diaspora.* She received her Magister degree in 2010 with a thesis on the history of Jewish interpretation of the Song of Songs, and her doctorate in 2016 with a dissertation on the Genizah fragments of the She'iltot Rav Aha. Her research interests include rabbinic and geonic literature, late midrashim and the Cairo Genizah.

Ronny Vollandt is Professor of Judaic Studies at Ludwig-Maximilians-Universität in Munich and director of the Munich Research Centre for Jewish-Arabic Cultures (http://www.lmu.de/jewisharabiccultures). Among his main research interests is the intercommunal transmission of knowledge, also the topic of his ERC Consolidator grant *MAJLIS: The Transformation of Jewish Literature in Arabic in the Islamicate World* (2021–2026). From 2019 to 2022, he was spokesperson of the CAS LMU research group *Textual Practices in the Pre-Modern World: Texts and Ideas between Aksum, Constantinople, and Baghdad*, together with Teresa Bernheimer.

Martin Wallraff (Dr. theol. Heidelberg 1997, Habilitation Bonn 2000) is Professor for the History of Ancient and Global Christianity at the Faculty of Protestant Theology of Ludwig-Maximilians-Universität in Munich. He has published widely on the transmission and canonisation of biblical texts, and in 2014 received an ERC Advanced Grant for the project *Paratexts of the Bible: Analysis and Edition of the Greek Textual Transmission*. His most recent monograph is *Die Kanontafeln des Euseb von Kaisareia: Untersuchung und kritische Edition* (de Gruyter, 2021).

INTRODUCTION
TEXTUAL PRACTICES: SYNOPSES AND LISTS[1]

Teresa Bernheimer and Ronny Vollandt

"In the beginning, there was the list," or so one might start a history of human writing. Lists are among the earliest written records; they are also among the earliest forms of scholarship. While a list may be defined as an enumeration of items, be they ideas, people, events, or terms, a synopsis is a particular kind of list, "a list in more than one dimension," as Martin Wallraff puts it in his contribution to this volume. To understand how lists and synopses were planned, produced, and consumed is to gain insight into the practices of what one might call the 'management of knowledge' in a time before our own. Lists and synopses entail

[1] We would like to thank the Center for Advanced Studies (CAS) at Ludwig-Maximilians-Universität Munich, particularly Managing Director Annette Mayer and Academic Coordinator Julia Schreiner, for providing the framework and financial support for our research focus *Textual Practices in the Pre-Modern World: Texts and Ideas between Aksum, Constantinople, and Baghdad*, which allowed us to organise a number of exciting interdisciplinary meetings, among them the workshops that led to this volume.

a variety of textual practices to allow storing, retrieving, selecting, and organising knowledge. Both make deliberate—yet not always explicit—choices as to what is included and excluded, thereby creating lasting hierarchies and canons.

The present volume is the product of two workshops on 'Synopses and Lists', held in 2019 and 2021 as part of the research focus 'Textual Practices in the Pre-Modern World: Texts and Ideas between Aksum, Constantinople and Baghdad', which was generously supported and funded by the Centre for Advanced Study (CAS) at Ludwig-Maximilians-Universität (LMU) Munich. The research focus examined the textual practices among the great intellectual traditions in pre-modern times: the ancient Near East, ancient philosophy, and the three monotheist religions Judaism, Christianity, and Islam. Aiming to understand how lists and synopses function in different types of literature, the workshops particularly looked to offer a historical and transcultural perspective, highlighting the centrality of lists and synopses as textual practice, that is, as a form of textual communication that is integral to scholarly writing.

The theoretical literature on lists has substantially grown in recent years. Two collected volumes should be particularly highlighted, as they offer a substantial bibliography and state-of-the-art discussion of list theory: *Forms of List-Making: Epistemic, Literary, and Visual Enumeration* and *Le pouvoir des listes au Moyen Âge*.[2] Lists, as the latter title states, play an important role in

---

[2] Barton et al., *Epistemic, Literary, and Visual Enumeration*; Anheim, *Le pouvoir des listes au Moyen Âge*.

knowledge-making, and thus in the creation of power structures; this aspect was already remarked upon in Jack Goody's chapter on lists in his seminal *The Domestication of the Savage Mind*, which has also formed a common background for the discussions in this volume.[3] Goody identified three kinds of lists that remain helpful in the broad categorisation (listing) of the subject: the inventory, a retrospective list that sorts and stores data; the shopping list, essentially a guide for future action, a plan, from which items can be struck off; and the lexical list, a proto-dictionary that is particularly prominent among early Mesopotamian writings. As Enrique Jiménez shows in his contribution to this volume, lexical lists underlie other early literary genres "at the genesis of writing." What all lists have in common is their emphasis on ordering, a sorting of items or ideas when speech is committed to writing.

So far, the emphasis of list studies has been on Western cultures. Thus, Umberto Eco's rich and inspirational *Il vertigine della lista* offers a discussion of a vast range of lists, from textual to visual and musical—though exclusively drawn from Western culture.[4] In his analysis, Eco suggests that lists are more than simple arrangements of items. They are a rhetorical device used to amplify a message, select and shape information, and create aesthetic appeal. Lists are "the origin of culture," our attempt to "make infinity comprehensible."[5]

The present volume aims to broaden the perspective by focusing on textual traditions from the eastern Mediterranean,

---

[3] Goody, *Savage Mind*, 80.

[4] Eco, *Il vertigine della lista*.

[5] Eco in Beyer and Gorris, 'Interview with Umberto Eco'.

where Eco's distinction between "practical" and "poetical" lists equally applies. In the present volume, however, the focus on the East is not exclusive, as we hope to emphasise a transcultural perspective and the universality of list-making as a textual practice among the great intellectual traditions of the pre-modern world. The common denominator as regards definition has been Robert Belknap's formulation of the term 'list' as "a formally organised block of information that is composed of a set of members."[6] Belknap argues that lists are not mere collections of items but rather a literary device with profound meaning. He suggests that lists serve as a tool for organising thoughts, ideas, and experiences, providing a sense of order and coherence; they have aesthetic, cognitive, and symbolic significance that contributes to the overall meaning and impact of a text. In this volume, Belknap's definition provides a starting point for the more specialised discussions that each context requires. Indeed, each of the 10 chapters begins with a brief review of lists and contextualisation as pertinent to the respective topic.

The volume opens with the contribution by Enrique Jiménez on 'Quotations from Lexical Lists and Other Texts in Later Mesopotamian Commentaries'. As Jiménez shows, lists represent the oldest, and most pervasive, scholarly genre in ancient Mesopotamia. Cuneiform commentaries, first attested in the first millennium BCE, can be regarded as a genre derived from lexical lists. Jiménez's paper studies the ways in which lexical lists are

---

[6] Belknap, *The List*, 15.

cited in commentaries, and compares them with quotations from texts other than lexical lists.

Lists in different genres are also the focus of Lennart Lehmhaus's contribution, 'A Rabbinic Epistemic Genre: Creating Knowledge through Lists and Catalogues'. Lehmhaus focuses on the variegated forms and functions of lists as adaptable containers as reflected in the practice of list-making in Jewish textual traditions from late antiquity, commonly known as rabbinic or talmudic literature. As he shows, rabbinic works deploy lists for different discursive purposes—exegetical, homiletical, narrative—embedded in their ancient Near Eastern surroundings and based on a long tradition derived from biblical and other ancient Jewish traditions. After a survey of the history of ancient Jewish lists, their broader cultural entanglements, and pertinent scholarship, Lehmhaus discusses some theoretical approaches to the literary and epistemological features of lists within three main frameworks: information, instruction, and enquiry. Lehmhaus argues that rabbinic texts deploy the versatility or affordance of the list not only for ordering knowledge, but also for the very process of knowledge, turning them into a powerful 'epistemic genre'. Consequently, lists do not serve as mere containers for knowledge that circulated apart from their usage. In fact, the rabbinic authors may have arrived at certain conclusions precisely in and through lists in which specific concepts or taxonomies were tried out before becoming more manifest or substantiated. This main argument is exemplified by focusing on complex types of list in two tractates of the Babylonian Talmud, which can be described as clusters, sequences, or, most compellingly, as catalogues.

A catalogue as a list, more precisely a book list, is also the focus of Liv Ingeborg Lied's 'The Unruly Books of Abdisho of Nisibis: Book Lists, Canon Discourse, and the Quest for Lost Writings'. Lied critically engages scholarship on the list of Old Testament books in Abdisho of Nisibis's (d. 1318) Syriac *Catalogue of the Books of the Church*. Focusing on the trajectories in scholarship that have focused on the Christian biblical canon and the lost books of early Judaism, the essay explores the entries that have proven challenging to this scholarship. The unruly entries of Abdisho's list fall into three categories: writings that are only known by title and which do not survive as extant and available texts, writings known by multiple titles, and entries that do not comply with the scholarly imagination of an Old Testament book. A new look at the epistemological and ontological status of these categories of entries provides a correction to the treatment of book lists by modern and contemporary scholars and a new appreciation of the many ways of knowing (about) books in a manuscript culture.

The contribution by Peter Tarras, 'A List in Three Versions: Revisiting al-Kindī's *On Definitions*', draws attention to the transmission process in the study of lists. Tarras examines a definition list in the Arabic philosophical tradition, a well-known text commonly attributed to the 'philosopher of the Arabs' al-Kindī (d. after 252/866). The study of this list, thought to stand at the beginning of the career of this literary format in that tradition, offers insights into the way in which Arabic philosophy emerged in the early Abbasid caliphate. However, the manuscripts that transmit it witness three divergent versions. Further, each version testifies not to a well-ordered text, but to a more or less loose assemblage of technical terms harvested from philosophy and related fields. This raises a number of questions as to the structure, function, and use of this text. This study attempts to show that these questions can be addressed fruitfully once we attend to the stratified compositional process from which the three versions of this text must have emerged. Its manuscript witnesses represent the latest stage in this process. After a brief survey of previous scholarship, the study thus begins with a review of the manuscript evidence, in order to make observations as to the text's codicological settings and paratextual features. It proceeds with an analysis of its different structural levels. The conclusion that can be drawn from this enquiry is that this definition list has not reached us as one unified literary entity, but in the form of three distinct historical artefacts, which owe themselves to the sum of the intentions of their users/producers.

Transmission is also a central theme in Matthew P. Monger's contribution. 'A Syriac List of the Names of the Wives of the Patriarchs in BL Add 14620' looks at the way in which scribal activity played a role in the transmission of lists as individual units—free from the work from which the knowledge was extracted. By viewing the list as its own composition, the function and transmission of the list become clearer. As the list is viewed as a work in its own right, the way in which the scribe interacted with the base text helps allows us to analyse the specific context in which the current list was produced. As Monger shows, the book of Genesis systematically omits the names of the women in the generations between Adam and Eve and Abraham and Sarah, but two different works from antiquity gave names to the women of each of these generations: Jubilees and the Cave of Treasures. The names of the wives of the patriarchs were then extracted and circulated in a number of different historical, linguistic, and manuscript contexts throughout antiquity and the Middle Ages, including in list form. The chapter provides an analysis of a Syriac list of the names of the wives of the patriarchs previously not discussed in scholarship, found in London, British Library Additional Manuscript 14620, fol. 30, and argues that the list in that manuscript is based on a list of the names of the wives of the patriarchs from the Jubilees tradition but supplemented at several points with knowledge that must ultimately come from the Cave of Treasures, making the list especially interesting in discussions of the transmission of the names.

The chapter by Teresa Bernheimer, 'Revisiting Lists in Early Islamic Historiography', examines lists as a crucial part of early Islamic historiography: lists provide the broad frameworks of organisation of the sources, and are ubiquitous in their content. As Bernheimer shows, lists in early Islamic historical works are not simply enumerations of people, events, or tax payments, but an important narrative strategy in the overall historiographic project of early Islam. Understanding lists as textual practice highlights their importance in the forging of a new cultural narrative and memory of early Islam, and emphasises their function as a principal scholarly form in historical writing.

Martin Wallraff's 'A List in Three Dimensions: The Case of Eusebius's Canon Tables of the Gospels' highlights the potential complexity of lists in ancient book culture. The canon tables of the gospels, composed by Eusebius of Caesarea in the first half of the fourth century, are a new form of synopsis: a list in three dimensions which uses both the extension (length and breadth) of a page in a codex, and the hypertextuality within the codex (intratextual references back and forth). In the antique culture of the book, this system raises the list to a new level of complexity. Given the extraordinary success of the device, to which many hundreds of extant copies in numerous languages attest, the impact on viewing habits and textual practices was enormous.

List documents of a very different kind are the subject of the contribution by Rebecca Ullrich, 'Lists of the Songs of Ascents (Pss 120–134) in the Cairo Genizah: Their Form and its Implications'. In the Cairo Genizah there are fragments containing lists of Psalms 120–34, the Songs of Ascents. All of them can be dated to the period from the tenth to the thirteenth century in Fustat. Given that these lists are single pieces in the Cairo Genizah, they have to be analysed without their specific context. Ullrich provides an introduction to list documents in the Cairo Genizah, noting that the most noticeable common feature of the lists examined is their small size. In addition, shorthand is used in all the fragments. Sometimes the place of the psalm in the prayer can be deduced from other entries. In some of them, the psalms were written on the back of the fragment, which suggests a secondary use of the paper. As a conclusion, Ullrich suggests that these lists were probably used in a private liturgical context and may have served as memory aids in prayer.

The possibilities of a rethinking of well-known lists when seen through the lens of other fields is exemplified in the contribution of Maroussia Bednarkiewicz, 'Regularity and Variation in Islamic Chains of Transmission'. Bednarkiewicz examines the *isnād*, a list of narrators' names which precedes an account about Islam's prophet or his companions, and indicates its origin. The content and the form of this list have been studied in different fields. Islamicists have scrutinised the names contained in the *isnād* in order to assess the authenticity of the following account and uncover potential fraudsters. Computer scientists, in turn, have focused on form: they attempted to exploit the regular succession of names and transmission terms to develop algorithms capable of distinguishing *isnād* from non-*isnād* texts. In her contribution, Bednarkiewicz opens a novel horizon and analyses the structural variations of the *isnād* within the old and universal context of list-making. A twofold methodology, combining traditional and computational text analysis, allows her to characterise the actual contours of the *isnād* in a large corpus of texts and propose a hierarchy of functions linked to the different variations observed.

The final contribution, 'Chapter Lists in Giant and Beneventan Bibles: Some Preliminary Remarks' by Marilena Maniaci, examines the so-called *capitula*, or chapter lists, that introduce the individual biblical books in the majority of Latin Bibles, particularly prior to the thirteenth century, when the 'Paris Bible' made its appearance and brought with it a new chapter subdivision of the biblical text. The Latin *capitula* briefly summarise, chapter by chapter, the contents of each section of the biblical text, or reproduce the words or the section's initial sentence. Several sequences or 'families' of lists are attested, which differ (even significantly) in the number, extension, and wording of the individual *tituli*, but also in the way they are arranged on the manuscript page and distinguished from the main text. The existence of different sets of lists for the same book, the textual instability of the individual chapter titles (*tituli*) and of their succession, even within the same set, and the not always linear relationship with the corresponding biblical text induce one to wonder about the chapters' functions and the exact meaning of their extensive—although not universal—presence among the paratexts of the Latin Bible between antiquity and the end of the monastic era. Maniaci's contribution, which is a prelude to a much wider study, aims to provide some examples of the potential interest of an in-depth analysis of the chapters, not only as a tool to highlight relationships between individual codices or operate groupings within specific strands of textual tradition, but also to deepen our knowledge of the practices of manufacture and transcription of the biblical text and of its accompanying paratexts.

QUOTATIONS FROM LEXICAL LISTS AND OTHER TEXTS IN LATER MESOPOTAMIAN COMMENTARIES

Enrique Jiménez

It is difficult to overstate the importance of lists in ancient Mesopotamian culture. Two genres are attested at the dawn of history, when writing was first invented:[1] administrative lists and lexical lists.[2] Lists constitute, therefore, the earliest scholarly genre in ancient Mesopotamia, and thus probably the oldest scholarly texts in world literature. It is remarkable, and unparalleled in other traditions, that the first written testimonies of a language are lexicographical treatises:[3] the complexities of a budding writing system, and the necessity to account for all its possible uses,

[1] In the so-called late Uruk period, ca 3200 BCE.

[2] According to the figures provided by Veldhuis, *Cuneiform Lexical Tradition*, 29, administrative documents constitute approximately 90 percent of all tablets and fragments from the Uruk IV and Uruk III periods; the rest (around 10 percent) are lexical lists.

[3] As van de Mieroop, *Philosophy before the Greeks*, 36–37, puts it: "Remarkably, the first works of Babylonian scholarship and thus the earliest in world history are lexicographic, that is, they are word lists. I use 'remarkably' because the extraordinary character of these works seems

 https://doi.org/10.11647/OBP.0375.01

explain the importance of the genre at the genesis of writing.[4] The role played by lists in the conception, standardisation, development, and dissemination of the cuneiform script conferred them a distinguished place in Mesopotamian written culture: in the more than three millennia of history of ancient Mesopotamian civilisations, from the invention of writing to the demise of cuneiform script around the turn of the eras, lexical lists of various types constituted the most important assignment given to scribal apprentices. One of the latest products of cuneiform culture, the so-called Graeco-Babyloniaca, contain chiefly excerpts

to be ignored not only by scholars surveying the world history of lexicography, but also by those specialists of Babylonian scholarship who have devoted much effort to the study of lexical lists. No other ancient culture developed lexicography at the moment its people started to write, and throughout antiquity lexicographic activity outside Babylonia always remained minimal."

[4] Veldhuis, *Cuneiform Lexical Tradition*, 28, notes: "We have to leave behind any implicit assumption that once you have a writing system you may use it for anything that involves language. We cannot expect any scribe to cross that bridge from pure accounting to using this symbolic system for something entirely different—not more than we expect anybody to use a cash register for writing poetry or for anything else than ringing up our groceries. The lexical lists, however, as haphazard and difficult to understand as they are, do cross that bridge and do use the symbols of writing as something that one can play with, that one can put to unexpected uses.... The lists are the first instances of the non-administrative uses of writing and as such demonstrate the flexibility and the potential of the system."

from lexical lists, some of them venerably old, written in cuneiform script on one side and in Greek transliteration on the other.[5]

Cuneiform commentaries, a genre first attested in the first millennium BCE, can be regarded as a product derived from the basic form of the lexical list. This genealogy is evident, in particular, in the fact that quotations from lexical lists constitute the foundation on which most commentaries are based. The goal of this paper is to study these quotations, and to compare them with quotations from texts other than lexical lists, in order to determine the degree of dependency of commentaries with the genre from which they derive.

1.0. The List Format and the List Science

The ubiquity of lexical lists in the cuneiform tradition decisively shaped Mesopotamian literature throughout its long history: the list became the default format of scientific texts in ancient Mesopotamia,[6] and genres such as divination treatises and law compilations can be seen as an expansion of the basic format of lexical lists. The list, with its typical laconism, became the vehicle for

---

[5] Proposals for the dating of the Graeco-Babyloniaca range from the second century BCE to the second century CE; see Oelsner, 'Überlegungen zu den "Graeco-Babyloniaca"', 150, with previous bibliography. On the Graeco-Babyloniaca in general, see Geller, 'The Last Wedge'; Westenholz, 'Graeco-Babyloniaca Once Again'.

[6] As perhaps first observed by Oppenheim, 'Zur keilschriftlichen Omenliteratur', 200: "[D]ie listenweise Zusammenstellung ist die charakteristische Darstellungsform wissenschaftlicher Arbeiten im keilschriftlichen Schrifttum."

grammatical and theological elucubrations. For instance, a famous list from the first millennium BCE equates the Babylonian Marduk with other gods of the Babylonian pantheon, in an apparent monotheistic move: each major god of the pantheon (in the first column) is said to be Marduk (in the second column) in a specific capacity (in the third column)—thus, Ninurta, a god traditionally related to agriculture, is Marduk of the pickaxe; Nergal, a warrior god, is Marduk of battle:

(1) BM 47406[7]

Ninurta	*Marduk*	*ša alli*
Nergal	*Marduk*	*ša qabli*
'Ninurta	Marduk	of the pickaxe
Nergal	Marduk	of battle'

Figure 1: BM 47406 (drawing from King, *Cuneiform Texts*, pl. 50.)

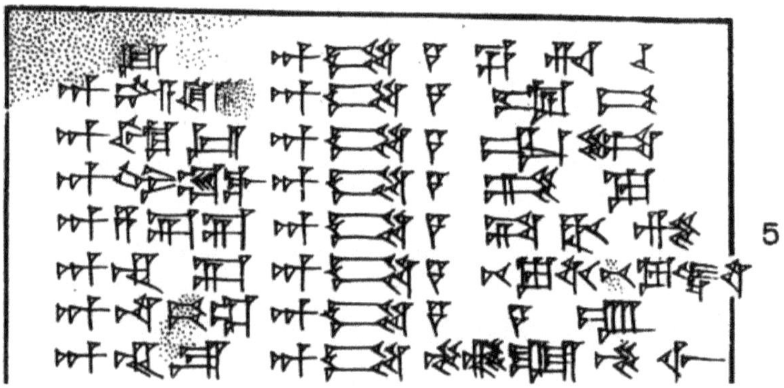

This monotheistic agenda was by no means the predominant one in the Mesopotamia of the first millennium BCE, but rather a mar-

[7] King, *Cuneiform Texts*, 24, pl. 50. Edition in Lambert, *Babylonian Creation Myths*, 264.

ginal view that only rarely surfaces in our written documentation.[9] The list must therefore reflect the theological elucubrations of an individual or a small community, yet these elucubrations are only given in the contrived, succinct style of a list. General principles ('all the gods are aspects of Marduk in a specific capacity') are typically never formulated in Mesopotamian scholarship: instead, the results of these principles are given ad nauseam. The absence of general principles was once seen as a major weakness in Mesopotamia scholarship, reflecting the incapacity of the Mesopotamians to think abstractly (their *Listenwissenschaft*)[10] and, therefore, the inferiority of their cultural products to those of

---

[9] As noted by Lambert, 'Babylonien und Israel', 78, "ein derartiger Monotheismus [war] im alten Mesopotamien eher ein Zeichen von religiöser Bigotterie und Fanatismus als von Aufgeklärtheit." On the marginality of monotheistic ideas in first-millennium Mesopotamia, see Lambert, 'Historical Development', 198; Lambert, 'Ancient Mesopo-tamian Gods', 121; Lambert, Babylonian Creation Myths, 265; Fadhil and Jiménez, 'Syncretistic Hymn to Marduk'.

[10] The expression was coined by von Soden, 'Leistung und Grenze', who states (p. 431) that the absence of general principles reflects the absence of abstract thinking: "Das zur genauen Beschreibung grammatischer Tatsachen und zur Aufstellung grammatischer Regeln notwendige Abstraktionsvermögen fehlte den Akkadern gänzlich; infolgedessen mangelte es auch in ihrer Sprache an Ausdrucksmöglichkeiten für grammatische Formulierungen in ganzen Sätzen." On the concept of 'Listenwissenschaft'—which Hilgert, 'Von "Listenwissenschaft" und "epistemischen" Dingen', 278, notes is one of the few neologisms coined by Assyriology that has found echo in other fields in the humanities—see, in addition to Hilgert, Visi, 'A Science of Lists?', 12–17; Veldhuis, *Cuneiform Lexical Tradition*, 19–23; Young, *List Cultures*, 27–30.

Western scholarship. As modern research sees the question, it is obvious that sophisticated general principles underlie lists such as the monotheistic Marduk list; the fact that these principles are not formulated is, therefore, just a matter of convention, a consequence of the prestige of the list format in ancient Mesopotamia.[11]

The prestige of the lexical tradition is perhaps best perceived through the uses that texts from other genres made of it. Numerous literary texts used lexical lists as a mine for rare words, unusual meanings, and recherché synonyms. As the "fullest repositories of a world viewed through the gauze of writing,"[12] lists provided readily accessible, well-arranged material suited to the needs of the Mesopotamian scribes. In particular, the heightened language of royal inscriptions is often peppered with rare words excerpted from lexical compilations. In the following example, from an inscription of King Sargon II of Assyria (721–705 BCE), the scribe has managed to use three extremely rare words to replace the nouns 'east', 'Šamaš' (the sun god), and 'Adad' (the storm god):

(2) Sargon II no. 43 ii 53[13]

mehret PÌRIG ŠU.DU$_7$ *ana* ^{d}SIG$_5$.GA *u* ^{d}LUGAL.DINGIR.RA (…) *talīmānī ina tēmīqi ušaqqī-ma*

---

[11] See, e.g., Machinist, 'Self-Consciousness in Mesopotamia', 200: "lack of explicitness in itself is not a method of thinking, but a mode of expression." See also Veldhuis, 'TIN.TIR = Babylon', 50.

[12] Michalowski, 'Negation as Description', 134.

[13] Frame, *Royal Inscriptions*, 229. The interpretation is due to Cavigneaux, 'Une crux sargonica'.

'Facing "east" (lit. "the perfect lion," PÌRIG ŠU.DU$_7$) I raised my two hands in prayer to "Šamaš" (lit. "the good god," ^{d}SIG$_5$.GA) and "Adad" (lit. "the king of the god(s)," ^{d}LUGAL.DINGIR.RA)'[14]

The first of these words translates literally as 'perfect lion'; its meaning 'east' is attested only in lexical lists, where it first appears in the archaic period and is transmitted throughout the entire cuneiform tradition, until Sargon II's scribe picks it up and uses it for the first time, hundreds of years after its incorporation into lexicography. The scribes of Sargon II were particularly fond of lexical *rarae aves*,[15] and found in the tradition of the lists a fertile ground for their poetic musings.

Lexical rarities were, however, also borrowed in the opposite direction: literary texts were excerpted by lexicographers, and the explanations they added entered the lexical tradition and were transmitted from generation to generation. For instance, a hymn to Marduk that was particularly popular in elementary education contains, towards its beginning, the hapax legomenon *abūšin*:

(3) 'Marduk 1' ll. 5, 7[16]

ša amāruk šibbu gapuš abūšin

---

[14] Throughout the translations in this chapter, elements in parentheses indicate authorial additions.

[15] For other quotations from lexical lists in inscriptions of Sargon II, see Hrůša, 'Die akkadische Synonymenliste malku = šarru', 17.

[16] Fadhil and Jiménez, 'Two Babylonian Classics', 167.

'(Marduk), you whose stare is a dragon, an overwhelming *abūšin*'

The word *abūšin* may have originated as a corruption of 'your strength' *vel sim.*,[17] although this is far from certain. Be that as it may, it is known in the lexical tradition already in around the thirteenth century BCE; that is, only a few centuries after the composition of the hymn that contains it. In the first millennium BCE, two different lexical lists explain that *abūšin* means *abūbu* 'flood'[18]—an ad hoc explanation that more or less works in the context of the hymn, but which appears to be incompatible with the rules of Akkadian morphology.[19] A rare word from a literary text, excerpted into a lexical list, was thenceforth transmitted within the lexical tradition.

On some occasions, lexicographers excerpted entire texts or sections thereof, and produced exegetical treatises that dealt with one specific text only. This practice is already attested in the first quarter of the second millennium BCE:[20] some lists from this period contain lemmata that come from specific sections of discrete texts with no extraneous material. These sorts of lists, however,

---

[17] This is the belief of Lambert, 'Notes on malku = šarru'.

[18] Jiménez, *Literary Texts*, no. 19.

[19] No other substantive ending in *-šin*, *-sin*, or *-šim* is known in Akkadian (all three endings are attested for *abūšin* in the manuscripts of the hymn and in the lexical tradition).

[20] For some cases, see Civil, 'Mesopotamian Lexical Lists'.

remained something of a rarity throughout the second millennium BCE;[21] the most common forms of citation from a literary text in a lexical list were glosses to individual entries integrated into larger lexical lists, such as the *abūšin* entry examined above. However, towards the end of the second or the beginning of the first millennium BCE this form of bespoke exegesis became exceedingly popular, and evolved into the genre known as Mesopotamian commentaries.

2.0. List and Commentaries

Mesopotamian commentaries represent the world's earliest cohesive group of exegetical texts. There are some 900 of them, the earliest dating to the eighth century, the latest to around 100 BCE.[22] The main difference between commentaries and lexical lists is that commentaries have an identifiable base text, which they seek to explain. Lexical lists, on the other hand, may

---

[21] In addition to the cases studied in Civil, 'Mesopotamian Lexical Lists', one may note the almost verbatim quotation of the list of weapons from *Gilgameš* in a small bilingual fragment from Emar, Msk.74166b; see Arnaud, *Recherches au pays d'Aštata*, 576. This was first noted by George, *Babylonian Gilgamesh Epic*, 813; see also Jiménez, 'La imagen de los vientos', 227–30.

[22] For an excellent description of the cuneiform commentaries, see Frahm, *Commentaries*. The Cuneiform Commentaries Project (CCP; https://ccp.yale.edu/) provides an introduction to the genre and annotated editions of a large selection of them. Almost all commentaries cited in this chapter are available on the CCP platform under the corresponding CCP number (e.g., CCP 3.7.2.J is found at https://ccp.yale.edu/3.7.2.J).

contain words excerpted from specific texts, such as *abūšin*, but they are not geared towards one text only. In commentaries, the base text is often first cited, and then explained.[23] The origin of Mesopotamian commentaries in lexical lists is perceivable, in particular, in their laconism: words and phrases are simply juxtaposed, separated by a colon (:), but hardly ever is the connection between the two words explained.[24] The majority of Mesopotamian commentaries (ca 70 percent), and almost every commentary cited in this paper, are devoted to the explication of the rich corpus of divination literature.

Some Mesopotamian commentaries are thus, essentially, small lexical lists, but compiled on the basis of one text only. For instance, the following commentary excerpts some lemmata from several chapters of its base text, the physiognomic collection known as *Alamdimmû*. In the commentary, written in a tabular format,[25] each line explains a specific lemma of the text (on the left-hand column in bold) with a one-word explanation (on the right-hand column). The lemmata are either logograms (i.e., Sumerian words used to represent Akkadian words, in small caps) or rare Akkadian words explained by means of more common

---

[23] Quotations from the base text are marked in bold type in the transliterations below.

[24] In the translations below, this connection is made explicit by means of words added in parentheses.

[25] Commentaries in the tabular format are sometimes called by their rubrics *ṣâtu*, as in the present case. The term *ṣâtu* is, however, used as a rubric also for commentaries with other formats, as discussed by Frahm, *Commentaries*, 55.

terms (in italics). Each short section deals with a specific chapter of the collection *Alamdimmû*, and the title of that chapter is given as a short rubric at the end of the section:

(4) BM 38788 obv. 2–10 (CCP 3.7.2.J)

(2) **SAG.HA.MA.AL**	*šar-hu*
(3) ***ku-um-mu-su***	*ra-áš-bi*
(4) **UMBIN BABBAR**	*na-ba-li*
(5) **UMBIN GE$_6$**	*ku-ra-ru*
(6) *ṣa-a-tú u šu-ut pi-i šá*	GÚ GÍD.DA
(7) **HÁŠ**	*em-šu*
(8) **HÁŠ**	*šap-ri*
(9) **ŠÀ.⸢MAH⸣**	*kar-šú*
(10) *ṣa-a-tú u ⸢šu⸣-ut pi-i šá*	GABA DAGAL.AŠ

(2) '*sag.ha.ma.al* (means) "proud"'
(3) '"fearsome" (means) "terrifying"'
(4) '*umbin babbar* (means) "*namālu*-disease"'
(5) '*umbin ge*$_6$ (means) "*kurāru*-disease"'

(6) Lemmata and oral explanations relating to 'If (his) neck is long' (= *Alamdimmû* IX)

(7) '*háš* (means) "abdomen"'
(8) '*háš* (means) "thigh"'
(9) '*šà.mah* (means) "stomach"'

(10) Lemmata and oral explanations relating to 'If (his) chest is wide' (= *Alamdimmû* X)

Some commentaries, such as this one, have all the appearance of being just another lexical list. Some were, in fact, perceived as just another lexical list: for instance, an excerpt from a commentary in tabular format was copied by a student on an elementary school tablet. Elementary education was primarily concerned with the memorisation of the traditional lexical lists, and commentaries played no role in it, as far as we can ascertain from the surviving school exercises. The commentary excerpted on the school tablet is similar to the one cited above, in that it comments on a large collection of omens, and is divided into sections corresponding to the chapters of the base text. It has, however, a much larger scale: it contains more than 550 entries. Its tabular format and large size confers it the appearance of a lexical list, which in turn granted it access to the category of school text, as if it were another lexical list.[26]

The fact that tabular commentaries look like lexical lists is hardly surprising: as heirs to the venerable Mesopotamian lexical tradition, commentaries are bound to reflect its conventions, most importantly its tabular format. Moreover, many of the entries that appear in tabular commentaries represent in fact quotations from lexical lists. For instance, the entry '*háš* (means) "abdomen"' in the text above is known from several of the most important traditional lexical lists.[27] The ways in which commentaries cite lexical lists—their ancestors, so to say—is particularly

---

[26] The commentary referred to here is the so-called 'Principal Commentary' on the collection of teratological omens known as *Šumma Izbu*; the school tablet that excerpts it is VAT 10071 (BWL pl. 73 = CCP 3.6.1.A.l). As noted by Frahm, *Commentaries*, 206: "Commentaries normally played no role in elementary education, and it is likely that the 'Principal Commentary' owes its exceptional inclusion in [VAT 10071] to the fact that it could be used as a lexical list in its own right."

[27] See the references in Oppenheim et al., *Assyrian Dictionary*, E 153b.

interesting for the study of the ancient Mesopotamians' reception of their own lexical tradition.

3.0. Lists Cited in Commentaries

Few commentaries cite lexical lists explicitly, i.e., the quotation is only rarely followed by a reference to its source. A few commentaries, however, refer to their source using the terms *ṣâtu*, literally 'excerpts', and *lišānu*, literally 'tongue'. As noted by E. Frahm, these terms refer probably to "bilingual lexical lists" and "monolingual lexical lists" respectively.[28] Other commentaries quote the title from the list they cite: this is the case in the following example, in which the lexical list titled 'Erimhuš' is cited (underlined) in support of an interpretation of the relatively rare verb *šarāru* 'to advance' as 'to run':

(5) IM 74410 (W 22312a) r 22–23[29]

> (22) ***i-šar-ru-*[*ur* :]** *i-la-as-su-um* : sag-gíd-i : sag-gíd-gíd-i : *ša-ra-ra* (23) *ši-t[a]r-ru-ru* *ina libbi*(ŠÀ) *erim*-huš** : sag : *a-ri* : *a-la-ku* : gíd : *šá-ra-ra* : *šá a-la-ku*
>
> '"He advances" (means) "he runs," (because) "*saggidi, saggidgidi* (means) 'to advance' (and) 'constantly to advance'," (it is said) in the (lexical series called) "Erimhuš," (the word *saggidi* can be analysed as) *sag*, (which means) "to progress," (in the sense of) "to walk," (and) *gid*, (which means) "to advance," (said) of "to walk."'

---

[28] Frahm, *Commentaries*, 89–90.

[29] Hunger, *Uruk* (SpTU 1), 83 (collated). For another edition, see Böck, *Die babylonisch-assyrische Morphoskopie*, 254–56.

The commentary first provides the explanation for a difficult verb in the base text: 'he advances' (*išarrur*), it states, means 'he runs' (*ilassum*). Then it proceeds to justify the explanation; the justification is based on a quotation from a lexical list, in which the verb *šarāru* and its form *šitarruru* are equated with the Sumerian words *saggidi* and *saggidgidi*. This quotation is stated to come from the lexical list 'Erimhuš'. Then the Sumerian verb is taken apart into its two constituents, which are explained individually: *sag* means 'to progress', in its meaning 'to walk', and *gid* means 'to advance', in its meaning 'to walk'. Both components of the Sumerian word, therefore, can be explained by means of verbs that mean 'to walk', whence the first connection offered ('"he advances" (means) "he runs"') is justified.

The passage from the lexical list 'Erimhuš' quoted in the commentary reads:

(6) 'Erimhuš' II 88–89[30]

sag-gíd-i	*ša-ra-ra*
sag-gíd-gíd-i	*ši-t[a]r-ru-ru*

The commentary, therefore, cites the lexical list 'in vertical', that is, first the entire left column and then the entire right column.[31] Other commentaries, such as the one excerpted in (7) below, cite them instead 'horizontally', that is, each Sumerian entry with its corresponding Akkadian explanation.

---

[30] Cavigneaux et al., *Series Erim-huš = anantu*, 31.

[31] 'Vertical' quotations are particularly common in quotations from the series 'Erimhuš'. See Frahm, *Commentaries*, 88–89 and 91n456; and Boddy, *Erimhuš*, 26–31.

The commentary cited above states the source of its quotation, but more frequently quotations are given without any indication of the source. This is the case of an interesting entry in a commentary on a chapter of the omen collection *Šumma Ālu*. According to the omen explained in the commentary, a pig repeatedly opening its mouth in front of a man foretells the infidelity of that man's wife. Commentaries on divination texts often attempt to connect the protasis with the apodosis of an omen, frequently on the basis of abstruse, extremely contrived equivalences. In this case, the commentary shows that the Akkadian word for mouth, *pû* (from 'the pig's mouth'), is equated in a lexical list with the Sumerian word múrub, which in the same list is also explained as Akkadian 'buttocks' and 'vagina'. The obvious implication is that a woman will open her genitalia in the same way that a pig opens its mouth, which justifies the connection between protasis and apodosis:

(7) DT 37 obv. 16b–18[32]

> (16b) *šumma*(DIŠ) *šahû*(ŠAH) *ana pān*(IGI) *amēli*(NA) (17) *pâ*(⌜KA⌝)-⌜*šú*⌝ *iptette*(⌜BAD*.BAD*⌝-*te*) *aššat*(DAM) *amēli*(LÚ) *it-ta-na-a-a-ak* : MÚRUB$^{mu\text{-}ru\text{-}ub}$ *pu-ú* : MÚRUB : *šu-uh-hu* (18) ⌜MÚRUB⌝ : *ú-ri šá sinništi*(MUNUS)
>
> '"If a pig repeatedly opens its mouth in front of a man, the man's wife will repeatedly have (illicit) sex" (= *Šumma Ālu* 49–34′): MÚRUB, (to be read as) *murub*, (means) "mouth," MÚRUB (means) "buttocks," (and) MÚRUB (means) "vagina."'

---

32 King, *Cuneiform Texts*, 41, 30–31; CCP 3.5.49.

The line in the commentary cites three entries of the lexical list titled 'Ura' in 'horizontal'. The entries can be found in the following passage from 'Ura':

(8) 'Ura' XV 21–24d[33]

^{uzu}ka	*pu-ú*	'mouth'
^{uzu}múrub	MIN (= *pu-ú*)	'ditto' (scil. 'mouth')
^{uzu}únu	MIN (= *pu-ú*)	'ditto' (scil. 'mouth')
^{uzu}un	MIN (= *pu-ú*)	'ditto' (scil. 'mouth')
^{uzu}múrub	*šu-uh-hu*	'buttocks'
^{uzu}múrub	*qin-na-tu*$_4$	'rump'
[^{uzu}múrub]	*bir-ti a-hi*	'armpit'
[^{uzu}múrub]	*ú-ru šá sin-niš-tu*$_4$	'female genitalia'

The entries from 'Ura' are quoted in the commentary without any specific indication of the source: given that lexical lists constituted the basis of schooling in ancient Mesopotamia, we may assume that they were quoted from memory and that the ancient audience would also have been able to identify them on sight.[34] Only three of the entries in the passage are quoted in the commentary, apparently the only three that were relevant for the discussion: with them, the exegete proves that the opened mouth of the pig in the protasis is connected with the infidelity of the man's wife in the apodosis.

---

[33] Landsberger, *Series HAR-ra = hubullu*, 6–7.

[34] Some of the quotations in commentaries contain mistakes typically caused by citing from memory, such as substitution of words by synonyms, or use of the wrong tense in verbs.

The two entries in commentaries given above clearly cite from one text, which is either identified explicitly or at least identifiable. A very considerable number of equations in commentaries, however, have no identifiable source. The lexical lists from ancient Mesopotamia are still being reconstructed from scores of scattered, broken fragments, and many of the as yet unidentifiable entries no doubt stem from hitherto unrecovered sections of these lexical lists.[35] In some cases, the quotations from lexical lists are so distorted that they are difficult to recognise. Thus, a commentary that seeks to demonstrate that every syllable of each of the 50 names of Marduk can be found in the wording of the final verses of the 'Epic of Creation' often resorts to perplexing homonyms, similar-sounding words, and similar-looking signs, in order to establish connections that are not attested anywhere else.[36] The majority of these equations cannot be identified: one may assume that the distorted form of the text quoted in the commentary has not yet been recognised, or else that as yet unrecovered lexical lists are quoted.

---

[35] For instance, it has been calculated that around 80 percent of the lexical series *Ea*, one of the most widespread in Mesopotamia in the first millennium BCE, has been recovered; whereas only 42 percent of the list *Aa* (an expanded version of *Ea*) can currently be reconstructed. See Civil et al., *Ea A = nâqu*, 152–54.

[36] As Lambert, *Babylonian Creation Myths*, 167, puts it: "every conceivable trick had to be used to pull off this tour de force." See the almost always unsuccessful attempts to correlate the equations in this commentary with lexical lists made by Genty, 'Les commentaires', 659–713.

On the other hand, in many other cases, the equations cited in commentaries are clearly not quoted from lexical lists, but from other types of sources.

4.0. Other Texts Cited in Commentaries

Commentaries occasionally quote texts other than lexical lists: laments, divination treatises, and magic, ritual, legal, and literary texts.[37] As with quotations from lexical lists, quotations from other genres only rarely identify their source explicitly. The majority of the quotations come from texts that were also copied on elementary school tablets, and which were, therefore, probably memorised by scribal apprentices at an early age. Since some of the quotations are marred by mistakes, one may assume that they were made from memory.

The following entry contains a quotation from the compendium called in antiquity 'Sidu', a collection of Sumerian–Akkadian bilingual proverbs and other miscellaneous material, in order to provide a context for the explanation of the rare word *qêlu* as *hepû* 'to smash':

(9) CCP 3.6.3.A ll. 28–30[38]

> (28) ***qé-e-el*** : *he-pu-ú* : KU$_5$.DU : *qé-e-el* : KU$_5$.DU : *he-pu-u* (29) *lìb-bu-ú ṣu-uh-hu-tú kur-ban-né-e su-un-šú ma-li šá i-qer-ru-ba-am-ma* (30) *i-né-ši-qa-an-ni a-qé-él-šú šá ina* ÉŠ.GÀR ^{m}*si-dù* E-*ú*

---

[37] For an overview of the texts cited in commentaries, see Frahm, *Commentaries*, 86–110.

[38] Finkel, 'Izbu VII Commentary'. See also Jiménez, 'Proverb from the Series *Sidu*'.

'(28) "*Crushed*" (= *Šumma Izbu* VII 164′) (means) "smashed," (since) *ku*$_5$.*du* means "*crushed,*" (and) *ku*$_5$.*du* (also) means "smashed," (29) as in "The dripping-eyed's lap is full of clods; (he says), 'Whoever approaches me and (30) kisses me, I shall *crush* him!'"—which is said in the Series of Sidu.'

The goal of the present quotation is to provide a context in which the rare verb *qêlu* is used, and in which its meaning 'to smash' is proved.

As stated above, in some commentaries the quotation is used for establishing a connection between the protasis and the apodosis of an omen. In example (7), the connection was established by means of a lexical list that provided some justification for the apparently arbitrary connection between the observed sign (a pig opening its mouth) and the given prognosis (infidelity). In another entry from the same commentary, the *explanandum* is an omen that states that if a pig is seen carrying a palm frond, the wind will rise. In order to justify the connection between the palm-carrying pig and the wind, the commentary cites a line from the anti-witchcraft series *Maqlû*, in which the date palm is described as '(the tree) that receives every wind':[39]

(10) DT 37 obv. 12b[40]

***šumma*(DIŠ) *šahû*(ŠAH) *ari*(^{giš}PA) *gišimmari*(GIŠIMMAR) *naši šāru*(IM) *itebbi*(ZI)** : *gišimmaru*(^{giš}GIŠIMMAR) *lim-hur-an-ni ma-hi-ir kal šá-a-*[*ri*]

---

[39] The epithet is probably due to the fact that palm branches sway with the slightest breeze; see Streck, 'Dattelpalme und Tamariske', 274.

[40] King, *Cuneiform Texts*, 41, 30–31; CCP 3.5.49.

'"If a pig carries a palm frond, wind will rise" (= *Šumma Ālu* 49–48′)—"May the date palm receive it, (the tree) that receives every wind!" (= *Maqlû* I 22).'

The quotation from an incantation in which the palm is called '(the tree) that receives every wind' thus justifies the connection between the palm-carrying pig and the rise of the wind. The incantation is quoted as a source of lexical knowledge, in order to extract from it an epithet of the date palm, which is then used by the exegete. The source of the quotation is not specified—nor does it need to be, since the only important aspect of the quotation is the fact that it connects the palm and the wind.

In the following entry, from a commentary on the poetic dialogue known as the 'Babylonian Theodicy', the commentator explains a common word, 'sage'. The goal of the commentary is therefore not to explain the meaning of the word, since it is clear enough, but rather to explain to whom the word refers. First, it states that 'sage' might refer to a scribe; the scribe who wrote this commentary often tries to demonstrate that he and his guild are referred to in the 'Theodicy', if one reads the text in the correct way. Second, he adds an alternative interpretation: 'sage' might be a metonym for the god of wisdom, Ea, who, in the line quoted in the commentary, is said to be the 'ears' (*uznu*, which in Akkadian also means 'intelligence') of another god:

(11) CCP 1.4 rev. 9

[mu-d] u-u : *tup-šar-ri* : [*m*]*u-du-u* : ^{d}⸢*é**-*a*⸣ ⸢:⸣ ⸢*uz*⸣*-*na-ka* ^{d}IDIM *u* ^{d}*dam-ki-an-n*[*a apkal nēmeqi* o o o o]

> '"[Sag]e" (refers to a) scribe; "[s]age" (refers to) Ea, (as in the line) "Your ears are Ea and Damkin[a, scholar(s) of wisdom...]"'

What is important in this quotation is, again, the fact that it provides the connection needed in the commentary: Ea equals wisdom, ergo Ea is the 'sage'. The context of the line quoted (a syncretistic hymn in which every god is said to be one body part of the god Ninurta), the fact that another god appears in it (Damkina, Ea's spouse), and the rest of the words of the quoted line are irrelevant; or relevant only inasmuch as they demonstrate that the line actually exists in a text. The only relevant aspect of the lines quoted is the one-to-one equation between Ea and 'wisdom', just as between 'palm' and 'wind' in the previous example.

5.0. Conclusion

The inescapable conclusion is that texts other than lexical lists are quoted in commentaries as if they were lexical lists, in order to extract from them the same information that lexical lists provide, namely one-to-one equations and, more rarely, contextualisation.[41] Since lexical lists are quoted far more commonly in Mesopotamian exegesis than texts from other categories, it seems safe to conclude that they represent the default source of commentarial explanations. Only if a particular equation was not

---

[41] Contextualisation, the goal of the quotation cited as (9), is also found in lexical lists. For instance, lexical lists occasionally have glosses, introduced by the determinative pronoun *ša* 'of' to distinguish between homonyms, or to indicate the semantic range of a given word. See Civil et al., *Ea A = nâqu*, 149–50.

available in the lexical tradition would Mesopotamian commentators resort to texts of other genres, and even then the texts would be quoted in order to extract from them the sort of information one would expect to find in a lexical list. The context of the lines cited, the character of the text in which they are contained, and even all words in the quotation not necessary for the explanation, are entirely superfluous: the only important aspect of the quotation is the lexical equation it provides.

The genre of commentaries had its origin in lexical lists, the time-sanctioned standard format of Mesopotamian scholarship. Even if not always expressed in tabular format, commentaries always betray their origins in their procedure: they explain A by B, occasionally adding C for contextualisation, but they never elaborate on the connection, nor do they express its purpose. Just as in the monotheistic list presented as (1), the lack of thematisation in commentaries does not mean that no underlying principle existed; rather, it reflects the conventions of the format. The principles and goals of the hermeneutic operations—the equation of all the gods with just one god; the demonstration that the predictions of the old divinatory treatises were justified—must have been discussed orally, but are never written down. Instead, only terse equations are given, a bare-bones version of an explanation. Centuries of transmission of lexical lists had taught the Mesopotamians that, if anything deserves to be recorded, it should be given the format of a list.

A RABBINIC EPISTEMIC GENRE: CREATING KNOWLEDGE THROUGH LISTS AND CATALOGUES

Lennart Lehmhaus

1.0. Lost in Lists

Despite the character of dryness, formality, and boredom usually associated with lists such as telephone books, index lists, or inventories, these hybrid textual forms are all around us and they play a crucial part in our lives. Eva von Contzen has aptly remarked that the "relative simplicity of the form accounts for its remarkable versatility, and also the difficulties one encounters when trying to come to terms with 'the' list as form."[1] On the one hand, lists are commonly deemed useful because they structure and emphasise important details in a broad range of contexts. Authors of lists link one item to another, thereby creating chains that can take on different structures, be of various lengths, and serve multiple functions (commercial, referential, mnemonic, etc.).[2] Lists can be rather simple, with single items—shopping

[1] Von Contzen, 'Theorising Lists in Literature', 41.

[2] Belknap notes: "Lists consist of arrangements of entries and have been used for varied purposes throughout history. Lists enumerate, account, remind, memorialize, order. Lists take a number of sizes, shapes, and

 https://doi.org/10.11647/OBP.0375.02

lists, guest lists, lists of ingredients. Or they may feature much more complex entries—from a library catalogue or a menu to a sequence of safety procedures. In both forms, they constitute epitomes of information received in a specific form that differs considerably both structurally and graphically from other surrounding (textual) discourse, which is predominantly narrative. We may think of an easily browsable bullet point list of three (five, ten) items in a textbook, a table of contents, or the navigation index for a website.[3] Accordingly, lists as "adaptable containers" selecting from a "mind-deep pool of possibility" often provide order within texts and cultural contexts.[4] On the other hand, their fluidity and potentially infinite openness also borders on excess and uselessness that challenges any order and structure with futility, disintegration, and collapse.[5]

---

functions, ranging from directories and historical records to edicts and instructions." Belknap, *The List*, 6; see also p. 34.

[3] Mainberger, 'Table of Contents', 20, stresses that many practical lists (timetables, dictionaries, tables of contents, conference schedules) have no direct relation to any continuous text, since their main purpose is extracting information or providing quick orientation rather than being read.

[4] Belknap, *The List*, 19.

[5] See Belknap, *The List*, 19; Mainberger, 'Ordnen/Aufzählen', 94–95. Compare the following remarks on postmodernist fiction, which hold true for many lists: "The lists… are direct confrontations with the arbitrary and capricious world of chance and chaos which lies beyond the man-made order." Alber, 'Absurd Catalogues', 352.

It is probably our own intimate acquaintance with these lapidary or expansive (e.g., music charts) formats whose everyday nature and ubiquity render their very existence as a discursive form, or even a genre, with a variety of functions almost invisible in most contexts.[6] But lists as a genre or a literary or textual form also have a long history which, according to some scholars, goes back to the incipient stages of writing and literary cultures.

In the present article, I focus on the forms and various functions of lists as adaptable containers as reflected in the practice of list-making in Jewish textual traditions from late antiquity, commonly known as rabbinic or talmudic literature.[7] These rabbinic works deploy lists for different discursive purposes (exegetical, homiletical, narrative) based on a long tradition derived

---

[6] Mainberger, 'Ordnen/Aufzählen', 97; Young, 'Un-Black Boxing the List'; Young, *List Cultures*.

[7] This corpus includes the early Mishnah (abbreviated as m) and its companion, the Tosefta, from Palestine in around the third century CE. Two later talmudic traditions commented and elaborated upon those earlier texts, often adding new material from their respective cultural background: the Palestinian or Jerusalem Talmud, from the sixth century; and the Babylonian Talmud (abbreviated as b), a vast tradition compiled between the sixth and eighth centuries in the region of today's Iraq. This body of texts is accompanied by other works subsumed under the label 'midrash', mainly from Palestine. These texts combine exegetical and homiletical approaches to the Hebrew Bible with ethical teachings and further discourse.

from biblical and other ancient Jewish traditions well embedded in their surroundings in the ancient Near East.[8]

First, I will briefly introduce the history of ancient Jewish lists, their broader cultural entanglements, and pertinent scholarship. Second, I sketch out some theoretical approaches to the literary and epistemological features of lists that outline their specific nature turning them into a powerful 'epistemic genre'. I argue that the rabbinic texts deploy the versatility or affordance of the list not only for ordering knowledge but also for the very process of knowledge production. Consequently, lists do not serve as mere containers for knowledge that circulated apart from their usage. In fact, the rabbinic authors may have arrived at certain conclusions precisely in and through lists in which specific concepts or taxonomies become manifest or substantiated. Following this, the main argument will be exemplified by focusing on complex types of list, which can be described as clusters, sequences, or, most compellingly, as catalogues. The findings will open up the discussion about rabbinic lists into the broader realm of the history of ancient knowledge and the place of the rabbis therein.

2.0. Premodern Jewish Approaches to Lists

Lists and enumerations of various forms can be found in almost all Jewish traditions, from the Hebrew Bible to the Middle Ages

[8] For a discussion of the concept of ancient Mesopotamian *Listenwissenschaft*, see Lehmhaus, 'Listenwissenschaft'; Hilgert, 'Von "Listenwissenschaft" und "epistemischen" Dingen'; Veldhuis, 'Elementary Education at Nipur'; Cancik-Kirschbaum, 'Writing, Language and Textuality'.

and beyond. However, scholarly engagement with this particular feature, while growing, is still limited.[9]

Scholars have mainly researched historical lists in the Bible, such as genealogies of biblical figures in Genesis or lists of kings and their royal houses, lists of priestly families, or lists of the tribes of ancient Israel.[10] Different lists include information about geography, the military, and administration, while others relate to ritual elements—ranging from features of the tent of congregation (tabernacle) or the temple, to ornamental details of the garment of the high priest (Exod. 27–28) or the markers of bodily fitness for the priestly office (Lev. 21.16–23)—and to religiously normative aspects—dealing with broad norms, as in the Decalogue, or with rather specific rules, such as Sabbath law (Exod. 31.12–17), intermarriage with converts, states and periods of ritual impurity (Lev. 15) or detailed dietary rules (Lev. 11.1–47).[11]

---

[9] For some preliminary studies, see Wünsche, 'Die Zahlensprüche'; Nador, 'Some Numerical Categories'.

[10] See Ron, 'Genealogical List'; Sergi, 'Alleged Judahite King List'. Compare Matthew P. Monger's study on the wives of the patriarchs in this volume.

[11] On biblical list-making, see Scolnic, *Theme and Context*, who focuses specifically on geographical knowledge and the itinerary list in Num. 33 that structures Israel's journey from Egypt into the promised land (see pp. 67–134). For military and administrative lists in the Bible, see, e.g., Ben Zvi, 'Levitical Cities'; Redditt, 'Census List'. On administrative lists in general, see Echterhölter, 'Jack Goody', 255–56; Young, 'Un-Black Boxing the List', 501–5; Young, *List Cultures*, 67–108.

Most scholarship, however, has refrained from touching upon discursive and epistemic dimensions or engaging with cultural and literary list theory.[12] Taking the list format for granted, they have focused on the content of lists compared with archaeological findings or non-Israelite traditions (Persian, Mesopotamian, or African).[13] Still, listing should also be seen as an instrument of religious instruction, with a prescriptive dimension, and as a marking of religious and cultural identity that creates a historical consciousness for and serves as the virtual collection of Israelite *Heilsgeschichte*, having a high value for generations of readers and interpreters to come.[14]

In the texts from the Dead Sea (Qumran), lists cover halakhic or ritual aspects and engage in the selection and exclusion of various others.[15] Similar to Greek lists, Qumranic texts also deployed lists to express cultural values and to define what was accepted by a certain group as authoritative tradition or textual

---

[12] For some issues of broader cultural and literary interest, see Coxon, '"List" Genre'; Tsumura, 'List and Narrative'; Golani, 'Three Oppressors'.

[13] See especially Deysel, 'King Lists'; Na'aman, 'Solomon's District List'. Von Contzen, 'Theorising Lists in Literature', 40, is also primarily interested in content or theme (e.g., names, places, species, mirabilia, treasures, alien nations, etc.).

[14] See Kirk, *Ancient Greek Lists*, 6. Compare the ordering of early Islamic history through lists, as discussed in Teresa Bernheimer's paper in this volume.

[15] See Golani, 'Three Oppressors'; Golani, 'New Light' (on false prophets). Compare the liturgical dimension in Rebecca Ullrich's study in this volume.

canon.[16] 'Canonisation' is important in later rabbinic discourse on 'external scriptures' or lists of forbidden targumim (Aramaic translations or paraphrases of Scripture).[17] Lists also played a crucial role for the appropriation of scientific knowledge, mainly calendrical and astrological/astronomical concepts, in various Second Temple traditions (Dead Sea Scrolls, Enoch) with a long afterlife (e.g., in late midrash).[18] From early on, ethical instruction through lists of virtues and vices—in manuals of conduct or midrashic ethical taxonomies—was a core feature of rabbinic tradition.[19]

As with classical Greek poetics, many studies have considered premodern Jewish lists as mere interjections or digressions but not as part of the central discourse, and so their format did not call for special attention.[20] However, the contrasting aspects

---

[16] See Noam, 'List of David's Songs'; Tzoref, '4Q252', on 4Q252 as a list of quotations and paraphrases from Genesis, sometimes supplemented by commentary. For Greek lists, see Kirk, *Ancient Greek Lists*, 2–3.

[17] See Alexander, 'Lists of Forbidden Targumim'. On canonisation, see the studies by Liv Ingeborg Lied and by Marilena Maniaci in this volume; or that of Martin Wallraff, on canon tables as an important step towards the 'sacralisation' of Christian writings.

[18] Reed, 'Ancient Jewish Sciences'; Jacobus, 'Calendars'; Stern, *Calendar and Community*.

[19] See Uusimäki, 'Ideal Ways of Living' (on Qumranic ethics); Schofer, 'Ethical Formation' (rabbinic ethical literature). For ethical lists in *Seder Eliyahu*, see Lehmhaus, 'Listenwissenschaft', 66–71; Lehmhaus, 'Making Moral Lists'.

[20] Cf. Asper, 'Katalog', 916 (epic catalogues).

of sequences of lists and their clear function of inclusion and exclusion has been highlighted by Jacob Neusner for early rabbinic texts.[21] Wayne S. Towner comparatively analysed the so-called 'enumeration of scriptural examples' in early midrashic literature as a versatile micro-format pointing towards an entanglement between a "science of lists" and a "science of (written) language/ scripture."[22] Roy Shasha's first form-critical study, shaped by the Frankfurt/Manchester school, accentuated the structural elements—a caption with a deictic (*we-ʾilu hen*; 'these are they') and/or a numerical reference ('three things do X', 'three things are X…') signalling items that follow in a list—and their functions and formats: simple or compound lists, series or combinations of several lists, or accumulations of lists addressing or contrasting more than one topic.[23] Although these features can also be found in abundance and in a more elaborated form in later talmudic and midrashic texts, the scholarship of rabbinic lists is still in its infancy.[24]

A special example of cultural curating and tradition-building can be found in the so-called *Maʿase Torah* (lit. 'the work of

---

[21] Neusner, 'Mode of Thought', sees *Listenwissenschaft* as the prevailing mode of reasoning in Mishnah and earlier midrashim (e.g., *Sifra*). Cf. Bernard, 'Listing and Enlisting' on tractate Avot.

[22] See Towner, *Rabbinic 'Enumeration'*.

[23] See Shasha, 'Lists in the Mishnah', 36–51 (definition), 52–79 (form-critical description).

[24] For some preliminary studies, see Keim, *Pirqei deRabbi Eliezer*, 209–11; Adelman, *Return of the Repressed*, 265–69, Noegel, 'Abraham's Ten Trials'; Lehmhaus, 'Listenwissenschaft'; Lehmhaus, 'Lore and Order'.

Torah') collections of simple or compound lists with a numerical caption.[25] These texts can be perceived as a long catalogue or 'encyclopedia' of lists which are sometimes contrastive and sometimes build up whole subtopics or thematic sections. Those range across different areas of knowledge including ethics, moral advice, elements of Jewish rituals and liturgy, biblical historiography or eschatology, and various branches of scientific knowledge (astrology/astronomy, dream interpretation, geography, geology, biology, botany, physics, and medicine). Those lists are often interspersed with biblical verses as proof texts, a phenomenon also known from other texts like *Seder Eliyahu*.[26] However, information from the Bible is not presented because of its special religious value but rather as scientific proof for taxonomies built through lists (types of plants, animal species, stones, etc.). Moreover, the texts' penchant for biblical history turns the lists at times into a rich resource for important events of Israel's history. Alternatively, they serve as a lexicon for place names or biblical and eschatological figures, or as a topical index.[27]

---

[25] This includes the work known as *Ḥuppat Eliyahu* ('The canopy of Eliyahu') and the *Midrash sheloshah we-ʾarbaʿah* ('Midrash of three and four'), as well as *Pirqe rabbenu ha-qaddosh* ('Chapters of our holy master'). The main portions of all texts feature lists with three or four items, but these are supplemented by other numerical lists, especially seven-item lists.

[26] See Lehmhaus, 'Listenwissenschaft', 66–71; Lehmhaus, 'Making Moral Lists'.

[27] See Lehmhaus, 'Listenwissenschaft', 71–83.

Instead of being mere compilations of earlier rabbinic teachings, the *Maʿase Torah* traditions have a unique nature that calls for studying them in their new historical contexts of early Islamic times and looking for structural parallels in Islamicate epistemic and literary culture(s).[28] The deliberate selection and variation of older lists indicates an openness for change and the ability of lists to be attuned to various discourses and contexts through extension, shortening, or alteration. Moreover, these traditions show that lists and enumerations are usually used and embedded in a practice bespeaking their potential to serve as epistemic tools of knowledge-making, a key aspect of this paper.[29]

3.0. List Theory, List Knowledge

Rabbinic texts contain lists within continuous texts and feature neither the specific vertical layout nor any other graphic detachment or emphasis (e.g., through other type or colour) discussed by scholars.[30] These lists, as a subform of the enumerative genre, but also as a "transmedial phenomenon,"[31] require a rather broad

---

[28] Such parallels might be found in ethical handbooks, compilations, and *florilegia* well embedded in the intellectual trends of the Abbasid period. On some similarities between early Islamic ethical traditions (*adāb*) and later rabbinic texts, see Lehmhaus, '"Hidden Transcripts"'; Lehmhaus, 'Making Moral Lists'.

[29] Mainberger, 'Ordnen/Aufzählen', 96.

[30] For a focus on the vertical and graphic layout of lists, see Mainberger, 'Table of Contents', 21; Mainberger, 'Ordnen/Aufzählen', 91–92.

[31] Kirk, *Ancient Greek Lists*, 3.

definition. Knowledge production through lists might take multiple forms. Commonly, lists and enumerations tend to compile items in a nominal sequence using single nouns or adjectives—be it names or characteristics of plants, objects, people, or the like.[32] The inclusive understanding of lists ranges from semantically linked enumerations and sequences of grammatically unconnected items (mostly nouns) to multi-column tables facilitating selective screening (e.g., timetables), or, finally, to catalogues with more detailed, at times narrative, expansions and explanations for each entry.[33]

Taking into account the versatility and the dynamic and fluid character of lists, the present discussion seeks to describe the interplay between the format of rabbinic lists and their possible functions. Most rabbinic lists have been compiled according to a certain system (alphabetically, numerically, geographically, chronologically, taxonomically, etc.) or following a thematic key (question), such as rabbinic lists of primordial things (*Pirqe de-Rabbi Eliezer*, ch. 3) or medical lists of what is beneficial or harmful for the body. Temporal-functional aspects, as in Goody's scheme, can help to parse the abundance of rabbinic lists: record-taking of the past; prescriptions of present or future actions

[32] Belknap, *The List*, 2.

[33] See Hoffmann, 'Aufzählungen', 91; Mainberger, 'Ordnen/Aufzählen', 91 (preferring enumeration over list); Kirk, *Ancient Greek Lists*, 7 ('list' as the most inclusive umbrella term). See also Young, 'Un-Black Boxing the List'; Young, 'On Lists and Networks'; Belknap, *The List*, 2: "A list of listings would include the catalogue, the inventory, the itinerary, and the lexicon."

(shopping lists or administration); and lexical lists with an encyclopedic intention of collecting knowledge. The three dimensions of these ideal types, however, are often inextricably interwoven. In Jewish traditions, one often finds a merging of chronological and administrative functions, as in genealogies or lists of kings and priests, and a blending of prescriptions and religious or cultural knowledge, as in the Decalogue or the larger body of biblical laws and their afterlife in later texts. Moreover, record-making through lists not only provides a sense of chronology and historical awareness but also inscribes these items into the broader collective cultural consciousness.[34]

Rabbinic lists often feature less than three items, specifically when couplets or doublets serve as internal substructures for more complex catalogues.[35] While list formats can switch between vertical, horizontal, or tabular (raster) orientation, enumerative lists in rabbinic literature always progress horizontally, and are connected, due to the structure of Semitic languages, by 'and' (-ו) instead of by commas or any other typographical marker.[36] This allows for greater grammatical coherence or even

---

[34] See Goody, 'What's in a List?', 129–45; Young, *List Cultures*, 23–43. For a thorough discussion of Goody's theory and its limitations, see Echterhölter, 'Jack Goody'; Kirk, *Ancient Greek Lists*, 4–8.

[35] Milic, *Stylists on Style*, 416.

[36] The studies in this volume regarding list practice in Syriac (Matthew P. Monger, Liv Ingeborg Lied), medieval Jewish (Rebecca Ullrich), and Islamic (Maroussia Bednarkiewicz, Peter Tarras, Teresa Bernheimer) traditions suggest that horizontal, enumerative lists may have prevailed

for a (narrative) list fully resembling a sentence, a structure which distinguishes it from a vertical list of simple nouns. In some cases, repetition of wording or even of whole phrases may serve to indicate a new item or entry.[37]

Rabbinic lists display a complex interaction between "the individual units that make up a list (what does it hold?) and the function or purpose of the list as a whole (how does it hold together?)."[38] In many lists, captions prefigure and shape the understanding of the following items, whereby the items and their hierarchy may support the initial clue, but can also surprise or cast doubt on its coherence. Consequently, lists become open to (re)interpretation and rearrangement, inviting reutilisations and transformations that alter or add structure, content, and commentaries.[39] This expandability of the list format dovetails with

---

over vertical or tabular list formats in many premodern writing cultures—also due the need to utilise writing space efficiently, linked to the scarcity and precious value of manuscript material.

[37] See Belknap, *The List*, 19, 23, 30, on the vertical orientation and the horizontal progress of literary lists. See also Belknap, *The List*, 28: "In polysyndeton all the constituents are joined by a conjunction, often the word and. The repetition of the conjunction serves to call equal attention to each item in the list, as well as to generate momentum."

[38] Belknap, *The List*, 16. Cf. Shasha, 'Lists in the Mishnah'.

[39] Mainberger, *Die Kunst des Aufzählens*, 20; Doležalová, 'Potential and Limitations'; von Contzen, 'Lists in Literature'. See also Belknap, *The List*, 30–31 (lists as "at once accretive and discontinuous"); and Müller-Wille and Charmantier, 'Lists as Research Technologies', 743–44: "the list was a handy means to present and preserve knowledge in a concise and structured yet open-ended manner."

rabbinic discourse that is simultaneously ordered and highly associative. Authors and compilers could thus expand or shorten lists, or populate existing lists with alternative items, sometimes introduced through the marker 'some even say'.

The importance of the site or location of lists, and their sudden or established appearance, becomes significant when the Babylonian Talmud or works like *Pirqe de-Rabbi Eliezer* feature whole sequences, networks, or clusters of lists.[40] For instance, b. Gittin 70a creates an accumulation of lists connected via the theme of what benefits or jeopardises the health of men, especially their virility and ability to procreate.[41] Another phenomenon, is the deliberate creation of opposites through contrastive lists as couplets or series, such as "six things heal a sick person from their illness" versus "ten things are liable to send the convalesced person back to their illness" (b. Avodah Zarah 28b–29a).[42]

---

[40] See von Contzen, 'Theorising Lists in Literature', 39; cf. Belknap, *The List*, 30, on serialisation. The third chapter of *Pirqe de-Rabbi Eliezer* consists almost entirely of lists structuring the various steps in the process of the creation. Chapters 6 to 8 also feature numerous lists explaining astronomical and cosmological aspects, such as the number and names of planets, constellations, and months, or the paths of the sun and the moon.

[41] The captions of the lists read: "six things you will do and die," "eight things beneficial in small but harmful in large quantities," "eight things that diminish the semen."

[42] Another example from the Babylonian Talmud, b. Berakhot 57b, contrasts "three things enter the body without benefiting it" with "three

While some scholars emphasise material writing practices and literacy as prerequisites for lists, others see lists rather as challenging "the common assumptions about a dichotomy between orality and literacy/writing" because it occupies "a liminal or interstitial space."[43] Epic catalogues, genealogies, chronicles, itineraries, and recipes for instruction were in premodern cultures likewise bound to the curriculum of oral teaching and transmission, mostly learned by heart. Deeply embedded in a primarily oral rabbinic culture, rabbinic lists may have emerged as a mnemonic device that builds a bridge between these oral and written traditions. Many lists and catalogues, as will be shown, rely on anaphora, "a word or phrase [that] repeats at the beginning of subsequent clauses," or use repeated phrases and key words—all of which would make them an apt instrument for oral transmission and instruction.[44]

4.0. Lists as Epistemic Tools: Information, Instruction, Enquiry

It is commonly agreed that lists, albeit in diverse forms and for different purposes, are almost always tied to the collection and transmission of information—thereby creating knowledge. Lists

---

things benefit the body without being absorbed by it." Cf. Belknap, *The List*, 30, on the opposite or asyndeton.

[43] Young, 'Un-Black Boxing the List', 501–2.

[44] Belknap, *The List*, 10. On the oral dimension of enumerations, see Mainberger, *Die Kunst des Aufzählens*, 64–75. See also Jaffee, 'Rabbinic Oral Tradition'; Hallo, 'Midrash as Mnemonic', on mnemonic devices in midrash as substituting for concordances or dictionaries.

can thus be perceived as artefacts whose content and structure may point the reader to underlying concepts and epistemologies or, at times, even to cultural peculiarities or the historical context of their production. Lists transmitted over time embody epistemic conventions within a certain culture and time in a specific locality.[45] Other scholars, however, hold that it "is the *practice* that determines what a list or catalogue is and is not. Taken on its own, it is undetermined and, although laden with facts, it is unable to reveal its significance."[46]

4.1. Information

Robert Belknap summarised two fundamental functions of lists regarding knowledge: referential and epistemic. On one hand, they serve as "repositories of information... in which information is ordered... and easily located. On the other,... its role is the creation of meaning, rather than merely the storage of it."[47]

In his seminal study, Towner had already commented that lists in Jewish texts often serve to systematise "observations about nature, geography and man, and as pedagogical and mnemonic tools for conveying this information to students and posterity."[48] And Annette Y. Reed stressed that several Jewish texts

---

[45] See Belknap, *The List*, 27; Young, 'On Lists and Networks'; von Contzen, 'Lists in Literature'. Goody, 'What's in a List?', 90, discusses lists that "permitted wider developments in the growth of human knowledge."

[46] Mainberger, 'Table of Contents', 20.

[47] Belknap, *The List*, 2.

[48] Towner, Rabbinic 'Enumeration', 4.

with scientific interest "encompass all varieties of knowledge," which they try to balance with "the epistemological monopoly of the Torah."[49] Similarly, many ancient lists or catalogues, with their classificatory purpose and advantages, went far beyond the ornamental and entertaining aspect.[50] While also demonstrating the authors' learnedness and artistry, they emphasised the cultural or religious value of objects and ideas, since "inclusion in a list endows an item with extrinsic value, thus making it worth re-listing."[51] While serving as circuits of knowledge, list-making entails complex procedures of selection, exclusion and inclusion, and ordering and classification that form the basis of a reality on which an empire or a ruling class can act.[52]

4.2. Instruction

Lists—especially catalogues, representing a culture or its parts in miniature—have a claim to closure or completeness. But more than just serving as a retrievable and condensed cultural storage device, they reproduce culture through a dynamic process of learning and teaching. This didactic use of lists can be witnessed in many traditions of the ancient Mediterranean and the Near

---

[49] Reed, 'Ancient Jewish Sciences', 22.

[50] See von Contzen, 'Theorising Lists in Literature', 35.

[51] Kirk, *Ancient Greek Lists*, 2.

[52] See Schaffrick and Werber, 'Einleitung', esp. 304–7; Young, *List Cultures*, 67–108; Mainberger, 'Table of Contents', 23–24. For lists in Pliny's encyclopedic work and its agenda of an all-encompassing Roman imperial superiority, see Carey, *Pliny's Catalogue of Culture*; Laehn, *Pliny's Defense of Empire*.

East,[53] often deeply connected to scribal education and the field of exegesis and interpretation, which can be also seen as the core expertise of the rabbinic sages.[54] Here, lists also functioned as an apt tool for the translation and explication of terms and their variants, such as names of measures, plants, stones, and so on.[55]

In some cases, ancient Egyptian, Babylonian, or Greek catalogues sometimes reference the titles and contents of other texts or objects included in certain physical collections or 'libraries' (e.g., the Library of Ashurbanipal). In other cases, their content conveys important implicit knowledge about the scope of a specific field of knowledge (a 'discipline'). As such, they allow for a (partial) reconstruction of the interest of later authors or even of the ancient curricula.[56]

---

53 For ancient Mesopotamia, see Cancik-Kirschbaum, 'Writing, Language and Textuality'; Veldhuis, 'Elementary Education at Nipur', 137–46. For ancient Egypt, see Hoffmann, 'Aufzählungen', esp. 122–23; Quack, 'Ägyptische Listen'.

54 See Neusner, 'Mode of Thought', 317–21, on *Listenwissenschaft* as the discursive backbone of the Mishnah, and Bernard, 'Listing and Enlisting', who sees the discourse of lists in Avot as a recruitment and training text for rabbinic students.

55 See Steinert, 'Catalogues, Texts and Specialists'; Hoffmann, 'Aufzählungen', 112–13. On the translation of plant names in talmudic texts, see Lehmhaus, 'Beyond Dreckapotheke'.

56 See Steinert, 'Catalogues, Texts and Specialists'; Steinert, *Medicine, Magic and Divination*. Compare the contributions by Liv Ingeborg Lied, Martin Wallraff, and Marilena Maniaci in this volume.

4.3. Enquiry

Lexical or scientific lists, catalogues, and encyclopedias often aim for a (partial) reproduction of the world by creating classificatory systems that reflect the underlying order or paradigms of knowledge in a given culture.[57] Going beyond the understanding of *Listenwissenschaft* as proto-science, recent studies have highlighted list-making and cataloguing as an epistemic practice with various functions. Transcending the practical focus of administrative lists, Mesopotamian authors dared to introduce more abstraction or intellectual playfulness, from which emerged new epistemic structures and ordering systems (e.g., alphabetical/phonetic).[58] Accordingly, thinking with and through lists involves some deliberate fragmentation of the world instead of a passive collection of things that already exist.

Ancient Jewish lists, among various other micro-forms, serve not only as 'containers' of previous tradition but also as methods of acquiring knowledge. Their specific hermeneutics and conceptualisations reflect a dynamic transmission process

---

[57] See Kirk, *Ancient Greek Lists*, 6, who discusses listing as knowledge production.

[58] Hilgert, 'Von "Listenwissenschaft" und "epistemischen" Dingen', esp. 277–309; Cancik-Kirschbaum, 'Writing, Language and Textuality'; Lehmhaus, 'Listenwissenschaft'; Echterhölter, 'Jack Goody', 248–49. Even scholars of early modern science have noticed that ancient Mesopotamian lists "group words by abstract categories like 'things of the heavens' and 'things of the earth' or, in an even more strikingly 'useless' manner, by initial sound"; Müller-Wille and Charmantier, 'Lists as Research Technologies', 744.

and active participation in wider discourses of ancient (scientific) knowledge. Lists create and (re)present patterns or concepts that guide the cognitive processes of their authors and their audience.[59] Such a process is triggered by the double nature of the list as being joined (the whole list) and a sequence of separate units (list items) in which each "possesses an individual significance but also a specific meaning by virtue of its membership with the other units in the compilation."[60]

The important potential of list-making has been observed in scholarship on early modern scientific practice. For the 'father of botanic taxonomy', the Swede Linnaeus, those "instruments of structured synopsis" became his central "research-enabling technology… to explore territories of the unknown." I will argue in the following that in rabbinic lists on varying topics, one may already find a similar "tendency to 'play around' with lists" and a "quasi-experimental approach" that turns cataloguing into taxonomic thinking. Accordingly, from early on, "lists exhibit the potential to generate the same kind of epistemic surplus that is so familiar today" from modern lab equipment.[61]

This description comes close to Gianna Pomata's approach to 'epistemic genres' in premodern sciences that will serve as a second theoretical underpinning for my discussion. In her view,

---

[59] See Young, 'Un-Black Boxing the List'. On knowledge-producing lists, see Pommerening, 'Bäume, Sträucher und Früchte', about ancient Egypt; Echterhölter, 'Jack Goody', esp. 248.

[60] Belknap, *The List*, 15.

[61] Müller-Wille and Charmantier, 'Lists as Research Technologies', 744–45.

these small text forms (e.g., recipes, case stories) do not constitute simple devices or containers for indexing and conveying already self-contained knowledge. Rather, they serve as powerful cognitive tools or vehicles that offer additional epistemic value and advance the broader project of the production of knowledge. Numerical list captions or guiding questions or categories resemble core features of what Gianna Pomata designates as 'epistemic genres', where they serve as "signposts indicating direction for further observation and enquiry."[62] Rabbinic lists and catalogues, as we will see, while facilitating the classification of phenomena, observations, or experiences, additionally "challenge extant knowledge formations, but also create new ones... (which amount to new ways of seeing and doing)."[63]

5.0. Knowledge-Making through Catalogues in Rabbinic Texts

In this main section, I will concentrate on a few examples where lists function explicitly as taxonomies or serve as flexible tools for epistemological purposes. In this sense, and similarly to many ancient and more recent (epic) catalogues, they both generate

---

[62] Pomata, 'The Medical Case Narrative', 8.

[63] Young, *List Cultures*, 26. See also Young, 'On Lists and Networks'; von Contzen, 'Limits of Narration', 257: "Lists, because they encapsulate the tensions and fascinations of narration and dis-narration, are a perfect way of throwing new light on the complex interplay of the creation of meaning in and through narratives, of involving the readers in the processes of sense-making, and, ultimately, of the inextricable connection between form and function that lies at the heart of all literature."

and transfer knowledge.[64] The following examples will demonstrate how a list-itinerary combines religious and medical knowledge, how lists explore and implement legal, medical, or ethical ideas, and how rabbinic authors appropriated a scientific subfield (pharmaceutics, dealing with simple remedies) and created a kind of encyclopedia or reference work. Due to limitations of space, I will only briefly mention here the knowledge-making function of lists that define concepts and create taxonomies. For example, a discourse ranging from the early Mishnah into the Babylonian Talmud strives for a classification system that defines behavioural patterns of the *shoteh* (lit. 'deviant', mentally ill or disabled) in a dynamic interplay with local knowledge and discriminatory labels and rules related to religious law. Other taxonomic lists refer to specific illnesses and seek to establish knowledge about their aetiology, symptoms, and possible therapeutic approaches. Different lists explore human behaviour by combining a sort of micro-sociological approach (character traits, motivations, etc.) with normative, prescriptive attitudes (morally right actions).[65] These taxonomical lists attest to the versatility of the format and the fluid continuum between lists, list clusters,

---

[64] See Belknap, *The List*, 10.

[65] On the *shoteh*, see Belser and Lehmhaus, 'Disability in Rabbinic Judaism', and Lehmhaus, 'Shoteh'; on illness taxonomies, see Lehmhaus, '"Curiosity Cures the Reb"', and Lehmhaus, 'Bodies of Texts'; on moral lists, see Lehmhaus, 'Listenwissenschaft', and Lehmhaus, 'Making Moral Lists'; on some similarities between early Islamic ethical traditions (*adab*) and later rabbinic texts, see Lehmhaus, '"Hidden Transcripts"'.

and expansive catalogues that often use guiding questions, 'headers', or narrative elements and proof texts for their epistemic project.[66]

5.1. Lists: Structuring Time, Organising Structure

One important feature of lists is their ability not only to store or stack list items together but also to structure actions. Consequently, lists impose order on and refigure time and temporality in the past, present, and future, or our awareness thereof.[67] One might think of the first aspect (the past) as in a catalogue of past events (a chronicle) or a list of specific key moments of Jewish history (i.e., *Heilsgeschichte*). The second aspect (the present) concerns the performance of lists and enumeration in the present which proceed in a specific temporary framework that might be stretched or prolonged, evenly clocked, or equipped with a varying and dynamic rhythm.[68] The last aspect (the future) can be exemplified by common shopping lists (or target lists or to-do lists), instruction manuals, or more elaborated catalogues of rules (e.g., law, etiquette, diet, and regimen) that aim at prescribing and codifying human behaviour and (re)actions.

One finds at least two of these temporalities—present and future—merged with other functions (prescription) and realised in a list on gestation in the talmudic tractate Berakhot, whose

---

66 For the list type that starts with a definitory question, see Shasha, 'Lists in the Mishnah', 42–43. See also Pomata, 'The Medical Case Narrative'.

67 See Mainberger, 'Table of Contents', 28.

68 See Mainberger, 'Ordnen/Aufzählen', 95.

main discourse revolves around rules for correct blessings and how to pray, albeit with many digressions.

Mishnah; m. Berakhot 9.3:

If someone's wife conceived and he said [a prayer]: Let it be [God's] will that my wife shall give birth to a male [child]—this is a prayer in vain....[69]

It has been taught [in a baraita]:

1. For the first three days, one should ask for [divine] mercy that [the seed] will not decompose.
2. From three to forty [days], one should ask for [divine] mercy that [the fetus] will be male.
3. From forty days to three months, one should ask for [divine] mercy that [the fetus] will not be a *sandal* (סנדל, lit. 'sandal') [i.e., a compressed fetus].
4. From three to six [months], one should ask for [divine] mercy that [the fetus] will not be stillborn.
5. From six to nine [months], one should ask for [divine] mercy that [the fetus] will come out safely.

[Interjection] However, does this plea for mercy have any effect?

Did not Rav Yitzhak, the son of Rav Ami say:

A. If a man emits seed first, [the woman] gives birth to a female [child].

B. But if the woman emits seed first, she gives birth to a male [child].

---

[69] Words in square brackets provide some additional information that makes the text more readable in English, while parentheses contain explanations of the preceding word or sentence.

> As it is said [in Scripture]: *If a woman emits seed she will give birth to a male [child] (Lev. 12.2).*
>
> [If that is the case,] what are we dealing with [regarding the prayer for a male child]?
>
> [This is only effective] when both (man and woman) emit seed at the same time.[70]

The trigger of this talmudic discussion unit (*sugya*) is the base Mishnah concluding that any prayer for the (male) determination of a future child's sex, a crucial issue in Jewish halakhic thought, is futile.[71] This initial objection to an action based on the overarching logic of the tractate (i.e., prayers on behalf of someone or for something) must have come as a surprise to the talmudic sages. The solution of R. Yosef, who introduced a biblical story of a miraculous sex transformation (Leah's daughter Dinah), does not satisfy the anonymous compilers of this talmudic tractate. Accordingly, they try to resolve the difficulties by resorting to a list on the development of the fetus taught in a source not included in the Mishnah, called a 'baraita'.

The list items or entries represent a more elaborate alternative, a set of useful prayers, rather than simple (and futile) wishes for a male child. All the advice is based on rather exact knowledge about the gestation process found in ancient Babylonian or Graeco-Roman texts on gynaecology and physiology. However, this knowledge is not theorised as such, but remains implicit. It is conveyed encapsulated in a list that relates specific time spans or periods from the moment of conception until birth to specific,

---

[70] b. Berakhot 60a.

[71] See Fonrobert, 'Regulating the Human Body'; Fonrobert, 'Sexed Body'.

potential dangers to the baby that prayer should help to avoid. Most instructions relate to being concerned about and praying for the unborn's survival (nos 1 and 4), healthy formation (i.e., not a 'sandal'; no. 3), and birth (no. 5). Only the second recommendation takes up the issue of determination of sex, which—according to other rabbinic texts and Graeco-Roman traditions—happens within the time span indicated (3–40 days).[72]

This list can be understood as belonging to the subcategory of the itinerary, in which actions are structured and ordered through time. Following Belknap, "the continuum of a single motion" or event (in this case, the pregnancy) "may be subdivided into discrete elements" (the various phases of the gestation process), and the development is expressed through an "elaborate listing of a series of events."[73] The catalogue of pregnancy prayers in b. Berakhot exemplifies the performative and processual aspects of prescriptive lists (recipes or therapies). In this, it shows how the "list and the narrative can work in tandem or, at times, merge closely together," since "how-to lists and recipes inform

---

[72] On rabbinic and Graeco-Roman embryology, see van der Horst, 'Seven Months' Children'; Kottek, 'Embryology'; Kessler, *Conceiving Israel*; Lepicard, 'The Embryo'; Shinnar, 'The Experiments of Cleopatra'. The concepts included gestation periods of different lengths for male children (40 or 41 days) and female children (80 or 81 days). For a brief discussion of Graeco-Roman embryological discourse, see Mulder, 'Ancient Medicine'.

[73] Belknap, *The List*, 3. The itinerary is similar to a recipe or a therapeutic instruction; the latter can be understood as a list of events or stages (of a journey) from illness to health.

you of the series of steps to be taken if you are to do something... as the potential narrative seems to become enacted."[74]

Moreover, all three aspects of lists mentioned by Goody merge here. One finds the chronology or record-taking aspect in the temporal scheme or structure of the stages of pregnancy, as well as the prescriptive dimension, as it indicates what to do when.[75] Simultaneously, it embodies the encyclopedic aspect through an accumulation of knowledge in a specific area (pregnancy or embryology) that can be transmitted and commented upon. Finally, it also has a cognitive or epistemological function. By including medical knowledge, it provides a reliable temporal framework for the appropriate prayers through which the microcosm of the human body and the macrocosm of divine creation are inextricably connected.

5.2. The Vade Mecum in b. Gittin as a Catalogue

In the tractate *Gittin* ('writs of divorce') of the Babylonian Talmud, one finds an elaborated cluster of lists, or rather a catalogue of recipes, which complies with the characterisation of cataloguing as a "major component of elaborate monumental works."[76] This large chunk of discourse—spanning over four printed folio pages—has been called by various scholars the 'Book of Remedies', while others prefer to call it a vade mecum or medical

[74] Richardson, 'Modern Fiction', 328. On the list as a proto-narrative, see Mainberger, 'Table of Contents'; von Contzen, 'Limits of Narration'; von Contzen, 'Theorising Lists in Literature'; Hoffmann, 'Aufzählungen'.

[75] Compare the study by Martin Wallraff in this volume.

[76] Belknap, *The List*, 10.

handbook.[77] Mark Geller, who has extensively worked on this long textual unit, described its main features. The list is structured following the location of diseases in the body, which complies with a common ancient way of structuring lists from head to toe; this prevailed in ancient Mesopotamian and Graeco-Roman medical traditions. Moreover, these entries ordered by body part illustrate the close connection between lists or catalogues and the physical equivalent in the empirical world. The body parts and their healing are represented and conjured via the list.[78]

The Gittin cluster comprises recipes for more than 40 ailments, and these all follow a stable pattern. Each entry introduces the ailment (-ל, *le-* 'for X') or the affected body part (e.g., 'for the head') followed by the instruction that the patient 'should take Y'.[79] While Aramaic dominates, certain elements (e.g., ingredients) or clues are delivered in Hebrew. This therapeutic advice

---

[77] See Veltri, *Magie und Halakha*; Freeman, 'Gittin "Book of Remedies"'; Geller, 'Akkadian Vademecum'; Geller, *Akkadian Healing Therapies*; Amsler, *Making of the Talmud*.

[78] See Kirk, *Ancient Greek Lists*, 8; this refers to Collins, *Magic in the Ancient Greek World*, 78–88, esp. 83–88, who highlights a connection between body part enumerations and healing ex-votos depicting body parts, on the one hand, and the frequent head-to-foot structure of medical lists and curse tablets, on the other.

[79] See Geller, 'Akkadian Vademecum'. Amsler, *The Babylonian Talmud*, 177–91, distinguishes recipes of this 'verb'-type, because of the imperative (e.g., 'bring…') from another style of recipe in which the remedies follow directly after the indicated ailment. For an ancient Egyptian parallel, see Hoffmann, 'Aufzählungen', 102, where the ailment is featured in the caption followed by various recipes.

can be very simple, featuring just one remedy, but often includes more sophisticated approaches. The recipes are completed with descriptions of plants and other *materia medica* (animal parts, stones, food, etc.) and instructions on how to prepare and apply the remedies. A remarkable feature of these recipes is that they include not only the application of drugs but also the use of bodily techniques, rituals, and incantations. As an illustration, consider the following brief example from the Gittin vade mecum:

> For a [sick] spleen:
>
> Let one take seaweed[80] (lit. 'that lying on the water') and let one dry it in the shade and let him (the patient) drink [the dried plant or a powder made from it] two or three times per day in wine.
>
> [alternative recipe] If not,
>
> let one take the spleen of a virgin kid and smear it on an oven and let him (the healer?, the patient?) stand near it and let him say, 'just as this one spleen is dried up, may that spleen of so-and-so[81] dry up'.
>
> [alternative recipe] And if not,

---

80 Printed text *šbbyny*, read as *škbyny*. The usual translation is 'seven leeches'—see Sokoloff, *DJBA*, 202—but this lacks any evidence from cognate languages. The translation here follows the reading of Geller, *Babylonian Medicine*.

81 Lit. 'X (patient's name) son of Y (name of the patient's mother)'. Compare b. Shabbat 66b: "Abayye said: 'An expert told it to me: [Individual] incantations [have to be] with the name of the mother.'"

> let one smear it between the brick layers of a new house, and let him say accordingly (i.e., as in the previous recipe).[82]

In this rather short entry for curing a sick spleen, one finds one piece of advice with a pharmaceutic or phyto-medical therapy ('seaweed' drunk in wine) and two instructions featuring an approach focusing on certain actions and pertinent formulas or incantations. This example also entails, like most other entries, a substructure that lists several alternative recipes. Thus, the straightforward introductory formula ('for X, take Y') is supplemented with another marker (ואילו לא, *we-ʾilu loʾ* 'and if not'). From the text itself, it is not entirely clear if this bridging formula is meant to indicate an alternative in case the first therapy fails or in case ingredients are lacking, or both.

However, in light of the present discussion focusing on list-making, I argue that the accumulation of alternative recipes for one ailment presents an apt strategy for collecting and cataloguing knowledge pertaining to ailments of various body parts or of the whole body (e.g., fever). The head-to-toe structure does not only figure in medical texts but can be also observed in poetical lists.[83] The 'for X' captions are easily browsable entry markers, similar to lemmata in a lexicon or encyclopedia, specifying the ailing body part or disease followed by the first or primary therapeutic instruction ('take Y'). The phrase *we-ʾilu loʾ* 'and if not' functions as a second, substructural marker highlighting every

---

[82] b. Gittin 69b, in Aramaic. The translation follows the reading of Geller, *Babylonian Medicine*. See also Geller et al., *Sourcebook*.

[83] Belknap, *The List*, 23–25.

alternative recipe. The catalogue consists, thus, of a lemma or entry ('for X') followed by a potentially open-ended sequence of various alternative therapeutic elaborations for the same item (ailment A: recipe 1; recipe 2; recipe 3 and recipe 3a; recipe 4; etc.). This order and its taxonomic structure conforms to what has been observed in a recent study:

> The catalogue, even if structured hierarchically by a taxonomic method, remains wedded to the simplest form of a list—that is, the arrangement of entries in a linear series that is read from top to bottom, while each individual entry is to be read from left to right.[84]

One basic difficulty of the Gittin catalogue of recipes in the Babylonian Talmud is that one cannot exactly discern its taxonomic hierarchy beyond the entries according to diseases or affected body parts. As already noted, from the text itself, it is not entirely clear if the alternative recipes are ordered on the basis of their expected or ascribed efficacy ('and if Y1 does not work, proceed to Y2') or if the order emphasises the availability of 'ingredients', which may not always have been readily available. The listing potentially also reflects the different therapeutic approaches from the easily procurable and rather pharmaceutical (plant-based) remedies to the more complicated cures, which often include prescribed actions and incantations.

---

[84] Müller-Wille and Charmantier, 'Lists as Research Technologies', 748. See also Hoffmann, 'Aufzählungen', 114. While linearity can be found in the talmudic catalogue, it does not comply with a vertical orientation (top to bottom).

Through this very structure, the catalogue also becomes an effective tool for actively exploring different approaches to and cures for the listed ailments. Besides this exploratory function, the catalogue also serves as a handbook for practical purposes. As such, it seems closer to similar collections (*euporista)* in Akkadian, Greek, Latin, and Syriac than to the rather complex pharmacological discourse in Galen and other medical authors, who like to theorise on anatomy and physiology before giving a treatment.

However, the Gittin cluster is not only a collection of existing knowledge: the very accumulation and condensation of information within the framework structure of the catalogue of recipes brings forth, shapes, and stabilises therapeutic insights. Consequently, such an endeavour also creates a field of expertise or a body of knowledge that is transmitted and serves as a pool of information from which future recipients can learn in various contexts (e.g., practice, instruction).[85]

Scholarship on the Gittin catalogue has often described it as an alien body within the talmudic discourse.[86] This would tally with Stephen Barney's observation that lists might appear as "in-

---

[85] See Steinert, 'Catalogues, Texts and Specialists', on how catalogues and lists shape and define whole fields of knowledge or ancient scientific disciplines. Hoffmann, 'Aufzählungen', 94–95, stresses the sequencing but also the limitation to the items contained in a list or catalogue that functions as a scaffold or skeleton of knowledge.

[86] See Freeman, 'Gittin "Book of Remedies"'; Veltri, *Magie und Halakha*; Geller, 'Akkadian Vademecum'.

truders" that interfere but also "potentially react with the narrative" in which they are embedded.[87] Accordingly, I argue that even if the list content has been derived from non-talmudic sources, the rabbinic authors sought to smoothly appropriate and integrate this catalogue by choosing multiple strategies. First, it seems very likely that the catalogue mostly contains therapies that were based on regional or local medical knowledge and practice (Mesopotamian, Mandean, Persian, etc.).[88] Second, the authors created dense connections on various levels: to a religious-medical discussion on the illness *qordiaqos* at the beginning of the chapter; a fading out of the core catalogue by adding some advice on diet and regimen ascribed to named sages; and through a discursive connection to narratives about a rabbinic sage and King Solomon, both related to therapies and the importance of knowledge.[89] In this, one may find some strategic resemblance to the ancient epic catalogue that "moves in and out, alternating grand sweep with intimate portrait. With narrative dynamism it also moves backward and forward in time."[90]

Finally, the breadth of the Gittin catalogue, the longest recipe cluster in talmudic texts, points us towards a notion of copiousness. On the one hand, it displays a wish for all-inclusiveness

---

[87] Barney, 'Chaucer's Lists', 190. Cf. Richardson, 'Modern Fiction', 328–29.

[88] See Geller, 'Akkadian Vademecum'. For the local character of knowledge production, see Cooper, *Inventing the Indigenous*.

[89] See Lehmhaus, 'Listenwissenschaft', 83–93. For a different strategy of embedding, see Amsler, *The Babylonian Talmud*, esp. 148–60.

[90] Belknap, *The List*, 11.

for this valuable encyclopedic compilation of recipes for the whole body. On the other, in the guise of long, almost excessive lists throughout history, the Gittin catalogue also interacts with its broader contexts by disrupting the usual halakhic discourse, adding new elements and parsing the rhythm of the chapter and the whole tractate differently.[91]

6.0. Conclusion

While some scholars prefer a dichotomy between poetic or literary lists and epic catalogues, on the one hand, and more pragmatic, everyday lists, on the other, many others challenge such a rigid distinction by analytically merging practical, poetic, and epistemic features.[92] As lists are "a powerful tool for propagating, but also revising, ingrained cultural systems of worth,"[93] rabbinic authors deployed them to transmit and modify the discourse of earlier halakhic traditions, adding new items and entering into a process of knowledge-making. Whether one considers rabbinic lists in the form of complex lists or broader catalogues, one notices "the joined but flexible nature of list components, operating somewhere between the extremes of detached isolation and rigid

---

[91] See Belknap, *The List*, 19; von Contzen, 'Limits of Narration'; Mainberger, 'Table of Contents', 20.

[92] Eco, *Die unendliche Liste*, 113; Belknap, *The List*. For a critique, see Kirk, *Ancient Greek Lists*, 4–8; von Contzen, 'Theorising Lists in Literature'.

[93] Kirk, *Ancient Greek Lists*, 2.

unification."[94] The items or entries display equality or difference, gradual differentiation (e.g. of symptoms, or recipes), or a process (therapies, embryological phases). Rabbinic lists "function to facilitate various forms of interaction between human beings... while also standing as a record or an index of... this interaction,"[95] especially when they are concerned with normative or legal questions (halakha) connected to medical or social issues (embryology, illness, therapies). Recent studies have stressed "the power of lists to stand in for objects, to act as the interfaces by which we access them. As a result, these lists become our experience of the things in them; more than just mediators or translations, they are, in some sense, the things themselves."[96] This happens, for example, with ingredients and other objects useful for the preparation of a remedy or the enactment of a therapy. Lists evoke the very materiality of the necessary objects but also conjure and reassure the involvement and reality of malevolent beings (e.g., demons) and apotropaic helpers.

Rabbinic lists and catalogues also challenge their readers to establish "connections, whether associative, temporal, or causal, between the separate items of the list as well as between the list and the surrounding narrative context."[97] The lists cast out their nets and form connections that expand into their broader contexts. For instance, taxonomic lists often draw on legal (halakhic)

---

[94] Belknap, *The List*, 27, discussing Nicholas Howe's description of the list as 'catenulate' in *Old English Catalogue Poem*.

[95] Young, 'Un-Black Boxing the List', 501–2, 505.

[96] Kirk, *Ancient Greek Lists*, 11.

[97] Von Contzen, 'Theorising Lists in Literature', 48.

triggers (healing on Shabbat; who can be deemed 'sane', etc.). As shown above, the catalogue of recipes in Gittin is anchored in various ways in its immediate chapter and the broader tractate.

Lists in rabbinic discourse interfere with or intrude into a different discourse—be it midrashic exegesis, homiletical speech, or talmudic halakhic discussion. However, although they are the discourse's other and stand out, they are well integrated and also possess a narrative rhythm of their own (e.g., the itinerary of pregnancy, the therapeutic instructions).[98] From ancient times on, we find lists either as proto-narratives inviting later elaboration or as index lists that condense information of an elaborated format into a brief enumeration. While we rarely find any narrative expansion of lists, rabbinic texts use simple lists to form more complex clusters and catalogues, as in the case of the Gittin vade mecum, or even a whole 'midrash of lists', as in the *Maʿase Torah* tradition. Lists lend themselves as if naturally to their expansion into catalogues or encyclopedic collections in which the former items of simple lists are transformed into entries featuring longer textual units, commentary, or even sub-lists.[99]

Rabbinic lists and catalogues should be studied in relation to their epistemic genre and their world-making/knowledge-producing function, since "cataloguing, listing, enumerating, and indexing can be perceived as attempts to order the world.... [L]ists are instances of cultural coherence and cultural identity; they are

---

[98] See von Contzen, 'Theorising Lists in Literature', 45–47, on the list as the narrative's other.

[99] On proto-narratives and lists as a pool of key terms, see Mainberger, 'Table of Contents', 19–20; Hoffmann, 'Aufzählungen', 117–21.

indicative of a particular view on the world."[100] Rabbinic lists can grant us a glimpse into the epistemic concepts underlying their knowledge. But, in fact,

> to list... is to do more than record; it is to display, to lay out, to arrange—to create reality—whether that be to represent a moment of complete awareness of the world or just to experiment, to conjure by naming.... By compiling, a writer can evoke for the reader an object or an action in all its definite and peculiar aspects.[101]

Simultaneously, the recipients are invited to decode the meaning of the list and its parts.[102] This seems to dovetail with rabbinic hermeneutics and reading practices which operate with gap filling and 'dialogical reading'.

But the discussion has shown that lists and catalogues do not function as simple containers or pools for accumulating the already known. Rather, through their structure or new captions that subsume surprising items, they can point towards new relations between parts of the body, illnesses, elements of nature, or social behaviour, which sometimes might even reflect a specific cultural embeddedness or certain historical circumstances. Here, list-making transcends the purpose of storing knowledge, and moves towards an 'epistemic game' of implicit questions and a

---

[100] Von Contzen, 'Theorising Lists in Literature', 35 (on Foucault).

[101] Belknap, *The List*, 19–20. See Kirk, *Ancient Greek Lists*, 2–3, on the ekphrasis function of the catalogue.

[102] Von Contzen, 'Theorising Lists in Literature', 49, 38. Cf. Mainberger, *Die Kunst des Aufzählens*, and Mainberger, 'Table of Contents', on the need to make sense and the necessary embeddedness into practice.

process of enquiry that facilitates the creation, discovery, and exploration of new insights and their potential relationships.[103] These aspects stand out in the rabbinic experimentation with new classification systems, such as taxonomies of illnesses, disabilities, or moral behaviours, or the alternative parsing of pregnancy and associated prayers. The rabbinic deployment of lists illustrates the "powerful potential that list-making has to open up new research agendas."[104]

In addition to the epistemological functions, "lists can carry objects across vast expanses of time and space,"[105] and thus one may use lists as a pool for another, more elaborated list, catalogue, or other format. The catalogue presents itself as an apt medium with some advantages over direct oral transmission or learning by doing or showing. This is a very prominent feature to be observed in the catalogue in Gittin and the whole genre of *euporista*, which sometimes border on becoming inclusive handbooks or encyclopedias of practical medical knowledge. As mentioned before, catalogues and encyclopedias may be understood as cultural inventories "which evoke, and ultimately create, the material world of another time."[106] Lists stabilise and underline

[103] See Echterhölter, 'Jack Goody', 243–45, who mentions, for instance, Borges's *Celestial Emporium of Benevolent Knowledge* or the Japanese *Pillow Book* in relation to fictitious and unordinary list categories.

[104] Müller-Wille and Charmantier, 'Lists as Research Technologies', 749. See also Kirk, *Ancient Greek Lists*, 8.

[105] Kirk, *Ancient Greek Lists*, 11. See also Müller-Wille and Charmantier, 'Lists as Research Technologies', 747–48.

[106] Kirk, *Ancient Greek Lists*, 14.

the cultural weight and importance of their contents. Their representation might "even supplant and supersede physical objects themselves."[107] In rabbinic catalogues, one finds knowledge and whole epistemic systems fixed, and these become accessible and transmittable between Palestine and Babylonia, and between late antiquity and later periods.

---

[107] Kirk, *Ancient Greek Lists*, 3. See also Young, *List Cultures*; Young, 'On Lists and Networks'.

THE UNRULY BOOKS OF ABDISHO OF NISIBIS: BOOK LISTS, CANON DISCOURSE, AND THE QUEST FOR LOST WRITINGS[1]

Liv Ingeborg Lied

A series of book lists survive from late antiquity and the Middle Ages. These lists have played an important role in the history of scholarship on early Jewish and Christian literatures, with a particular impact on discourses about Christian canons and on attempts at recovering the lost books of early Judaism. These academic trajectories focus on scale and categorisation; that is, the imagined ranges and confines of (late) ancient literatures. The allure of the book lists is that they give scholars a sense of order and control, providing tools for dealing with the vast expanses, the gaps, and the complexities of long-gone literary worlds.[2]

[1] This chapter was written during my stay at the Centre for Advanced Study at the Norwegian Academy of Science and Letters in Oslo in 2020–21.

[2] Belknap, *The List*, xii; Gilhus, 'Betydningen av religiøse lister', 46. The literature that theorises lists, list-making, and cataloguing is substantial. In addition to Belknap and Gilhus, I have benefited from engaging with

 https://doi.org/10.11647/OBP.0375.03

In this chapter, I will explore scholarship on one selected book list: the list[3] in Abdisho of Nisibis's Syriac *Catalogue of the Books of the Church* (henceforth, the *Catalogue*).[4] My focus is on the latter part of the first section of entries in the *Catalogue*: the writings Abdisho[5] ascribes to the Old Testament. I will reiterate the trajectories of scholarly interpretation of this section, which focus on the Christian biblical canon and the lost books of early Judaism, paying particular attention to the entries that have proven challenging to previous research. The first category of these entries includes writings that are only known to modern and contemporary scholars by title, and which do not survive as extant and available texts. The second category contains writings known by multiple titles. The third and final category consists of

---

Goody, *Savage Mind*; Spufford, *Cabbages and Kings*; Chartier, *Order of Books*; Eco, *Infinity of Lists*.

[3] Following Belknap, I apply the term 'list' to refer to "a formally organized block of information that is composed of a set of members" (Belknap, *The List*, 15). I will use the term in particular to talk about the cluster of entries in Abdisho's section on the Old Testament. I refer to his complete work as a 'catalogue', including more "descriptive enhancement" than a list (Belknap, *The List*, 2).

[4] ܡܐܡܪܐ ܕܐܝܬ ܒܗ ܡܢܝܢܐ ܕܟܠܗܘܢ ܟܬܒܐ ܥܕܬܢܝܐ. Vatican City, Biblioteca Apostolica Vaticana, MS Vat. sir. 176, fol. 26r.

[5] Abdisho of Nisibis is in all due likelihood a historical person. It is also likely that he was responsible for, or that he took part in, the making of the *Catalogue*. It is probably unlikely, though, that he alone would be responsible for the work. Since my key interest in this chapter is not the historical figure or his oeuvre, but the 'author function' associated with the name Abdisho of Nisibis, it is enough for my current purposes to know that this work has been ascribed to him.

those entries that do not comply with the scholarly imagination of an Old Testament book. It is my contention that a new look at the epistemological and ontological status of these categories of entries in the list will provide a crucial correction to the treatment of book lists by modern and contemporary scholars. My engagement with the unruly entries of the *Catalogue* will provide a new appreciation of the many ways of knowing (about) books and critically examine the scholarly imagination of late antique and medieval literatures.

1.0. Abdisho's *Catalogue of the Books of the Church*

Abdisho of Nisibis[6] (d. 1318) was the bishop of Sinjar and Beth ʿArbaye, and the metropolitan of Nisibis and Armenia in the latter decade of the thirteenth and the first decades of the fourteenth century.[7] Several works are associated with him,[8] including the

[6] He is also referred to as Abdisho bar Brikha, and sometimes in alternative spellings: ʿAbdishoʿ; Ebedjesus; ʾbd Jeshua.

[7] All dates are CE, unless otherwise noted. On the life of Abdisho, the works associated with him, and his importance in the Syriac tradition, see, for example, Wright, *Short History*, 285–89; Baumstark, *Geschichte der syrischen Literatur*, 123–25; Van Rompay, 'Past and Present', 96–97; Kaufhold, 'Introduction', xii–xiv; Brock, *Brief Outline*, 69; Varghese, 'Mar Oudisho'; Childers, 'ʿAbdishoʿ'.

[8] Other extant works associated with Abdisho are the *Nomocanon*, the *Pearl*, the *Treatise on the Rule of Ecclesiastical Judgements*, and *Paradise of Eden* (see, e.g., Brock, *Brief Outline*, 69). In the last section of the *Catalogue*, Abdisho lists his own writings. If we assume that all of these writings at some point existed as extant texts, several of his works are now lost. Note, though, that we do not have to take this for granted.

Catalogue, or more precisely, a "*memra*, which contains a catalogue of all the books of the church."[9] The *memra*[10] has been dated to the year 1298, but also to the early fourteenth century.[11] In this metrical treatise,[12] and as the title indicates, Abdisho lists all of the writers and writings that he identifies as belonging to the literary history of the East Syriac tradition.[13]

Abdisho describes the goal of the *memra* in the introductory section:

> ܡܟܬܒ ܐܢܐ ܡܐܡܪܐ ܬܡܝܗܐ܀ ܕܒܗ ܟܬܒ̈ܐ ܐܠܗ̈ܝܐ. ܘܟܠ ܣܝ̈ܡܐ ܕܒܬܪ̈ܝܐ.
> ܕܟܠ ܩܕ̈ܡܝܐ ܘܐܚܪ̈ܝܐ. ܣܕܪ ܐܢܐ ܘܩܕܡ ܦܘ̈ܢܝܐ܀ ܥܡ ܡܟܬܒ̈ܢܐ ܡܕܒܪ ܐܢܐ.
> ܘܕܐܝܠܝܢ ܐܬܟܬܒܘ ܘܒܐܝܢܐ ܙܒܢ. ܘܟܕ ܥܠ ܐܠܗܐ ܬܟܝܠ ܐܢܐ. ܡܢ ܡܘܫܐ ܗܐ
> ܡܫܪܐ ܐܢܐ܀[14]

[9] See n. 4. This is the title that appears in Vat. sir. 176, fol. 26r, dated 1476, available at https://digi.vatlib.it/view/MSS_Vat. sir.176, image 29 (accessed 4 November 2021).

[10] In this chapter, I translate the term ܡܐܡܪܐ *memra* as 'treatise'. This is potentially a reductionist translation of the Syriac term. Abdisho's text is metrical, and hence it is possible that 'metrical homily' would be more precise.

[11] Badger, *Nestorians*, 392; Kaufhold, 'Abraham Ecchellensis', 119.

[12] The *memra* follows the seven-syllable metre of Ephrem of Nisibis; Kaufhold, 'Abraham Ecchellensis', 130.

[13] The 'East Syriac tradition' refers to the traditions associated with the Church of the East. The Church of the East developed after 410 in the Sassanian Empire, outside the church structures of the Roman Empire. Resulting from the Christological controversies in the fifth and sixth centuries, the Church of the East follows the dyophysite Christology of Theodore of Mopsuestia. See Brock and Coakley, 'Church of the East'.

[14] All translations are mine. The text in the manuscript is richly dotted. I have only kept those dots that are necessary to convey the semantic

> I write an admirable treatise in which I will arrange before the reader the divine books and all the ecclesiastical tracts of all past and present [writers]. I record the names of the writers and [the writings] they wrote and in what manner. And trusting God, behold, I begin with Moses.

In this section, Abdisho explains that the *memra* will arrange all of the past and present divine books and ecclesiastical tracts, and he adds that he will record the names of the writers and their works, as well as the type (format, genre) of the writing in question.[15] As promised, he starts with Moses and the five books of the Law and continues to record the categories of writings of the Old Testament. After recording these writings, he continues with the New Testament. He then lists the 'Greek Fathers',[16] which both the East and West Syriac Churches hold as authorities. Next, Abdisho catalogues the writings of the 'Syriac Fathers';[17] that is, the Syriac writers and writings that are acknowledged by the East

meaning of the text. In addition, I have also kept all delimitation marks. The dotting can be seen in the digital images referred to earlier.

[15] The *Catalogue* applies a set of different terms to talk about the listed entries. In the opening paragraphs, Abdisho states that he will list 'the divine scriptures' (ܟܬܒ̈ܐ ܐܠܗܝ̈ܐ) and 'the ecclesiastical tracts' or 'booklets' (ܣܝ̈ܡܐ). In the list of the Old Testament, Abdisho applies the words ܣܦܪܐ and ܟܬܒܐ with high frequency. These terms are indeed commonly used to talk about 'books' in Syriac. (See my definition of 'book' below.) He also applies ܬܫܥܝܬܐ 'history' and ܡܬܠܐ 'proverb, fable' in this section. These terms may refer to different literary formats (see the discussion below). In other parts of the *Catalogue*, he also applies a wide range of other terms to render the genres of the entries.

[16] ܐܒܗܬܐ ܝܘܢ̈ܝܐ. Vat. sir. 176, fol. 28v.

[17] ܐܒܗܬܐ ܣܘܪ̈ܝܝܐ. Vat. sir. 176, fol. 28v.

Syriac tradition, ending with Abdisho himself. In the concluding paragraph of the *Catalogue*, he notes that he has recorded works ascribed to writers that spoke 'by the Spirit'.[18]

The present study is a study of one singular manuscript—Vatican City, Biblioteca Apostolica Vaticana, MS Vat. sir. 176—and its representation of the *Catalogue*. This manuscript is dated 1476 and is among the oldest manuscripts of this text that survive. I understand the representation of Abdisho's *Catalogue* in this particular manuscript as meaningful and interesting in its own right—regardless of the existence of potential 'variants' in other manuscripts.[19]

1.1. Abdisho's Old Testament and Its Latter Part

In this chapter, I will focus on the latter part of Abdisho's list of Old Testament writings. After listing the five books of the Law—which are associated with Moses—Abdisho continues with Joshua, Judges, Samuel, Kings, Chronicles, and Ruth. He then lists the Psalms of David, the Proverbs of Solomon, Qohelet, the Song of Songs, Ben Sira, Wisdom, and Job. He records all of the major and minor prophets, in addition to Judith, Esther, Susanna,

---

[18] ܒܝܕ ܪܘܚܐ. Vat. sir. 176, fol. 38r (image 45). Note that Badger reads 'the books which we have seen' (*Nestorians*, 379). This is not correct; or at least, it is not attested in Vat. sir. 176.

[19] Indeed, several manuscripts containing Abdisho's *Catalogue* survive (see, e.g., Kaufhold, 'Abraham Ecchellensis'), but in this study I neither attempt to cover all of these manuscripts nor the variance to which they attest. A critical edition of the *Catalogue* is still missing, and a comprehensive study of variance across the parts of the manuscripts that include the list of Old Testament writings remains a desideratum.

Ezra, and ܕܢܝܐܝܠ ܙܥܘܪܐ. This latter entry is likely to either be a reference to Young Daniel[20] or to the additions to Daniel; that is, Bel and the Dragon and maybe the Song of the Three Youths.[21] At this point, Abdisho lists the following writings:

> ܘܐ ܐܓܪܬܐ ܕܒܪܘܟ ܘܟܬܒܐ. ܕܡܫܠܡܢܘܬܐ ܕܩܫܝ̈ܫܐ. ܘܕܝܘܣܝܦܘܣ ܟܬܘܒܐ. ܡܬ̈ܠܐ
> ܘܬܫܥܝܬܐ ܒ̈ܢܝ ܫܡܘܢܝ܀ ܘܟܬܒܐ ܬܘܒ ܕܡܩܒ̈ܝܐ. ܘܬܫܥܝܬܐ ܕܗܪܘܕܣ ܡܠܟܐ.
> ܘܟܬܒܐ ܕܚܘܪܒܢܗ ܐܚܪܝܐ. ܕܐܘܪܫܠܡ ܕܒܐܝ̈ܕܝ ܛܛܘܣ܀ ܘܟܬܒܐ ܕܐܣܝܢܬ
> ܐܢܬܬ. ܝܘܣܦ ܟܐܢܐ ܒܪ ܝܥܩܘܒ. ܘܟܬܒܐ ܕܛܘܒܝܐ ܘܛܘܒܝܛ. ܙܕܝ̈ܩܐ
> ܐܝܣܪܝܠ̈ܝܐ܀ ܗܫܐ ܕܫܠܡܬ ܥܬܝܩܬܐ. ܢܫܪܐ ܚܕܬܐ ܒܥܘܕܪܢܬܐ.
>
> And the Epistle of Baruch and the Book of the Tradition of the Elders. And of Josephus the Writer, Proverbs, and the History of the Sons of Shamuni. And next the Book of the Maccabees and the History of King Herod and the Book of the Last Destruction of Jerusalem by Titus. And the Book of Aseneth the Wife of Joseph the Just, Son of Jacob, and the Book of Tobias and Tobit, Righteous Israelites. Now that the Old [Testament] is ended, the New [Testament] will begin.[22]

---

[20] See London, British Library, Add MS 18715, fols 239v–241v.

[21] For suggestions and discussion, see, Schmoldt, 'Die Schrift', 25–27; DiTommaso, *Book of Daniel*, 110–11; Haelewyck, 'Le canon', 163; Kraft, 'Daniel'; Brock, 'The Young Daniel', 267; Minov, 'Syriac', 116–17; Van Rompay, 'The Syriac Canon', 152.

[22] I understand the *waw* ('and') as the main marker of division between discrete entries of the list. Or to be precise, the *waw* both separates the basic units *and* binds them together as items of the same list (see Belknap, *The List*, 27–28). I understand the use of the dot and double dot graphemes mainly as indications of a reading break, supporting the syllabic metre.

This last part of Abdisho's list of Old Testament writings includes entries that are easily identifiable from Syriac and other linguistic traditions, and also includes a spectrum of entries that are harder to pin down. In fact, this section of Abdisho's list embodies several of the challenges that we face when we read and use medieval book lists. How have scholars so far understood the entries in this section? And how have they treated the section in their research?

2.0. Canon and Lost Books: A History of Interpretation

In the following, I will focus more closely on two of the main research trajectories that have directed the interpretation and use of the entries in the section. As mentioned in the introduction, the first trajectory is a discourse of canon, while the second is the search for and recovery of lost, Jewish books.[23]

[23] Both trajectories depend on the publication of two early editions of the Syriac text of Abdisho's *Catalogue*: Abraham Ecchellensis's 1653 edition and Latin translation (*Ope Domini Nostri*) and Giuseppe (Joseph) Simone Assemani's 1725 edition, translation into Latin, and commentary (*Bibliotheca Orientalis*). Assemani's work, in particular, has impacted later scholarship. For other, later editions, see Kaufhold, 'Abraham Ecchellensis', 129–33. It is likely that Vat. sir. 176 was one of the manuscripts that Assemani used in his edition. Kaufhold (p. 122) has suggested that Ecchellensis based his edition primarily on Rome, Biblioteca Nazionale, MS 1194. Note that Ecchellensis makes several changes to the Syriac text he edited, such as changing the order of the books of the Old Testament (Kaufhold, 'Abraham Ecchellensis', 130).

2.1. A Discourse of Canon

As the earlier quotation shows, Abdisho clearly marks the end of the Old Testament after Tobit: "Now that the Old [Testament] is ended, the New [Testament] will begin."[24] However, this latter section of entries leading up to Tobit includes several writings that scholars interested in questions of canon have found to be difficult to pin down and not necessarily identifiable as 'Old Testament books'. This has led them to produce auxiliary hypotheses to explain the presence and location of these books in the order of entries. I refer to the structuring presumptions, interests, and priorities that unite the contributions of this trajectory and that determine their approach to the *Catalogue* as a 'discourse of canon'. This is one of the dominant approaches in the history of academic study of Abdisho's *Catalogue*. In the following, I will present a selection of previous research contributions, focusing on some of the most influential. These contributions all participate in an explicit or implicit negotiation about what entries belong, or do not belong, in the scope of a Christian authoritative collection of biblical books.[25]

His editorial practice deserves to be studied in its own right in a separate study.

[24] The phrasing 'the Old'/'the New' (without 'Testament') is a commonplace in Syriac literature.

[25] The research on, in particular, the Christian biblical canon and its closedness/openness is immense. See, emblematically, the contributions to McDonald and Sanders, *The Canon Debate*. See also Gallagher and Meade, *Biblical Canon Lists*, esp. xii–xxii, 1–7, 17–29. For further discussion on the meta-level, see Rine, 'Canon Lists', 811–16.

In 1852 George P. Badger published *The Nestorians and Their Rituals*, which included the first English translation of the *Catalogue*.[26] The pages that include the translation of the treatise's list of Old and New Testament books include a feature that is not present in the rest of the publication: Badger adds a running list in the left-hand margin where he lists the common English names of the biblical books mentioned in Abdisho's *Catalogue*. However, when he arrives at the last section of the Old Testament, he mentions only three books—Baruch, Maccabees, and Tobit—all of which were well known to English-reading audiences as apocryphal or deuterocanonical books. However, this selection leaves out six of the writings that Abdisho mentions in the latter section of his Old Testament. Although Badger includes them in the running text of the English translation next to his marginal list, this graphic exclusion efficiently keeps them outside the order of Protestant and Catholic canonical books.[27]

In a footnote, Badger addresses the entries that he did not include in his list in the left margin. This footnote deserves to be cited in whole:

> The 'Narratives', and several of the other works enumerated in this paragraph, are probably legends such as are frequently met with in the East. Some of these are written with much pathos, and from epic poems, set to the most plaintive chants. The Legend of Joseph is very common among Mohammedans as well as Christians, and many

[26] Badger, *Nestorians*, 361–79.

[27] Note that Badger does the same in his list of New Testament books. He excludes the Diatessaron, which Abdisho listed at the end of his New Testament; Badger, *Nestorians*, 363.

> strolling derweeshes obtain a living by reciting it from house to house.[28]

The footnote shows that Badger disregards the entries that he avoids in his own list as "legends" from "the East." This footnote displays a heavy orientalising rhetoric, underscoring pathos, chanting, strolling, commonalities among "Mohammedans," and the economic benefits of stereotypically exotic performers. This rhetoric efficiently constructs these entries in Abdisho's list as something wholly other than 'proper' Old Testament books.

The entries in the latter part of Abdisho's list were not only challenging to researchers of the nineteenth century but are also demanding for more recent research contributions. Albert-Marie Denis referred to the last section of Abdisho's list of Old Testament books in his *Introduction aux pseudépigraphes grecs d'Ancien Testament*, which was published in 1970.[29] In this book, Denis aims to give an overview of Old Testament Pseudepigrapha surviving in Greek.[30] At pages xiv and xv, he includes a synoptic list

---

[28] Badger, *Nestorians*, 362.

[29] Denis, *Introduction*, xiv–xv.

[30] The term 'Old Testament Pseudepigrapha' is commonly used in research literature to refer to writings ascribed to Old Testament figures and story clusters that are part of neither the Hebrew Bible nor the deuterocanonical/apocryphal writings. The term is most often, but not exclusively, used in reference to Jewish writings from the Second Temple period.

of Christian apocryphal writings[31] mentioned in some of the major book lists surviving from late antiquity and the Middle Ages. Denis lists four entries from the *Catalogue*: "(Aḥiqar)," "(4 Mach.)," "Livre des Mach.," and "Asénath."[32] Just like Badger, his use of Abdisho's list is selective, and he leaves five entries out. However, Denis makes a different selection from Badger, based on the categorisation that directs his work. Given that Denis's synoptic list is a list of Christian Apocrypha, his list excludes, first, the biblical books that Protestant and Catholic traditions share with the Hebrew Bible and, second, the deuterocanonical writings. This leads Denis to exclude the Epistle of Baruch (which he probably understood as the Book of Baruch) and Tobit.[33] He is left with four potentially apocryphal/pseudepigraphal

[31] Denis uses the term 'apocryphes' to denote a corpus other than the deuterocanonical writings. In other words, he considers lists of Christian 'Apocrypha' as a place to look for potentially lost 'Old Testament Pseudepigrapha'.

[32] Note that Denis mentions "(Aḥiqar)" and "(4 Mach.)" in parentheses. The parentheses probably indicate that this is his interpretation of the title in the source. As the heading and footnotes in the synoptic list show, Denis did not consult the Syriac text of Abdisho's list—he was fully dependent on Assemani's translation. He explicitly called the list "Assemanus" and the footnotes provide Assemani's Latin translations of the titles of interest (e.g., "Josephi Scribae proverbia" and "Historia filiorum Samonae"). Denis also uses parentheses when he refers to "(Jub.)"—i.e., Jubilees—in the listing of books of the Gelasian Decree. This is his interpretation of the Latin title, "Liber de filiabus Adae Leptogeneseos, apocryphus."

[33] It is unclear why he includes (and what he means by) "Livre des Mach." 1–2 Maccabees are part of the deuterocanonical writings, which

writings from Abdisho's list. A side effect of Denis's focus on Pseudepigrapha and the frame of canonical categorisations is that he passes over in silence those entries that fit neither of these categories. If you read Denis's synoptic list only, there is no way of knowing that Abdisho's list also includes other items: the Book of the Tradition of the Elders, the Proverbs associated with Josephus the Writer, the History of the Sons of Shamuni, the History of King Herod, and the Book of the Last Destruction of Jerusalem by Titus.

In 'The Reception of Peshitta Chronicles', David Philips explores the potential canonical status of Chronicles in the Syriac traditions.[34] In the second half of his article, Philips explores the input of a category of writers that he refers to as "theoreticians of canonicity," among them Abdisho of Nisibis. Philips calls attention to the writings of Abdisho's Old Testament and refers to the last section as "a mixed bag of books," adding that "it is among these that we find the Epistle of Baruch, Maccabees and Tobit." He then focuses in on the reference to "Josephus 'the Narrator'" in this section, including the implications of this for the understanding of the *Catalogue* as a witness to the East Syriac biblical canon. It is noteworthy that Philips's otherwise thorough investigation of Abdisho's *memra* makes no mention of the other books in the "mixed bag." He names all of the books of Abdisho's Old Testament, with the exception of the Book of the Tradition

---

he otherwise avoids. It is possible that Denis understands the entry as the larger, multivolume Book of Maccabees, but note that he does mention "(4 Mach.)" explicitly.

[34] Philips, 'Reception', 288–91.

of the Elders, the History of the Sons of Shamuni, the History of King Herod and the Book of Aseneth the Wife of Joseph the Just, Son of Jacob. Thus these books are passed over in silence again.[35]

In 'Le canon de l'Ancien Testament dans la tradition syriaque', Jean-Claude Haelewyck also engages Abdisho's *memra* to explore surviving witnesses to an East Syriac canon. He starts by listing the writings of Abdisho's Old Testament, but similar to his predecessors he mentions only three of the entries in the latter section: the Epistle of Baruch, the Book of Maccabees, and Tobit. He then moves on to the other entries in the section, arguing that Abdisho must apply the concept of divine books in the broad sense in his *memra* and that the list of Old Testament books is "entrecoupée de la mention d'oeuvres extra-canoniques" and that the *memra* thus includes books that are canonical and books that are not.[36]

Finally, in 'The Syriac Canon' (a subsection of 'The Canonical Histories of the Deuterocanonical Texts'), Lucas Van Rompay frames his discussion using the same discourse of canon that we have witnessed earlier, but he provides a quite different interpretation. He sees a growing receptiveness towards deuterocanonical books in the Syriac traditions in the twelfth and thirteenth centuries and understands Abdisho's list of Old Testament books as one of the indications of this. Van Rompay includes the books

---

35 Philips, 'Reception', 288–91. He also makes no note of 'Young Daniel'.

36 Haelewyck, 'Le canon', 163–64.

"not found elsewhere" in his treatment and concludes that the status of these books "remains uncertain."[37]

In summary, the unruly items in Abdisho's list of Old Testament books have challenged scholars who have applied the list in service of a discourse of canon. However, given that many entries in the list do not fit the matrix of a biblical book, and do not even fit a 'pseudepigraphon', most scholars[38] have either recategorised, reinterpreted, exotified, excluded, or passed over them in silence. The result is that they have left behind significant blank spots.

2.2. A Discourse on 'Lost Books'

The quest for lost books has long traditions in the academic disciplines that study Second Temple Jewish writings, and for good reasons.[39] This field of study is characterised by a particularly challenging source situation, because late antique and early medieval Jewish communities themselves stopped transmitting a

---

[37] Van Rompay, 'The Syriac Canon', 152.

[38] Van Rompay is an exception.

[39] The academic interest in a systematic and comprehensive recovery of Second Temple Jewish writings started in the sixteenth century (1573–75) with de'Rossi's *Light of the Eyes* (esp. pp. 86–92). The interest grew during the eighteenth, nineteenth, and twentieth centuries. See, for example, Fabricius, *Codex Pseudepigraphus*, and its second edition, *Codicis pseudepigraphi*; Whiston, *Collection*; Migne, *Dictionnaire des apocryphes*; James, *Lost Apocrypha*.

large share of these writings.[40] Some of them went out of circulation and were forgotten,[41] while others were adopted, transmitted, and preserved throughout the Middle Ages primarily by Christian communities in the Middle East, North Africa, and central Asia.[42] However, many of these writings were not known as extant texts to the budding academic communities in Europe and North America until the eighteenth and nineteenth centuries, when large numbers of manuscripts were taken to Europe, bringing copies of hitherto unattested writings to the attention of scholars there.[43] Earlier generations of scholars knew references to these writings through citations in late antique works and because they were mentioned in the variety of book lists that were extant in linguistic traditions such as Greek, Latin, Arabic, Armenian, and Syriac. This means that, on many occasions, scholars were aware of mentions of works before they encountered extant texts.

---

[40] This is the case for the writings of Flavius Josephus and Philo of Alexandria, as well as the so-called Apocrypha and Pseudepigrapha.

[41] The finding of the scrolls in the caves close to the Dead Sea displayed several examples. See, e.g., Himmelfarb, 'The Pseudepigrapha in Greek', 263–64.

[42] Some writings have later reappeared in chance finds and archaeological digs; for example, the Dead Sea Scrolls and the fragments from the Cairo Genizah.

[43] The practice of transferring manuscripts from monasteries and digs in the Middle East to Europe was part of the colonial practices of the eighteenth, nineteenth, and twentieth centuries. These practices are currently heavily debated. See, among others, Mazza, 'Papyrology and Ethics'; Stewart, *Yours, Mine, or Theirs?*.

The book lists have played a particularly crucial role in the retrieval and identification of writings categorised as Apocrypha and/or Pseudepigrapha.[44] In the earliest phases of scholarship on these writings, the lists impacted the scholarly imagination of the contents and reach of an early Jewish literature that was presumably once in existence, parts of which scholars considered to be 'lost' because they were unaware of extant and available texts.[45] When extant texts of these writings did occasionally appear in the newly available manuscript materials, the lists became tools to identify copies in these manuscripts.[46] Although other entries in the lists remained undocumented, the experience that extant

[44] I apply the term 'apocryphal' in *one* of the ways in which it is used in late antique and medieval sources, namely to refer to books that are either contested, condemned, or not seen as equally suitable reading (often, public reading) as other scriptural books. This means that I am not addressing the deuterocanonical books, referred to as Apocrypha in Protestant traditions, which have been and are part of (some) Christian canons. Note that the term 'pseudepigraphal' occurs as a native ascription in some of the lists too, to describe a feature of individual books (namely, that they are, according to the one who put the list together, falsely ascribed to a biblical figure). The use of the term 'Pseudepigrapha' to encompass a collection of books (a 'literature') is an early modern invention, though, which starts with Fabricius in 1713. So, books referred to as apocryphal in the sources may be referred to as pseudepigraphal in scholarship, and the books falling under these categories may thus be overlapping.

[45] For the earliest phase, see, in particular, the publications by Fabricius, Whiston, Migne, and James, cited above.

[46] This has been the case, for example, for the Testament or Assumption of Moses, books ascribed to Enoch, and 2 Baruch and 3 Baruch.

texts could be recovered in surviving manuscripts strengthened the idea that the entries in the lists were indeed indications of lost writings that were still waiting to be found. In this epistemological matrix, writings still known only by mention in the book lists became a 'lost book' by default; hence, it was assumed that the titles mentioned in the lists referred to discrete literary entities—books that once were written and read by Jewish communities.[47]

The book lists that European scholars were most familiar with were, typically, some of the Greek and Latin ones.[48] Although available in Latin translation since 1635, Abdisho's *memra*

---

[47] See, for example, Denis, *Introduction*; Charlesworth, 'Introduction', xxi–xxiii (as well as the selection of entries in the volumes); Charlesworth, 'Foreword', xiv–xv. For a discussion, see Stone, *Ancient Judaism*, 174–76, 188–89, 192; Reed, 'Introduction to Forgetting', 13–16, 19–21.

[48] In particular, the Greek *Apostolian Constitutions*, the List of Sixty Books, the Stichometry of Nicephorus, and the list in the Pseudo-Athanasian *Synopsis of Holy Scripture*, as well as the Latin Gelasian Decree. See, e.g., Fabricius, *Codex Pseudepigraphus*, 16, 799–800, 801–2, 1116–17; Migne, *Dictionnaire des apocryphes*, xx; Whiston, *Collection*, 476, 481; James, 'Lost Apocrypha', 8–9; Kraft, 'James's *The Lost Apocrypha*', section 'Lists and Stichometries'. It should be noted, though, that many of the early volumes on lost Apocrypha/Pseudepigrapha drew heavily on Fabricius's work on the lists and thus often applied the books lists only indirectly: see, e.g., Migne, *Dictionnaire des apocryphes*, xxix–lxxii; Whiston, *Collection*, e.g., 444, 449, 462. The Armenian lists associated with Samuel of Ani and Mechichtar of Airivank and a selection of Slavic lists also figure in the research literature, many of them already in the early twentieth century; see, for example, James, *Lost Apocrypha*, 11; Denis, *Introduction*, xiv–xv; Kraft, 'Lists and Stichometries'.

was not brought into the search for potentially lost Apocrypha/Pseudepigrapha until 1970, when Denis included it in his synoptic list of apocryphal writings. Indeed, Denis's interest in Abdisho's treatise was part of his project to create a more comprehensive view of the Greek Pseudepigrapha, including "les fragments de pseudépigraphes perdus."[49] However, as I pointed out earlier, Denis left out several items from Abdisho's list that could have been considered "perdus," but did include four writings that qualified for him as Apocrypha/Pseudepigrapha.

In the first two decades of the twenty-first century, Robert A. Kraft worked on a project called the New M. R. James Project, which aimed to publish an updated, digital version of Montague R. James's seminal book, *The Lost Apocrypha of the Old Testament: Their Titles and Fragments Collected, Translated and Discussed* (1920).[50] Kraft aimed to make a collection point online, a "new, electronic, James"[51] that could easily be "expanded, corrected and reshaped."[52] Kraft's project enters into the long tradition of attempts to search for lost Apocrypha/Pseudepigrapha. Indeed, it takes the shape of a revision of James's catalogue of lost apocryphal books and Kraft applies the vocabulary of "known and lost

[49] This is the heading of part 2 of Denis's book.

[50] Kraft, 'James's *The Lost Apocrypha*'.

[51] Kraft, 'Eve'.

[52] It is interesting to note how the digital age offers a new potential, and a new yearning, for comprehensiveness. The format makes for a never-ending project—"an open-ended electronic resource."

writings" to grasp the variety that he encounters.[53] The book lists are important sources for this work,[54] and among the writings he refers to are the entries in Abdisho's treatise.[55] Under the rubric "References to 'lost' or suppressed writings associated with respected persons or groups," Kraft mentions the Traditions of the Elders, the History of Aseneth, and "'Proverbs of Josephus' [=Aesop]."[56] In other words, in this presentation, these three entries are portrayed as lost 'parabiblical texts'.

In the entry 'Syriac' in *A Guide to Early Jewish Texts and Tradition in Christian Transmission*, Sergey Minov provides a helpful overview of early Jewish writings in Syriac transmission. In the section on "Lost Works, Works Only Partly Preserved in Syriac, or Never Translated into Syriac," Minov includes the Book of the Tradition of the Elders from Abdisho's list.[57] He comments that "although no Syriac work bearing such title has been discovered so far, it seems unlikely that Abdisho invented it."[58] In other

---

[53] For the perspective of 'lost' in Kraft's project, see, for instance, his description of "known or lost writings" ('Reviving'); his presentation of the book ascribed to Og/Ogias ('Og and the Giants'); and his description of lost or suppressed writings ('Parabiblical Literature').

[54] See, e.g., 'Lists and Stichometries' and '"Parabiblical" Titles from Lists'.

[55] Kraft uses the name Ebed Jesu.

[56] Kraft, 'Parabiblical Literature'.

[57] Note that he does not include the History of King Herod. Note, also, that this is also the only entry in Abdisho's Old Testament that Assemani does not comment on in his edition and commentary (*Bibliotheca Orientalis*, 7).

[58] Minov, 'Syriac', 135.

words, Minov argues that it is likely that it once existed and, thus, should now be considered to be lost. In the list of "Works Discussed" at the beginning of Minov's entry,[59] the Book of the Tradition of the Elders appears alongside writings that are extant in Syriac. Therefore, this contemporaneous list serves to reify the claimed book in Abdisho's medieval list.

In summary, this second trajectory of engagement with Abdisho's Old Testament is part of an established scholarly discourse of lost Jewish books. This discourse construes the entries in the list as books that at some point had extant and available texts associated with them. In this matrix, the titles are traces of identifiable but lost writings that are defined first and foremost by their potential of being more than just names on a list.

3.0. 'Books Known Only by Title', Writings Known by Multiple Titles, and Entries That Are Not Books

As suggested in the introduction to this chapter, some writings mentioned in Abdisho's list are known only by title, others are known by multiple titles, and yet other entries in his Old Testament probably do not refer to books but refer instead to other literary formats. When the term 'book' is used in scholarship, it often refers to a literary entity that is conceived as a discrete and identifiable work that has a relatively substantial block of text associated with it. In the relevant scholarly fields, the most common example of this usage of the term is the conception of the

---

[59] Minov, 'Syriac', 96–97.

biblical book. Hence, the three categories that I will explore are all unruly and, in various ways, in conflict with the model biblical book. I focus on precisely these categories because they bring out the implicit epistemologies of the scholarship that has focused on the biblical canon and on presumed lost books.

First, when I apply the concept 'books known only by title' in the following I refer to writings that are unknown to us today in the shape of an extant text. These claimed books are known through (and are thus dependent on) another medium in which they are named and sometimes described or categorised. I apply the concept to stress the aspect of the entries in the list that actually remains and which is there for us to study: we know the names of claimed writings. Thus, we have access to a cognitive placeholder—the conceived textual object—regardless of whether or not these claimed books at some point also had extant texts attached to them.

Second, it is well known among manuscript scholars that the identification of a writing often varies from one manuscript to another. The identification may even vary within the same manuscript.[60] Title variation is also familiar to scholars who focus on literary texts. The same literary work may circulate under many names.[61] Therefore, there is good reason to suspect that

---

[60] See, e.g., Sharpe, *Titulus*, 8–9.

[61] There are many examples of this phenomenon. One pertinent example is the book (if that is really what all of these names refer to) that we today commonly refer to as Jubilees. This book has circulated as, for instance, Leptogenesis/Parva genesis, Life of Adam, Apocalypse of Moses, The Testament of the Protoplasts, and potentially Jewish Histories.

some of the names that appear in book lists are variant names of known works. On occasions, it is also possible that some lists may mention the same writing under two different names or that one and the same title may bring different writings to mind for different readers.

Finally, the general preference in previous research for the book as the presumed foundational unit of the list also warrants attention. On many occasions, the book category is fitting and helpful. However, the literary formats of ancient writings were richer and more varied and this may very well be reflected in late ancient and medieval lists.[62] For instance, independently circulating smaller pieces—that may at some point have been extracted from a larger whole—also circulated as autonomous literary entities. A named entity may sometimes refer to several different formats, which suggests that it may not even have been entirely clear what format a title in a list would refer to.

3.1. Revisiting Abdisho's Old Testament

The three categories introduced above will help me to illustrate the complexity involved in engaging with the latter part of Abdisho's list of Old Testament writings. My goal here is not to determine, once and for all, what literary work an entry refers to but rather to display the potential for interpretation.

The first entry in this section is the Epistle of Baruch. Peshitta Old Testament codices often include two epistles ascribed

---

[62] Cf., for instance, Mroczek, *Literary Imagination*; Lied, 'Between "Text Witness"'; Monger, 'Many Forms of Jubilees'; Larsen, *Gospels before the Book*; Spittler, 'Vienna Hist. Gr. 63'.

to Baruch: the First Epistle of Baruch the Scribe and the Second Epistle of Baruch.[63] The text of the epistle that these codices refer to as the First Epistle is very similar to the one that makes up chapters 78–86 of 2 Baruch. The Second Epistle is the name the Peshitta gives the writing known elsewhere as the Book of Baruch, Baruch, or, in modern nomenclature, 1 Baruch.[64] The entry 'the Epistle of Baruch' in Abdisho's list may in theory refer to either of these epistles. Thus, this entry exemplifies one of the challenges of reading the list, as suggested earlier: the same title may refer to more than one discrete writing. Badger understood the title as a reference to the Book of Baruch (that is, the Second Epistle).[65] However, it is just as likely that this is a reference to the First Epistle and that Abdisho understood the Second Epistle (the Book of Baruch) to be implied by the entry 'Jeremiah'. Whereas the Book of Baruch is included in the larger cluster of Jeremiah literature in several manuscript traditions, the Syriac Peshitta tradition is the only one that includes the First Epistle in that cluster. Hence, it stands out, and it is possible that it has thus been mentioned separately.

The second entry is a puzzle. In the manuscript Vat. sir. 176, fol. 26v, Abdisho records it as the Book of the Tradition of the Elders. This entry is an example of a book known to us by title only. It is mentioned in Abdisho's *Catalogue* but it appears

---

[63] See, Lied, 'Between "Text Witness"'.

[64] Cf., Ecchellensis, *Ope Domini Nostri*, 4–5.

[65] Badger, *Nestorians*, 362.

nowhere else. It is thus uncertain to what it refers. Abraham Ecchellensis understood it as a rubric, introducing the rest of the writings that follow after it rather than as a reference to a discrete book.[66] Giuseppe Simone Assemani suggested that the entry refers to the Mishnah, and his hypothesis has later been mentioned (sometimes acclaimed) in subsequent scholarship.[67] Minov offered another interpretation, pointing to similarities found in quotations of a rabbinic work in a preface to a Christian Arabic catena on the Pentateuch.[68]

Following the Book of the Tradition of the Elders, Abdisho lists Josephus the Writer, Proverbs. The syntax of the sentence is unusual, probably due to the syllabic metre. It is possible to interpret the expression as 'Proverbs of Josephus the Writer',[69] or as a statement of the name of Josephus the Writer followed by references to more works ascribed to him, the first being Proverbs. Note that the Syriac term, ܡܬܠܐ, can also mean 'fable' or 'parable'.[70] The entry may thus refer to proverbs, fables, or parables ascribed to the figure Josephus. As we shall soon see, several of the entries that follow the mention of the Proverbs are traditionally associated with Flavius Josephus. Thus, it is likely that

[66] Ecchellensis, *Ope Domini Nostri*, 4–7.

[67] Assemani, *Bibliotheca Orientalis*, 6–7; Haelewyck, 'Le canon', 163; Van Rompay, 'Past and Present', 80–81. Francis Borchardt has suggested that it may be a reference to Pirqe Avot.

[68] Minov, 'Syriac', 135.

[69] Kraft, 'Parabiblical Literature', understands it in this way.

[70] I apply the term 'proverb' to ensure consistency in my translation. The Syriac word is also used in the title of the Proverbs of Solomon.

Flavius Josephus is the writer that Abdisho had in mind. If so, then the Proverbs associated with Josephus the Writer is the second example of a book that is known to us only by title. However, Assemani and several other scholars have suggested that the entry may be a reference to Aesop's Fables, given that Syriac and Arabic sources sometimes ascribe these fables to Josephus. The name Aesop was mixed up with Iosippos/Josephus and the fables became associated with him.[71] Denis's interpretation of the entry as "(Aḥiqar)" builds on this idea: the Greek Life of Aesop draws on the story of Aḥiqar.[72]

The next entry, the History of the Sons of Shamuni, refers to a literary formation of the well-known narrative of the Maccabean martyrs and their mother, who is often called Shamuni (Shmuni) in Syriac sources.[73] This narrative enjoyed a widespread circulation among Syriac Christians in a variety of shapes. This very fact constitutes a challenge when we interpret entries in a book list: the title 'The History of the Sons of Shamuni' may refer to at least three different extant writings or textual forms.[74] The narrative about the sons of Shamuni is often associated with 4 Maccabees, as suggested for instance by Denis.[75] 4 Maccabees

---

[71] Assemani, *Bibliotheca Orientalis*, 7. See DiTommaso, *Book of Daniel*, 110–11; Brock, 'Aesop'. Hence, the entry is potentially an example of the re-attribution of a writing to another author.

[72] Brock, 'Aesop'; Brock, 'Aḥiqar'.

[73] See, in particular, Brock, 'Eleazar'; Witakowski, 'Mart(y) Shmuni'.

[74] Forness, 'First Book of Maccabees', 120–22.

[75] Milan, Biblioteca Ambrosiana, MS B 21 inf.; London, British Library, Egerton MS 704.

is almost entirely devoted to the narrative, and sometimes this literary content is reflected in the title that scribes gave this book.[76] However, the 'history', ܬܫܥܝܬܐ, of the sons of Shamuni may be a reference to an excerpt from 2 Maccabees that also includes the narrative. For example, an additional marginal heading in the copy of 2 Maccabees in London, British Library, Add MS 14446, fol. 90r, identifies the section of the text as such: "The History of Shamuni and her sons and Eleazar, Elder and Priest."[77] The extract from 2 Maccabees sometimes circulated independently, as is the case in London, British Library, Add MS 12172, fols 188v–192r. Hence, we do not know precisely to what writing or what format the entry in Abdisho's list refers.[78]

Next is the Book of the Maccabees. This is a multivolume work and the number of volumes ascribed to it in Syriac manuscripts and book lists varies from two to five.[79] Hence, although the identification of the reference in Abdisho's list is unproblematic and affirmed by several of the scholars mentioned earlier,

---

76 See, for example, 'Shamuni and Her Seven Sons and Eleazar, Their Teacher' (Milan B 21 bis inf., fols 312v, 320r).

77 ܬܫܥܝܬܐ ܕܥܠ ܫܡܘܢܝ ܘܒܢܝܗ ܘܐܠܥܙܪ ܣܒܐ ܘܟܗܢܐ.

78 In addition, several hymns, homilies, and narrative poems bear similar titles. For an overview, see Witakowski, 'Mart(y) Shmuni', esp. 157, 158. See additionally Minov, 'Syriac', 122; Young, 'The Anonymous Mēmrā'.

79 See the helpful overview in Haelewyck, 'Le canon'. See also Forness, 'First Book of Maccabees', 100–1, 123; and Van Rompay, 'Syriac Canon', 142–45.

the number of volumes and thus the range of the reference remains unclear. Abdisho also includes a list of Old Testament books in another of his works, the *Nomocanon.* In that writing, he lists three volumes of the Book of Maccabees. Thus, it is possible that this is the imagined extent of the entry in the *Catalogue* too. However, given that there are many differences between the lists in the *Nomocanon* and the *Catalogue,* this remains uncertain.

The History of King Herod follows the Book of Maccabees. This is the second entry in the list that is referred to as a 'history'. Once again, we are dealing with a writing that we know only by title. Many of the scholars that have dealt with Abdisho's list have overlooked this entry. For instance, it is the only entry in the section that Assemani does not comment on.[80] Likewise, none of Badger, Denis, Philips, Kraft, or Minov note its existence. A possible reason for this omission is that traditions about King Herod are more commonly associated with the New Testament and hence the entry seems to be misplaced or does not fit the categories that the scholars are investigating (that is, the Old Testament, Old Testament Pseudepigrapha, or other early Jewish books). A potential interpretation of the entry is that Abdisho has singled

---

[80] Assemani, *Bibliotheca Orientalis,* 7.

out one of the sources that Josephus mentions in *Jewish Antiquities*: the so-called Memoires of Herod.[81] However, this remains a hypothesis only.[82]

The Book of the Last Destruction of Jerusalem by Titus is, in all due likelihood, a reference to book 6 of the *Jewish War*, by Josephus. In the Syriac Codex Ambrosianus (Milan, Biblioteca Ambrosiana, MS B 21 inf. and bis inf.), the book is copied under this title. It is also referred to as the fifth volume of the Book of Maccabees.[83] Thus, this entry refers to a writing identified by several different names.

The second to last entry Abdisho records is the Book of Aseneth (Asyat) the Wife of Joseph the Just, Son of Jacob. This is the book that contemporary scholars most often refer to as Joseph

[81] *Jewish Antiquities* 15, 174. Josephus mentions the Memoires of Herod and a world history in 144 volumes associated with Herod's court historian Nicholas of Damascus (*Jewish Antiquities* 16, 184–87, and elsewhere). See Siegert, 'Minor Jewish Hellenistic Authors'.

[82] See Siegert, 'Minor Jewish Hellenistic Authors', 346.

[83] The title of the volume in the Codex Ambrosianus is 'Memra of the Last Destruction of Jerusalem' (fol. 320v). The two running titles say 'The Fifth Memra of Josephus on the Destruction of Jerusalem' (fols 323v–324r) and 'The Fifth Book. Which Relates to the Last Destruction of Jerusalem' (fols 328v–329r). The subscription of the Book of Maccabees on fol. 330r says '...the fifth [volume] on the last destruction of Jerusalem by Titus son of Vespasian, King of the Romans'. See Forness, 'Narrating History'; Lied, *Invisible Manuscripts*, 72–73. For the occurrence of *Jewish War* in Deir al-Surian, MS Syr. 9 (9A+B), see Van Rompay, 'Flavius Josephus' *Jewish War*'.

and Aseneth.[84] This name is somewhat misleading, though, because the book is just as often ascribed to Aseneth as to Joseph in medieval manuscripts. Consequently, this entry is another example of a writing circulating under several names in late antiquity and the Middle Ages. The identification remains confusing—even to modern scholars.[85] As pointed out earlier, Badger notes that the "Legend of Joseph" is common among "Mohammedans" and Christians. This note probably refers to the entry for the Book of Aseneth the Wife of Joseph the Just, Son of Jacob, but it is unclear why Badger chooses to interpret the entry as the "Legend of Joseph."

The last entry in the section, the Book of Tobias and Tobit, Righteous Israelites refers to the book that English naming conventions identify as Tobit. This book is infrequent in Syriac Old Testament codices, and Abdisho leaves it out of his other list of

[84] This name has been in use since at least the early twentieth century; see, e.g., Brooks, *Joseph and Asenath.* Joseph and Aseneth survives in two Syriac manuscripts: London, British Library, Add MSS 17202 and 7190.

[85] Among the names are: History of Aseneth; Book of Asyat; Prayer(s) of Aseneth; History of Aseneth and Joseph; Prayer of Joseph and Aseneth; Tale of Joseph the Just and of Asyat his Wife; Story of Joseph and Aseneth; and potentially also Prayer of Joseph. This latter name would probably be the result of a mix up with the Prayer of Joseph mentioned, among other places, in the Annals of Michael Glycas, in Eusebius, *Praeparatio evangelica* VI, 11 (James, *Lost Apocrypha*, 33–34), and in several medieval book lists. For an overview of the various titles, see Burchard, *Untersuchungen.* Note that although a large number of the titles suggest that Aseneth is the main figure of the tale, the conventional English name prioritises Joseph; see Kramer, *When Aseneth Met Joseph.*

Old Testament writings in the *Nomocanon*.[86] However, the book appears, for instance, in the twelfth-century pandect[87] Cambridge, Cambridge University Library, MS Oo. 1.1,2, and it is mentioned by some Syriac writers.[88] The title The Book of Tobias and Tobit does not appear in Syriac manuscript copies of the work.[89] While there is little doubt that this entry refers to the Book of Tobit, it is possible that the title formula aims to highlight the narratives associated with Tobias within it.[90]

As this brief presentation suggests, the entries in the latter part of Abdisho's Old Testament embody qualities that have made them confusing to scholars, and are incompatible with established epistemological frames and dominant discourses. Some

---

[86] See Mai, *Scriptorum veterum*, 183–84; Perczel, *The Nomocanon*; Haelewyck, 'Le canon', 152; Van Rompay, 'The Syriac Canon', 152.

[87] A pandect is a (perceived) full Bible codex.

[88] See, e.g., the list in Michael the Great's *Chronicle*, VI, 1; see Van Rompay, 'The Syriac Canon', 143–45, 151–52, 155.

[89] See Lebram, 'Tobit', 1. Indeed, the mention of Tobias in the title is rare in other linguistic traditions as well; see Weeks et al., *The Book of Tobit*, 62–63. However, the Greek Stichometry of Nicephorus refers to the book as "Tobit, which is also (called) Tobias" (Τωβήτ ὁ καί Τοβίας).

[90] Tobias is the most important figure of the book. See, for instance, the miniature in CUL Oo. 1.1,2, fol. 234r (https://cudl.lib.cam.ac.uk/view/MS-OO-00001-00001/501, accessed 18 January 2021), that portrays Tobias, Raphael, and the fish. The miniature is found at the beginning of the copy of the Book of Tobit and is used to mark the start of a new literary or layout unit, serving as an aid to retrieval and memory or interpretation. This suggests that identifying the book with the narrative of Tobias would be relatively common.

explanatory models may increase our understanding of the section. I offer these models as heuristic tools. Although none of them will explain all of the features of the section, they all shed some additional light on it.

First, as mentioned earlier, Syriac Christians ascribed many of the entries in this section to Flavius Josephus. The History of the Sons of Shamuni, the Book of Maccabees, the Book of the Last Destruction of Jerusalem by Titus, the Book of Aseneth the Wife of Joseph the Just, Son of Jacob, and the Book of Tobias and Tobit, Righteous Israelites have all at some point been associated with him.[91] In addition, and as suggested above, it is possible that the History of King Herod is a reference to a (fictitious) book mentioned in *Jewish Antiquities*. If so, then all of the books that follow the mention of Josephus's name in Abdisho's list bring his oeuvre to mind.[92] Given the overall logic of Abdisho's *Catalogue*, this would not be a surprising find. Abdisho states explicitly in

---

[91] See, e.g., the titles and running titles in Milan B 21 bis inf., mentioned above. BL Egerton 704 connects the History of Shamuni (e.g., 4 Maccabees) explicitly to Josephus; Deir al-Surian Syr. 9 connects 3 Maccabees to him. Likewise, several late antique and medieval writers attribute Maccabees to him. See Bensly and Barnes, *Fourth Book of Maccabees*, xiii–xiv; van Peursen, 'La diffusion', 202–3; also Assemani, *Bibliotheca Orientalis*, 7–8; DiTommaso, *Book of Daniel*, 110–11; Vollandt, 'Ancient Jewish Historiography', 73; Minov, 'Syriac', 112–14; Siegert, 'Minor Jewish Hellenistic Authors', 344–46. Note, though, that I have not been able to confirm that Tobit is associated with Josephus in Syriac sources. This remains Assemani's claim.

[92] Cf. Ecchellensis, *Ope Domini Nostri*, 7.

the introductory paragraphs that he "record[s] the names of the writers and [the writings] they wrote."

Second, it is possible that Abdisho gathers together writings that contain examples of, or that are ascribed to, ideal figures in ancient Israel. The section contains entries that are associated with a major biblical scribe (Baruch), hero martyrs (the Maccabean martyrs), an exemplary convert (Aseneth), and righteous and wise people (that is, the Elders, Joseph the Just, and Tobias and Tobit) of the Jewish tradition. Abdisho even refers to some of them explicitly as such: the section ends with the mention of Tobias and Tobit, "Righteous Israelites." An important interpretational key is that Syriac Christians would commonly interpret figures and narratives of the Old Testament as 'the old covenant' and as models and forerunners of the new covenant. For example, the Maccabean martyrs were often understood as the forerunners of Christ.[93] Aseneth could have been understood in light of the category of the holy women of the Syriac traditions, as well as a prototypical convert.[94] As I have pointed out elsewhere, a reason for Baruch's relative success among Syriac Christians may be his portrayal in several writings as the scribe that transmitted the knowledge of the old covenant to those who dwell "across the

[93] See Young, 'Anonymous Mēmrā', 329. See, furthermore, Forness, 'First Book of Maccabees', 120–22.

[94] See the manuscript context of this writing in BL Add 17202. According to Minov, it is located between biblical genealogies and the story of Constantine's conversion in Pseudo-Zachariah Rhetor's *Ecclesiastical History* ('Syriac', 111). See Brock and Harvey, *Holy Women*, 38; Wright, 'After Antiquity', esp. 71–72.

river [Euphrates]," bringing to mind Syriac Christians themselves.[95] Likewise, the story about Tobias and Tobit is set in ancient Nineveh and Media.

Third, it is likely that Abdisho's list of Old Testament writings implies chronological order.[96] The overall logic of the *Catalogue* suggests that this may be the case: Abdisho starts with the Old Testament and he ends with his own oeuvre. While not all of the individual entries of the latter section of the Old Testament comply with this logic,[97] a chronological logic makes sense if we accept the suggestion that the majority of them are writings ascribed to Flavius Josephus. Syriac Christians considered Josephus as an authoritative source to the major events of the first century—the birth and life of Jesus (implied by the History of King Herod) and the fall of the Second Temple in Jerusalem (implied by the Book of the Last Destruction of Jerusalem by Titus).[98] If so, then Abdisho extends his Old Testament or time of the old covenant all the way up to the first century CE. He thus links the Old and New Testament chronologically, letting the New take over where the Old ends.[99]

---

[95] Lied, *Invisible Manuscripts*, 258.

[96] Cf. Philips, 'Reception', 289–90.

[97] Tobias and Tobit is a case in point.

[98] For an overview, see Lied, *Invisible Manuscripts*, 71–74.

[99] A potential fourth explanatory model is that Abdisho was familiar with the way of organising the latter part of East Syriac Old Testament manuscripts that survives today in some seventeenth-century pandects. The latter collection of these full Bible manuscripts is called Maccabees

4.0. Unruly Books, Scholarly Priorities, and Abdisho's Old Testament

The two research trajectories that I have discussed in this chapter have one feature in common: neither of them fully approaches the entries in Abdisho's list of Old Testament books as intrinsic parts of the work they are part of, that is, the *Catalogue of the Books of the Church*. This means that instead of allowing the *Catalogue* itself to be the primary context for an interpretation of the inclusion of entries in it, the *Catalogue* is mined in the service of a project external to it. This approach is indeed common and can in some settings be fruitful, but only if the immediate literary context is also satisfactorily taken into account. As the earlier presentation shows, a focus on the three categories of books known only by title, writings known by multiple titles, and entries in the list that are not necessarily books highlights that this is not always the case.

4.1. Canon—or Heritage?

The publications that are guided by a discourse of canon have approached Abdisho's Old Testament with the Protestant and Catholic biblical canons as authoritative comparanda (Badger),

and includes 1–3 Maccabees, Chronicles, Ezra-Nehemiah, Wisdom, Judith, Esther, Susanna, Epistle of Jeremiah, First Epistle of Baruch, and Second Epistle of Baruch. Two arguments are against this explanation: first, too many entries in Abdisho's list are left unexplained; and second, the only surviving evidence for this collection dates to centuries after Abdisho's *Catalogue*.

to argue for the canonicity in the East Syriac tradition of a particular book while dismissing others (Philips), by questioning the legitimacy of Abdisho's understanding of "divine books" (Haelewyck), and even by protecting the category of Old Testament Pseudepigrapha from potential "unreal" books (Denis). As my earlier presentation shows, this has led them to either exclude, reinterpret, exotify, or silence those entries that do not fit their matrix. This move is particularly clear in the case of Badger. He uses all of the tools in his orientalising tool box to label the unruly entries as improper.

It is important to note that the list of Old Testament entries in Abdisho's *Catalogue* is arguably not a biblical canon list. In fact, Abdisho includes a list that would be more fruitfully approached as such in the *Nomocanon*. The list in the *Nomocanon* differs from the one that he included in the *Catalogue*; for instance, it is more restrictive in scope.[100] In contrast, the *Catalogue* provides an ordering of "the books of the church."[101] I share Van Rompay's judgement that Abdisho's *Catalogue* is a profiling of the

---

[100] Abdisho's list of biblical books in the *Nomocanon* is probably reproduced from the *Apostolic Canons*. See Mai, *Scriptorum veterum*, 183–84; Philips, 'Reception', 291; Haelewyck, 'Le canon', 152; Van Rompay, 'The Syriac Canon', 152; Gallagher and Meade, *Biblical Canon Lists*, 134–41.

[101] For a more comprehensive discussion of Syriac book lists and the biblical books in particular, see Haelewyck, 'Le canon'; Van Rompay, 'The Syriac Canon'; Gallagher and Meade, *Biblical Canon Lists*, 134–41. For other types of lists transmitted in Syriac manuscripts, see Matthew P. Monger's contribution to the present volume.

East Syriac literary tradition at around the year 1300—as someone at a given time and place conceived of it.[102] In this sense, it is a heritage list. In some regards, and particularly in some of its sections, the *Catalogue* is indeed selective and exclusive: it limits itself to figures and books that are widely acknowledged as authoritative within the tradition.[103] In other regards, the list is characterised by comprehensiveness and inclusivity. For instance, Abdisho includes the Diatessaron in his New Testament—in addition to the four Gospels. Furthermore, he is generous in his inclusion of contemporaneous East Syriac writers and books to the extent of being sweeping. The inclusion of 'histories' in the *Catalogue* points in the same direction. The history is a common genre in the Syriac traditions and an overview of Syriac literature would not be complete without them.[104] The fact that the entries in the *Catalogue* are ordered chronologically and in the shape of a list creates an impression of an unbroken chain of writers in the East Syriac tradition. Each entry is genealogically linked to the next and together the entries make up a comprehensive whole.

Thus, Abdisho's list of Old Testament writings is part of a catalogue that reflects someone's perception of East Syriac literary history. In such a heritage list, the Old Testament serves as

---

[102] Van Rompay, 'Past and Present', 96. In other words, the *Catalogue* does not offer a bird's eye view on East Syriac literature as it objectively was.

[103] See, in particular, his treatment of "the disciples of the Apostles."

[104] Van Rompay, 'Past and Present', 80–81. See Minov, 'Syriac', 118–19, for an overview of other 'histories' related to the Old Testament narrative world: History of Job, History of Jonah, History of Joseph.

the starting point. It is construed as the first category of East Syriac literature.[105] The inclusion of the Old Testament serves constructions of the antiquity of the tradition, of continuity, and of golden beginnings. The entries that Abdisho included in his Old Testament served these goals—their inclusion was not guided by canon, but by a notion of heritage.

4.2. 'Lost Books'?

The publications associated with the second research trajectory have another goal and thus meet other challenges than those met by the publications of the first trajectory. Their goal is to recover an early Jewish literature. To meet that goal, they trace entries in the *Catalogue* that may once have been Jewish books. Ironically, in contrast to the first trajectory that tends to make the unruly entries invisible, the second trajectory may end up making these entries hyperreal and creating an imagination of Jewish literature that is out of proportion.

The project of recovering early Jewish literature demands that entries in books lists can be pinned down as extant texts and as 'real writings'. A book that is known only by title and which does not survive as an extant text can either be disregarded as 'unreal' or 'false' due to its lack of an extant text (and thus considered irrelevant to the project), or it can be construed as a 'lost book', assuming that all entries by default were books that had texts associated with them.

---

[105] The Old Testament often serves as the beginning of Syriac historiography and the origin of the literary tradition. See Debié, 'Syriac Historiography', 94–95, 98, 103, 105.

This approach is challenged by some of the entries that I have discussed above, which may never have circulated as extant and available texts that were materially present in the world as layout units in manuscripts. It is possible that entries such as the History of King Herod refer to a fictitious book, which is embedded in a literary text. Another challenge is that publications of the second trajectory will easily fall prey to what I would call the 'one-to-one fallacy'. If we are to argue the existence of an early Jewish book based on an entry, then we must imagine a one-to-one relationship between an entry and an identifiable and discrete (sometimes hypothetical) extant text, and we also have to trust that the copying and transmission of the *Catalogue* has not affected the rendering of the entries. As my presentation has showed, many of the entries in the latter part of Abdisho's Old Testament may refer to a selection of potential texts; this is the case for the Epistle of Baruch, the Proverbs, and the History of the Sons of Shamuni. There is no clear one-to-one relationship between these entries and discrete target texts. In addition, given the general priority of the book format—particularly for entries that are catalogued as part of the Old Testament—the entries that the list ascribes to other formats (such as 'histories' and 'proverbs' or 'fables') quickly also become 'books'. The risk is that the publications of the second trajectory disregard the potential ontological multiformity of these entries in the *Catalogue*. For example, the History of the Sons of Shamuni may refer to 4 Maccabees, but it may also refer to an independently circulating, excerpted, narrative cluster.

5.0. The Various Ways of Knowing about Books

In this chapter, I have argued that Abdisho of Nisibis's *Catalogue of the Books of the Church* is best understood as someone's late thirteenth-century conception of the East Syriac literary heritage. In other words, the *Catalogue* provides a heritage list, and is not a canon list. Furthermore, the list does not provide an objective account of East Syriac literature as it once was. The list reflects the knowledge and the judgement of the list-maker(s) and the surrounding community at a certain point in time—which is mediated by the later scribes who copied and recopied the *Catalogue*. If scholars engage book lists such as Abdisho's *Catalogue* to mine them for historical information about books or categories of books that were once in existence, then it is vital to, first, take the book list into account as a piece of literature in its own right—that is, as a work that may not have been designed to answer the questions that modern and contemporary scholars would like to pose to it. Second, it is equally important to keep in mind that the list consists of names of writers and the titles of their writings. These names and titles are sometimes all that we have, and there is no direct link between them and identifiable texts outside the literary universe of the list. While we may harbour a deep longing for filling in the blanks, it may be equally beneficial—not least to our academic imagination of past literary landscapes—to allow the entries to remain unruly.

The three categories of unruly entries that I have explored in this chapter provide intriguing indications of the various ways of knowing (about) the writings that are represented in a book list. It is of course likely that a learned figure such as Abdisho read and handled (alternatively: heard read) many of the writings that he lists in his *Catalogue*, and that he thus knew them as extant and available texts. However, it is unlikely that this is the case for all of the entries that he includes. Van Rompay has suggested that Abdisho may not actually have been familiar with all the writers and writings he listed and that he may sometimes just have "quoted from memory or copied some vague reference."[106] Indeed, the character of a number of the entries in the *Catalogue* suggests that Abdisho knew many of them only by mention. As pointed out above, he treats some entries in a highly sweeping manner—"Bar Yaqub/Bar Shahaq,[107] he has one book; Damanais, he has treatises"[108]—and he also includes "a book that Paqor wrote."[109] This way of knowing about writings, maybe by hearsay, allows for misunderstandings, layers of interpretation, and the inclusion of entries that may never have existed elsewhere. Moreover, as suggested in this chapter, some of the writings that Abdisho lists may be fictitious. The line between writings known only by mention and writings that were fictitious can be difficult to draw. Alternatively, the inclusion of fictitious books may have served rhetorical purposes, filling in perceived gaps in the comprehensive account of East Syriac literary history.

In my view, there is nothing peculiar about this multifaceted way of knowing (about) writings. On the contrary, I would

---

[106] Van Rompay, 'Past and Present', 96–97.

[107] Vat. sir. 176, fol. 38v, has Bar Yaqub. Berlin, Staatsbibliothek, Sachau MS 312, fol. 60r, has Bar Shahaq.

[108] ܒܪ ܝܥܩܘܒ ܐܝܬ ܠܗ ܟܬܒܐ. ܕܡܢܝܣ ܐܝܬ ܠܗ ܡܐܡܪ̈ܐ܀ (Vat. sir. 176, fol. 39v).

[109] ܘܟܬܒܐ ܕܣܡܗ ܦܩܘܪ܀ (Vat. sir. 176, fols 40v–41r).

consider it to be highly common. In any attempt at profiling East Syriac heritage literature, we should expect to find entities that had different epistemological statuses for the list-maker(s). In a manuscript culture, where manuscripts and thus physical copies of writings were less frequent than in a print culture, a learned person would know about writings in many ways.[110] That person may have heard about and maybe yearned for several works that he or she would never see or handle. The conception of the literature of a tradition would far exceed what any person or local community would physically engage. Hence, when the goal is to provide a list of the books of the church, the imagination of a comprehensive literature would invite the inclusion of entities whose ontological and epistemological status were indeed varying.

---

[110] Of course, this is still so. We are constantly imagining, referring to and talking about the literature that we think about as 'ours', and that literature includes several books we have never read.

A LIST IN THREE VERSIONS: REVISITING AL-KINDĪ'S *ON DEFINITIONS*[1]

Peter Tarras

Philosophical texts come in many shapes: as treatises, epistles, and commentaries, to name but a few. But the list is not a typical or common format used by philosophers—and for a good reason.[2] Listing things, on the face of it, does not seem to have much in common with philosophical activity (apart from listing examples maybe, which, of course, is not specific to philosophy). Listing things may even seem to be the exact opposite of what philosophical writing is about.[3] Still, there is not a small number of types of philosophical lists that come to mind if we take a look at the

[1] This study could not have been written without the generous support and advice of the following people: Peter Adamson, Hanif Amin Beidokhti, Zeno Bampi, Dag N. Hasse, Paul Hullmeine, Andreas Lammer, Liv I. Lied, Adel Sidarus, Cristina Tomé, Sarah Virgi, Ronny Vollandt, and Vevian Zaki. I would like to express my particular gratitude to Rotraud Hansberger who read and commented upon three versions of this study. I dedicate it to my children Josef and Esther, who were born in between its first draft and its final version.

[2] Gabriel, 'Literarische Form', does not discuss the list as a literary format of philosophy.

[3] Compare Enrique Jiménez's discussion of *Listenwissenschaften* in his contribution to this volume.

 https://doi.org/10.11647/OBP.0375.04

Arabic tradition. Some authors have composed annotated bibliographical lists, for example of Aristotle's writings;[4] some important works were transmitted together with or contain annotated chapter lists;[5] some authors build their arguments on painstakingly compiled doxographical lists;[6] there are the lists of so-called isagogic ('introductory') questions inherited from Greek late antiquity; together with these, one might also consider ques-

[4] One important example is al-Kindī's *Epistle on the Quantity of Aristotle's Books and What Is Required for the Attainment of Philosophy* (*Risāla fī Kammiyyat kutub Arisṭūṭālīs wa-mā yuḥtāj ilayhi fī taḥṣīl al-falsafa*), which has a hybrid format including commentarial as well as encyclopedic elements insofar as it not only discusses the contents of Aristotle's books, but also the hierarchic order of the sciences that they cover. On this text, see Endress and Adamson, 'Abū Yūsuf al-Kindī', 158–59. On early Arabic catalogues of Aristotle's books and their Greek models, see Hein, *Definition*, 263–381.

[5] The most prominent example is probably the list of 142 'headings of questions' (*ruʾūs al-masāʾil*) following the prologue of the so-called *Theology of Aristotle*; see Adamson, *The Arabic Plotinus*, 42–48. Another well-known example is the 'enumeration of chapters' (*iḥṣāʾ al-abwāb*) transmitted together with Abū Naṣr al-Fārābī's *Principles of the Opinions of the Inhabitants of the Virtuous City* (*Mabādiʾ ārāʾ ah al-madīna al-fāḍila)*; see Richard Walzer's commentary in al-Fārābī, *On the Perfect State*, 331–32. Both lists go beyond mere enumeration.

[6] This feature permeates, for instance, Saadia Gaon's (d. 330/942) *Book of Beliefs and Opinions* (*Kitāb al-Amānāt wa-l-iʿtiqadāt*), in which almost every chapter is prefaced with a doxography. For a discussion of one of Saadia's doxographies, see Davidson, 'Saadia's List'.

tions-and-answers texts, a format which was often used for introductory purposes as well.[7] The best-studied example of lists in Arabic philosophy, however, is the terminological or definition list. Lists of this type are compilations of technical terms pertaining to philosophy and related fields such as mathematics or medicine. Roughly speaking, these lists offer philosophical glossaries. That is to say, glossaries riddled with all sorts of peculiarities.

The aim of this study is to take a close look at one such definition list thought to stand at the beginning of the career of this literary format in Arabic philosophy. This list is commonly attributed to the 'philosopher of the Arabs' (*faylasūf al-ʿarab*) Abū Yūsuf Yaʿqūb b. Isḥāq al-Ṣabbāḥ al-Kindī (d. after 252/866). I shall refer to it here as *On Definitions*.[8] Al-Kindī is one of the pioneering figures of Arabic philosophy, inaugurating a tradition that not only continued late ancient philosophical thought in a

---

[7] Daiber, 'Masāʾil wa-Adjwiba'.

[8] The designation *On Definitions* is a workaround, since the text bears three different titles or designations in three different manuscripts, a fact that will be discussed in more detail in section 3. I shall not use the title *On Definitions* in order to denote a hypothetical abstract entity (or archetype), but as a sort of umbrella descriptor for three different instantiations of this presumed archetype. What is more, none of the attested titles or designations was known to al-Kindī's bibliographers. As I argue elsewhere, the set of definitions of philosophy that we find in one of these manuscripts (referred to here as MS Istanbul), together with a few other items in the list of this witness, very likely formed the textual nucleus of what was to become *On Definitions* and what might have been a propaedeutic text in the tradition of late ancient Alexandrian introductory literature; see Tarras, 'Textual Genesis'.

new language, but impressed its very own character upon this heritage. *On Definitions* promises to offer, through the lens of terminology, insights into the way in which al-Kindī carried out the intellectual project of enculturating Greek philosophical and scientific knowledge in the Islamic environment of the early Abbasid caliphate. It appears to have had model character for later definition collections of prominent figures such as Abū Yaʿqūb Isḥāq b. Sulaymān al-Isrāʾīlī (or Isaac Israeli, d. between 320/932 and 344/955–56), the Ikhwān al-Ṣafāʾ (or Brethren of Purity, fl. fourth/tenth century), and Abū ʿAlī ibn Sīnā (or Avicenna, d. 427/1037). In a process of adaptation, excerption, and translation, *On Definitions* also became the substrate of Hebrew and Latin texts, making it an important link in a chain of Greek–Arabic–Hebrew–Latin knowledge exchange.[9]

Here, I am interested in questions concerning the structure, purpose, and use of *On Definitions*. As I shall argue, these are closely related to the textual practices it imposed upon its readers

---

[9] The Jewish philosopher Isaac Israeli composed his own *Book of definitions and descriptions* (*Kitāb al-Ḥudūd wa-l-rusūm*), which exhibits a number of textual parallels to *On Definitions* and other Kindian texts, as demonstrated by Altmann and Stern, *Isaac Israeli*, 3–78. The Arabic original has survived only fragmentarily. It was translated twice into Hebrew; see Altmann and Stern, *Isaac Israeli*, 5–7. Gerard of Cremona (d. 1187) translated the text into Latin. His translation was later revised by Dominicus Gundisalvi (d. after 1181); see Hasse and Büttner, 'Notes'; Hasse, 'Double Translations'. The Latin version of Israeli's *Book of Definitions* was used, for instance, by Thomas Aquinas (d. 1274); see Guttmann, *Die philosophischen Lehren*, 20.

and, thus, offer important insights into the emergence of *On Definitions* in its present shapes, in three versions witnessed by three manuscripts. In other words, the ways in which it was produced and the ways in which it was used converged more than once in its transmission history, leading to what we have before us now. It was the list format, possibly more than other formats, that invited participation in the enterprise of collecting useful definitions and terminological explanations. The three often-lamented haphazard instantiations of *On Definitions* make clear that it is the product of several stages of reworking and interpolation, defying our modern expectations concerning authorial dramaturgy. What I attempt to show is that some of the questions that are still open concerning its structure, function, and use can be addressed fruitfully once we attend to the stratified compositional process from which *On Definitions* must have emerged.

In the following, I propose to subject *On Definitions* to a distant reading of sorts; that is, my primary concern will be with the way in which *On Definitions* was used and produced as a text. I shall begin with a quick survey of previous scholarship, followed by a review of the manuscript evidence in order to make some observations as to the text's codicological settings and paratextual features. I will then offer an analysis of its different structural levels. Finally, I will turn to the text's users and the traces they left and argue that, once we are forced to acknowledge properly that *On Definitions* has not reached us as one unified literary entity, we realise that its three versions must each be understood as embodying the sum of the intentions of its users and producers.

1.0. Status Quaestionis

A swift glimpse at previous scholarship may suffice to give an impression of the problems that interpreters of the text and its versions have had to face. The study of al-Kindī's thought was put on a firm textual basis for the first time in the 1950s with Muḥammad ʿAbd al-Hādī Abū Rīda's two-volume edition of his philosophical writings.[10] The edition is based on the unique collection of Kindiana in Istanbul, Süleymaniye Kütüphanesi, Ayasofya MS 4832 (henceforth MS Istanbul),[11] which transmits *On Definitions* together with 32 other Kindian works on philosophical, astronomical, meteorological, and other scientific topics.[12] In 1959, Samuel Stern published a short article drawing attention to another witness of *On Definitions*: London, British Library, Add MS 7473 (henceforth, MS London).[13] Lamentably, the text offered not even one-third of what is found in MS Istanbul. However, it allowed Stern to draw two important conclusions:

---

[10] Abū Rīda (ed.), *Rasāʾil al-Kindī al-falsafiyya.*

[11] The importance of this manuscript was first highlighted by Ritter and Plessner, 'Schriften'; see also Krause, 'Stambuler Handschriften islamischer Mathematiker'. More recently, see Hullmeine, 'Ayasofya 4832'. The manuscript is available in a facsimile edition: Sezgin, *Codex Ayasofya 4832*. One huge disadvantage of this reproduction, however, is that foliation was cut out.

[12] See Hogendijk and Käs, 'Survey'; Hullmeine, 'Ayasofya 4832'.

[13] Stern, 'Notes'.

first, the list of definitions in MS Istanbul was apparently incomplete;[14] second, the list in MS London had attracted material that is evidently not by al-Kindī. In 1982, a third witness was brought to light by Felix Klein-Franke: Lisbon, Academia das Ciências, Série Vermelha MS 293 (MS Lisbon).[15] In this manuscript, the text of *On Definitions* exceeds the 98 definitions of MS Istanbul by 11 items, while having roughly half of the definitions in common with it. In the last third, MS Lisbon exhibits an accumulation of redundancies; that is, it lists quite a number of curious double definitions for terms that have already been defined earlier on. Klein-Franke highlights that these definitions are interpolations.[16] As demonstrated more recently by Joshua Olsson, they most likely derive from ʿAlī b. Sahl Rabban al-Ṭabarī's (d. ca. 250/864) medical encyclopedia *Paradise of Wisdom* (*Firdaws al-ḥikma*).[17]

The welcome unearthing of new textual witnesses had thus brought with it some intricate questions. What was the original form of *On Definitions*? Had such an original ever existed at all?

---

[14] Stern, 'Notes', 34, deduced the incompleteness of the MS Istanbul version from the absence of the "important definition" of 'universal intellect' (*al-ʿaql al-kullī*), which is, however, a misreading. MS London clearly, but also mistakenly, reads: الفعل الكُلّي (*al-fiʿl al-kullī* 'universal action'). The correct reading is offered by MS Lisbon: 'universal definition' (*al-ḥadd al-kullī*). Despite the corrupt text of MS London, Stern's observation remains valid.

[15] Klein-Franke, 'On Definitions'.

[16] Klein-Franke, 'On Definitions', 194.

[17] Olsson, 'Ḥudūd'.

What was its intended purpose? How was this purpose affected by the text's transmitters, readers, and users? Are later changes discernible as such? Is *On Definitions* to be viewed as the intellectual property, as it were, of one or many authors?

To be sure, *On Definitions* was copied and transmitted together with other important works by al-Kindī, especially in the Kindiana collection of MS Istanbul, and two of the three manuscripts explicitly ascribe the text to al-Kindī. However, it obviously cuts a poor figure within the Kindian corpus. In the 1970s, two re-editions with French translations were published by Michel Allard and Daniel Gimaret. Allard comments that the definitions "se suivent sans que l'on puisse déclarer entre elles aucun ordre."[18] He was willing to interpret this as a sign of the text's didactic function, having served some sort of introductory purpose. Gimaret, however, rejects this interpretation, concluding that, if the text is to be ascribed to al-Kindī at all, it must represent some sort of "brouillon laissé tel quel" or "aide-mémoire."[19] In 1975, Tamar Frank dedicated a doctoral thesis to *On Definitions*, expressing similar worries: "The treatise is apparently incomplete; there is no introduction of any kind, nor even a dedication or address which might give some indication of the purpose or the audience for which it was intended."[20] Peter Adamson and Peter Pormann, who more recently worked out an extremely useful commented English translation that takes into account all

---

[18] Allard, 'L'Épître', 49.

[19] Gimaret in al-Kindī, *Cinq épîtres*, 10.

[20] Frank, '*Book of Definitions*', 11.

three manuscript witnesses and their differences, are somewhat undecided as to the text's purpose.[21] They point out, however, that *On Definitions* "is not a discursive treatise or epistle, like al-Kindī's other works, but a list of entries which could have gone through many redactions, probably already in al-Kindī's circle."[22] By contrast, in her study of Arabic philosophical definition works, Kiki Kennedy-Day does not concern herself with any of these questions and simply asserts that it was written "for interested beginners in philosophy."[23]

These hermeneutical problems demonstrate that its stratified compositional process reveals *On Definitions* as an 'open' or even 'opened' text. Adopting this terminology from Israel Ta-Shma's description of Hebrew manuscripts as "open books,"[24] one could say that, like open books, open texts

> were not meant by their authors to serve as final statements, but rather as presentations of an interim state of knowledge or opinion, somewhat like our computerised databases, which are constantly updated and which give the user a summary of the data known at the time of the latest updating.[25]

By contrast, an 'opened text' would be one "which appears prima facie to be 'open', but was not meant originally to be so: it has

[21] Adamson and Pormann, *Philosophical Works*, 297.

[22] Adamson and Pormann, *Philosophical Works*, 299.

[23] Kennedy-Day, *Books of Definition*, 21.

[24] Ta-Shma, 'The "Open" Book'.

[25] Ta-Shma, 'The "Open" Book', 17.

actually been 'opened up' by its readers, not by the author."[26] The manuscript witnesses of *On Definitions* clearly represent different stages of 'updating' and it is its 'openness' that raises questions concerning structure, function, and use. In approaching these questions, therefore, it is necessary to first get a better idea of the manuscripts that transmit the text.[27]

2.0. Manuscript Tradition

All three manuscripts have in common that they are well-planned collections of texts. In general, their scope is scientific and philosophical. Both MSS Istanbul and London include mathematical, astronomical/astrological, and philosophical texts, whereas MS Lisbon more strictly focuses on philosophical literature. All three manuscripts are multiple-text manuscripts;[28] that is, they are, first

---

[26] Ta-Shma, 'The "Open" Book', 18.

[27] After the completion of this study, Paul Hullmeine brought to my attention another copy of the text in the manuscript Bursa, Hüseyin Çelebi Yazma Eser Kütüphansei, MS 1194. The text of this fourth witness is again not identical to any of the three known so far and constitutes a fourth version. We are currently working on an edition of it; see Hullmeine and Tarras, 'A New Manuscript Witness.'

[28] Recently a distinction between composite and multiple-text manuscripts was suggested to replace ambiguous descriptors such as *majmūʿ* or its Western equivalents such as *miscellany*, *recueil*, or *Sammelhandschrift* that fail to distinguish between customised and personalised user-produced manuscripts that assemble texts in accordance with the owner's needs, and manuscripts that are collections of texts due to the binding; see Friedrich and Schwarke, 'Introduction'.

of all, codicological units. However, MS Istanbul was not produced in a single production process (i.e., it is not a production unit), since some of the texts, including *On Definitions*, were added later to fill blank folio pages.[29] All three manuscripts transmit *On Definitions* with other Kindiana; MS Istanbul in particular exhibits a conscious effort to assemble a collection of al-Kindī's works. MS London offers documentary information about the antigraph, dating to 531/1136, from which *On Definitions* was copied together with al-Kindī's *On the Rule of the Arabs and Its Duration* (*Risāla fī l-Mulk al-ʿarab wa-kamiyyatihā*). This is actually the earliest date that can be assigned to the manuscript transmission of *On Definitions* and its connection to the Kindian corpus. In the following, I will give a non-exhaustive description of these manuscripts, highlighting some of the features that are important with respect to the textual transmission of *On Definitions*.[30]

---

[29] The manuscript still has a number of blank folios; see Hullmeine, 'Ayasofya 4832'.

[30] Exhaustive descriptions of MSS Istanbul and London are provided by the Bavarian Academy of Sciences and Humanities project Ptolemaeus Arabus et Latinus (http://ptolemaeus.badw.de); see Hullmeine, 'Ayasofya 4832'; José Bellver, 'Add. 7473'. For MS Istanbul, see also Reisman and Bertolacci, 'Thābit ibn Qurra', 725–28; Rashed and Jolivet, *Œuvres philosophiques*, x–xi. For MS Lisbon, I rely on the information given by Sidarus, 'Un recueil'; recently the manuscript was thoroughly described by Esmaeili, 'Sciences of the Ancients', 199–202. The information derived from these sources was checked against digital reproductions of all three manuscripts. I am grateful to Peter Adamson, Paul Hullmeine, Cristina Tomé, and Sarah Virgi, who made accessible to me reproductions of MSS Istanbul and Lisbon. Digital images of MS London

2.1. MS Istanbul

Content: 66 works on mathematics, astronomy, astrology, meteorology, medicine, and philosophy by various authors.

Paper; II + 232 folios (foliation in Hindu-Arabic numerals in red ink, counting from fols 1 to 150 and starting anew on fol. 153r; foliation in European-Arabic numerals in pencil); 220 × 125 mm; 29–32 lines per page; in four places (fols 57r–57v; 191v–193r; 206v–207v [*On Definitions*]; 228r–229r) varying number of lines; black and red ink; ownership notes and table of contents on fol. 1r; second table of contents on fol. 153r.

Script: Naskh (one main hand, later additions by different hands).

Date: fourth/tenth–fifth/eleventh century; later additions (eighth/fourteenth century).

MS Istanbul is a multiple-text manuscript, consisting of three parts and compiled by at least four different scribes. Hellmut Ritter dated the manuscript to the fourth/tenth–fifth/eleventh century on palaeographical grounds.[31] One of the later additions dates to the eighth/fourteenth century. *On Definitions* is also a later addition, yet the text was copied again by a different scribe (probably the same who copied the undated text on fols 228r–229r and completed the table of contents on fol. 153r). Thus, our text was inserted some time between the fourth/tenth and eighth/fourteenth centuries, possibly later. The oldest ownership

are available online via Qatar Digital Library: https://www.qdl.qa/en/archive/81055/vdc_100023601232.0x000001 (accessed 29 June 2021).

[31] Ritter and Plessner, 'Schriften', 363.

note (fol. 1r) states that the codex came into the possession of one Ibn al-Ḥammāmī Abī Zayd b. ʿAlī on 19 Rajab 568 (6 March 1173).[32] One of the ownership notes states that it used to be part of Avicenna's library, which, if true, would confirm a late fourth/tenth-century or early fifth/eleventh-century date for the initial production of the codex. A second note even claims that the main scribe was al-Shaykh al-raʾīs himself.[33] Part 2 starts with a new folio numbering (1–76 in Hindu-Arabic numerals) on fol. 153r and a table of contents, bearing the title *al-juzʾ al-awwal min kutub wa-rasāʾil Yaʿqūb b. Isḥāq al-Kindī wa-fīhi sittūn muṣannafan* 'first part of the books and epistles of Yaʿqūb b. Isḥāq al-Kindī comprising 60 works'. Of these 60 works, however, the manuscript contains only 33. The table of contents was numbered in advance from 1 to 60 in *abjad* numerals. A first hand added the first 20 titles, up to al-Kindī's *Book of Demonstration concerning the Proximate Agent Cause for Generation and Corruption* (*Kitāb al-Ibāna ʿan al-ʿilla al-fāʿila al-qarība li-l-kawn wa-l-fasād*). Interestingly, in the manuscript, two non-Kindian works follow this text. A later hand, possibly the same that copied *On Definitions*, added 10 more titles to the table of contents, apparently overlooking *On Definitions*, which was then noted in the box numbered 52 (نب). This procedure suggests the following scenario: a first scribe consciously planned an anthology of al-Kindī's works, which was to include 60 works in total. This scribe managed to

[32] Ritter and Plessner, 'Schriften', 363n1; Hullmeine, 'Ayasofya 4832'.

[33] The two notes are discussed in Rashed and Jolivet, *Œuvres philosophiques*, x; Reisman and Bertolacci, 'Thābit ibn Qurra', 726–27; Şeşen, 'Manuscrits philosophiques', 669.

collect 30 works, of which he recorded the first 20 in the table of contents. He left some folios blank before and after al-Kindī's *On First Philosophy* (*Kitāb fī l-Falsafa al-ūlā*, fols 196r–206r = 43b–53b). One later scribe disregarded the plan of his predecessor and used this space to include the two non-Kindian works, while another scribe inserted *On Definitions* after *On First Philosophy* and completed the table of contents.

Within the Kindiana collection, *On Definitions* is the twenty-fourth work. It begins with a *basmala*, a concise title and ascription: *risāla li-l-Kindī fī ḥudūd al-ashyāʾ wa-rusūmihā* 'epistle by al-Kindī on the definitions of things and their descriptions'. *On Definitions* comprises 98 definitions. The text ends with an explicit: *tammat al-risāla bi-ḥamd Allāh wa-mannihī* 'the epistle ends with the praise to God and His blessing'. Abū Rīda already pointed out that the scribe's hand differs from the one that copied the preceding and the following work. According to him, the text was slipped in for economic reasons in order to make use of the empty space.[34] This is certainly the reason for the extremely dense appearance of the later additions. The first additional text in the volume is a *Risāla fī Ruʾyat al-kawākib bi-l-layl lā bi-nahār* ('On [why] stars are seen at night and not during daytime') ascribed to Avicenna (but probably by Abū l-Barakāt al-Baghdādī).[35] According to the colophon of this text, the copying was completed in 755/1345–46. Even though *On Definitions* is a later addition as

[34] Abū Rīda, *Rasāʾil*, 163; see also Ritter and Plessner, 'Schriften', 369.

[35] Hogendijk and Käs, 'Survey', x; Reisman and Bertolacci, 'Thābit ibn Qurra', 726n34.

well, we have no indication that it also dates to the eighth/fourteenth century. It is clear, however, that its scribe consciously chose a shorter text that could be copied on two to four folio pages.

2.2. MS London

> Content: 20 works on mathematics, astronomy, astrology, meteorology, history, *adab*, and philosophy by various authors.
>
> Paper; I^a + 85 folios + I^b (foliation in Hindu-Arabic and European-Arabic numerals; quires numbered in epact numerals); 215 × 155 mm; 27 lines per page; black and red ink; text occasionally restored; ownership statement and table of contents on fol. 1r.
>
> Script: Naskh.
>
> Date: Dhū al-Qaʿda 639/May 1242.

MS London is a multiple-text manuscript produced by one scribe. *On Definitions* has no title and is simply referred to as *fuṣūl* 'sections'. Neither is it ascribed to any author. The text is preceded, however, by one of al-Kindī's works, namely his *On the Rule of the Arabs* (fols 175v–178r). This text's colophon is found on the same folio as the beginning of *On Definitions* (fol. 178r) and discloses that it was copied from a manuscript dated Rabīʿ al-Awwal 531/November–December 1136. From the same manuscript, the scribe also copied Apollonius of Perga's *On Pine-like Shapes* (*Fī Ashkāl al-ṣanawbariyya*, fols 164v–172v) and Abū Maʿshar's *Discourse on Astrological Indications* (*al-Qawl fī Namūdhārāt*, 173r–175v). The colophons of both texts specify that the copying took place "in the western area of the city Mahdiyya" (*bi-nāḥiyat al-*

maghrib bi-madīnat al-Mahdiyya), which, as José Bellver suggests, might be the coastal city of the same name in Tunisia.[36] The incipit of *On Definitions* reads as follows: "I have found these sections in the antigraph like this, so I copied them" (*wajjadtu hādhihi l-fuṣūl ʿalā nuskhat al-aṣl hākadhā fa-naqaltuhā*).[37] This means that the scribe copied this selection of texts from an anthology that already offered this arrangement. He does not bother to start the text with a *basmala* or title, which must also reflect the shape in which he found the text in his model. The explicit reads: "the sections end" (*tammat al-fuṣūl*). Hence, the 38 definitions of this text witness formed a textual unit appended to al-Kindī's *On the Rule of the Arabs*. Twenty-five definitions accord with definitions given in MSS Istanbul and Lisbon. A further set of 13 definitions exclusively concerns eschatological terminology, which Samuel Stern traced back to the *Epistles* of the Ikhwān al-Ṣafāʾ.[38] *On Definitions* covers only two folio pages. The incipit as well as the *mise-en-page*, however, suggest that *On Definitions* was not included as a space filler, but rather purposefully integrated as part of the compositional plan of this one-volume library. This indicates that the eschatological definitions, which Stern identified as spurious material, were not appended by the scribe of this manuscript, but already transmitted together with

---

[36] Bellver, 'Add. 7473'.

[37] Stern, 'Notes', 31, translates: "The following paragraphs were found in the copy which I used as my model, and so I transcribed them." In my translation, I have corrected Stern's transcription (*wajjadtu* instead of *wujidat*, p. 31n1) as well as his understanding of *hākadhā*.

[38] Stern, 'Notes', 34–37.

the 'common core' of all three manuscripts in the sixth/twelfth-century antigraph.

2.3. MS Lisbon

Content: 16 works on philosophy and one work on pharmaceutics.

Paper; III[a] + 85 folios + III[b] (foliation in European-Arabic numerals); 175 × 125 mm; 17 lines per page; black and red ink; occasional notes in Arabic, Arabic Garshuni, and Portuguese.

Script: Naskh.

Date: Rabīʿ al-Awwal 750/May–June 1315.

MS Lisbon is the second volume of a two-volume multiple-text manuscript (Série Vermelha MSS 292+293). It was copied by one al-Mubārak b. Ismāʾīl b. Muḥammad al-Kutubī al-ʿAbbāsī al-Baghdādī al-Mutaṭabbib during his travels between Aleppo and Alexandria in the eighth/fourteenth century (on the specific dating, see below). Adel Sidarus has pointed out that the texts assembled in this manuscript testify to "[l']intérêt évident du compilateur pour… écrits sur la terminologie philosophico-scientifique."[39] It forms the miniature library of a bookseller (*kutubī*) and physician (*mutaṭabbib*) who brought together a carefully designed collection of useful medical and philosophical writings. The manuscript was brought to the attention of scholars for the

[39] Sidarus, 'Un recueil', 185.

first time in 1982 when Klein-Franke published a diplomatic edition of *On Definitions*.[40] The text is transmitted under al-Kindī's name, but the title differs from the one given in MS Istanbul: *Risāla fī l-Asmāʾ al-mufrada* ('Epistle on technical terms'). As highlighted by Sidarus, *On Definitions* is not the only work on terminology in the manuscript. It also contains an excerpt from Abū Ḥayyān al-Tawḥīdī's *Exchange of Ideas* (*Muqābasāt*, fols 39v–44v) according with chapter 91 of that work, which itself offers a list of definitions that actually draws on *On Definitions*.[41] Similarly, the manuscript used to include an excerpt on terminological issues from Abū l-Barakāt al-Baghdādī's *Carefully Considered Book on Philosophy* (*al-Kitāb al-Muʿtabar fī l-Ḥikma*), which is now missing.[42] Further, it includes a number of (Pseudo-)Avicennian works that deal with terminological issues, as for instance a text entitled *On the Definition of the Soul* (*Fī Ḥadd al-nafs*, fols 62v–66r) that immediately precedes *On Definitions*, or works that have an encyclopedic scope, as for instance the *Epistle on the Entirety of the Parts of the Sciences of the Ancients* (*Risāla fī Jamīʿ aqsām*

---

[40] Klein-Franke, 'On Definitions'. Unfortunately, the editor failed to give the manuscript's shelfmark, rendering futile later attempts at comparing the (not flawless) edition against the manuscript; see Adamson and Pormann, *Philosophical Works*, 238n58; Olsson, '*Ḥudūd*', 247n8, 256.

[41] Stern, 'Notes', 38–42; Adamson and Pormann, *Philosophical Works*, 299.

[42] Sidarus, 'Un recueil', 185.

ʿulūm al-awāʾil, fols 1v–6v)[43] that opens the volume. Another, rather extensive definition work is found at the beginning of volume 1 (Série Vermelha MS 292, fols 1v–32r), bearing the title *Treatise on the Description of Divisions and Definitions* (*Maqāla fī Dhikr l-furūq wa-l-ḥudūd*). The manuscript's table of contents attributes this text to the East Syrian physician Ibn al-Tilmīdh (fl. sixth/twelfth century), yet Sidarus suggests the fifth/eleventh-century physician Abū l-Ḥasan Saʿīd b. Hibat Allāh b. al-Ḥasan (d. 495/1101) as its author who is mentioned in the colophon.[44]

On the last line of fol. 66r, the text of *On Definitions* begins with the title. After the *basmala* and a short prayer, the following eight folio pages offer 109 definitions. According to the colophon (fol. 70r), the text was copied in Alexandria "on a Thursday morning in the month Rabīʿ al-Awwal" by the aforementioned al-Mubārak b. Ismāʾīl. The subsequent date, written in a documentary hand, is hard to decipher, as it is also in other colophons of the volume. Previous scholars, including one of the manuscript's owners, suggested a range of dates. According to Sidarus, the manuscript was produced in 764–65/1363–64.[45] Hinrich Biesterfeldt read the date of the colophon of the Pseudo-Avicennian *Parts of the Sciences*, the first text in the volume, as "a Saturday evening in the month Rabīʿ al-Awwal of the year 615" (*nahār al-*

[43] On this work, see Esmaeili, 'Sciences of the Ancients'; Biesterfeldt, 'Eine arabische Klassifikation'.

[44] Sidarus, 'Un recueil', 185.

[45] Sidarus, 'Un recueil', 180.

jumʿa al-thānī [*sic*] *rabīʿ al-awwal sana khamsat ʿashara sitt miʾa*),[46] which would correspond to 2, 9, 16, or 23 June 1218. Below the colophon of our text, a modern hand written with a fine quill has given the following translation into Portuguese: "it was written in Alexandria in [the year] 705 of the Hegira, which corresponds to [the year] 1306 of the Christian era."[47] This reader note was left in June 1810 by the Franciscan polyglot translator João de Sousa (Yūḥannā l-Dimashqī, d. 1812), in whose possession the manuscript was at that time.[48] If de Sousa's reading were correct, the text would have been copied on 24 September or 1, 8, or 15 October 1305 (not 1306). However, he seems to have had a hard time deciphering the dates as well and must have changed his mind while sifting through the manuscript. On the flyleaves at the beginning (III^{a}v) and end of the codex (III^{b}v), he gives the date 605/1206, though the first was corrected from what seems to have been 705/1306. The correct reading, however, as recently argued by Mohammad Esmaeili, is *khamsat ʿashara wa-sabʿ*

---

46 Biesterfeldt, 'Eine arabische Klassifikation', 265; the English translation is mine.

47 *Foi escrito em Alexandria em 705 da Hegira = = que corresponde ao* [sc. *ano*] *de 1306 de Christo*. I am grateful to Sarah Virgi for her remarks on how to understand the note.

48 On João de Sousa, see Figanier, *Fr. João de Sousa*; Sidarus, 'Introduction'; Braga, 'Os manuscritos árabes'.

mi'a, that is, 715/1315.[49] Hence, *On Definitions* was copied on 13, 20, or 27 June or 4 July 1315.

3.0. Structure

Having obtained a better understanding of the codicological settings of *On Definitions*, I shall now turn to its structure both as a physical and as an abstract entity. I will consider it on the following three levels: on a visual or representational level, on a syntactic level, and on a semantic level.

The list format provides the text's basic structure. Following the directionality of the Arabic script (right to left, top to bottom), this format generally functions according to two principles, a vertical and a horizontal one: the vertical structure is imposed upon the text by the successive listing of entries, which is itself organised graphically by the use of paratextual markers. None of our manuscripts makes use of paragraph breaks; that is, new entries do not start on a new line. The horizontal structure is provided by the definitional content and organised syntactically. If one compares the manuscripts with their modern editions and translations, it can easily be noticed that these structural principles are enhanced by adding further elements like numbering, dashes, punctuation, paragraph breaks, and so on. All these elements serve the purpose of navigating the reader through the text. When compared to its modern instantiations, the manuscript versions of *On Definitions* give a rather messy impression.

---

[49] Esmaeili, 'Sciences of the Ancients', 200–201. I would like to thank Vevian Zaki for discussing the date of the colophons of MS Lisbon with me.

Yet already the copyists employed certain strategies of navigation. In my concluding remarks, I will return to these scribal techniques and discuss the way in which they reflect a change in the text's use.

3.1. Visual Structure

In all three manuscripts, the text of *On Definitions* is written out en bloc without paragraph breaks. This is a very common and economic—that is, space-saving—way of representing lists in manuscripts (see the contribution by Matthew P. Monger in this volume). No other visual means of enhancing the text's structure were employed. In MS Istanbul, the copyist uses the common feature of paragraph marks (*fawāṣil*) in the shape of the letter *hāʾ* (an abbreviation for *intihāʾ* 'end') to separate the different entries from one another.[50] The copyist of MS London employed blank spaces to provide a visual structure that helps in distinguishing the respective items. The blank spaces have been left for the purpose of later insertion of textual dividers, which was never carried out. A similar approach was followed by the copyist of MS Lisbon, though occasionally he also used *hāʾ*-shaped dividers, assuming the form of a dotted circle.

What stands out in MS Lisbon is the red underlining used to mark the *definienda* of each item and, thus, enhance the text's vertical structure. This paratextual feature, however, was added semi-automatically, since in a number of cases the *definienda* are left without marking. In other cases, the spacing between words

---

[50] See Gacek, *Arabic Manuscripts*, 269–70.

was mistaken for the beginning of a new definition. Red ink is used with a similar intention also in the definition list extracted from Tawḥīdī's *Exchange of Ideas*. It was probably added by a later hand, possibly one of its later owners, and testifies to the way in which readers of *On Definitions* interacted with this text as a concrete physical entity. This interaction affected only the text's surface, as it were. But in a few instances, their interactions go beyond this mere representational level.

In MS London, the definition of 'imagination' (*tawahhum*) has been divided into two entries. The scribe's testimony quoted above suggests that this is how he found the text in his model. What seems to have happened, however, is that the scribe of the model realised after a while that he had copied only half of the item's text. Scribal cancellations in MSS Istanbul and Lisbon testify to the difficulties the copyists experienced when trying to locate again the definition they were copying. In MS London, this common problem of manuscript copying effectively led to a longer list of definitions, that is, a slightly different text. Inadvertently (or so it would seem), Stern later undid the copyist's correction by overlooking the second definition of 'imagination' in MS London.[51]

Considerations of an economic nature have affected the text's shape as well. In MS Istanbul it was copied on three blank folio pages, giving it an extremely dense impression (the last folio

---

[51] The manuscript reads: *a<l-t>awahhum huwa quwwa nafsāniyya mudri<k>a li-l-ṣūra al-ḥissiyya* ('imagination is a psychic faculty perceiving sensible forms in the absence of their matter'). This is the second part of the definition, which is missed in Stern, 'Notes', 22.

of the text has 49 lines, while the facing page to the left starting with a new text has 32 lines). The explicit suggests that the number of definitions was not dependent upon the available space. The shortness of the version in MS London, however, could be explained that way. In the antigraph of this manuscript, *On Definitions* could actually have served as a space filler.

3.2. Syntactic Structure

We must assume that readers similarly interacted with the text on an even earlier temporal level. At that point, their interaction was to affect it as an abstract entity. This can be demonstrated if we turn to the horizontal structure of the syntax. In most cases, the definitions are nominal sentences, starting with a definite noun (marked by the definite article *al-*),[52] the *definiendum*, which is then followed either by a personal pronoun (*huwa/hiya*) that functions as the copula, a definite or indefinite predicate noun, or a relative pronoun (*mā, alladhī, allatī*) that connects the *definiendum* to the entry's definitional content. In some cases the *definiendum* is followed by a finite verb. We may take as an example the definition of 'soul' (*nafs*):

> *al-nafs tamāmat jirm ṭabīʿī dhī āla qābila li-l-ḥayāt wa-yuqāl hiya istikmāl awwal li-jirm ṭabīʿī dhī ḥayāt bi-l-quwwa wa-*

[52] In one case the lack of the definite article rightfully gives occasion to doubt the text's soundness; see Adamson and Pormann, *Philosophical Works*, 335n181.

> *yuqāl hiya jawhar ʿaqlī*[53] *mutaḥarrik min dhātihī bi-ʿadad muʾallaf*
>
> The soul is the perfection of the natural body, possessing organs and being receptive of life. And it is said: it is the first perfection of the natural body, possessing life potentially. And it is said: it is an intellectual substance, self-moving by a harmonious number. (MS Istanbul)
>
> *al-nafs tamāmat jirm ṭabīʿī dhū āla qābil li-l-ḥayāt bi-l-quwwa*
>
> The soul is the perfection of the natural body, possessing organs and being receptive of life potentially. (MS London)
>
> *al-nafs tamāmat jirm ṭabīʿī dhī āla qābila li-l-ḥayāt*
>
> The soul is the perfection of the natural body, possessing organs and being receptive of life. (MS Lisbon)

What is really striking here is that the text of MS Istanbul is about three times as long as that of the other two versions. The additional text is introduced by the phrase *wa-yuqāl* ('and it is said'), which also recurs a second time in the same entry. Both times it is followed by the copula (*hiya*) allowing to introduce two further nominally structured definitions. The seemingly harmless phrase *wa-yuqāl*, which turns up 11 times in MS Istanbul, functions as an editorial marker, that is, it marks editorial interferences where further explanatory material has been added. Other such editorial phrases are *wa-ayḍan* ('and also') or the expression *wa-yursamu ayḍan bi-annahū* ('and it is also described in that'), which occurs in MS Lisbon. On a syntactic level, these phrases indicate textual additions. Editorial markers are traces of intervention and

---

[53] MS reads: عقل; cf. Adamson and Pormann, *Philosophical Works*, 328n64.

neatly separate the textual core of a definition from later additions. There is, however, no way to tell when these additions were made. It is by no means the case that MSS London and Lisbon only transmit core definitions, though editorial markers are completely absent from MS London. For instance, the definition of 'opinion' (*raʾy*) in MSS Istanbul and Lisbon is a prolonged version with two instances of *wa-yuqāl*. This, in my view, indicates that the scribes, not of our present manuscripts, but possibly of their models, performed some sort of selection, which led to the simultaneous inclusion of core and prolonged definitions in the version of MS Lisbon, while MS London evinces a prevalence of concise core definitions. In this case, they effectively interacted with earlier readers who were responsible for the editorial interventions.

There are other syntactic elements that equally indicate a stratified compositional process. Some took place before the respective definitions became part of *On Definitions*. The version of MS Lisbon offers a curious set of double definitions. Each of these differentiates the definitional content by qualifying one part as defined "with respect to instruction" (*min jihat al-taʿlīm*) and a second part as defined "with respect to nature" (*min jihat al-ṭabʿ/al-ṭibāʿ*). Different views have been voiced concerning this peculiarity. According to Klein-Franke, the definitions exhibiting this feature have to be considered as interpolations.[54] Adamson

[54] He adds the unsubstantiated claim that these "were at the head of a similarly arranged but unknown list of definitions"; Klein-Franke, 'On Definitions', 194. Olsson, '*Ḥudūd*', 255–56, misquotes Klein-Franke by adding "[i]n the same manuscript."

and Pormann comment that in these cases "the first definition is a looser but more intuitive one intended for beginners, whereas the second is technical and more strictly accurate."[55] This is partly confirmed by one of the definitions of 'definition', which also employs the editorial phrase *wa-yuqāl*: "the definition is a brief statement that indicates the essences of things. And it is said: it is a brief statement [that indicates] the nature of the existing thing" (*al-ḥadd qawl wajīz yadullu ʿalā ḥaqāʾiq al-ashyāʾ wa-yuqālu qawl wajīz* [*yadullu*] *ʿalā ṭabīʿat al-shayʾ al-mawjūd*).[56] Essence (*ḥaqīqa*) and nature (*ṭabīʿa*) are Arabic equivalents to the Aristotelian *to ti ēn einai*, which, according to *Posterior Analytics* II.3 (90b4), the definition is supposed to indicate. Thus, the second part of the double definitions, marked by the phrase *min jihat al-ṭabʿ/al-ṭibāʿ*, consists of definitions that accord or at least seek to accord with the Aristotelian definition of 'definition'. The part marked by the phrase *min jihat al-taʿlīm*, however, does not necessarily indicate a didactic purpose, but simply seems to introduce additional material. If we consider the distinction between *min jihat al-ṭabʿ/al-ṭibāʿ* and *min jihat al-taʿlīm* as a pair of editorial phrases, it becomes clear that it also allowed for opening up the text of the definition proper for secondary material of an explanatory or doxographic nature. In the definition of 'soul' in the version of MS Istanbul, for instance, the first *wa-yuqāl* introduces a

---

55 Adamson and Pormann, *Philosophical Works*, 335n168.

56 Edition from Klein-Franke, 'On Definitions', 215, lines 12–13; translation slightly modified from Adamson and Pormann, *Philosophical Works*, 311.

clarification of the essentially Aristotelian definition, while the second *wa-yuqāl* introduces a Platonic definition.[57]

3.3. Semantic Structure

The list format of *On Definitions* also implies a peculiar semantic structure with clear consequences for the way in which *On Definitions* ought to be read. Adamson and Pormann already highlighted that certain argumentative features suggest that "*On Definitions* should be read as a philosophical treatise, not merely as a neutral guide to terminology."[58] This, however, is contradicted by the many blatantly non-argumentative features of our definition list. In my view, this heterogeneity is best described applying the concept of 'discreteness' or 'discontinuity'. I borrow this terminology from Markus Asper's discussion of Greek scientific list texts, including collections of philosophical definitions.[59] Asper defines 'discrete texts' as a discontinuous string of terms or sentences, meaning that a discrete text is made up of unconnected parts (compare the designation *fuṣūl* 'sections' in MS London) whose relation is not explicitly specified.[60]

---

[57] In a similar way, Andreas Lammer has argued with respect to the double definition of 'nature' that it supplements the Aristotelian understanding of nature as a principle of motion and rest with the Philoponean understanding of nature as a power (*quwwa*) inherent in bodies. See Lammer, 'Defining Nature'; Lammer, *Avicenna's Physics*, 257–59.

[58] Adamson and Pormann, *Philosophical Works*, 298.

[59] Asper, *Griechische Wissenschaftstexte*, 57–61; see also 64–71. I am grateful to Dag Hasse for drawing my attention to this book.

[60] Asper, *Griechische Wissenschaftstexte*, 57.

It should be noted that the respective elements of discrete texts can nevertheless form continuous sub-elements. MS Istanbul includes a number of rather extreme examples of this, which are not actually definitions of any kind, but disquisitions on a given philosophical concept or issue, like the long entries 'human virtues' (*al-faḍāʾil al-insāniyya*) and 'philosophy' (*falsafa*). In contrast to continuous texts (like philosophical treatises), discrete texts are not meant to be read, but to be consulted. The version of MS Istanbul especially constitutes a hybrid between discrete and continuous texts, which is certainly one reason why it is so difficult to pin down its actual purpose. Typically, discrete texts are consulted for certain units of information, while continuous texts have to be understood as a coherent whole. Asper points out that discrete texts, such as lists, can only function as tools of knowledge transmission if their readers are already familiar with the systematic context, that is, they have to have implicit systematic knowledge in order to make the right use of the text.[61] For this reason, it has been rightly argued that *On Definitions* cannot be a mere reference list for beginners.

What complicates matters further is that certain sets of definitions are certainly connected, thus implying again a continuous rather than a discontinuous reading. The following sets of definitions form semantic clusters in one, two, or all versions of *On Definitions*:

---

[61] Asper, *Griechische Wissenschaftstexte*, 58–59.

First cause (*al-ʿilla al-ūlā*), intellect (*al-ʿaql*), nature (*al-ṭabīʿa*), soul (*al-nafs*), body (*al-jirm*), origination (*al-ibtidāʿ*), matter (*al-hayūlā*), form (*al-ṣūra*), element (*al-ʿunṣur*);

Act (*al-fiʿl*), action (*al-ʿamal*);

Quantity (*al-kamiyya*), quality (*al-kayfiyya*), relative (*al-muḍāf*), motion (*al-ḥaraka*), time (*al-zamān*), place (*al-makān*);

Imagination (*al-tawahhum*), sense (*al-ḥāss*), sensation (*al-ḥiss*), sensitive faculty (*al-quwwa al-ḥissiyya*), sensible (*al-maḥsūs*);

Deliberation (*al-rawiyya*), opinion (*al-raʾy*);

Will (*al-irāda*), love (*al-maḥabba*);

Necessary (*al-wājib*), possible (*al-mumkin*), impossible (*al-mumtaniʿ*);

Truth (*al-ṣidq*), falsehood (*al-kidhb*);

Eternal (*al-azalī*), natural causes (*al-ʿilal al-ṭabīʿiyya*), celestial sphere (*al-falak*);

All (*al-kull*), entirety (*al-jamīʿ*), part (*al-juzʾ*), some (*al-baʿḍ*);

Opinion (*al-ẓann*), determination (*al-ʿaẓm*), certainty (*al-yaqīn*);

Multiplication (*al-ḍarb*), division (*al-qisma*);

Medicine (*al-ṭibb*), heat (*al-ḥarāra*), cold (*al-burūda*), dryness (*al-yubs*), moisture (*al-ruṭūba*);

Curve (*al-inthināʾ*), breaking (*al-kasr*), compression (*al-ḍaghd*), attraction (*al-injidhāb*);

Difference (*al-khilāf*), otherness (*al-ghayriyya*);

Occurring (*al-ḥaṭar*), impulse (*al-sāniḥ*), occurrence (*al-khāṭir*);

Love (*al-maḥabba*), passion (*al-ʿishq*), desire (*al-shahwa*);

Anger (*al-ghaḍab*), hatred (*al-ḥiqd*), rancour (*al-dhahl*), laughter (*al-ḍāḥik*), contentment (*al-riḍā*);
Humanity (*al-insāniyya*), angelity (*al-malʾakiyya*), bestiality (*al-bahīmiyya*);
This world (*al-dunyā*), the other world (*al-ākhira*), death (*al-mawt*), place of return (*al-maʿād*), resurrection (*al-qiyāma*), awakening (*al-baʿth*), hell (*al-jahannam*), congregation (of the dead) (*al-ḥashr*), *ṣirāṭ*,[62] reckoning (*al-ḥisāb*), reward (*al-thawāb*), punishment (*al-ʿiqāb*), heaven (*al-janna*);
Generation (*al-kawn*), corruption (*al-fasād*);
Indication (*al-dalīl*), enquiry (*al-istidlāl*), term (*al-ism*), *fawt* (?),[63] judgement (*al-qaḍīya*), speech (*al-qawl*);
Individual (*al-shakhṣ*), species (*al-nawʿ*), property (*al-khāṣṣa*);
Definition of land animal (*ḥadd al-māshī*), definition of biped (*ḥadd dhī l-rijlayn*);
Definition of matter (*ḥadd al-hayūlā*), definition of nature (*ḥadd al-ṭabīʿa*), definition of fire (*ḥadd al-nār*);
World (*al-ʿālam*), all (*al-kull*).

It is not hard to see how the grouping of these sets came about. Generally, they form thematic units. Some of these are groups of

---

[62] This is the name of the bridge that in Islamic eschatological imagination has to be crossed to enter paradise.

[63] MS Lisbon reads: ہوت. Ed. Klein-Franke reads: فوت (*fawt*, 'escape'). Adamson and Pormann, *Philosophical Works*, 335n181, note that the *definiendum* lacks the definite article and, thus, does not accord with the common syntactic structure of the definitions. They suggest to emend the word to *ṣawt* ('sound') and assume a lacuna at the beginning of the definition.

related medical or mathematical terms. One of the most outstanding groups is the set of 13 eschatological terms (this world, the other world, etc.) found exclusively in MS London. As demonstrated by Stern, this set derives from the Ikhwān al-Ṣafāʾ's forty-first epistle.[64] According to him, its inclusion in *On Definitions* happened "by some accident" and rests upon "the sole authority of a copyist who set down these excerpts at second or third hand."[65] It is true that this set of definitions, like the ones that were taken from al-Ṭabarī in the version of MS Lisbon, does not help in understanding al-Kindī's supposed aim in composing *On Definitions*, but it is instructive as to the way in which this text, or rather its versions, must have emerged in the first place. The list format must have invited its readers to participate in the enterprise of collecting useful definitions or terminological explanations. On the other hand, the presence of such sets does not preclude the possibility of others originally going back to al-Kindī. A case in point is the first set, especially the sequence 'first cause', 'intellect', 'nature', 'soul', which mirrors the Plotinian emanationist scheme. As pointed out by Adamson, this sequence appears in the prologue of the *Theology of Aristotle*, very likely authored by al-Kindī himself, as well as in his *Sayings of Socrates*

---

[64] Edition and English translation in Baffioni and Poonawala, *Epistles 39–41*.

[65] Stern, 'Notes', 37.

(*Alfāẓ Suqrāṭ*).[66] It cannot be accidental that this set of definitions stands at the beginning of all three versions of *On Definitions*.

Another feature some of these sets exhibit, undermining again the text's discreteness, is internal cross-referencing. Some definitions work with terms defined elsewhere. If one follows these cross-references, the respective definitions become visible as snippets of theory-building. Adamson has demonstrated this with respect to the set 'occurring', 'impulse', and 'occurrence'.[67] Another striking example is the set 'sense', 'sensation', 'sensitive faculty', and 'sensible'. These sets function as a sort of mini-lists within the lists of the three versions. They also presuppose a closed theoretical frame, which means that they work somewhat like the 'philosophical lexicon' of Aristotle's *Metaphysics* V: they offer coherent (or at least interrelated) philosophical analyses of concepts, rather than lexicographical explanations of the meanings of the terms defined.[68] This brings us to the important question of the function of *On Definitions*.

4.0. *On Definitions* and Its Users

We have seen that *On Definitions* is a text closely associated with the Kindian corpus. Some scholars have doubted its authenticity, but most are content to assume that it was produced by al-Kindī

---

[66] Adamson, 'al-Kindī', 75n87; see also Klein-Franke, 'On Definitions', 199; Adamson and Pormann, *Philosophical Works*, 298; Frank, '*Book of Definitions*', 21.

[67] Adamson, 'al-Kindī', 66–75; esp. 67–68.

[68] See Barnes, 'Platonic Lexicon', 296; see also Asper, *Griechische Wissenschaftstexte*, 64–71.

or his circle on the basis of original compositions and available translations, with the qualification that some of its versions have incorporated later material that does not belong to this initial production process. Still, the purpose and structure of *On Definitions* has so far remained elusive. Its three versions prompt questions concerning the extent to which the supposed original text was manipulated by later transmitters. Looking back at the previous discussion, what can our findings tell us about *On Definitions* and the textual practices from which its three versions emerged?

Our survey of the manuscript evidence has shown that all three versions were copied as textual units; that is, the shape of the text in our manuscript witnesses does not owe itself to the selection of the respective scribe, though this cannot be excluded for the manuscripts from which they themselves copied. *On Definitions* was transmitted together with other Kindian texts at the latest in the sixth/twelfth century and explicitly ascribed to al-Kindī in two versions. It was integrated into collections of scientific and philosophical works. Since al-Kindī was a prolific writer on matters of astronomy/astrology, we find *On Definitions* in two collections that display a strong interest in these disciplines. Hence, the manuscript evidence gives us some clues as to the interests of the premodern readers of *On Definitions*: they were largely concerned with mathematics (including astronomy/astrology) and philosophy; some may have come across the text while trying to collect al-Kindī's writings; others were interested more generally in texts on scientific and philosophical terminology.

The scribes of the three manuscripts employed very common methods to enhance the text's visual structure, either by means of paragraph marks or blank spaces. This was certainly necessary in order to more easily navigate the text. Paragraph marks would have allowed the readers to find at least the beginnings of the respective entries. One of the users of MS Lisbon used red underlining, facilitating even more a reading practice that must have consisted in looking up certain units of information. This suggests that the text was in fact used as some sort of reference work—that is, that it was used as a discrete or discontinuous text, to use Asper's terminology. On the other hand, *On Definitions* is not a comfortably usable reference work, since it can be hard to find the term that is being sought and some terms have more than one definition in disparate places. Further, some subunits within the lists must be read as continuous text, calling for a different reading practice.

The fact that *On Definitions* indicates different approaches to reading certainly has to do with the stratified nature of its textual genesis. We have seen that there are clear signs of editorial intervention. Earlier transmitters of the text seem to have understood it not so much as a reference work, but as a sort of notebook, a list that takes stock of philosophically interesting items, which could be supplemented as needed. *On Definitions* functioned as a premodern database, which went through different updates in the course of its transmission. Both the editorial phrases and textual additions of prolonged definitions as well as the definitions that came from other identifiable sources testify to this use of *On Definitions*. With these additions and modifications, it was not only the shape of the text of *On Definitions* that evolved over time. Its meaning as a text evolved as well, especially as far as it depended on the use made of it.

For comparable lists of definitions, like those mentioned at the beginning of this study, authors penned introductions, which could serve as a sort of user manual. Such introductory texts could specify the purpose and use of the list and provide a closed theoretical frame for it. This task was neither achieved nor apparently aimed at for *On Definitions*. The question of what al-Kindī intended with this text cannot be answered, since we do not have an introduction by al-Kindī. It is also wrongly put, since al-Kindī was after all not the sole author of the text. What our material mainly tells us is what the text's users intended to do with it. Theoretical unity is sometimes presupposed by lists, but as something hinted at, made explicit outside the text of the lists themselves (compare Martin Wallraff's deliberations on three-dimensionality in this volume). In other words, certain definitions and sets of definitions do not develop a theoretical framework, but make use of one that could be found, for instance, in the texts from which they were excerpted. The three versions of *On Definitions* were shaped by different agents involved in the compositional process from which they emerged as three distinct historical artefacts. This does not preclude that al-Kindī was involved in this process at some early point as well, but we have no reason to hypothesise that *On Definitions* had a fixed function that could be related to al-Kindī. This also means that *On Definitions* cannot have been an exclusively, nor even predominantly, didactic text.

It is a text that had to serve more than one need in the course of its history. A modern need for ascription—in our case to al-Kindī, the famed first 'philosopher of the Arabs'—tends to overshadow this characteristically premodern feature.

A SYRIAC LIST OF THE NAMES OF THE WIVES OF THE PATRIARCHS IN BL ADD 14620

Matthew P. Monger

The final extant folio of London, British Library, Add MS 14620[1] contains a section labelled ܫܡܗ̈ܐ ܕܢܫ̈ܐ ܕܐܒܗ̈ܬܐ 'The names of the wives of the fathers'. Here, we find a list of the names of many of the pre-Abrahamic wives and mothers who are mentioned but unnamed in the book of Genesis. This text bears a close resemblance to other lists and texts containing the names of the wives of the patriarchs found in several different linguistic and manuscript contexts, most notably the well-known Syriac text found in London, British Library, Add MS 12154, fol. 180.[2] The names of the

[1] See Wright, *Catalogue*, 800–3. See also Minov, 'A Syriac tabula gentium', where this text is discussed. Minov's article was not available until this present chapter was in the final stages of publication. Accordingly, it was not consulted during the primary research for this contribution.

[2] This manuscript was first published in Ceriani, *Monumenta Sacra et Profana*, ix–x. The list has subsequently been published in a number of studies on Jubilees; see Charles, *Ethiopic Version*, 183; VanderKam, *Jubilees*, 1:8–9. London, British Library, Add MS 12154 is written in the Estrangelo script, while BL Add 14620 is written in the Serto script.

 https://doi.org/10.11647/OBP.0375.05

wives of the patriarchs provide a fascinating example of the transmission of lists and extracted material in antiquity and the Middle Ages because of the wide distribution of sources. Lists found in Hebrew, Greek, Syriac, and Armenian sources share names ultimately derived from Jubilees, a Jewish work from the Second Temple period.

The text of BL Add 14620 is a fascinating case in this connection, as it is not merely a copy of a list of the names of the women as known from Jubilees, but a synthesis of names from Jubilees and at least one other source—a tradition related to the Syriac Cave of Treasures. This conflation of different textual traditions in list form raises several practical and theoretical questions that I would like to investigate in this chapter. Thus, following an edition and translation of the text, I will explore the place of this particular text within the larger tradition and circulation of the names of the wives of the pre-Abrahamic patriarchs. Then, I will move on to a more theoretical discussion of two subjects that arise from this particular list: the transmission of lists as individual units, not only as representations of the works from which they were initially extracted; and the way in which the scribal practice of list-copying may be interrupted by the insertion of new knowledge. In order to situate the text of BL Add 14620 within the larger transmission history of the names of the wives of the patriarchs, I will begin with a brief overview of the

---

References to Syriac words in BL Add 12154 will be given here in Estrangelo to maintain the visual and material difference between the two manuscripts.

Jubilees and the Cave of Treasures traditions related to the names.

1.0. The Names of the Wives of the Patriarchs

The book of Genesis leaves much to the imagination when it comes to the identities of the wives of the patriarchs. Few women are named in Genesis and the pre-Abrahamic genealogies provide only the patriarchal line, following a standard formula concerning their lives and offspring, which can be exemplified by the information on Seth, the son of Adam and Eve:

> When Seth had lived one hundred five years, he became the father of Enosh. Seth lived after the birth of Enosh eight hundred seven years, and had other sons and daughters. Thus all the days of Seth were nine hundred twelve years; and he died.[3]

The lack of names for the wives and mothers is systematic in the generations between Adam and Eve and Abraham and Sarah. However, scattered throughout narrative, exegetical, historiographical, and chronological sources in late antiquity and the Middle Ages, we find different names given to the unnamed women of the biblical stories. In some cases, one or two women are given names, as is the case in sources such as 1 Enoch,[4] the Genesis Apocryphon,[5] the Testament of Levi,[6] and the Babylonian

---

[3] Gen. 5.6–8, translation following the New Revised Standard Version.

[4] Edna is the name of Enoch's wife in 1 En. 85.3.

[5] Batenosh is the name given to Lamech's wife in 1QapGen II, 3.

[6] Melka, the wife of Levi, is mentioned in T. Levi 11.1.

Talmud.[7] Other, more comprehensive narratives were also composed that filled in more of the gaps found in the text of Genesis. Two works, Jubilees and the Cave of Treasures, contain names for many unnamed women mentioned or alluded to in Genesis. For example, the section of Jubilees corresponding to the verses about Seth from Genesis cited above looks like this: "And in the fifth week of the fifth jubilee, Seth took ʾAzura, his sister, as a wife. And in the fourth year of that week, she bore for him Enos."[8]

The names given to the women are not the same in all these sources, nor do they have a common origin. For example, different names are given to the wife of Noah in a large number of sources, prompting a 1941 article entitled 'The One Hundred and Three Names of Noah's Wife'.[9] The names as found in Jubilees and in part in the Cave of Treasures are the most widely transmitted of the ancient names, being found in various later works, especially of historiographical or exegetical nature, in Jewish, Christian, and Muslim contexts.[10]

1.1. Jubilees

The most widespread tradition of the names of the wives of the patriarchs is connected to Jubilees, which was composed during

---

[7] b. Bava Batra 91a records the names of the mother of Abraham, Samson's mother and sister, and the mothers of David and Haman.

[8] Jub. 4.11; translation from Wintermute, 'Jubilees', 35.

[9] Utley, 'Noah's Wife'.

[10] Tal Ilan, 'Biblical Women's Names', has given the most comprehensive analysis and presentation of the sources and traditions. The Jubilees tradition is also analysed in depth in Lipscomb, 'Tradition'.

the second century BCE. Jubilees is witnessed in Hebrew in several fragmentary manuscripts from Qumran dating to the first centuries BCE and CE, but the text that we today know as Jubilees is based on the Ethiopic text of Jubilees extant in Geʿez from the fourteenth century CE.[11] The work retells the events of Genesis and the beginning of Exodus but differs significantly from the Hebrew Bible and adds a number of details, including the names of many of the women who are unnamed in Genesis. Throughout the sections that correspond to the Genesis genealogies, Jubilees gives names to each of the wives of the pre-Abrahamic patriarchs and the wives of the 12 sons of Jacob and the daughter of Pharaoh.

Jubilees is extant as a complete work only in Ethiopic, but a Greek translation must have existed at one point, and large portions of the book are extant in Latin.[12] Numerous citations and allusions are found in a variety of works written in Greek, as well as in Syriac and Arabic. The nature of the Jubilees material in works of a historiographical nature indicates that material from Jubilees was extracted and circulated much more widely than the

---

[11] As only a small portion of the Hebrew text of Jubilees is preserved, it is impossible to determine the exact shape and extent of the work or its text in Hebrew. As the Ethiopic text is a translation of a translation (Greek), it is prudent to allow for a certain amount of redaction and/or literary growth from the Hebrew version to the Ethiopic; Monger, '4Q216'. A more traditional discussion of the manuscript traditions of Jubilees can be found in VanderKam, *Jubilees*, 1:1–16.

[12] Hanneken, 'Book of Jubilees'.

work as a whole.[13] There is no consensus as to whether or not Jubilees as a whole was ever translated into Syriac,[14] but the names of the wives of the patriarchs in Syriac are explicitly connected to Jubilees in the title of the text in BL Add 12154: ܫܡܗ̈ܐ ܕܢܫ̈ܐ ܕܪ̈ܝܫ ܐܒܗ̈ܬܐ ܡܕܒܪ̈ܢܐ ܐܝܟ ܟܬܒܐ ܕܠܘܬ ܥܒܪ̈ܝܐ ܗܘ ܕܡܬܩܪܐ ܝܘܒܠܝܐ. 'the names of the wives of the patriarchs according to the book which among the Hebrews is called Jubilees'.[15]

While some individual names from the Jubilees tradition can be found in a large number of texts, a few ancient texts show knowledge of and interest in all of the names. Many names are found in historiographical works, such as the tenth-century Muslim work *Tarikh al-rasul wa-l-muluk* 'History of prophets and kings' by Muḥammad ibn Jarīr al-Ṭabarī, a Byzantine chronicle referred to as the *Eklogē historion*,[16] a Medieval Hebrew chronicle titled *Toledot Adam*,[17] and a number of Armenian chronicles.[18] While these texts do include many of the same names under discussion here, the function of the names in historiographical texts is necessarily different from in a list. Even though the chronicles

---

13 Adler, *Time Immemorial*, 229–34; Monger, 'Many Forms of Jubilees'.

14 On the possibility of Jubilees having been extant in its entirety in Syriac, see Tisserant, 'Fragments syriaques'; Hilkens, *Syriac Chronicle*, 51–84.

15 BL Add 12154, fol. 180.

16 Lipscomb, 'Wives of the Patriarchs', 91.

17 This text, composed by R. Samuel Algazi, is referred to as al-Gazi in Ilan, 'Biblical Women's Names'.

18 Stone, *Abraham*, 29–35; Stone, *Angels and Biblical Heroes*, 51–64.

and world histories may be organised as lists or list-like texts,[19] the purpose of collecting the names in a list outside of any narrative of history or chronology must be to highlight this knowledge, whereas names included in the historiographical texts only supplement the larger goal of describing the lines of history. Thus, of more interest here are the manuscripts that contain lists or list-like texts where the names appear. Among these are two Hebrew manuscripts that contain the names as independent units;[20] a Greek catena manuscript from the tenth or eleventh century, containing text and commentary to Genesis and Exodus, that contains the names of the wives of the patriarchs in the margins;[21] a number of Armenian manuscripts with the names in list form;[22] and the two Syriac manuscripts already mentioned.

1.2. Cave of Treasures

In contrast to Jubilees, Cave of Treasures was composed in Syriac and is extant in full in Syriac. Translations and adaptations of Cave of Treasures are also found in Arabic, Ethiopic, Coptic, and Georgian.[23] Like Jubilees, Cave of Treasures retells the book of Genesis but then continues up until the time of Jesus and is thus

---

[19] See the discussion of historiographical texts as lists in Teresa Bernheimer's contribution to this volume.

[20] The Fahri Bible, Sassoon collection MS 368; see Harkavy, 'חדשים גם ישנים', 58. Munich, Bayerische Staatsbibliothek, Cod. hebr. 391 (olim 421), fol. 91v; see Perles, *Beiträge*, 90.

[21] Basel, Universitätsbibliothek, AN III 13.

[22] Lipscomb, 'Tradition', 149–63.

[23] See the overview in Toepel, 'Cave of Treasures', 532–34.

clearly a Christian work. Cave of Treasures has two different methods for recording the names of the pre-Abrahamic women. In a few instances, women are given names in the narrative, such as the sisters/wives of Cain, Abel, and Seth and the wives of Noah and Terah,[24] whereas all of the others—in addition to the aforementioned—are presented in a list that is included as a single section that serves to clarify the lineage of Mary, mother of Jesus, because "neither the Greek nor the Hebrew or Syriac writers, however, could show from where each one of them took his wife and whose daughter she was."[25] In other words, the genealogy of Christ—from a matrilineal perspective—is the motivation for the complete list in Cave of Treasures.

The list is not witnessed in any other earlier texts, and there are disagreements between the list found in the genealogy of Mary and the names given in the narrative, which may indicate that the list and the narratives were composed separately before their inclusion in Cave of Treasures. For example, the list in Cav. Tr. 44 differs from the narrative when it comes to the names of the wives of Terah.[26] There is also wide variation in the manuscripts as to the names of the wives of Terah in Syriac as well as in the ancient versions.[27] The text of BL Add 14620 further complicates the picture and will be discussed in detail below.

---

[24] Cav. Tr. 5.21–32; 14.3; 28.16–17.

[25] Cav. Tr. 44.

[26] The genealogical list is found in chapter 44, with the wives of Terah being mentioned in Cav. Tr. 44.32. In the narrative, the wives of Terah are named in Cav. Tr. 28.17–18.

[27] Ri, *La caverne des trésors*, 222–23, 334–61.

It is difficult to determine to what extent some or all of the names are part of older traditions than the works in which they are first witnessed. In some cases, such as those mentioned above found in 1 Enoch, the Testament of Levi, and the Genesis Apocryphon, the names are at least as old as the oldest attestations of Jubilees, which shares the same names for the same matriarchs. Thus, it seems possible—or even likely—that these particular names were known and in circulation prior to the composition of Jubilees. It also seems possible that at least the genealogical list in Cav. Tr. 44 could have been extant prior to its inclusion in Cave of Treasures. Further, the names in the narrative sections of Cave of Treasures could also be part of an older tradition. The fact that there are different traditions of the names of the matriarchs extant seems to suggest that there was no single early tradition that was transmitted. Names of figures from the Hebrew Bible are generally very stable in their transmission into Syriac and Arabic contexts, suggesting that the names of the matriarchs were not in wide circulation in the early centuries of the Common Era. Parts of Jubilees were clearly known in several Syriac contexts,[28] but the names of the matriarchs in Syriac texts are more often related to Cave of Treasures than Jubilees. Clearly, some later authors did know of both traditions, as BL Add 14620 suggests, but the earliest circulation of the names of the matriarchs is not reliant on widespread knowledge of the text of Jubilees.

---

[28] Tisserant, 'Fragments syriaques'; Brock, 'Abraham and the Ravens'.

In any case, Jubilees and Cave of Treasures retain different names for the individual matriarchs, and names from both traditions have been transmitted into a variety of literary contexts, such as historiographical works and lists in different types of manuscripts. Given the fact that the names appear in such a variety of textual and manuscript contexts, the question arises as to whether the information was transmitted through the works where the names appear or by other means. In order to further evaluate this question, I will give a more detailed analysis of the manuscript and the manuscript context of the current list before moving on to a presentation of the text itself.

2.0. BL Add 14620: Manuscript and Manuscript Context

BL Add 14620 consists of the remains of a once larger Syriac codex, now reduced to 30 folios representing parts of five quires, though the codex originally seems to have contained at least 14 quires.[29] The codex is a regular-sized vellum codex, approximately 25 × 18 cm in dimensions, which William Wright dates paleographically to the ninth century.[30] The contents of the codex

[29] The manuscript quires are numbered in standard Syriac style, with each quire being marked on the recto of the first folio and the verso of the final folio. The fact that only four quire markers remain in the manuscript—ܝܐ '11', ܝܒ '12', ܝܓ '13', and ܝܕ '14'—indicates that the original codex had at least 14 quires. See Wright, *Catalogue*, 800.

[30] Wright, *Catalogue*, 800.

are miscellaneous in nature, including philosophical texts, extracts from the sixth book of Eusebius's *Ecclesiastical History* and Epiphanius's *On Weights and Measures*, as well as a number of other texts related to theological, philological, and historical topics. This type of anthology is common in the Syriac manuscript tradition, which contains a large number of collections of excerpted material. Many of the excerpts found in these manuscripts are portions of works known from other contexts, such as theological treatises by Greek or Syriac church fathers, historiographical works, and interpretations of biblical passages or topics.

The section containing the list of the names of the wives of the patriarchs is found at the end of the final extant page, fol. 30v. The text immediately follows a treatise on the peoples, languages, and scripts associated with the table of nations found in Gen. 10.[31] The text, attributed to David of Bet-Rabban, is entitled ܡܛܠ ܫܪ̈ܒܬܐ: ܕܒ̈ܢܝ ܢܘܚ 'Concerning the generations of the sons of Noah'. It is a re-evaluation of which nations belong to which descendant of Noah. This type of interpretation of the table of nations from Gen. 10 is relatively common, being found in the targumim, Josephus, Eusebius, and many other places.[32] In fact, the text of BL Add 14620 claims that "many have attempted to

[31] The text is fully edited and discussed in Minov, 'A Syriac Tabula Gentium'.

[32] The most comprehensive study of the text and its reception can be found in Borst, *Der Turmbau von Babel*.

give an interpretation of the generations of the sons of Noah, including Eusebius of Caesarea."[33]

William Wright understands the list of the matriarchs as being part of the text concerning the generations of the sons of Noah, though this is uncertain. Nearly the entire manuscript is written in continuous text, with little space allotted between texts. Each new textual unit is introduced with the word ܛܘܒ *tob*, a common marker of a new text in Syriac. As it appears in the manuscript now, the title of the final section is rubricated, and the text begins with ܛܘܒ. Thus, it is graphically and lexically marked as a new section in the same way as the other units of the manuscript. Regardless of how we view the connection of the names of the wives of the patriarchs to the preceding text, the subject of the text fits neatly with the explication of Gen. 10, as the line of Terah is discussed in Gen. 11. Furthermore, the subject as a whole seems to fit within the broader interests of the compiler of the texts in BL Add 14620, which have an exegetical and historiographical tendency.

A final issue that should be dealt with is whether the remaining text is all that was originally copied into this manuscript. The list of the names of the wives of the patriarchs is the final text of the manuscript in its current state, but the quire structure of the original manuscript points towards fol. 30 not being the final folio of the manuscript. It appears that there were at least 14 quires containing 10 leaves each, as quire numbers are found throughout the manuscript, and the quire numbers mark both the

[33] BL Add 14620, fol. 29 I 22–25.

beginning *and* the end of the quires. Thus, it is possible that our text continued onto a now lost folio. In support of the text having once continued is the fact that our current version of the list of the names of matriarchs does not include all of the names known from Jubilees or the other sources to the Jubilees tradition. On the other hand, several sources do not include all of the names of the matriarchs, and it is possible that the current text was intended simply to fill the space available. Further, there is a blank line between the names of the wives of the sons of Noah and the short section on the wives of Terah (see fig. 1). This could be an indication that this text was purposefully placed at the end of this page in order to fill the remaining space. The jump directly from the wives of the sons of Noah to the wives of Terah also points towards this text being purposefully more compact than other sources.

Figure 1: A close-up of the text as found in London, British Library, Add MS 14620, fol. 30v; © The British Library Board

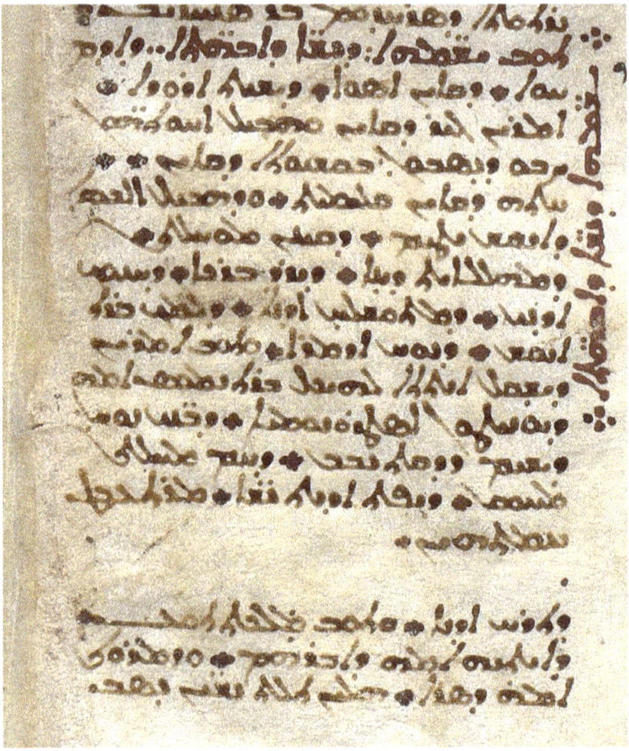

3.0. Text and Translation

London, British Library, Add MS 14620, fol. 30v b

ܬܘܒ ܫܡ̈ܗܐ܇ ܕܢ̈ܫܐ ܕܐܒ̈ܗܬܐ ܕܐܕܡ	(26)	Again, the names of the wives of the fathers. Of Adam,
ܚܘܐ ܀ ܕܩܐܝܢ ܐܣܘܐ ܀ ܕܫܝܬ ܐܪܘܙܐ ܀	(27)	Eve. Of Cain, *ʾSwʾ*. Of Seth, *ʾRwzʾ*.
ܐܡܪܝܢ ܕܝܢ ܕܩܐܝܢ ܘܗܒܝܠ ܐܚ̈ܘܬܗܘܢ	(28)	However, they say that Cain and Abel

ܪܓܘ ܕܢܣܒܘܢ܆ ܒܥܫܝܢܘܬܐ ܕܩܐܝܢ ܀	(29)	wanted to marry their sisters, it was the stubbornness of Cain.
ܚܬܗ ܕܩܐܝܢ ܩܠܡܝܬ ܀ ܘܕܗܒܝܠ ܐܠܒܘܕܐ	(30)	The sister of Cain was *Qlmyt*. And of Abel, *ʾLbwdʾ*.
ܕܐܢܘܫ ܢܛܝܡ ܀ ܕܩܝܢ ܡܘܚܠܬ ܀	(31)	Of Enosh, *Nṭym*. Of Kenan, *Mwhlt*.
ܕܡܗܠܠܐܝܬ ܕܝܢܐ ܀ ܕܝܪܕ ܒܪܟܐ ܀ ܕܚܢܘܟ	(32)	Of *Mhllʾyt, Dynʾ*. Of Jared, *Brkʾ*. Of Henock,
ܐܕܢܝ ܀ ܕܡܬܘܫܠܚ ܐܕܢܐ ܀ ܕܠܡܟ ܒܪܬ	(33)	*ʾDny*. Of Methuselah, *ʾDnʾ*. Of Lamech, *Brt*
ܐܢܘܫ ܀ ܕܢܘܚ ܐܙܡܪܐ ܀ ܘܠܒܬܪ ܐܡܪܝܢ	(34)	*ʾNwš*. Of Noah, *ʾZmrʾ*. Later, they say
ܕܢܣܒ ܐܢܬܬܗ ܠܗܝܟܠ ܒܪܬ ܢܡܘܣ ܐܡܗ	(35)	that he married his wife *Hykl*, daughter of Namos, the mother of
ܕܝܘܢܛܘܢ ܐܣܛܪܘܢܘܡܐ ܀ ܕܒܢܝ ܢܘܚ	(36)	Yonton the Astronomer. Of the sons of Noah:
ܕܫܡ ܙܕܩܛܢܒܒ ܀ ܕܚܡ ܡܚܠܬ	(37)	Of Shem, *Zdqtnbb*. Of Ham, *Mḥlt*
ܡܚܘܩ ܀ ܕܝܦܬ ܐܕܢܛܢܫܐ ܀ ܡܪܬܥܒܛ	(38)	*mḥwq*. Of Japhet, *ʾDntnšʾ*. *Mrtʿbṭ* was
ܚܡܬܗܘܢ ܀	(39)	their mother-in-law.
·	(40)	.
ܕܬܪܚ ܐܕܢܐ ܀ ܘܠܒܬܪ ܡܠܟܬ ܬܘܐ	(41)	Of Terah, *ʾDnʾ*. Then there was *Mlkt twʾ*,
ܕܐܝܬܝܗ ܐܡܗ ܕܐܒܪܗܡ ܀ ܘܙܡܪܘܬ	(42)	who was the mother of Abraham. And *Zmrwt*

ܐܡܗ ܕܣܪܝ ܀ ܘܗܠܝܢ ܬܠܬ ܢܫܝܢ ܢܣܒ (43) was the mother of Sarai. These three women he took.

4.0. Textual Notes

Line 26: The title of this section, ܠܘܬ ܫܡ̈ܗܐ܂ ܕܢ̈ܫܐ ܕܐܒ̈ܗܬܐ ‘The names of the wives of the fathers’, is found both in the text of the column and in the margin adjacent to the beginning of the text. This is the practice throughout this manuscript. The exact wording of the title is different from that of BL Add 12154, which reads ܫܡ̈ܗܐ ܕܢ̈ܫܐ ܕܪ̈ܝܫ ܐܒܗ̈ܬܐ ܡܕܒܪ̈ܢܐ ܐܝܟ ܟܬܒܐ ܕܠܘܬ ܥܒܪ̈ܝܐ ܗܘ ܕܡܬܩܪܐ ܝܘܒܠܐ ‘The names of the wives of the patriarchs according to the book which among the Hebrews is called Jubilees’.

Line 27: ܐܣܘܐ *ʾSwʾ* is the name of the wife of Cain here, which matches BL Add 12154, and is similar to the most common form found in many Greek sources, Ἀσουάμ *Asouam*, but differs from the Ethiopic text of Jubilees, which has *Awan*.[34]

ܐܪܘܙܐ *ʾRwzʾ* is the name given to Seth’s wife, but the spelling in our text differs from the normal form of the name of Seth’s wife, which is ܐܙܘܪܐ *ʾZwrʾ* in BL Add 12154 and the majority of the other sources. Only in the Arabic Genesis catena[35] do we find

---

[34] Table 1 gives the names in the two Syriac manuscripts as well as (Ethiopic) Jubilees.

[35] Printed in de Lagarde, *Materielen*, and referred to as *Arabic Midrash* in Ilan, ‘Biblical Women’s Names’, this work is a widely attested Arabic text of Genesis with running commentary in the catena style. See further Graf, *Geschichte der christlichen arabischen Literatur*, 284–89.

a similar form: ارزون *ʾArzwn* is found in the Arabic script[36] and ܐܪܙܘܢ *ʾArzwn* in the Garshuni.[37] The variance is likely due to a pointing error or misreading of a Syriac text as the letters *zayn* and *rīš* in the Serto script of BL Add 14620 are identical in form except for the dot over the *rīš*.

Lines 28–30: Following the names of the wives of Cain and Seth, the text continues with the phrase ܐܡܪܝܢ ܓܝܪ 'Indeed they say', followed by several lines of text that are not part of the Jubilees names tradition, but are related to the sisters and wives of Cain and Abel in the Cave of Treasures tradition. This is the first of several places where BL Add 14620 deviates from the Jubilees list tradition known from BL Add 12154 and the other lists. The phrase 'Indeed they say' serves as an introductory formula for information that comes from a different source to the base text, marking a transition from one source to another. The same phrase is used in precisely the same way—also introducing the information related to Cave of Treasures—in lines 34–36. This formulaic introduction may be a simple acknowledgement of the fact that this information supplements or contradicts the information in the text, or it may also indicate that the scribe here is referring to an oral source. A similar situation occurs in BL Add 12154, in the final line of the text where the name of the daughter of Pharaoh who rescued Moses is named. According to Jubilees, Josephus, and a number of ancient sources, her name was

---

[36] See inter alia Paris, Bibliothèque national de France, Arabe 17, fol. 59v II 13.

[37] See inter alia Munich, Bayerische Staatsbibliothek, Cod. arab. 235–26v 5.

Tharmuth(i), a name which BL Add 12154 records as ܬܪܡܘܬܝ. Following the name Tharmuthi, BL Add 12154 adds the words: ܐܝܟ ܐܚܪ̈ܢܐ ܕܐܡ ܪܥܘܣܐ 'According to others, *R'ws'*'. The name *R'ws'* is known from a number of Syriac sources, such as Ishodad of Merv and Bar Bahlul. While the phrasing is different in the two Syriac manuscripts, the clear demarcation of information as coming from a different source shows the scribal desire to distinguish between sources of information.

The names given to the sister-wives of Cain and Abel in BL Add 14620, ܩܠܡܝܬ *Qlmyt* and ܐܠܒܘܕܐ *'Lbwd'*, are found in Cave of Treasures, though the form of the name here, *'Lbwd'*, is different to in Cave of Treasures. This form is found in one other text, the tenth-century *Syriac Lexicon* of Bar Bahlul,[38] who also gives an alternate form for the wife of Enosh.

The names of the daughters of Eve and Adam from Cave of Treasures are the most widely received of the names of the wives of the patriarchs in the Middle Ages. They appear in the Apocalypse of Pseudo-Methodius, which was one of the widest read and copied Syriac texts and was later used as a source for the *Historia Scholastica*, which in turn had great influence on the European vernacular Bibles that developed in the twelfth century. The question of who Cain, Abel, and Seth marry is well known in antiquity and is commented on in the Babylonian Talmud and Midrash Rabbah, as well as Jubilees, Cave of Treasures, and other retellings of Genesis.[39] In this current text, we are presented with

[38] Duval, *Lexicon syriacum*, 604.

[39] *b. Yebam.* 62a; *Midr. Gen. Rab.* 22.7; Jub. 4.1–11; Cav. Tr. 5.18–32.

the name of Cain's wife in the Jubilees tradition but are also given part of the story about who Cain and Abel were to marry according to Cave of Treasures. In Cave of Treasures, the background for the purported first murder is rooted in a conflict over who gets to marry Cain's twin sister. Cain approaches Adam to ask permission to marry his own twin because he claims she is the more beautiful of the two. Adam rejects this as an abomination and sends Cain and Abel to the cave of treasures to make an offering to atone for their sin. It is assumed that it is this offering that we read about in Gen. 4, where God favours Abel's offering, and Cain subsequently kills Abel.[40] The text of BL Add 14620 reflects this tradition not only in the names of the twins but also in that it says: "They wanted to marry their sisters—it was the stubbornness of Cain."

The entire section following the words 'Indeed they say' is absent in all the other lists from the Jubilees tradition, but BL Add 14620 is not the only source that records both of these traditions, as we find both sets of names in two Arabic works. Al-Ṭabarī mentions both traditions in his *Tarikh al-rasul wa-l-muluk*, and the names were also known to the tenth-century Christian author Saʿīd ibn Baṭrīq—also known as Bishop Eutychius of Alexandria—who mentions both in his *Annales*.[41]

Line 31: The name of Enosh's wife here is different to in other sources in the Jubilees tradition: ܢܛܝܡ *Nṭym*. In Jubilees and all the other lists, we find the name *Noʿam*. However, the name

[40] This episode is found in Cav. Tr. 5.21–24.

[41] Eutychius, *Annales*, 110. Al-Ṭabarī, *Annales*, 146, 167; translation in Rosenthal, *The History of Ṭabarī*, 316–17, 336–37.

Nṭym is found in the tenth-century *Syriac Lexicon* of Bar Bahlul, where she is identified as being the wife of Enosh.[42] We have already seen that Bar Bahlul records the name of the sister of Abel as *ʾLbwdʾ*, meaning that there are two direct connections between BL Add 14620 and Bar Bahlul. Further, Bar Bahlul also includes the name of the daughter of Pharaoh that is recorded in BL Add 12154, as mentioned above. The presence of the name confirms the spelling here, but as the Jubilees form is not mentioned, and there are no other known sources that record *Nṭym*, it is difficult to trace the transmission into BL Add 14620.

Line 32: The manuscript gives the name of this patriarch as ܡܗܠܠܐܝܬ *Mhllʾyt* where we would expect ܡܗܠܠܐܝܠ *Mhllʾyl*.

Lines 33–34: The form of the name of the wife of Lamech, ܒܪܬ ܐܢܘܫ *Brt ʾNwš*, corresponds more closely to the form known from the other sources in the Jubilees tradition than to the Syriac BL Add 12154, which gives her name as *Enoshi*. The form is best understood as a Syriac form of the Hebrew name *Bat Enosh* witnessed in the Genesis Apocryphon. Here, the Hebrew word *bat* 'daughter' is translated to Syriac *bart* 'daughter'.

Line 34: The name of Noah's wife here is ܐܙܡܪܐ *ʾZmrʾ*. BL Add 12154 has ܐܡܙܪܐ *ʾMzrʾ*, the common form in the Jubilees tradition. It is likely that the form in BL Add 14620 is the result of a scribal error where the *mīm* and the *zayn* were transposed.

Lines 34–36: After the name ܐܙܡܪܐ *ʾZmrʾ*, another section of material not related to Jubilees is introduced. Again, we find the

---

[42] Duval, *Lexicon syriacum*, 1241.

introductory phrase ܐܡܪܝܢ ܠܡ 'Indeed they say', and the information in the following lines is related to Cave of Treasures, as in line 28 above. The name for Noah's wife given in the section is *Hykl*, daughter of Namos. The name *Hykl* itself suggests a connection to the Cave of Treasures tradition, but more striking in this context is her association with Yonton the Astronomer. Yonton as a figure is first attested in Cave of Treasures, where he is the fourth son of Noah. After the flood, he moves to the east, where he is associated with astronomy and magic. Yonton passes his knowledge down to Nimrod, who is the purported founder of the Persian and Babylonian cultures. Nimrod's connection to Yonton later plays an important role in Cave of Treasures in the story of Jesus's birth. In Matt. 2.1–12, we read about the 'magi from the east' who interpret the rising of a star as a sign of the birth of a king. In Cave of Treasures 45.1–11, the magi are specifically connected to the knowledge of Nimrod and thus to Yonton. Cave of Treasures goes to great lengths to make clear that the astronomy practised by Nimrod and the magi was connected to the divine revelation that had been passed down to Yonton from Noah, his father.[43]

Line 38–39: The text here is difficult to make sense of. The word ܡܪܬܥܒܬ *mrtʿbṭ* is unclear, but given the focus of the text here on names, I read it as a name. The second word is also ambiguous. It could read 'their mother-in-law' or perhaps 'their heat/

[43] For a discussion of the figure of Yonton, see Gero, 'Fourth Son of Noah'; Toepel, 'Yonton Revisited'.

passion/anger'. Again, given the nature of the text I have translated here with a family term, 'their mother-in-law'.[44]

Line 40: After the names of the wives of the sons of Noah, there is a blank line with only a dot at the right edge of the column. This is very uncommon in this manuscript, but there are at least two possible explanations for its function here. It may be that the dot was placed in order to fill the space in the column so that the final lines of the text would fill to the bottom of the page. Another explanation is that the scribe was aware that he was skipping a number of generations between Japhet and Terah and thus marked the large section he skipped with this single dot and a blank line. In either case, the dot appears precisely where the text skips from the sons of Noah to Terah.

Lines 41–43: The final three lines of the text are devoted to Terah and his wives. The first name, *ʾDnʾ*, is the common name for Terah's wife in the Jubilees tradition and matches what is found in BL Add 12154. Following this, two further names are given. Neither name corresponds to any ancient source I am aware of. In Jubilees and the other lists, there are no further names given for the wives of Terah. Cave of Treasures and a number of other ancient sources do speculate that Terah had to have had at least two wives based on a reading of Gen. 20.12, where Abraham explains that Sarah is his sister, the daughter of his father but not his mother. What is noteworthy here is the fact that after giving the names of the three wives of Terah—*ʾDnʾ*, *Mlkt twʾ* the mother of Abraham, and *Zmrwt* the mother of Sarah—the text

[44] Cf. Minov, 'A Syriac Tabula Gentium', 71, who reads the text here as phrase meaning 'Lord, increase their fury'.

makes clear that Terah "took these three women (as wives)." Thus, the text does not envision two wives for Terah but three. While we are not able to identify what the source of the information here is, it is worth noting that the traditions surrounding the names of Terah's wives are among the most fluid in Cave of Treasures. The names of the two wives of Terah are found twice in Cave of Treasures, both in the narrative about Abraham in Cav. Tr. 29, and in the genealogy of Mary in Cav. Tr. 44. The name of the first wife is fairly consistent in both passages, ܝܘܢܐ *Ywn*ʾ in the East Syriac tradition and ܝܘܥܐ *Yw*ʿʾ in the West Syriac tradition. The name of the second wife is more unstable. Her name appears as different variations of ܢܗܪܝܬ *Nhryt* in Cav. Tr. 29, but as ܫܠܡܘܬ *Slmwt* in the East Syriac tradition and ܡܣܡܬ *Msmt* in the West Syriac tradition.[45]

Despite the fact that we cannot identify the source behind the names of the two additional wives of Terah, it is still clear that the text conflates information from at least two sources, the base text of names from Jubilees and the secondary tradition giving different names to the mothers of Abraham and Sarah.

---

[45] For the Syriac texts, see Ri, *La caverne des trésors*, 222–23, 334–61.

Table 1: The names of the wives of the patriarchs in BL Add 14260, BL Add 12154, Jubilees,[46] and Cave of Treasures[47]

BL Add 14260	BL Add 12154	Jubilees	Cave of Treasures	Associated Patriarch
ܚܘܐ *Ḥw*ʾ	ܚܘܐ *Ḥw*ʾ	Ḥewwa	ܚܘܐ *Ḥw*ʾ	Adam
ܐܣܘܐ ʾ*Sw*ʾ	ܐܣܘܐ ʾ*Sw*ʾ	ʾAwan	— —	Cain
ܩܠܡܝܬ *Qlmyt*	— —	—	ܩܠܝܡܬ *Qlymt*	Cain
ܐܠܒܘܕܐ ʾ*Lbwd*ʾ	— —	—	ܠܒܘܕܐ *Lbwd*ʾ	Abel
ܐܪܘܙܐ ʾ*Rwz*ʾ	ܐܙܘܪܐ ʾ*Zwr*ʾ	ʾAzūra	ܩܠܝܡܬ *Qlymt*	Seth
ܢܛܝܡ *Nṭym*	ܢܐܘܡ *N*ʾ*wm*	Noam	ܚܢܐ *Ḥn*ʾ	Enosh
ܡܘܚܠܬ *Mwḥlt*	ܡܚܠܠܘܬ *Mhllwt*	Muʾaleleth	ܦܝܪܬ *Pyrt*	Kenan
ܕܝܢܐ *Dyn*ʾ	ܕܝܢܐ *Dyn*ʾ	Dinah	ܨܚܦܛܪ *Ṣḥpṭr*	Mahalalel
ܒܪܟܐ *Brk*ʾ	ܒܪܟܐ *Brk*ʾ	Bāraka	ܕܘܝܪ *Dwyr*	Jared
ܐܕܢܝ ʾ*Dny*	ܐܕܢܝ ʾ*Dny*	ʾEdni	ܙܕܩܝܢ *Zdqyn*	Enoch
ܐܕܢܐ ʾ*Dn*ʾ	ܐܕܢܐ ʾ*Dn*ʾ	ʾEdna	ܣܟܘܬ *Skwt*	Methuselah
ܒܪܬ ܐܢܘܫ *Brt* ʾ*nwš*	ܐܢܘܫܝ ʾ*Nwšy*	Betenos	ܩܝܦܪ *Qypr*	Lamech
ܐܙܡܪܐ ʾ*Zmr*ʾ	ܐܡܝܙܪܐ ʾ*Myzr*ʾ	ʾEmzara	— —	Noah
ܗܝܟܠ *Hykl*	— —	—	ܗܝܟܠ *Hykl*	Noah
ܙܕܩܬܢܒܒ *Zdqtnbb*	ܙܕܩܬܢܒܒ *Zdqtnbb*	Sedeqetelebab	— —	Shem
ܡܚܠܬ ܡܚܘܩ *Mḥlt mḥwq*	ܢܚܠܡܚܘܩ *Nḥlmḥwq*	Naʾeltamaʾuk	— —	Ham
ܐܕܢܬܢܫܐ ʾ*Dntnš*ʾ	ܐܕܢܬܢܫܐ ʾ*Dntnš*ʾ	ʾAdataneses	— —	Japheth
ܐܕܢܐ ʾ*Dn*ʾ	ܐܕܢܐ ʾ*Dn*ʾ	ʾEdna	— —	Terah
ܡܠܟܬ *Mlkt*	— —	—	ܝܘܢܐ *Ywn*ʾ	Terah
			ܣܠܡܘܬ *Slmwt*	Terah
ܙܡܪܘܬ *Zmrwt*	— —	—	ܢܗܝܪܬܐ *Nhyrt*ʾ	Terah

[46] The Names from Jubilees are normalised from the Ethiopic following Wintermute, 'Jubilees'.

[47] There are two recensions of Cave of Treasures that reflect different spellings of the names, and there is also disagreement between the two

5.0. Format and Style

The format of Syriac lists varies between two common typologies. Some lists are formatted stichographically, each entry appearing on a separate line, but the majority are written in running text without demarcation from the surrounding text. In such cases, entries are generally distinguished by diamond-shaped four-point rosettes (⁘), which are often also marked in red ink. The list in BL Add 14620 belongs to the latter group, with running text with rosettes placed between each new item in the list, as can be seen in figure 2. This stylistic feature is also found in BL Add 12154, as seen in figure 3.

Figure 2: Rosettes in London, British Library, Add MS 14620, fol. 30v; © The British Library Board

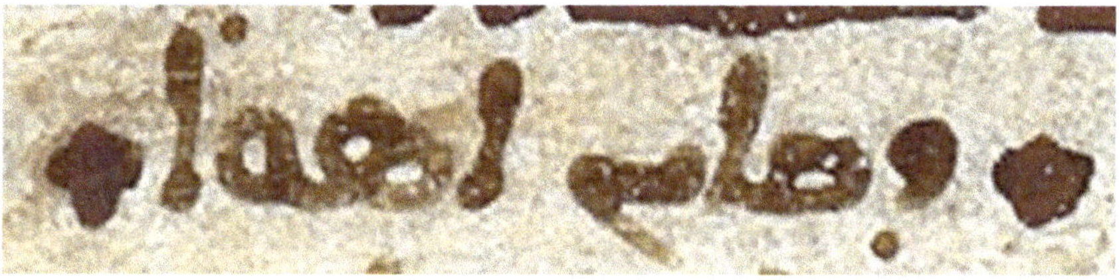

Figure 3: Rosettes in London, British Library, Add MS 12154, fol. 180r; © The British Library Board

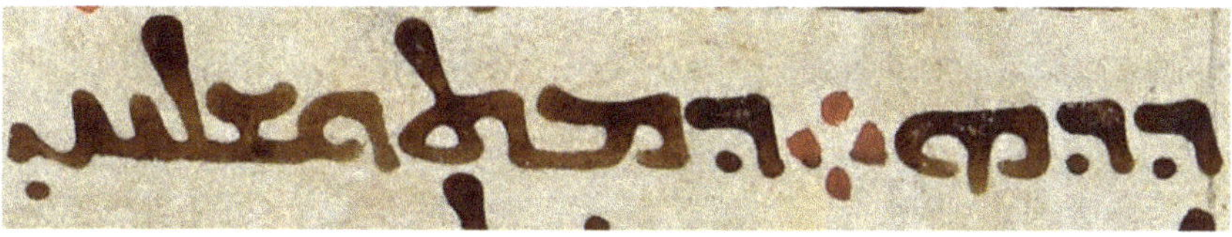

Syriac traditions. Further, the names in the various translations and adaptations of Cave of Treasures do not always correspond to any Syriac form. The table gives the names from the Western Syriac tradition.

There are, however, a number of features about the format and style of the text in BL Add 14620 that differ from BL Add 12154. In BL Add 14620, each set of names is introduced simply by the prefixed particle ܕ 'of', repeating the formula *of X, Y* for each set of names. BL Add 12154 includes the word ܐܢܬܬܗ 'the wife', repeating the following formula throughout: *the wife of X, Y*. In this way, BL Add 14620 is closer to the Armenian lists, which also tend to omit the word for 'wife' throughout,[50] while BL Add 12154 is similar to the two Hebrew lists Sassoon collection MS 368 and Munich, Bayerische Staatsbibliothek, Cod. hebr. 391, which both include the word 'wife' (or an abbreviation of it) for each entry, as well as the marginal notes in Basel, Universitätsbibliothek, AN III 13.

Another difference between the two Syriac texts is that BL Add 14620 does not include the relationship between each matriarch and her husband. The text of BL Add 12154 supplies these relationships following each set of names and is clearly based on the same details found in Jubilees. Basel AN III 13 also includes the same genealogical information as BL Add 12154. No other list or list-like source includes all this information from Jubilees.

Further, the scope of BL Add 14620 also differs from that of BL Add 12154. In our current text, the names of the wives of the patriarchs from Arpachshad to Nahor are not mentioned. This is similar to the texts of the Hebrew manuscripts Sassoon 368 and BSB Cod. hebr. 391, which both omit all or the majority of these names. Other traditions, however, such as the BL Add 12154, the

[50] See Lipscomb, 'Tradition', 149–51; Stone, *Adam and Eve*, 165.

Armenian, and the Greek, all include the generations from the flood to Terah.

A final point that is relevant here is the fact that, while the conflation of names from the Jubilees and the Cave of Treasures traditions is only found in list form in BL Add 14620, several Arabic texts that are not lists do also show knowledge of both traditions. In a historiographical text, Saʿīd ibn Baṭrīq includes the names of the wives of Cain, Seth, Shem, Ham, and Japhet from Jubilees and the names of the wives of Cain and Noah from Cave of Treasures. The widely attested Arabic Genesis catena similarly gives the names of the wives of Cain, Seth, and Noah from Jubilees and the wives of Cain, Noah, and Terah from Cave of Treasures. Common for all of these sources is that, in addition to a few names from Jubilees, the texts give names only to the women who are given names in the narrative portion of Cave of Treasures, not in the genealogy of Cav. Tr. 44. The text that comes closest in scope to BL Add 14620 is the *Tarikh* of al-Ṭabarī, where we find an almost identical situation. Al-Ṭabarī weaves different traditions together throughout his work, including the names of the wives of the patriarchs from Adam to the sons of Noah and the wife of Terah from Jubilees, in addition to the wives of Cain, Seth, and Terah from Cave of Treasures. There is a clear difference in genre between the list in BL Add 14620 and the historiographical and exegetical Arabic texts, but the conflation of material from the Jubilees tradition and the Cave of Treasures tradition is more at home in the Arabic context than in the other lists.

6.0. Discussion

As we have seen in the preceding, BL Add 14620 can be situated textually both within the transmission history of *lists* of the names of the wives of the patriarchs and within the wider transmission of material from Jubilees and Cave of Treasures. The other lists are more or less uniform in their inclusion of names from the Jubilees tradition, while BL Add 14620 conflates Jubilees and Cave of Treasures throughout. Further, the fact that there are a number of differences in layout, syntax, and content makes it difficult to place BL Add 14620 in comparison to the other lists. A question that arises in this connection is how this tradition was transmitted so widely. W. Lowndes Lipscomb, in his article on the Armenian version of the list of the names of the wives of the patriarchs, suggests that the Hebrew manuscripts are all related and that they derive directly from Hebrew Jubilees, whereas all of the other versions are descended from a Greek *Vorlage* that is based on knowledge, not from Jubilees itself, but from one of the Greek chronographers, tentatively identified as the Greek chronicler Annianus.[51] It seems to be the common view that material transmitted from Jubilees to later Greek, Syriac, Armenian, and Arabic contexts passed through the Greek chronographers. The problem with this view as I see it is that the majority of Greek texts prior to the ninth century include only the names of the wives of Cain and Seth. Only a single extant Greek chronicle includes the names of all or nearly all of the wives of the patriarchs,

---

[51] Lipscomb, 'Tradition', 153–55. Cf. Adler, *Time Immemorial*, 229–34; Gelzer, *Sextus Julius Africanus*.

the *Eklogē historion* found in Paris, Bibliothèque national de France, Grec 854. The names in *Eklogē historion* are very close to what is found in the margins of the Greek catena Basel AN III 13. So close, in fact, that J. T. Milik claims: "Je ne doute guère que le glossateur utilisait un exemplaire de l'"Εκλογὴ Ἱστοριῶν."[52] I am not convinced that the glossator actually used a copy of the *Eklogē historion,* but it seems likely that both texts share a common Greek source, quite possibly in list form.

Also relevant to this discussion are the names that are used by al-Ṭabarī. Al-Ṭabarī has much of his Cave of Treasures material from earlier sources and does not seem to use Jubilees traditions except for the names of the wives of the patriarchs. Material from Cave of Treasures is found in many Arabic historiographical and religious texts, so the presence of this material is unsurprising. The inclusion by al-Ṭabarī of names taken from the Jubilees tradition that correspond so closely to the scope of BL Add 14620, and the clear juxtaposition of names from different traditions, put BL Add 14620 closer to al-Ṭabarī than any of the other sources.

All of this suggests that the names may have been transmitted *separately* from the rest of the Jubilees material in the chronicles and universal histories. Based on the available evidence, I believe it is much more likely that the context where we find many or all of the names of the wives of the pre-Abrahamic patriarchs are related to a list tradition that transmitted the names separate from other Jubilees material. It is simply not plausible that all of the lists of the names of the wives of the patriarchs

---

52 Milik, 'Recherches'.

represent individual instances of extraction. Once a list was developed, the list could itself be transmitted entirely independently of the work from which it was extracted. So, when we deal with lists such as the one in BL Add 14620, we must keep a clear theoretical focus on which situation we are discussing.

If this is the case, then it adds to our understanding of the way in which knowledge was transmitted in list form and also gives us a clearer understanding of the way in which knowledge may be extracted from a given work and circulated independently from the work itself. The latter is an important theoretical point in the study of ancient texts and their reception: the reception of themes, ideas, or even specific texts from a given work does not imply the reception of the work itself. As extraction and list-making were common practices in scribal contexts, the transmission of knowledge in list form into novel contexts is evidence of the transmission of knowledge rather than the transmission of a specific literary work.

In conclusion, I want to dwell for a moment on what this case says about the production and transmission of lists and extracts. My claim here is that BL Add 14620 relies on a base text that is a list of the names of the wives of the patriarchs from the Jubilees tradition, that this list was either very similar to the current text or was more comprehensive but was condensed by the scribe, and that the base text was augmented with information from other sources known to the scribe. By viewing the base text as a work in its own right—free from Jubilees—we can more easily understand the simple scribal interventions made by the scribe of BL Add 14620. The addition of knowledge from Cave of

Treasures shows that the scribe sought to articulate both faithfulness to the received text but also to include important information that supplemented or contradicted the base text. The list form facilitates this addition of information in a way that may not be natural in other formats. Items in a list may easily be moved, reordered, and emended by a scribe in the process of copying, making conflations as seen in this list very simple. This particular expression of the list is thus situated within the Syriac–Arabic context of the ninth century and is evidence of one particular expression of a literary tradition that appears throughout the manuscript cultures of Christianity, Judaism, and Islam in late antiquity and the Middle Ages.

REVISITING LISTS IN EARLY ISLAMIC HISTORIOGRAPHY[1]

Teresa Bernheimer

Despite the impressive advances in tools to access and analyse the source material, and new possibilities in the field of digital humanities, the controversies regarding the origins and early history of Islamic historical texts remain unsolved. The debate about the reliability of the source material, allegedly compiled from earlier sources, but extant only in later synthetic forms, has long dominated the field. As I have written on in more detail elsewhere, the most controversial question in the field of Islamic historiography has long been: to what extent can sources compiled decades or centuries after the events they claim to describe be used to reconstruct the origins and early history of Islam?[2] While the answers to this question continue to be varied, even the most sceptical historians have usually regarded lists as early and authentic. What can, moreover, be agreed upon is that lists form a crucial part of early Islamic historiography: they provide the

[1] Many thanks to Antoine Borrut and Hannah Hagemann, as well as the participants of the two workshops on 'Textual Practices in the Pre-Modern World' at CAS LMU for their comments and suggestions on an earlier draft of this paper.

[2] Bernheimer and Bayhoum-Daou, 'Introduction', 1.

 https://doi.org/10.11647/OBP.0375.06

broad frameworks of organisation of our sources, and are ubiquitous in their content.[3]

Indeed, the common denominator of the three main categories of Islamic historiography suggested by Chase Robinson—biography, prosopography, and chronography—is the "list framework."[4] Biographical and prosopographical works are essentially lists of people fleshed out with additional information;[5] chronography is thought to have grown out of lists of caliphs, which were

---

[3] The corpus of early Islamic historiography is vast, and its formation a complex phenomenon. A good introductory summary to the topic is Humphreys, 'Taʾrīkh': "The bulk of early Arabic historical texts (or more precisely, texts which claim to be early) have not come down to us in their original form but are only preserved as citations and paraphrases in a corpus of digests and compilations assembled between the mid-3rd/9th century and the early 4th/10th century.... It is true that much apparently archaic material can be dug out of the encyclopaedias and biographical dictionaries of later centuries, but this does not alter the nature of the problem. Given the present state of the evidence, then, we can determine what Arabic historiography had become by the end of Islam's first three centuries, but recovering the earlier phases of historical thought and writing has proved an extremely elusive problem."

[4] Robinson, *Islamic Historiography*, 55ff.

[5] How kinship lines are drawn, who is included and excluded, is more a matter of design than it first appears—particularly in the Islamic context, where the whole genealogical arrangement is built around Islam and its Prophet; see Bernheimer, *The ʿAlids*, 16. For the particular problems of Islamic prosopography, see Ahmed, *Religious Elite*, 6–21.

known from Ancient Near Eastern tradition and were circulating in the contemporaneous Syriac sources.[6]

Beyond these broad organisational frameworks, the ubiquity of lists of all kinds is a striking feature of early Islamic historical works. In the following contribution, I will revisit these 'lists as content': I want to rethink lists in early Islamic historiographical works as textual practice, that is, as a form of textual communication that is integral to scholarly writing and the creation of a historical narrative. Lists are not simply enumerations of people, events, or tax payments, but an important narrative strategy in the overall historiographic project of early Islam. Understanding lists as textual practice highlights their importance in the forging of a new cultural narrative and memory, and their function as a principal scholarly form.[7] Indeed, the long tradition

[6] Robinson, *Islamic Historiography*, 47: "The scheme itself may be explained as an expansion of skeletal lists of caliphs, which we know from the Syriac tradition to have been circulating in the middle of the eighth century, and whose use in the mature tradition is frequently betrayed. Indeed, listing—not only caliphs, but also governors, judges, and other officials—appears to have been among the *akhbārīs*' earliest enthusiasms, and one which survived the rise of the synthetic forms of the ninth century." For questions of origins and influence between early Islamic and Syriac lists, see Borrut, 'Vanishing Syria' (with a Syriac caliphal list at pp. 48–49, which appears to be based on an Umayyad era Arabic-Islamic list).

[7] For a discussion of 'cultural memory' in premodern societies, see Assmann, *Das kulturelle Gedächtnis*. In the historical study of Islam, some recent studies have notably engaged with memory studies: Borrut, *Entre mémoir et pouvir*; Savant, *The New Muslims of Post-Conquest Iran*; and

of lists in the writings of Near Eastern societies forms an important backdrop to this discussion.[8]

Before examining two examples of lists in some of the main historiographical works in more detail—lists of those who died in the battle of the Ḥarra, and the administrative lists for the reign of ʿAbd al-Malik—I will briefly recapitulate how lists have thus far been understood in the scholarship, and offer some alternative perspectives.[9]

1.0. Lists as Content

Provocatively, one might say that early Islamic historiography could be reduced to two forms of writing: reports and lists. Reports (in the historical context usually called *khabar*, pl. *akhbār*; in the religious or legal context usually called *ḥadīth*, pl. *aḥādīth*)

Vacca, *Non-Muslim Provinces under Early Islam*. See also Borrut and Cobb, *Umayyad Legacies*, for a brief introductory discussion.

[8] For the importance of lists since the dawn of scholarly writing, see the contribution of Enrique Jiménez in this volume.

[9] For the purpose of this contribution, I have chosen a few representative chronographies for close examination. They are universal (rather than local) histories, and date to the formative period of Islamic historiography, usually taken to end in the early tenth century. These are: the *Kitāb al-Muḥabbar* of Muḥammad ibn Ḥabīb (d. 245/860), edited by Ilse Lichtenstädter; the *Taʾrīkh* of Khalīfa ibn Khayyāṭ (d. 240/854), edited by Akram ʿUmarī, by Suhayl Zakkār, and by M. N. Fawwāz; the *Taʾrīkh* of al-Yaʿqūbī (d. 283/897), edited by M. Th. Houtsma; the *Ansāb al-ashrāf* of al-Balādhurī (d. 279/892), edited by W. Madelung (vol. 2) and by M. Schloessinger (vol. 4b); and the monumental *Taʾrīkh al-rusul wa al-mulūk* by Muḥammad b. Jarīr al-Ṭabarī (d. 310/923), edited by de Goeje et al.; there is also a 39-volume translation of this final work.

have received lots of attention, both in medieval Arabic and modern scholarship. They are composite of an *isnād* (the chain of transmission, itself a list—in the historical *akhbār*, the *isnād* is often incomplete or altogether absent) and a *matn* (the body text, which may also contain a list). The study of *akhbār* and *aḥādīth,* collectively known as the *ʿilm al-rijāl* 'science of the transmitters' (as the reliability of the transmission became a central issue), produced whole libraries of supporting literature, including the genesis of entire genres, such as biographical dictionaries of all kinds.[10]

Lists, on the other hand, have received little attention—in both medieval Arabic scholarship and in the modern context. Indeed, there is no clear technical term in Arabic for a list: the term might be *tasmiya*, *shajara*, *jadwal*, *qāʾima*, or another word, depending on its shape, purpose, and content.[11] Where they have been the subject of scholarly attention, lists have usually been mined for information (particularly the prosopographical and biographical lists), rather than examined for their significance in the overall corpus.

The main explanation in the scholarship for the existence of lists in Islamic historical writing has focused on their origins.

---

[10] For a discussion of the *isnād* as a list and recent scholarship on *aḥādīth*, see the contribution of Maroussia Bednarkiewicz in this volume. For the development of biographical literature, see Muranyi, 'Zur Entwicklung der *ʿilm al-riǧāl*-Literatur'.

[11] The meaning of these terms may not have been stable over time, either; thanks to Julia Bray for suggesting some of these terms.

The explanation seems to be that lists are remnants of government records that were compiled from the earliest days of Arab rule, and especially from the Umayyad period (661–750 CE); these lists found their way into the composite historical works of the Abbasid period, where they were either included as lists or fleshed out with *akhbār*. As Robert Hoyland summarises:

> There had been an increasing emphasis, during the first Abbasid decades, on giving some chronological order to narratives of early Islam. Conversely and coincidentally, there was a move to flesh out *lists compiled from government records that had been kept since mid-Umayyad times, regarding the names of holders of high office and notable events for each year* [emphasis added]. From such, Ibn Shihāb al-Zuhrī (d. 742) had drawn up a list of 'The Years of the Caliphs'; soon after, such works included pilgrimage leaders, governors, and judges. Names of those who had fallen in battle may also have been inscribed. Then, in the early 9th century, al-Haytham b. ʿAdī (d. 822) and Abū Ḥassan al-Ziyādī (d. 857) composed a 'History according to Years' (*Taʾrīkh ʿalā sinīn*), presumably a compendium of year by year notices. Finally, with the 'History' of Khalīfa b. Khayyāṭ (d. 854) and especially the 'History of the Prophets and Kings' of Muḥammad b. Jarīr al-Ṭabarī we see a full marriage between literary narrative (*akhbār*) and official annals and records (*taʾrīkh*).[12]

A brief search among the extant documents dated to the early Islamic period indeed reveals a great number of lists. The Arabic Papyrology Database, currently the most comprehensive database for early Arabic documents, gives over 1,300 items classified

---

[12] Hoyland, 'Historiography in the First Abbasid Century', 215–16.

as 'list, account'.[13] Among the documents dated to the first centuries of Islamic rule, there are lists of people or goods; number lists (recording payment sums or weights, and so on); and lists of place names (villages that paid a certain tax). Two fascinating examples, both dated to the seventh century, are a bilingual Greek–Arabic papyrus that gives a list of villages in the al-Bahnasā region where alms payments had been distributed to the poor and needy;[14] and a long (three-folio) papyrus listing names of people according to different (tribal?) groups, possibly relating to military payments.[15]

Clearly, many of the early Arabic list documents are records of some sort of administrative concern (tax registers of various kinds, registers of those who received alms payments or paid a certain tax, expenses for the detachment of soldiers, and so on),

---

[13] This number includes documents written on materials of all kinds, and for the entire period covered by the database; see https://www.apd.gwi.uni-muenchen.de/apd/show_new.jsp. Indeed, there might be many more, which for some reason were classified in another category. I am grateful to Michail Hradek and Leonora Sanego for additional references on the documentary sources.

[14] P.Khalili inv. 68 recto. The document was edited by Khan, *Arabic Papyri*, 49–56.

[15] P.Mil.Vogl. 6. This unusual document was edited by Grohmann, 'Arabische Papyri', 252–59. For a discussion of the document, see also Sijpesteijn, 'Archival Mind', 165; and Sijpesteijn, 'Army Economics' (where she suggests at p. 256 that the document "might be part of a *dīwān*").

reflecting, as Petra Sijpesteijn has argued, the "Muslim bureaucratic instinct."[16] What is important to note for the present purposes, however, is that few, if any, of these list documents have actually been related to lists in the composite historical works.[17] Clearly, there is more to the ubiquitous inclusion of lists in early Islamic historiography than pure administrative interest.

Indeed, there are a great many lists in the early Islamic historiographic works that serve no obvious administrative purpose at all. For instance, one important work of early Islamic historiography is the *Taʾrīkh* ('History') of Ibn Wāḍiḥ al-Yaʿqūbī (d. after 295/908), a caliphal history of the later ninth century that is striking in its clear authorial voice.[18] It includes genealogical lists (such as the children of ʿAbd al-Muṭṭalib, a forefather of the prophet Muḥammad), lists of suras revealed in Mecca or Medina (2:32–33, 43), lists of battles, and lists of those who participated or died in them. There are also lists of missions to foreign rulers (2:82), lists of scribes (2:88), and lists of the wives of the Prophet (between twenty-one and twenty-three women; 2:93), those who

---

[16] Sijpesteijn, 'Archival Mind', 165.

[17] How documents generally relate to the composite historical works is a subject for urgent further examination. In al-Yaʿqūbī's *Taʾrīkh*, for instance, the account of the drawing up of the stipend registers (*dīwān*, pl. *dawāwīn)* under ʿUmar ibn al-Khaṭṭāb appears to have been pieced together from various sources. If among these sources there were actual documents is unclear; in any case, documents or fragments of documents of ʿUmar's *dīwān* are not known to be extant. See al-Yaʿqūbī, *Taʾrīkh*, 2:175 (translation, 3:783).

[18] For a discussion of the distinctively Shiʿi authorial voice, see Anthony, 'Ibn Wāḍiḥ al-Yaʿqūbī'.

resembled the Prophet (2:131), and the Fatimas who bore the Prophet (2:135). What is striking in these lists is that they are all vested in the creation of a new Islamic world view—at times describing it (such as the list of the garrison cities in the reign of ʿUmar ibn al-Khaṭṭāb, 2:176), but at the same time clearly also creating and delineating it (as in the list of religious scholars that he includes at the end of each caliph's reign).[19]

While the lists in al-Yaʿqūbī's work are impressive, the master list-maker among the early historians is Muḥammad ibn Ḥabīb (d. 245/860), a ninth-century scholar whose *Kitāb al-Muḥabbar* is one of the earliest surviving attempts to arrange *akhbār* chronologically and place them in a broader historical context.[20] It is full of curious lists: there is a list of men who lost their eye in battle; one of people who limped; lists of people whose mother was a Christian or Abyssinian woman; lists of people who bought their freedom; one of all those who were the Prophet's relations only by the fact that they were related to one of the Prophet's wives; lists of women who had three husbands or more (indeed of great interest to understand certain kinship networks that are usually hidden in the patrilineal genealogies);

[19] Though outside the scope of this paper, it should be noted that the lists in the first part of al-Yaʿqūbī's work, on the pre-Islamic period, are also part of this definition/creation project. Here al-Yaʿqūbī includes wide-ranging and often curious lists, such as lists of books by Hippocrates (1:107; translation, 2:360), lists of Yemeni tribes (1:229; 2:508ff.), and a long list of the names of the poets of the Arabs (1:304; 2:586), to mention but a few.

[20] See Tayyara, 'Ibn Ḥabīb's *Kitāb al-Muḥabbar*', which examines Ibn Ḥabīb's role in the formation of Islamic universal histories.

lists of women who did homage to the Prophet, and women among the *mushrikūn* (six women who did not become Muslims together with their husbands); lists of the sons-in-law of the caliphs; lists of people who were crucified, and those whose heads were cut off; and a list of the *rāwīs* of Imraʾ al-Qays. Ilse Lichtenstädter, who first edited the *Kitāb al-Muḥabbar* in 1939, notes that there are so many lists in Ibn Ḥabīb's works that he seems to have written "for the sake of classifying and catalogueing [*sic*] his material in a systematical way."[21]

But was the classifying and cataloguing of material really the main purpose of such lists? Lists organise and structure information, thus appearing to be exhaustively inclusive, or ruthlessly exclusive; but in fact they are neither. They also give a certain 'scientific' character to the narrative, they appear to give 'data'—"thereby reducing the proportion of uncertain or ambiguous knowledge," as Lichtenstädter concludes in her study of the *Kitāb al-Muḥabbar*.[22] But of course, then as now, data are far from unambiguous.

Julia Bray suggests that Ibn Ḥabīb's many lists were meant "to throw up a new order of data, relational as opposed to narrative or declarative."[23] In her examination of lists in the *Kitāb al-*

---

[21] Lichtenstädter, 'Muḥammad ibn Ḥabîb', 4.

[22] Cited in Bray, 'Lists and Memory', 211. Bray also notes on lists: "The mental reflexes which they (i.e., lists) harness in the reader are not entirely spontaneous; indeed, lists often cut across the grain of familiar, lazy thought and are a form of conceptual training, or an attempt at it" (p. 214).

[23] Bray, 'Lists and Memory', 222.

Muḥabbar and in Ibn Qutayba's (d. 889) *Kitāb al-Maʿārif*, a fascinating work of the late ninth century generally considered more of a literary than a historical work (though its explicit purpose is to provide a historical handbook), Bray suggests that we should understand lists as mnemonics—that is, systems for improving and assisting the memory: "They tell us what it is essential that we should know, and are structured to help us memorize it."[24] Lists, Bray says, are part of the "attempt to fashion a new kind of cultural memory."[25] In the context of Islamic historiography, this may indeed be the point: the forging of a cultural memory that relates all narrative, of whatever form or genre, to the 'covenant, betrayal, and redemption' paradigm that underlies Islamic historiography.[26]

To illustrate differences and congruences in the list material and their role in the construction of narrative, I want to look at two examples in more detail: the lists of those who were killed in the battle of the Ḥarra; and the lists of those who led the pilgrimage for the reign of the famous Umayyad caliph ʿAbd al-Malik (d. 705), the builder of the Dome of the Rock, and in many

---

[24] Bray, 'Lists and Memory', 212–13: "The whole of Ibn Qutayba's *al-Maʿārif* claims to be mnemonic." See also Bellino, 'History and Adab', for an argument for the educational/pedagogical aspect of the *Kitāb al-Maʿārif.*

[25] Bray, 'Lists and Memory', 226.

[26] For the 'covenant, betrayal, and redemption' paradigm, see Humphreys, 'Taʾrīkh'. The discussion has been taken further by Georg Leube, 'Subversive Philology?', who suggests viewing early Islamic history as "a contested cultural memory." See also Borrut, *Entre mémoir et pouvir*, esp. ch. 4.

ways the architect of what was to become the Islamic state and administration.[27]

2.0. Those Killed in the Battle of the Ḥarra

The battle of the Ḥarra (*ḥarra* means a basalt desert, "a district covered with black broken stones, which looks as if it had been burned by fire") refers to a battle outside Medina, near a place called Ḥarrat Wāḳim, in 63/683, during the reign of the Umayyad caliph Yazīd b. Muʿāwiya. Some of the old Arab elites—Anṣār and Muhājirūn—rebelled against the caliph, his ostentatious lifestyle, and the hereditary succession of the Umayyads, according to one version of the account.[28] In the overall historiographic picture, this does not seem like a particularly important battle—no significant turn of events, for instance. And yet, the list (here called a *tasmiya*) of those who were killed in the battle of the Ḥarra is immediately striking to anyone reading the *Taʾrīkh* of Khalīfa ibn Khayyāṭ (d. 240/854). It is organised by kinship group, and in the edition by Zakkār the list runs to 22 pages.[29] Ibn Khayyāṭ, whose *Taʾrīkh* is the first annalistic chronology ex-

[27] Robinson, *ʿAbd al-Malik*.

[28] Veccia Vaglieri, 'al-Ḥarra', gives further references, and also the names of all those listed as killed in the battle according to Ibn Saʿd's *Ṭabaqāt* (a lot of names, but not nearly as many as listed by Ibn Khayyāṭ); for a contextual discussion see Kister, 'The Battle of the Ḥarra', and Rotter, *Die Umayyaden und der zweite Bürgerkrieg*, 40ff.

[29] In the al-ʿUmarī edition, it is slightly less—see Khalīfa ibn Khayyāṭ, *Taʾrīkh* (al-ʿUmarī, ed.), 1:231–44—though there are fewer notes.

tant, starts his account of the year 63 (682–83): "In this year occurred the affair of the Ḥarra." He gives a few accounts of what happened, before listing those who were killed, page after page. The section ends with the statement: "The total number of the Anṣār who were killed came to 173 men. The total number of the Quraysh and the Anṣār who were killed came to 306 men," though, as Carl Wurtzel points out in his examination of the work, in the list Ibn Khayyāṭ names 166 casualties among the Anṣār and 149 among the Quraysh—a total of 315.[30]

Al-Yaʿqūbī in his *Taʾrīkh* does not give a list of names, but says only that "few people in it [in the city] were not killed" and generally keeps the account short.[31] A list of those who died is also included in al-Balādhurī's *Ansāb al-ashrāf*, though a much shorter one: he gives the names of six *ashrāf* 'nobles' (all of whom are included in Ibn Khayyāṭ's list) and says that altogether about 700 men were killed from the Quraysh and about the same number from among the Anṣār.[32]

That it did matter to know who died in the battle of the Ḥarra, and the side on which they fought, is indicated also by Muḥammad b. Jarīr al-Ṭabarī (d. 310/923), the grand doyen of Islamic historical writing. Al-Ṭabarī does not give a list of those killed, but includes a report that gives some indication that there

---

[30] Wurtzel, *Khalifa ibn Khayyat's History*, 104n479: "Most of the individuals listed by Khalifa were not significant enough to merit an entry in his *Ṭabaqāt*." Translations are based on Wurtzel.

[31] Al-Yaʿqūbī, *Taʾrīkh*, 2:298 (translation 3:943–44).

[32] Al-Balādhurī, *Ansāb al-ashrāf*, 4/2:43.

continued to be a fierce disagreement over who was on the right and the wrong side of history:

> Ḥaṣṣān b. Mālik (fighting for the Umayyads) remained in the Jordan district and said, "Oh people of Jordan, what do you witness for Ibn al-Zubayr and those who were killed of the people of the Ḥarrah?" They replied, "We bear witness that Ibn al-Zubayr is a hypocrite (*munāfiq*) and those of the people of the Ḥarrah who were killed are in hell." "And what do you witness for Yazīd b. Muʿāwiya and those who were killed at the Ḥarrah?," he said. They answered, "We witness that Yazīd was in the right and those of us who were killed are in heaven."[33]

Al-Ṭabarī's account reads like the reformulation in account form of the lists in other historical works—the reordering of data into narrative or declarative form, as opposed to relational, a reversal of what Julia Bray suggested for Ibn Ḥabīb's many lists. Why, given the countless battles of the early Islamic period, those who participated in the battle of the Ḥarra were given so much space in some of the works is difficult to ascertain. As Georg Leube has recently shown in his prosopographical study of the Kinda tribe, the recurring motives of the early Islamic material are often not related to the plot, but reflections of contextual debates and controversies of the world of early Islam.[34] The same might be argued for our lists. As a textual practice, the lists embellish the narration just like the motives and topoi of the *akhbār*.

---

[33] Al-Ṭabarī, *Taʾrīkh*, 2:469 (translation by Hawting, 10:50).

[34] Leube, *Kinda in der frühislamischen Geschichte*. The foundational work on topoi in early Islamic historiography remains Noth, *Quellenkritische Studien*.

Moreover, while the listed names may at some point have been relevant, in the composite works of the Abbasid period it seems more likely that they should be read as "archives of cultural identity," as Christian Junge has called it.[35] Clearly, the lists of those who died in the battle of the Ḥarra highlight the Arab and Muslim origin of early Islam, functioning as (perhaps constructed) mnemonics not of a specific moment or persons, but of a perception of the origins and early history of Islam.

3.0. Administrative Lists for the Reign of ʿAbd al-Malik

While the sources include a great variety of lists whose purpose is difficult to discern, there are some that obviously reflect and reinforce the new structures of the Islamic state: lists of governors, judges, and other officials. In the annalistic histories, these lists are usually found at the very end of each year—al-Ṭabarī, for instance, closes his account of a given year with a note on who led the pilgrimage and who was appointed to a governorship or judgeship. In addition, he sometimes gives more detailed lists: the entry for the year 78/697–98, an important time in the consolidation of the Umayyad state, is mostly comprised of a list of "[t]he officials whom al-Hajjāj appointed in Khurāsān and Sijistān, and why he appointed whom he did, with further details."[36] As the heading already indicates, the list is interspersed

---

[35] Junge, 'Doing Things with Lists'.

[36] Al-Ṭabarī, *Taʾrīkh*, 2:1032 (translation by Rowson, 22:177ff).

with *akhbār*, in which the powerful but controversial governor of the East, al-Hajjāj, is made to justify his choice in direct speech.

Such lists of the main administrators of the Islamic state are included in all of the early historiographies. Ibn Khayyāṭ ends each year with those who led the winter or summer campaigns, and those who led the pilgrimage; after the death of each caliph, he gives detailed lists of the governors, judges, frontier commanders, secretaries, and attendants who served during the reign, and a list of prominent individuals who died in the period. So for instance, for the year 86/705, the year that ʿAbd al-Malik died, he firsts lists some of the governors (Medina, Mecca, Yemen, Basra, Kufa, Khurasan, Sijistan); then the judges (Basra, Kufa, Medina, Syria); then the remaining governors (Sind, Bahrain, Oman, Egypt, Ifriqiyya, al-Jazira, Armenia and Azerbaijan, al-Yamama); the summer raids; the Syrian districts; those who led the pilgrimage; the head of the police force (*shurta*); the secretary for correspondence; the head of taxation and the army (*al-kharāj wa al-jund*; here he says that Sulayman b. Saʿd, a *mawlā* of the Khushayn, a clan of the Qudaʿa, was the first to use Arabic for the records of the Syrian *dīwān*); the secretaries of the official seal, the treasuries, and the warehouses; the chamberlain; the head of the guard.[37]

Tobias Andersson has suggested in his recent study of the *Taʾrīkh* that these administrative lists highlight Ibn Khayyāṭ's Sunni perspective "by bringing the continuity of the caliphate

[37] Wurtzel, *Khalifa ibn Khayyat's History*, 161–70.

and its institutions to the foreground."[38] He further elaborates that "the list sections had two important functions besides their main purpose of structuring available administrative material: first, to provide non-narrative data within a caliphal rather than annalistic framework and, second, to illustrate the continuity and coherence of the caliphal organisation over time."[39]

While the demonstration of coherence and continuity may well be an important aspect, the practice of including lists is certainly not exclusively Sunni. Though his lists are less comprehensive, the Shiʿi historian al-Yaʿqūbī also gives the main postholders at the end of each caliph's reign in his *Taʾrīkh*. He similarly lists those who led the pilgrimage, the military campaigns, and the *fuqahāʾ* 'legal scholars' and the learned men of the time—usually his lengthiest list.[40] As Sean Anthony has recently argued, al-Yaʿqūbī "filled his chronicle with narratives crafted to resonate with the vision of the early Islamic community cultivated by the Shiʿa;"[41] a close analysis of his lists, in particular of the lists of legal scholars and learned men, may well add to our understanding of his Shiʿi perspective in the creation of a cultural memory.

---

[38] Andersson, *Early Sunni Historiography*, 8. An important list with regard to the Sunni perspective on early Islam is the order of the Rightly Guided Caliphs, i.e., the successors to Muḥammad as head of state; see Melchert, 'Rightly Guided Caliphs'.

[39] Andersson, *Early Sunni Historiography*, 187.

[40] For the reign of ʿAbd al-Malik, see 2:336, translation 3:987–89.

[41] Anthony, 'Ibn Wāḍiḥ al-Yaʿqūbī', 31; see also Daniel, 'al-Yaʿqūbī'. Many thanks to Hannah Hagemann for sharing these (and many other) texts.

4.0. Conclusion

There is not yet a good understanding of why the authors and compilers of early Islamic historical works included so many lists. In this short contribution I have tried to start a new conversation, arguing that lists in Islamic historiography are indeed part of the textual and narrative practices of authors and compilers: they are carefully constructed and selected, and just like the topoi and motives of *akhbār*, adapted to fit the specific overall project.

The kinds of lists that are included may give us insight into individual interests and perspectives, and help uncover the assumptions, background, and world view of the authors and compilers. Ibn Khayyāṭ's training as a biographer and genealogist is apparent throughout the *Taʾrīkh*, where lists shape the overall framework of the work and form a large part of its content. Similarly, Ibn Ḥabīb's interest in genealogy—and in particular matrilineal relations—is clearly discernible in his many lists of people, wives, and Fatimas.[42] Al-Yaʿqūbī, who is also famous for his work on geography, includes lists of irrigation channels, garrison towns, and foundations of the Arabs, besides his many other lists that may reflect a Shiʿi perspective.

In all, cataloguing and systematising knowledge is certainly an important aspect of lists in early Islamic historiography; but the role of lists as a textual practice of scholarship *par excellence,* and their purpose in the overall historiographic project of early

---

[42] His own situation may have been relevant here, as his claim to Arab-Islamic distinction may have come via his mother, who is said to have been a client (*mawlā*) of the Prophet's clan; see Tayyara, 'Ibn Ḥabīb's *Kitāb al-Muḥabbar*', 1.

Islam, the forging of a new Islamic narrative and cultural memory, deserve a whole lot more attention.

A LIST IN THREE DIMENSIONS: THE CASE OF EUSEBIUS'S CANON TABLES OF THE GOSPELS

Martin Wallraff

1.0. Synopses and Lists

One of the last books of Umberto Eco (1932–2016) is entitled *Il vertigine della lista*. In this book, the Italian scholar makes a few clear-sighted remarks on lists on the occasion of a series of initiatives at the Louvre in Paris in 2009. The Italian title has been translated rather freely into English as *The Infinity of Lists* and, even worse, into German as *Die unendliche Liste*.[1] These translations reduce the subject to one particular phenomenon: endless, unlimited lists, like the list of the stars in the sky, the list of species in biology, the list of Guinness World Records. However, the book does not deal with this kind of list only. It talks about the *vertigine*, the feeling of dizziness, even of very banal, limited lists of everyday life; their tendency to completeness; their partial and partially failing attempts at establishing order in the world.

Eco does not distinguish between open and closed lists but what he calls practical and poetical lists. The first is a limited

[1] Eco, *Il vertigine della lista*.

 https://doi.org/10.11647/OBP.0375.07

catalogue of "objects in the world," like the shopping list or the catalogue of a library. The latter, the poetical lists, are drawn up "because something cannot be enumerated, it eludes the possibility of control and naming."[2] An example for this kind of list would be the litany of saints in the Roman Catholic liturgy. "Saint so-and-so pray for us"—the litany goes on like this for a long time. Obviously, the time is limited, and the number of saints is limited, but the intention is to enumerate 'all saints'.[3]

In any case, a list is an enumeration of single items, which may or may not be presented in some sort of tabular layout. We are used to seeing lists in the form of a list, but they do not lose their character if they are displayed differently.

Now, what is a synopsis, as opposed to a list? I would suggest the following definition: a synopsis is a list of higher order. Or to be more precise: a list in more than one dimension. The shopping list is a limited enumeration of items in one row. This row can be displayed in various manners, but it remains a row, that is, a file or series of items. A menu in a restaurant is a different situation (fig. 1, *top left*). You can read it in two directions: vertically to see what they have, horizontally to see what price corresponds to what dish. This kind of information actually requires a tabular layout. It would lose its sense if it was arranged differently, for example all dishes as a continuous text, and then all prices as a continuous text.

---

[2] Eco, *Il vertigine della lista*, 117. My translation.

[3] Cf. Knopp, 'Sanctorum nomina seriatim'.

Figure 1: Lists and synopses in everyday life: (*top left*) a menu (Gaststätte Atzinger, Munich); (*bottom left*) a timetable (Schifffahrtsgesellschaft des Vierwaldstättersees [SGV] AG, Lucerne); (*right*) a table of contents (from Eco, *Il vertigine della lista*)

This is even more evident in a more complex case like a timetable (fig. 1, *bottom left*). You have a vertical axis with places around Lake Lucerne, and a horizontal axis for times and ships on the lake. The information can also be given differently, such as with the search function of an online timetable, but if you want to see everything on one page, you have to choose this or a very similar layout of a synopsis: a list in two dimensions on the two dimensions of a rectangular page. The concept of page is important here.

The same is true for the classical case in which theologians use the term synopsis, namely the juxtaposition of parallel pericopes from the Bible, mostly from the gospels. This has become so classical that we even call three of these texts the ‘synoptic gospels’, because they can conveniently be arranged in three parallel columns in order to be ‘seen together’ (Greek *sun-horaō*), the etymology of synopsis. Vertically, the sequence of each text is maintained, horizontally the parallels can be compared.[4]

Can there be more than two dimensions, more than the length and breadth of a page? I would argue, yes, and the table of contents of a book may be an example (fig. 1, *right*). At first sight, it is a straightforward table like the menu of a restaurant. Two columns (or three if the chapter numbers are counted) with two possible reading directions, horizontal and vertical. However, this case is more complex. Chapter 12 has the beautiful Italian title ‘La Wunderkammer’, and we learn from the table that it starts at p. 200. Miraculously, the Wunderkammer corresponds to a round number. Now, it is clear that this is not the sort of consideration that the list is meant for. The number 200 is not significative in itself, but it refers to something other, to a concrete place in the same object, in the same book. This is the difference between Wunderkammer in the book and Weisswurst in the menu. Once you learn that the latter costs €7.20, you are done, whereas page 200 has a deictic value. It refers to something else, to a third dimension outside the two dimensions of a flat page. In contemporary language this could be called a link, even if you cannot click on it (in a good e-book, you can).

---

[4] The layout as well as the terminology go back to Johann Jakob Griesbach (1745–1812) and his 1776 edition of the New Testament; see Stallmann, *Johann Jakob Griesbach*, esp. 44–48.

All this is not new. We get lists in one, two, and three dimensions already in antiquity. I would argue that no one mastered this technique better than Eusebius of Caesarea. He has rightly been called an impresario of the codex.[5] I would also call him an impresario of the list. And within the work of Eusebius no other list is more sophisticated—and more beautiful!—than the canon tables of the gospels. In what follows, I will give a very brief introductory explanation of what canon tables are about and how they can be used, an 'instruction manual', as it were. Then there will be three more short sections to illustrate their synoptic character.

2.0. What Are Canon Tables About?

As an example, I use a twelfth-century manuscript that has recently been purchased by the Byzantine collection of Dumbarton Oaks in Washington, DC (fig. 2).[6] It is a beautiful book, and the canon tables are even more beautiful. These pages are so delicate and so full of sweet and eye-catching details that you may not feel the need to ask for any practical purpose. Their raison d'être is their beauty, and even without any utility it is nice that they are there for the joy of readers, of the person who commissioned the book in the first place, and maybe even of the artist who produced them. Yet they are useful as well; despite their splendour,

---

[5] Grafton and Williams, *Transformation of the Book*, 178 (in the subtitle of the relevant chapter).

[6] Washington, DC, Dumbarton Oaks, MS 5 (BZ.2009.033, Gregory/Aland no. 678), https://nrs.harvard.edu/urn-3:DOAK.MUS:4740200 (accessed 6 December 2021).

these are ultimately very sober and boring tables of numbers. They serve the same purpose as a modern synopsis of the gospels; that is, they help to find parallel passages in the four gospels.[7] Each number stands for a passage in one of them. In the case of fig. 2, there are three columns for the three gospels of Matthew, Luke, and John, and each line is an equation of similar passages. To give just one example, line 10 of the left system contains the numbers ϟζ—σια—ρε (in Arabic numerals, 97—211—105). These numbers can be found at the margins of the text in the book, and they would lead to the following parallel passages (in the New Revised Standard Version):

Matt. 10.39 (= section 97)	Luke 17.33 (= section 211)	John 12.2 (= section 105)
Those who find their life will lose it, and those who lose their life for my sake will find it.	Those who try to make their life secure will lose it, but those who lose their life will keep it.	Those who love their life lose it, and those who hate their life in this world will keep it for eternal life.

These verses are not identical, but they basically convey the same message.

---

[7] To name just a few elements of essential bibliography: Nestle, 'Die Eusebianische Evangelien-Synopse'; Nordenfalk, *Die spätantiken Kanontafeln*; Wessel, 'Kanontafeln'; O'Loughlin, 'Harmonizing the Truth'; Crawford, *Eusebian Canon Tables*; Wallraff, *Die Kanontafeln*.

Figure 2: A page of Eusebius's canon tables, canons III and IV; Washington, Dumbarton Oaks, MS 5 (GA 678), fol. 3v (© Dumbarton Oaks, Byzantine Collection, Washington, DC)

The whole system is relatively sophisticated. There are a total of 10 tables for the various constellations of four or three or two parallels. Furthermore, there is a short letter accompanying the tables, in which the system, its purpose, and its usage, is explained (the 'Epistula ad Carpianum').

Dozens or even hundreds of Greek copies of Eusebius's work survive, and many more would have existed. Sometimes they are of modest quality, but in many cases they are of stunning splendour and preciosity. Some of the best pieces of medieval book illumination have been accomplished in the context of these modest and sober tables.

And there is not only Greek. Gospel books in virtually all languages of the ancient world were furnished with these tables. Splendid examples can be found in Latin, Armenian, Ethiopic, Syriac, and other languages.[8] In all the corresponding cultures the biblical text travelled together with these tables for many centuries. They were part of the reading experience for many generations of Christians, and they shaped the way in which the Bible was perceived.

It is no exaggeration to say that no other text of antiquity has been copied more often than the canon tables and the accompanying letter—the only exception being the Bible itself. Strangely enough, the favourable situation of transmission contrasts with an unfortunate printing history. Before my own critical edition (which appeared in 2021), only one edition was primarily based on manuscript evidence, and that appeared 500

[8] See the summary overview in Wallraff, *Die Kanontafeln*, 147–64.

years ago, edited by Erasmus of Rotterdam (1519). All subsequent prints (up to and including the standard edition of the New Testament by Nestle-Aland) did nothing but enrich the text with good and bad conjectures, partial evidence, new errors, and misprints.[9]

A thorough study of the text itself is worthwhile. There are many interesting things to discover, both for the New Testament itself and for the origin of the canon tables. The canon tables are remarkable not only because they bring us to the origins of Christian book illumination,[10] but also for their textual evidence—if indeed we want to call these pages and pages of just numbers 'a text'. Some people might disagree, but I would argue that they are a text in the strictest possible sense of the word: *textus* comes from *texere* and means woven. What we normally call a text should really more accurately be called a *filum*, that is, a row of letters and words, one after the other, a one-dimensional chain or string. In this sense, the gospel book contains four single *fila* on the life of Jesus Christ: four independent, yet partially parallel accounts of the same events. The invention of this synoptic system creates links between them; they are interwoven by means of cross-references from one to the other which creates a web or

---

[9] Erasmus's *editio princeps* of the New Testament of 1516 did not contain the canon tables. They were added in the second edition of 1519, *Novum testamentum omne*, 100–108. The modern edition is Wallraff, *Die Kanontafeln*, 175–89; remarks on the history of research and previous editions are found there at pp. 164–72.

[10] See Nordenfalk, 'Beginnings of Book Decoration'; and, of course, his monograph of 1938, *Die spätantiken Kanontafeln*.

textile structure that is symbolically visible in the canon tables at the beginning of the book. This is a *textus* par excellence, by means of which the four gospels become the *one* Gospel, with a capital G. Several interwoven *fila* become one *textus*.

James O'Donnell has called the numbers in these tables "the world's first hot links."[11] The formulation may be somewhat too trendy, but it is not entirely wrong. These numbers point to, refer to, different points in the book. To use them, one has to go continuously back and forth in the text. You would probably use your fingers, or small pieces of paper, to mark the various texts that you are reading almost simultaneously, synoptically. The use of canon tables is not meant for continuous reading of long passages of text, but rather for short consultation. You use them not to read, but to look things up. It is a very scholarly way of using the text. If you were not prepared to turn pages all the time, canon tables would be useless. You must have actual pages (or an electronic structure) to use them. The text must be available in a medium that allows fast and immediate access to any given passage. I stress this point because there is no way of using such a device with the Holy Scripture of Judaism, that is, with a scroll. It is technically impossible to use the fingers, or other bookmarks, to mark two, three, or even four different points in the text and consult them almost simultaneously in a scroll.

This point is so important because the medium of the book (or, in technical terms, of the codex) was relatively new at the beginning of the fourth century. This is the time when the canon

---

[11] Quoted in Grafton and Williams, *Transformation of the Book*, 199.

tables originated. Eusebius made use of the new media of his time in a clever and intricate way. This brings me to my third section.

3.0. The Codex in Early Christianity

The codex, as a new form of material support for texts, originated around the first century of the Christian era. The debate on its origins and about its relationship with Christianity is long and old, and there is no need to elaborate on this point here.[12] Suffice it to say that the affinity between Christianity and the codex is very old. Already in the second and third centuries, the predilection of Christians for the new medium is statistically verifiable. On this basis, it has to be asked what the codex actually meant to Christians, what this choice implied for them, and, viewed from the other side, how Christians used the codex, how they adapted it to their needs, and how the medium changed in the process. The first Christian books were rather modest brochures made of papyrus. Scholars have spoken of the antique equivalent of 'paperbacks'. The typical dimensions of a page can be around 15 × 15 cm.[13]

Now, when we come back to the canon tables, things change. At the beginning of the fourth century we find codices that are entirely different from the modest booklets on papyrus.

---

[12] See Wallraff, *Kodex und Kanon*, 13–18.

[13] On early codices in general, see Cavallo, 'Libro e pubblico', 85; on early Christian books ('religion of the paperback'), see Stroumsa, 'Early Christianity'. A well-preserved example of such a booklet is Pap. Bodmer 2 (= P^{66} Aland). The codex measures 16.2 × 14.2 cm; it contains the gospel of John.

In the fourth century, some of the most celebrated Christian books of all times originate, artefacts like the Codex Sinaiticus or the Codex Vaticanus.[14] Size, weight, quality, quantity of text, value—everything is different. Some of these manuscripts consist of many hundred pages. The term ‘megacodices’ is appropriate. What originated as a functional and inexpensive carrier medium, has now become a sumptuous and representative object. What does this all mean for the canon tables?

First, it means that the single biblical books (the book of Genesis, the book of Isaiah) are now joined into one book. The many *biblía* become the one Bible: the word ‘Bible’ is actually a collective plural of *biblíon*. Therefore, the four gospels are also united in one book.[15] The plurality and unity of the gospel becomes an issue. Second, the conjunction of a group of Christian writings with the old Holy Scripture of Judaism lets some rays of holiness from the latter also shine on the former. Christians now have Holy Scriptures as well—as implied in the diptych ‘Old and New Testament’. Third, these large codices are less likely to be owned and used by a single private person, certainly not during travel or in other situations of daily life. They are meant for congregations or libraries, therefore for liturgical or scholarly use.

Eusebius’s invention of the canon tables presupposes all these innovations. It has been an enormous success for centuries,

---

[14] The bibliography on these famous manuscripts is enormous. I limit myself to one recent title: Andrist, ‘Au croisement des contenus’.

[15] See Hengel, *Die vier Evangelien*. However, little attention is paid there to aspects of material culture, and in this sense, the work of David Trobisch, *First Edition*, is of fundamental importance (pace Hengel).

because it responded precisely to the new features in an ingenious way: four gospels in one book, a look-and-feel of holiness, scholarly use. I will elaborate on these points in my final section, but in order to understand Eusebius's work properly, we need to come to the more technical questions of the synoptical list as such.

4.0. Tabular Layouts

The canon tables did not appear out of the blue. Although they were highly innovative, there were precursors and presuppositions. The main innovation in Eusebius's system is the idea of arranging material in tables. In a recent book, Megan Williams and Anthony Grafton have rightly pointed out that Eusebius's most important predecessor was the *Hexapla* of the great Christian exegete and theologian Origen.[16] He drew up a synopsis of the various versions of the Hebrew Bible. The idea was to juxtapose the Hebrew original (along with a transliteration) and all relevant Greek translations in neighbouring columns. The six—sometimes even seven, eight, or nine—columns make use of the entire space of a wide double page of a codex. Of course, in theory it would be possible to implement this same idea in the medium of a scroll as well. However, it would require an enormous amount of scrolling all the time, and there is no evidence that the *Hexapla* ever existed in this form.[17] In fact, the type of reading

[16] *Pars pro toto* I mention only two titles: Grafton and Williams, *Transformation of the Book*, 86–132; Dorival, 'La forme littéraire'. Both concentrate more on the overall shape than on issues of the content.

[17] See Grafton and Williams, *Transformation of the Book*, 102–5.

required is different: Origen's invention is not meant for normal, 'edifying' Bible reading, and even less for liturgical purposes. It is an aid for philologists, who study variants of textual transmission and translation. The typical reader would already have known the text from elsewhere, and he would have had a specific problem or question that he wished to pursue. Very much like the canon tables, the *Hexapla* is for consultation, rather than bedside reading.

The next example brings us even closer to the canon tables. This is not so much about reading, but about understanding by means of synoptic comparison. Long before inventing the canon tables, Eusebius had used this kind of layout to revolutionise historiography. His first major scholarly work was a universal chronicle.[18] He was not the first Christian author in this field, and actually the material basis of his work is not much richer than that of his third-century predecessor Julius Africanus. The strong term 'revolutionise' is appropriate for Eusebius because the innovation was the tabular layout: in his chronological 'canon', Eusebius arranged all the lengthy lists of kings of various peoples in such a way that contemporary events in each reign were parallelised. The work has come down to us only in its Latin and Armenian translation, and fig. 3 shows a double page in an early Latin codex with no less than seven columns. The synchronism of the history of the Assyrians, the Hebrews, the Athenians etc. becomes visually clear. The *fila regnorum* of the single national histories are interwoven into one history of humankind. This list is

---

[18] See Burgess and Tougher, 'Eusebius of Caesarea'. The visual aspects are emphasised in Rosenberg and Grafton, *Cartographies of Time*, 15.

in two dimensions, and in this sense somewhat less complex than the canon tables of the gospels.

Figure 3: The history of humankind in synoptic columns, Eusebius, chronicle, Latin translation; Oxford, Bodleian Library, MS Auct. T.2.26, fols 50v–51r (© Bodleian Library, Oxford)

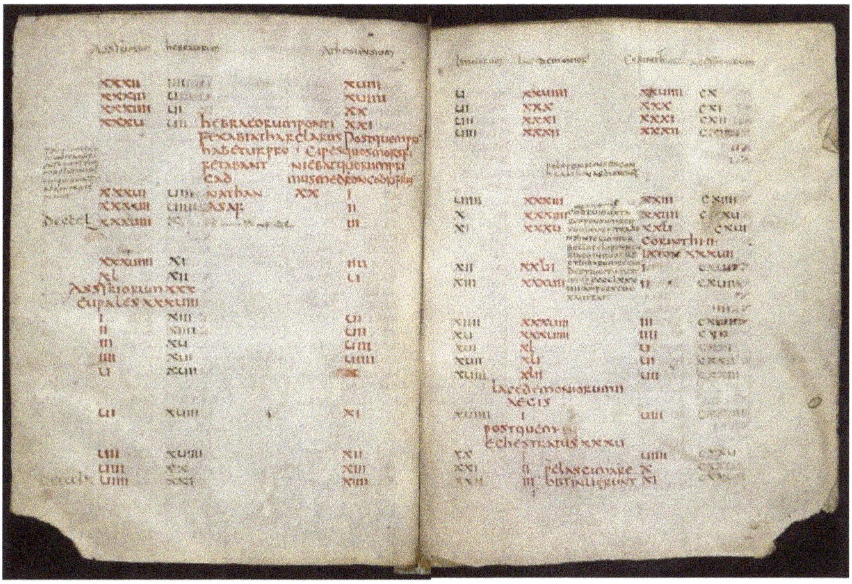

However, there is a predecessor for the third dimension as well, that is, the 'hypertext' aspect, the fact that texts are represented by numbers, which have the character of cross-references or 'hot links'. Only the deictic aspect of numbered references gave the system the slenderness to actually work. Some predecessors of Eusebius had the same basic idea—the only difference had been that they arranged actual texts rather than numbers. The four gospels were lumped together into one text by Tatian in his

Diatessaron.[19] A few years later Ammonius, somewhat more sophisticated, had drawn up a sort of synopsis, in which he juxtaposed various parallels for each passage of Matthew.[20] The result was not only cumbersome to handle, it also ruined the integrity of the holy text, at least for the three gospels after Matthew. In the words of Eusebius: "The coherent sequence of the three was destroyed as far as the network of reading is concerned."[21] The expression 'network of reading' or 'web of reading' is quite unusual, and I think it is remarkable. It points to what I would call a typically late antique reading experience: the texture of reading, 'text' in its literal meaning. Only the grid of deictic numbers allowed for both: organic, continuous reading as well as cross-references of intertextuality.

Already in an earlier work Eusebius had used this specific innovation. In what may be called 'the canon tables of the psalms', numbers are listed, not full texts (fig. 4). It is a very simple list. In several sections the psalms written by David, Solomon, and so on are listed.[22] This is not a synopsis, there is no vertical

[19] See the contributions in Crawford and Zola, *Gospel of Tatian.*

[20] The only source on this work is Eusebius's 'Epistula ad Carpianum', in which the predecessor is briefly mentioned at the beginning (§2). Crawford, 'Ammonius of Alexandria', provides a detailed analysis, although I do not agree with his conclusions in all aspects; see Wallraff, *Die Kanontafeln*, 22–24.

[21] ...ὡς ἐξ ἀνάγκης συμβῆναι τὸν τῆς ἀκολουθίας εἱρμὸν τῶν τριῶν διαφθαρῆναι ὅσον ἐπὶ τῷ ὕφει τῆς ἀναγνώσεως. 'Epistula ad Carpianum', §2 (line 6 in Wallraff, *Die Kanontafeln*).

[22] See Wallraff, 'Canon Tables of the Psalms'.

and horizontal reading direction, no comparison between columns. The material could also be arranged differently, for example in continuous text, without losing the information. However, it refers to textual units outside the page. It presupposes the numbered subdivision of the Psalter, and it must be possible to go back and forth easily. This list is also in two dimensions, albeit not on the physical extension of a page. It is an important presupposition for the extremely complex composition of the canon tables of the gospels.

Figure 4: Canon tables of the psalms; Oxford, Bodleian Library, MS Auct. D.4.1, fols 24v–25r (© Bodleian Library, Oxford)

5.0. Symphony of the Gospels

As I said before, in a megacodex like the Sinaiticus you can physically perceive something of the beauty and of the holiness of the biblical text. It is almost literally of imperial sumptuousness. Constantine ordered 50 copies at the scriptorium of Caesarea for the churches of the new capital founded by him: even if there is no evidence that the Sinaiticus was one of them, it may be *like* one of them.[23] At the same time, it must have contained the canon tables. Unfortunately, the tables themselves have not been preserved, yet they must have existed, as the marginal numbers of the Eusebian system show.[24] Thus, this is the earliest preserved attestation of the whole work—which is quite remarkable. Which other late antique text is physically attested at a distance of maybe one generation after it has been written?

The reason why I insist on this codex is that the scholarly apparatus and complicated cross-reference system did not prevent the manuscript from serving any purpose such a manuscript could possibly serve. It may well have been used for liturgical worship in one of the Constantinopolitan churches. It may well have been used by the emperor as a prestigious gift to a noble person. It may well have been read by a devout Christian, provided that he or she could afford such a precious Bible. All this would not have been true for Origen's *Hexapla*, which was targeted only at a scholarly market; as is well known, this market is

---

[23] The imperial letter is preserved in Eusebius, *Vita Constantini* 4,36; Eusebius complied (4,37). However, it should be noted that the letter does not speak of 50 *Bibles* (let alone pandects like the Codex Sinaiticus). Previous research was often based on false implicit assumptions. Likewise, it was often—baselessly—assumed that Sinaiticus actually belonged to the group produced in Caesarea.

[24] See Wallraff, *Die Kanontafeln*, 139–40.

very narrow and restricted—less promising for a great success during many centuries to come.

Eusebius's canon tables were so successful because they did not destroy the integrity of the sacred text. To the contrary: they highlighted its sanctity in a specific way. There is reason to think that a feature which is preserved in several manuscripts was already a part of the archetype. In a tenth-century manuscript in Venice, a splendid series of canon tables ends with a page with a beautiful tholos (*tempietto*). Carl Nordenfalk had already observed in 1938 the striking similarity of this tholos in some Greek manuscripts with similar images in very different cultures and traditions. Very similar motifs at the end of the canon tables can be found in Armenian, Ethiopic, and Latin manuscripts (fig. 5). When seeing these pictures on one page, one should always bear in mind that these illuminated manuscripts originated at a distance of several hundred years and several thousand miles from one another. This similarity would be difficult to explain if these motifs did not have common roots. According to Nordenfalk, they might even go back to the Eusebian archetype[25]—and this opinion has never been seriously questioned. I think there is additional evidence in its support, and that comes from its inscription.

---

[25] Nordenfalk, *Die spätantiken Kanontafeln*, 102–8.

Figure 5: Tholos in Greek, Ethiopic, Armenian, and Latin gospel books: (*top left*) Venice, Biblioteca Nazionale Marciana, Marc. I 8 (GA U / 030), fol. 3r; (*top right*) Abba Garima gospel book I (today bound in gospel book II, f. 258v; from McKenzie and Watson, *The Garima Gospels*); (*bottom left*) Yerevan, Matenadaran, cod. 3474, fol. 5v (from Buschhausen and Buschhausen, *Codex Etschmiadzin*); (*bottom right*) Paris, Bibliothèque nationale de France, lat. 8850, fol. 6v (Soissons gospel book)

In the Venice manuscript we read: *Hypothesis kanonos tēs tōn euaggelistōn sumfōnias*. Literally (and badly) translated, this states: 'Purpose/structure of the canon of the symphony of the evangelists'. I have not translated *sumfōnia* here, because it is a meaningful term, although 'harmony' would probably render the idea better in modern languages. A careful analysis of the oldest textual witnesses shows that this inscription too must be very old; in all likelihood it also goes back to the archetype. This is corroborated by the fact that the Ethiopic version also contains a very similar inscription in many copies.[26]

The inscription is partly similar to certain formulations in Eusebius's letter accompanying the canon tables, and so one might think that somebody developed it on this basis at a later stage. However, this seems unlikely, since 'symphony' is not used there, but there is a close parallel in Eusebius's *Church History*, where he also speaks of the "symphony of the evangelists."[27] This is actually Eusebian language; hence, it seems likely that the tholos was already there in the archetype and that it was explained and accompanied by this inscription.[28]

---

[26] Wallraff, *Die Kanontafeln*, 100.

[27] *Historia ecclesiastica* 6,31,3 (referring to Julius Africanus); see also 1,7,1; 2,10,2.

[28] See the overview of various positions of the text in Wallraff, *Die Kanontafeln*, 96–97.

There are, by the way, also manuscripts in which only the inscription has been preserved, not the tholos. One example is the gospel book at Dumbarton Oaks.[29]

What does this all mean, and why is it important whether the inscription is old or not? It is so important because it can be seen as the key to Eusebius's theological intention for the whole project. The tholos, as well as the inscription, expresses well the way in which Eusebius wanted to resolve the old problem of the plurality and unity of the gospels. There is one Jesus, but there are four similar accounts of his life. Earlier attempts at uniting these four literary units by Tatian and Ammonius had failed. Eusebius found a way of maintaining the integrity of each gospel, and at the same time of uniting them in one text or, maybe better, hypertext. This unity becomes concrete and visible for a non-expert as well, even for a reader who does not really understand or care about the complex scholarly system of numerical cross-references. The four columns of the tholos carry one common roof, and the inscription stresses the harmony of the four gospels. The curtains between the columns both conceal and open the way to the sanctuary (see, e.g., the famous Ejmiacin gospel book of the tenth century in Armenian, bottom left in fig. 5). This is a truly worthy doorway to the holy text. Maybe the most beautiful visual expression of this idea can be found in the Rossano codex, written in the sixth century on purple parchment (fig. 6). Images of the

---

[29] Dumbarton Oaks MS 5, fol. 7v (at the beginning of the 'Epistula ad Carpianum').

four evangelists are integrated into one endless chain; in the middle, the Eusebian inscription of the symphony of the gospels gives a hermeneutical key.

Figure 6: Tondo with four evangelists' portraits; Rossano, Museo Diocesano e del Codex (GA Σ/042), fol. 5r (© Museo Diocesano e del Codex, Rossano)

Not only did the scholarly lists not destroy the holy text, rather they highlighted it. Eusebius's invention was an important step in the process of the 'sacralisation' of Christian holy writings. The invention is so ingenious, and maybe it was so successful, because it allowed for different approaches that did not exclude one another: the spiritual, the aesthetic, and the scholarly aspect were all present in one book, so they might appeal to different readers, in different situations.

LISTS OF THE SONGS OF ASCENTS (PSS 120–134) IN THE CAIRO GENIZAH: THEIR FORM AND ITS IMPLICATIONS

Rebecca Ullrich

The Cairo Genizah[1] contains hundreds of thousands of fragments. Many of these fragments contain lists that have received considerable research attention. However, others still require in-depth study. These include eight fragments with lists containing the Songs of Ascents (Pss 120–34), which were often recited during the morning prayer of the rite of Eretz Israel; this section of the morning prayer is known as תפילת השיר (*tefillat ha-shir* 'the prayer of the song'). The fragments will be examined here in relation to the morning liturgy of the rite of the land of Israel.

[1] A genizah is a place where, strictly speaking, texts containing the Hebrew name of God are deposited. Ritual items such as tefillin and mezuzot, as well as profane text and material, were also deposited in genizahs, and texts in other languages can also be found there. Probably the most famous genizah is the Cairo Genizah, which has been researched from the late nineteenth century on. The Cairo Genizah was located in the Ben Ezra Synagogue, Fustat, and followed the rite of the land of Israel in the Middle Ages. Most of the surviving fragments from that genizah date from the eleventh century CE and later.

 https://doi.org/10.11647/OBP.0375.08

Thematically, Pss 120–34 include the “return from exile, the re-establishment of the community in Judah, the centrality of Jerusalem, Zion, and the Temple and the future of the Davidic dynasty.”[2] All 15 psalms have the heading *shir ha-maʿalot* (שיר המעלות) or *shir le-maʿalot* (שיר למעלות). From this heading comes the name Songs of Ascents or Songs of Degrees. The Mishnah explains the meaning of the headings in Sukkah 5.4 and Middot 2.5 and their relation to the 15 steps that led to the temple. The Songs of Ascents have received considerable attention during the development of the Jewish liturgy and have always been (again) part of the liturgy, although regionally and temporally at different places in the liturgy. The complete set of the abovementioned 15 psalms, or each psalm from the set, is still recited today during various rites at different times.[3] In medieval Egypt, the Songs of Ascents were recited during the morning prayers of the congregation of the land of Israel, in the *tefillat ha-shir*, until the gradual displacement of the rite of the land of Israel by the Babylonian rite at the end of the thirteenth century.[4]

The lists of the Songs of Ascents from the Cairo Genizah are particularly relevant in this liturgical context, as they provide

---

[2] Berlin, *Jewish Study Bible*, 1411.

[3] See Nulman, *Encyclopedia of Jewish Prayer*, 303–4.

[4] See the findings of Vered Raziel-Kretzmer, ‘How Late’, who, on the basis of prayer book fragments attributed to a scribe from the last decade of the thirteenth century, showed that although he followed the Babylonian rite, he still adhered to elements of the rite of Eretz Israel, such as the recitation of the *tefillat ha-shir* (Pss 120–34) and the Ten Commandments for Shabbat morning service.

partial information about the position of the Songs of Ascents in the prayer. At the same time, the fragments of prayer books can be used to assign the lists to specific occasions during the prayer. That such lists were written to aid prayer and memory during recitation is evident from the nature of the prayer books. In the Genizah manuscript Oxford, Bodleian Library, MS Heb. g. 2, which presents the rite of the land of Israel, the following text is found, along with the timing of recitation of the Songs of Ascents during prayer. The text starts on fol. 5b and continues to fol. 6a.

> ...ברוך אתה יי אלהינו מלך העולם [האל] המהולל בפי עמו ומשובח ומפואר בלשון כל חסידיו ובשירי דויד בן ישי עבדך נ[הללך] ונשבחך ונרוממך ונגדלך ונזכיר את שמך מלכינו אלהינו יחיד חי העולמים משובח ומפואר עדי עד שמך ברוך אתה יי מהולל הת[שבחות] יהי כבוד כולה תם שירו לאלהים זמרו שמו תם שיר המעלות אלשיר כול אלי כל הנשמה תהלל יה הללויה יהללוך יי אלהינו...[5]

> "...Blessed are You, God our God, King of the world, the Almighty, whose praise is spoken through the mouth of His people, who is praised and glorified through the tongues of those who are devoted to Him in love. With the songs of David, son of Yishai, Your servant, let us praise You, let us glorify You, let us magnify You, let us remember Your name, our King, our God, the only one who lived eternally, let Your name be praised and glorified forever: Blessed are You Adonai, praised by praises." [Then follows] the whole of *yehi khevod*, then (Ps. 68.5): "Sing to God, chant hymns to his name." This is followed by the Songs of Ascents, the song in its entirety, until (Ps. 50.6) "Let all that breathes praise the Lord. Hallelujah...."

---

[5] Fleischer, *Eretz-Israel Prayer*, 233; my translation.

This shows that, in this case, the Songs of Ascents are only mentioned, but their text was assumed to be known. Only the text of the blessings is written down in full in this example. That there was a need for the text of the Songs of Ascents is shown by a list on fol. 80b of the manuscript:

שיר המעלות אל יי בצרתה לי

שיר למעלות אשא עיני אל ההרים

שיר המעלות שמחתי באומרים לי

שיר המעלות לדוד אליך

שיר

שיר

שיר[6]

A song of ascents. To the Lord in my distress[7]

A song for ascents. I turn my eyes to the mountains

A song of ascents. I rejoiced when they said to me

A song of ascents. Of David.[8] To you

A song

A song

A song

The scribe enters the text of the opening verse for each of the Songs of Ascents here as a memory aid for the order of the texts.

---

[6] Fleischer, *Eretz-Israel Prayer*, 240.

[7] The translation of the Hebrew Bible throughout the article is based on Berlin, *Jewish Study Bible*.

[8] "Of David" belongs to the previous psalm. The scribe of the lines probably wrote down the biblical text from memory and switched the verses.

The list then ends for unknown reasons. If such a list is already integrated into a prayer book manuscript,[9] it is not surprising that such lists are also found as independent fragments in the Cairo Genizah. This also provides an insight into the possible practice of relying on 'memory cards' during prayer, probably as a support for memory.

In the following section, an overview of the types of lists in the Cairo Genizah is given, in order to analyse the lists within the broader context of the Cairo Genizah. Then an analysis of the fragments containing lists with the Songs of Ascents (Pss 120–34) and their liturgical classification follows.

1.0. Lists in the Cairo Genizah

The lists in the Cairo Genizah are a treasure trove of data, which provides numerous research insights. This is demonstrated by the extensive research focusing on the lists in the Cairo Genizah. For further classification of the lists, the categorisation of the entire source material of the Cairo Genizah must be considered first.

Often mentioned here is the categorisation elaborated by Goitein,[10] in which he follows a Western approach to categorisation.[11] The first category of sources is called the documentary corpus. It includes fragments with administrative and economic content. The purpose and nature of lists in the documentary corpus are varied. Often, for example, only personal names are

---

[9] Albeit by a secondary scribe and not the scribe of the main text of the prayer book.

[10] See Goitein, *Mediterranean Society*, 1:9–14.

[11] See Frenkel, 'Genizah Documents', 139.

listed. This may be a memorial list to show an ancestral line,[12] or a listing of persons who have received benefits or still owe money,[13] for example. In other lists, possessions or books are listed. For example, Nehemiah Allony collected book lists, offering a glimpse not only into book production and the book trade but also teaching rooms, for some of these lists were intended to be followed as a curriculum and used as templates for the books to be studied.[14]

Another list class was examined by Mark R. Cohen, comprising charity lists, donor lists, and alms lists. He writes:

> Inert though they appear, the lists divulge much about the dynamics of the Jewish public welfare system.... Among other things, the beneficiary and donor lists permit us to make a rough socioeconomic taxonomy of the poor and nonpoor, relying on the fact that people are often recorded with their occupation (X the grave digger, Y the physician, for instance).[15]

Yet other lists contain ingredients for medical recipes.[16] Also, numerous trousseau lists, in which the dowry of brides was listed with the respective values of the items, are found among the documents of the Cairo Genizah.[17] Several researchers have tried to

---

[12] E.g., Cambridge, Cambridge University Library, MS T-S 8J11.2.

[13] E.g., CUL T-S NS J76; CUL T-S Misc. 8.2.

[14] Allony, *Jewish Library*. See also Frenkel, 'Book Lists', and literature cited there.

[15] Cohen, *Voice of the Poor*, 107–8. See also Cohen, *Poverty and Charity*.

[16] See Lev, 'Drugs'.

[17] Goitein, 'Three Trousseaux'.

estimate the percentage of the lists in the texts of the Cairo Genizah; most recently, Jessica Goldberg estimated that "at least 10 percent of paper fragments from the documentary corpus contain lists."[18]

The second source category is known as the literary corpus. Books or book fragments are assigned to this category. Mostly, literary and religious content is found here. This corpus in theory includes lists that do not fall under the documentary corpus; however, a clear classification is not always possible, so certain fragments can be classified as belonging to both corpora. Clearly belonging to the literary genre are the word lists of biblical books,[19] as well as, for example, verse lists or lists of piyyutim and sequences of halakhic passages. Among them are also lists of mishnaic and talmudic texts in which the tractates in the orders and the chapters deviate from the present arrangement.[20]

There are also lists that include Hebrew–Arabic glossaries of biblical texts. Meira Polliack has highlighted the value of these lists for linguistics, Bible translations, and commentaries,[21] while Judith Olszowy-Schlanger has examined a glossary of difficult words from the Babylonian Talmud.[22]

---

[18] Goldberg, 'Lists'.

[19] See Russell, 'Armenian Word List'; and also Shivtiel, 'Judaeo-Romance'.

[20] See, e.g., CUL T-S K3.5; CUL T-S K3.7; CUL T-S K3.8; CUL T-S NS 329.448.

[21] Polliack, 'Bible Translations'.

[22] Olszowy-Schlanger, 'Glossary'. For glossaries in medieval Arabic, see Vollandt, 'Glosses of Hebrew'.

The purpose of this paper is to examine lists that can be categorised as liturgical. For this purpose, the lists containing the Songs of Ascents (Pss 120–34) were identified among the fragments of the Cairo Genizah. In some cases, these lists include other contents as well, and, based on the psalms and any additional material, the purpose of these lists will be examined. The lists are viewed here as literary products of their environment.[23] Since they are understood as literary products, they can also be examined and interpreted through a literary analysis. The criteria would include, for instance, the arrangement of the list entries as well as a comparison of the list content. First, however, we turn to a classification of the object of study, that is, the Songs of Ascents and the purpose they served during the tenth through thirteenth centuries in Fustat.

2.0. Liturgical Framework in Fustat between the Tenth and Thirteenth Centuries

The Cairo Genizah contains writings from all the regional congregations of the period between the tenth and thirteenth centuries. This period witnessed three major congregations in Fustat, all of which have their liturgical costumes: the congregation of the land of Israel, which had its centre in the synagogue where the Cairo Genizah was discovered; the Babylonian congregation; and the Karaite congregation. This paper focuses on the Babylonian congregation and on the congregation of the land of Israel,

---

[23] This approach was also followed by Miriam Frenkel in the analysis of three different types of fragment: a letter, a court record, and a report of events. See Frenkel, 'Genizah Documents', 139.

which share some liturgical traditions but also differ in many ways. Divergences can be identified, for example, in the morning liturgy, in terms of length, texts included and to be recited, and the arrangement of these texts. For the study of Jewish liturgy, the Cairo Genizah is very important. Only because of the Cairo Genizah are we aware of details of the rite(s) of the land of Israel, which would otherwise have been lost.

The rite of the land of Israel and the Babylonian rite coexisted until the twelfth or thirteenth century. Gradually, however, the former rite was replaced by the latter.[24] There are many reasons for this, the most notable of which are the diminishing influence of the Palestinian academies and the gradual predominance of the Babylonian Talmud and its rites.

3.0. The Songs of Ascents in the Medieval Palestinian Liturgy in the Rite of Eretz Israel

The Songs of Ascents were recited during the morning prayers of the congregation of the land of Israel, in the section known as *tefillat ha-shir*.[25] This section is not found in the morning prayers in the Babylonian rite. In that rite, Pss 145–50 are recited, in the section called *pesuqe de-zimra* ('chapters of praise').[26] Thus, while the Babylonian rite inserts only the last six chapters of the book of Psalms into the morning prayer, the fragments from the Cairo

---

[24] See Raziel-Kretzmer, 'How Late', 309–36.

[25] Fleischer, *Eretz-Israel Prayer*, 215–57, dedicated a separate chapter to the rite of the land of Israel and in particular to the *tefillat ha-shir*.

[26] For a discussion of the origin of the *pesuqe de-zimra* in the Babylonian rite, see Langer, 'Early Emergence'.

Genizah pertaining to the rite of the land of Israel show other sections of the Psalms, in particular the liturgical use of the Songs of Ascents, Pss 120–34, in the *tefillat ha-shir*.

It should be noted that the *tefillat ha-shir* was not a stable prayer entity and tended to change its position in the morning prayers.[27] In addition, its scope also varied. It could be either one single stretch of 31 connected psalms, Pss 120–50; or else divided into Pss 120–36 and Pss 144–50. A third version places the Songs of Ascents at the beginning of the morning prayer, as an introduction, so to speak.[28]

These differences between the psalms included in the *tefillat ha-shir* and its position in the morning prayer result mainly from the days on which it is recited. There are differences between the recitation on weekdays and on Shabbats and holidays. Vered Raziel-Kretzmer describes the differences as follows:

> On Shabbats and holidays, the *shir ha-maʿalot* are further expanded to include Pss 135–36 and are recited before the *pesuqe de-zimra* of the rite of the land of Israel. The land of Israel tradition of the *pesuqe de-zimra* differs in that it includes the seven last psalms (Pss 144–50), rather than six that are customary, and consists of the psalms and the concluding blessing alone. The opening berakhah, the יהי כבוד (*yehi khevod*, 'May the glory'),[29] the ויברך דוד (*wa-yevarekh*

[27] Raziel-Kretzmer and Ben-Dov, 'Qumran Psalter', 306–8.

[28] See Raziel-Kretzmer and Ben-Dov, 'Qumran Psalter', 309.

[29] Catena of 18 verses, recited in the *pesuqe de-zimra* section of the morning service in the Babylonian rite.

> *David*, 'And David blessed'),[30] and the אתה הוא יי לבדיך (*ata hu adonai levadekha*, Neh. 9.6) are missing, compared with the Babylonian rite. The concluding berakhah is similar to יהללוך (*yehallelukha*, 'All Thy works praise Thee')... and not to ישתבח (*yishtabach*, 'praised be Your name forever').[31]

On weekdays, the *tefillat ha-shir* is even detached from the *pesuqe de-zimra* and placed before the *birkhot ha-shachar*, at the very beginning of the morning prayer.[32]

4.0. The Analysis of These Liturgical Lists

Lists are primarily characterised by their writers. On the one hand, lists can represent pure transcripts, if it can be assumed that the writers agreed with the pre-existing content. On the other hand, a scribe can also take the liberty to design a list according to his or her own preferences. This may be the case, for example, when a list containing the Songs of Ascents is adapted to the regional needs of the congregation. Therefore, it is helpful to identify the creator of a list; there may be further information available about the writer, or more fragments from the same writer. In some cases, the writers of the lists taken from the Cairo Genizah are indeed known—for example, if they sign or mark a list or can be identified by their handwriting. Unfortunately, this

---

[30] This prayer consists of 1 Chron. 29.10–13 and Neh. 9.6–11, and is recited in the daily morning prayer.

[31] Raziel-Kretzmer, 'How Late', 318; my translation. *Yishtabach* is the concluding blessing of the *pesuqe de-zimra* section in the morning service.

[32] Raziel-Kretzmer, 'How Late', 319.

is not the case with the lists presented in this paper. Nevertheless, in the case of unknown writers, an attempt can be made to determine the characteristics of the writer with the help of the following analytical approaches, from which in turn conclusions can sometimes be drawn about further aspects of the list.

When it comes to list fragments from the Cairo Genizah, it must be considered that, as a rule, the context of the lists is completely missing. For example, they are not (any longer) bound into a manuscript and exist only as an independent fragment. Thus, the study of the liturgical lists containing Pss 120–34 must address how manuscript fragments can be interpreted when there is no immediate context. To this end, a fragment with a list can only be studied with an auxiliary context. Within this auxiliary context, all references that can be found and deciphered are to be understood. In this paper, further fragments from the Cairo Genizah are included as auxiliary contexts—for example, fragments from prayer books, depicting, for instance, the morning liturgy of the rite of the land of Israel.

A material examination of the fragment can also contribute to the interpretation of a list. For example, considerable insight may be gained if a list is part of a comprehensive manuscript, in the context of which it can be interpreted. Likewise, a list could have served as the table of contents of a prayer book. It is more difficult if there are only individual pages without any context, although even here the material aspects of the list can still be investigated. For example, it may have served as a personal note, or perhaps even as a mnemonic device for a liturgical context.

After considering the material aspects, the next step is to analyse the purpose of the list. What is the purpose of entries in the list? Is this list an official document or is it intended for a private purpose? Does it serve as a summary or as a memory aid? In the context of worship, lists were used for personal orientation for the sequence of prayers. They were also used for listing and collecting passages, which could then be edited and embedded in a new text. Aside from this, lists helped in systematising the existing knowledge in the existing texts. These purposes could be greatly expanded and used to reflect on the individual uses of lists.

Similarly, the design of a list can provide valuable insights. Here, for example, it is possible to look at the written form, especially the use of abbreviations or ornaments. Graphic elements can also be analysed to help with understanding a list. Likewise, the list structure can prove to be relevant. For example, lists may have an alphabetical arrangement (e.g., the alphabetical arrangement of piyyutim in CUL T-S K3.12 or of Bible verses in CUL T-S D1.35) or a thematic arrangement (e.g., CUL T-S D1.76, containing biblical and rabbinic passages on Shabbat). In addition, entries may be presented consecutively, or one below the next.

Particularly helpful is the analysis of the content of lists, remembering that the entries included in a list were determined by criteria set before the list was written. Among other things, it is important to note the entries that were made, and the relationship of the entries with each other.

This paper examines those lists in the Cairo Genizah that include a particular group of psalms, the Songs of Ascents. In addition to the psalms, these lists also contain short entries of other biblical passages or passages from the liturgy. This raises the question of the context of these lists and why they were created.

In the course of the analysis, it will be shown that these lists are to be seen in a liturgical context, and so allow at least a limited view into liturgical procedures. Thus, our understanding of the practices of the congregation members during the morning liturgy of the congregation of the land of Israel in Fustat in the tenth through thirteenth centuries can be expanded upon. More specifically, it is apparent that, even then, lists in the form of small slips of paper were used as mnemonic devices for the service. In order to arrive at this conclusion, existing research findings are first presented in the following section. Then selected lists will be examined and studied, fusing the analytical approaches described in this section.

5.0. Existing Research on Lists Containing the Songs of Ascents

The study of the rite of the land of Israel as reflected in the Cairo Genizah has a long tradition. For the Songs of Ascents, the *tefillat ha-shir*, and the lists to be discussed in this paper, studies by Jacob Mann, Ezra Fleischer, and Kim Phillips are particularly relevant.[33]

---

[33] Further findings can be expected from the as yet unpublished dissertation by Vered Raziel-Kretzmer, 'Palestinian Morning Service'.

In 1925, Jacob Mann was one of the first to study the peculiarities of the morning liturgy of the rite of the land of Israel.[34] He analysed several fragments and pointed out that the rite of the land of Israel differed considerably from the Babylonian rite. In particular, the inclusion of the Songs of Ascents in the morning liturgy in the rite of the land of Israel is a distinctive feature.

Ezra Fleischer was the first to examine the Songs of Ascents in the liturgy of the congregations of the Cairo Genizah in his work 'Eretz-Israel Prayer and Prayer Rituals as Portrayed in the Geniza Documents'. He devoted an entire chapter to the Songs of Ascents in the liturgy. He analysed prayer book fragments that contain a much more elaborated text than the lists considered in this paper, and found a remarkable result when analysing certain fragments of the Cairo Genizah: depending whether the recitation was taking place on a weekday, on Shabbat, or on a holiday, the liturgy and the position taken by the Songs of Ascents differed. Therefore, on the basis of his analysis, it is possible in some cases to assign lists of the Songs of Ascents to certain days (weekdays or Shabbats). Moreover, by comparing a list with his analyses of the formulated prayer book fragments, it is also possible to determine where the Songs of Ascents were to be recited, that is, their position in the liturgy.

In a short article titled 'A Shorthand Psalter: T-S A43.8', produced as one of a series of Cambridge University Library fragments of the month, Kim Phillips examined the fragment CUL T-S

---

[34] Mann, 'Genizah Fragments'.

A43.8, basing his work on that of Mann and Fleischer. This small fragment is only 10 × 12 cm. Phillips assumes that

> it was a personal production for individual use in personal and liturgical contexts. We can imagine a worshipper using this very codex in the Morning Service a thousand years ago, occasionally glancing at the abbreviated text as a sufficient aid to assist him in the recitation of Psalms he had been reciting from his youth.[35]

6.0. Liturgical Lists in the Cairo Genizah Containing the Songs of Ascents

A total of eight fragments that contain lists of the Songs of Ascents and are to be seen in a liturgical context were found for this paper. All are from the Cambridge University Library:[36]

CUL T-S A40.34 (joins with CUL T-S AS 41.28)
CUL T-S AS 41.28
CUL T-S Ar.37.77
CUL T-S Misc. 10.184
CUL T-S NS 218.41
Mosseri VII 192.2 (joins with Mosseri VII 192.3)
Mosseri VII 192.3
CUL T-S NS 203.2

Ezra Fleischer and Kim Phillips have already shown, on the basis of some of these fragments, that these lists are to be seen in a liturgical context. Nevertheless, it is necessary to adopt a new

---

[35] Phillips, 'T-S A43.8'.

[36] It is of course possible that more fragments will be identified containing lists of the Songs of Ascents in the future.

perspective on these lists, since they have been considered neither as lists nor in the context of that particular technique of textual production with its own implications. In addition to building on this previous research, additional fragments from the Cairo Genizah are examined.

An essential feature of the lists in these fragments is their design, especially their graphic presentation. Signs are placed in these liturgical lists that are helpful for the reader. In addition, the scribes presuppose, to varying degrees, textual knowledge of the psalms, since they sometimes abbreviate the psalms or list only the first words of the psalms.

6.1. CUL T-S A40.34 and CUL T-S AS 41.28

The first fragment is CUL T-S 40.34 (fig. 1). It measures 22.5 × 8.4 cm and is written on paper. The lower end of the paper strip is detached. The text of the Songs of Ascents is shown on the front side:[37]

א׳ ש׳ ה׳ אל יי בצרת לי	1. A s[ong] of a[scents]. To the Lord in my distress
ב׳ ש׳ ה׳ למעלות אשא עיני	2. A s[ong] for a[scents]. I turn my eyes
ג׳ ש׳ ה׳ לדוד שמחתי באומרים לי בית יי נלך	3. A s[ong] of a[scents]. I rejoiced when they said to me, “We are going to the House of the Lord.”

[37] Only the first lines of the fragment are shown here to illustrate the layout of the list.

ד׳ ש׳ ה׳ אליך נשאתי את עיני הישבי בשמים	4. A s[ong] of a[scents]. To You, enthroned in heaven, I turn my eyes.
ה׳ ש׳ ה׳ לדוד לולי יי שהיה לנו יאמר נא	5. A s[ong] of a[scents]. Of David. Were it not for the Lord, who was on our side, let declare

Figure 1: Upper part of CUL T-S A40.34, showing Pss 120–24 of a numbered list of the Songs of Ascents (reproduced with the kind permission of the Syndics of Cambridge University Library)

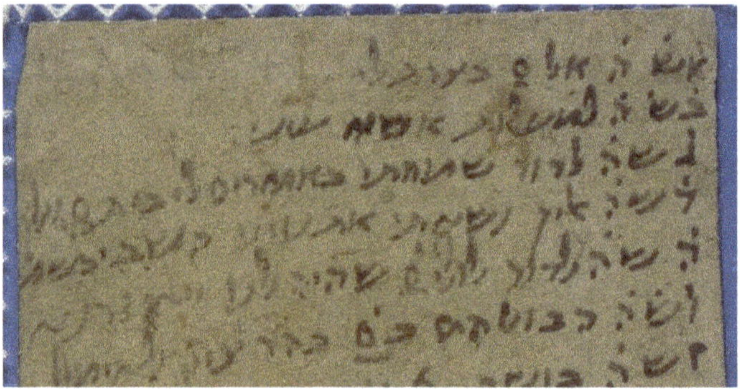

This manuscript presents a numbered list. The Songs of Ascents (Pss 120–34) are assigned the numbers 1–15, written using Hebrew letters and identified by overdots. The words שיר המעלות (*shir ha-maʿalot*) are abbreviated using the letters *shin* and *heh*. Then, throughout the set, the remaining text of the first verse of the respective psalm follows. Interestingly, Ps. 135 is omitted, and the list continues with Ps. 136. Commenting on this, Ezra Fleischer writes: “One does not know why Ps. 135 (שעומדים) was not included. Surely, he had no difficulty recalling this passage.

The liturgical, mnemonic purpose of the list cannot be doubted."[38] Thus, the omission of this psalm from the list can only be an oversight and does not indicate an actual omission in the rite.

In the case of Ps. 136, not only the opening verse is quoted, but a total of 22 verses are quoted in full (up to v. 22). However, the refrain of the psalm is omitted. The fragment ends at this point.

In the course of searching for other lists in the Cairo Genizah that contain the Songs of Ascents, the lower part of this paper strip was found (CUL T-S AS 41.28). It seamlessly complements the upper part, and contains Ps. 136.23, but Ps. 136.24–26 are missing. Afterwards, the initial verses of Pss 137–40 follow. The author flipped the paper top-to-bottom and continued to write on the back of this fragment: the beginning verse of Ps. 140 is written again, followed by Pss 141–42. Then the fragment passes seamlessly into the verso of the fragment CUL T-S A40.34. There are still the beginnings of Ps. 142.1–3 and Pss 143–44. The rest of the verso of this fragment is blank.

The position of the text of this fragment in the liturgy is unclear. The continuous presentation of Pss 120–44 indicates that it could have been recited on a weekday or on Shabbat.[39] The absence of Pss 145–50 is notable, and so is the absence of these very verses in the next fragment.

---

[38] Fleischer, *Eretz-Israel Prayer*, 240; my translation.

[39] See above and Raziel-Kretzmer, 'How Late', 319.

6.2. CUL T-S Ar.37.77

The next fragment is made of paper and measures 15 × 7 cm; it is also in a rather small format. The writing is almost completely faded in some places.

This list is written in the manner of continuous text and contains some graphic separations. Abbreviations and the end of a psalm are marked with overdots and colons, respectively.

שיר ה׳ אלי״י בצרתה: ש׳ למ׳[40] אשא עיני:	A song of a[scents]. To the Lord in distress (Ps. 120.1): A s[ong] for a[scents]. I turn my eyes (Ps. 121.1):
ש׳ ה׳ לדוד שמחתי: ש׳ ה׳ אליך נשאתי[41] את עינ׳	A s[ong] of a[scents]. Of David. I rejoiced (Ps. 122.1): A s[ong] of a[scents]. To You, I turn my eyes (Ps. 123.1):
ש׳ ה׳ לד׳ ש[42] לולי י״י:	A s[ong] of a[scents]. Of David. Were it not for the Lord (Ps. 124.1):
ש׳ ה׳ הבוטחים: ש׳ ה׳ בשוב י״י	A s[ong] of a[scents]. Those who trust (Ps. 125.1): A s[ong] of a[scents]. When the Lord restores (Ps. 126.1):

[40] ש׳ למ׳ added above the line.

[41] נשאתי added below the line.

[42] Here a probably accidental spelling of the letter ש, the first letter of שמחתי, the first word of Ps. 122, which also begins with שיר המעלות לדוד.

	[43]… …
מז׳ לד׳ יי קראתיך: מז׳ לד׳	A p[salm] of D[avid]. I call You, Lord (Ps. 141.1): A p[salm[44]] of D[avid].
בהיותו במע׳: מז׳ לד׳ יי	While he was in the cave. (Ps. 142.1): A p[salm] of D[avid]. O Lord,
שמע תפילתי: לדויד ברוך	hear my prayer (Ps. 143.1): Of David. Blessed is
יי צורי:	the Lord, my rock (Ps. 144.1):

In this notation of the verses, no attention is paid to the meaning of the biblical verse. Moreover, only the first words that seem necessary to identify the psalm are quoted, a form of shorthand.

In this list, Ps. 136 is omitted. It can therefore be assumed that Pss 135 and 136 were possibly regarded as a unit and, thus, only the beginning of Ps. 135 was written.[45] Another possibility is that Ps. 136 was not quoted; however, this needs further clarification. The fragment ends with the first words of Ps. 144.

6.3. CUL T-S Misc. 10.184

The third fragment is also very small, measuring only about 16.4 × 25.5 cm. The characteristic of this fragment is its graphic design. It lists the opening verse and the closing verse of each

---

[43] Only the first and last lines of the fragment are shown here to illustrate the layout of the list.

[44] The text of the Hebrew Bible says *maskil* and not *mizmor*.

[45] See also the discussion in b. Pesahim 118a.

psalm and then graphically separates it from the next list entry by a horizontal line (see fig. 2).

Figure 2: Psalms separated by a horizontal line in CUL T-S Misc. 10.184; top of the list including Ps. 5.2 and Ps. 59.17, then the first and last verses of Pss 120–122 (reproduced with the kind permission of the Syndics of Cambridge University Library)

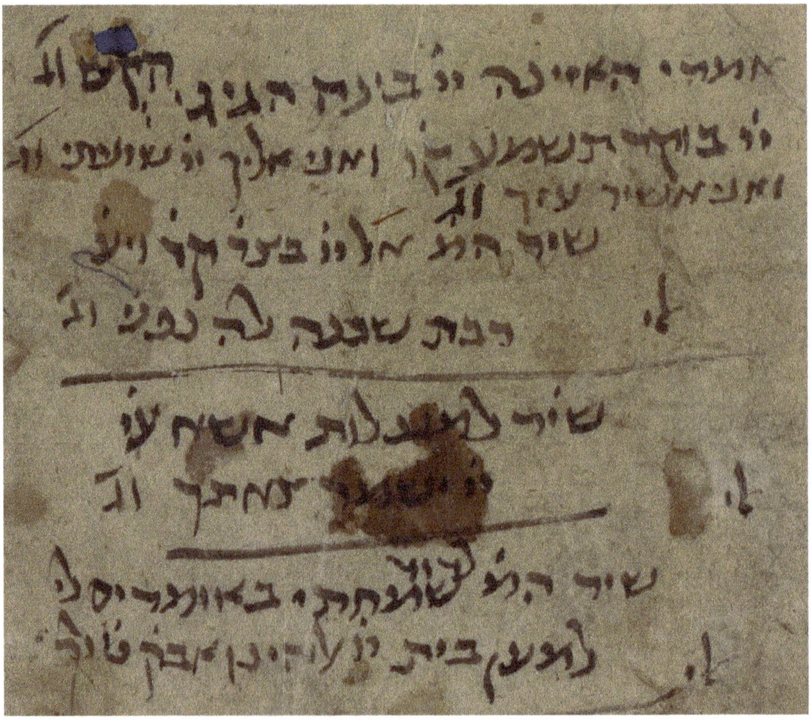

The fragment begins with the verses “Give ear to my speech, O Lord; consider my utterance. Hear the sound of my cry, my King and God, for I pray to You. Hear my voice, O Lord, at daybreak” (Ps. 5.2–4) and “But I will sing of Your strength, extol each morning Your faithfulness; for You have been my haven, a refuge in time of trouble” (Ps. 59.17). These verses are followed by the listing of the Songs of Ascents. The fragment contains Pss 120–45 in their entirety.

Having Ps. 5.2–4 and Ps. 59.17 as opening verses is also found in the fragment London, British Library, Or. 5557E, fols 12–13.[46] There, as in the fragment here, these verses precede the Songs of Ascents. The British Library fragment also gives a clue as to when the reading of the *shir ha-maʿalot* should take place. The fragment reads:

> And afterwards (after the *birkhot ha-shachar* ['the blessings of the morning']) one says the song here on Shabbat morning and on holidays, and on the fast day Kippur and on the feast of the Commandments and on the feast of Shavu'ot and on the feast of Sukkot and on New Year's Day one says the song before saying *barukh she-amar.*[47]

From comparison of the Genizah fragment and the fragment from the British Library, it can be concluded that CUL T-S Misc. 10.184 has its context in the morning prayer on Shabbats and feast days.

6.4. CUL T-S NS 218.41

The fourth fragment is written on a paper measuring only 13 × 16 cm. It is a bifolium, two pages of which are blank. The list is written without abbreviation signs above the letters. The entries are separated by blank spaces (fig. 3).

---

46 For this fragment, see Fleischer, *Eretz-Israel Prayer*, 236–37.

47 My translation.

Figure 3: Psalms separated by blank spaces in CUL T-S NS 218.41a; top of the list including Ps. 5.2 and Ps. 59.17 followed by Pss 120–23 (reproduced with the kind permission of the Syndics of Cambridge University Library)

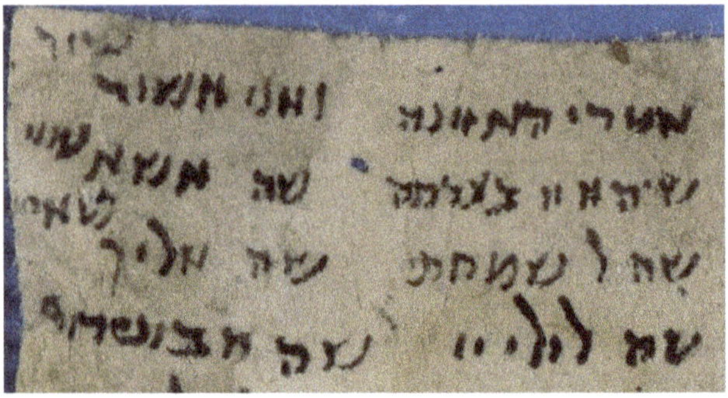

(verso)

אמרי האזינה ואני אשיר עוזיך	Give ear to my words [Adonai] (Ps. 5.2), and I will sing of Your strength (Ps. 59.17)
ש ה א יי בצרתה ש ה אשא עיני	A s[ong] of a[scents]. In distress (Ps. 120.1) A s[ong] of a[scents]. I turn my eyes (Ps. 121.1)
ש ה ל שמחתי ש ה אליך נשאתי	A s[ong] of a[scents]. I rejoiced (Ps. 122.1) A s[ong] of a[scents]. To You, I turn (Ps. 123.1)
	…[48]

[48] Only the first lines of the fragment are shown here to illustrate the layout of the list.

Like fragment CUL T-S Misc. 10.184, this fragment begins with the first words of Ps. 5.2, "Give ear to my words [Adonai]," followed by the first words of the verse Ps. 59.17, "But I will sing of Your strength." On the back, after the citation of Ps. 144, follow the *wa-yevarekh David*, *barukh she-amar*, and *yehi khevod*. The last entry in the list is the *mizmor shir* (fig. 4).

Figure 4: End of the list of the Songs of Ascents in CUL T-S NS 218.41b, where other sections of the morning prayer are mentioned (reproduced with the kind permission of the Syndics of Cambridge University Library)

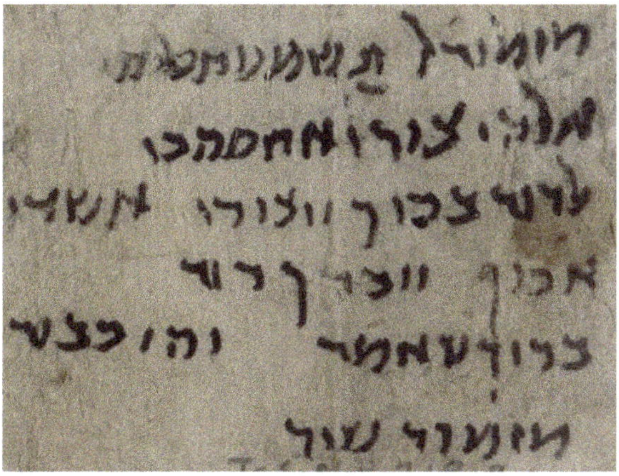

(recto)

…	…
מזמור ל יי שמע תפלתי	A psalm of [David]. O Lord hear my prayer: (Ps. 143.1)
אלהי צורי אחסה בו	
לדוד ברוך צורי אשרי	Of David. Blessed is my rock. (Ps. 144.1) Happy (Ps. 144.15)
אמן ויברך דוד	Amen. *Wa-yevarekh David.*

יהי כבוד ברוך שאמר *Barukh she-amar.*
Yehi khevod.
מזמור שיר *Mizmor shir* (Pss 145–50)

From this fragment, information can be drawn about the position of the Songs of Ascents in the morning prayer. They precede the *wa-yevarekh David* ("And David blessed," 1 Chron. 29.10–13), followed by *barukh she-amar* ("Blessed be he who spake"), and *yehi khevod*[49] ("May the glory of the Lord endure forever; let the Lord rejoice in His work," Ps. 104.31); that is, the Songs of Ascent occur before the opening elements of the morning prayer. Finally, following these opening elements is another section of Psalms, the *mizmor shir* (מזמור שיר) or Pss 145–50, known from the Babylonian version of the morning prayer.[50] Thus, the psalms enclose the first official section of the morning liturgy.

Like the fragment CUL T-S Misc. 10.184, this fragment places the reading of the Songs of Ascents before the *barukh she-amar*. Thus the list also seems to reflect the recitation on Shabbats and holidays.

6.5. Mosseri VII 192.2 and 192.3

The two fragments Mosseri VII 192.2 and 192.3 are the fragments from which the least information can be extracted. Mosseri VII 192.3 shows the beginning of a list of the Songs of Ascents from Pss 120–25. The word 'song' (שיר *shir*) is repeatedly seen on the

---

[49] A passage comprising 18 verses mostly from the book of Psalms, today recited daily in the *pesuqe de-zimra* section of the morning prayer.

[50] Raziel-Kretzmer and Ben-Dov, 'Qumran Psalter', 307.

right, which is then connected by a line to the initial words of each psalm (fig. 5). These initial words are offset from the repetition of the word 'song', so the stroke is necessary to visually draw an auxiliary line of association. After Ps. 125, no further psalm beginning seems to have been added, since there is also no longer a stroke for assignment. This is also shown by the fragment Mosseri VII 192.2, which contains only a repeated sequence of the word 'song'.

Figure 5: Lines connecting the word *shir* 'song' with the opening verse of each psalm in Mosseri VII 192.3 (reproduced with the kind permission of the Syndics of Cambridge University Library)

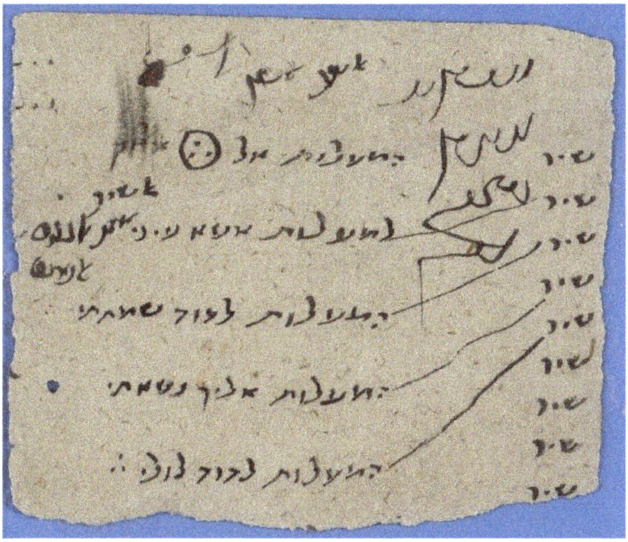

The fragments are incomplete and cut or detached. It can be assumed that originally the list was written on paper, and a text in Judaeo-Arabic was written on the reverse side afterwards when the paper was reused. This later text is a note on both fragment parts to inform the judge Moses that the Parnass Abū l-Nās is responsible for the provision of bread. Such a secondary use of paper and splitting of fragments is not uncommon in the Cairo Genizah, and it reflects the frequent reuse of previously written material at the time.

6.6. CUL T-S NS 203.2

A particularly pronounced form of shortening of the text is evident in the fragment CUL T-S NS 203.2 (fig. 6). This fragment is also very small, measuring only 8 × 8 cm. It has already been identified and edited by Ezra Fleischer.[51] The listing extends over five lines.

Figure 6: Mnemonic from Pss 120–35 on CUL T-S NS 203.2 (reproduced with the kind permission of the Syndics of Cambridge University Library)

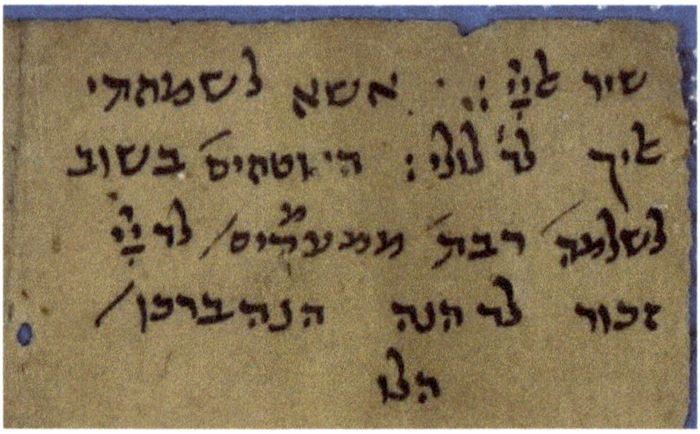

שיר אל יְיָ: אשא ל׳ שמחתי
אליך לד׳ לולי: הבוטחים בשוב
לשלמה רבת ממעמ[52]קים לד׳ יְיָ
זכור לד׳ הנה הנה ברכו
הלו

---

[51] Fleischer, *Eretz-Israel Prayer*, 240–41.

[52] מ added above the line.

Here, there is neither an explanation of what the list is supposed to be nor any classifying words, as in the other lists presented so far.

Rather, as Fleischer noted, the order of the Songs of Ascents is listed here in a mnemonic fashion.[53] Mostly, only a single word from the opening verse of the Songs of Ascents appears. Strung together, these words make no sense, unless one understands them as a mnemonic. Fleischer also noted the absence of Ps. 128 from this listing. If one reconstructs this mnemonic enumeration and inserts the further text of the psalms, the following picture arises:

> שיר [המעלות] אל יי בצרתה לי: [שיר למעלות] אשא [עיני]: [שיר המעלות] ל[דוד] שמחתי: [שיר המעלות] אליך [נשאתי את עיני]: [שיר המעלות] לד[וד] לולי [יי שהיה לנו]: [שיר המעלות] הבוטחים [ביי]: [שיר המעלות] בשוב [יי את שיבת ציון]: [שיר המעלות] לשלמה [אם יי לא יבנה בית]: [שיר המעלות] רבת [צררונו]: [שיר המעלות] ממעמקים [קראתיך יי]: [שיר המעלות] לד[וד] יי [לא גבה לבי]: [שיר המעלות] זכור [יי לדוד]: [שיר המעלות] לד[וד] הנה [מה טוב ומה נעים]: [שיר המעלות] הנה ברכו [את יי]: הלו.[54]
>
> A song [of ascents.] In my distress: [A song for ascents.] I turn [my eyes]: [A song of ascents.] Of [David.] I rejoiced: [A song of ascents.] To You [I turn my eyes]: [A song of ascents.] Of D[avid.] Were it not [for the Lord, who was on our side]: [A song of ascents.] Those who trust [in the Lord]: [A song of ascents. When the Lord] restores [the fortunes of Zion]: [A song of ascents.] Of Salomon. [Unless the Lord builds the house]: [A song of ascents.] They have often [assailed me]: [A song of ascents.] Out of the depths

[53] Fleischer, *Eretz-Israel Prayer*, 241n99.

[54] Fleischer, *Eretz-Israel Prayer*, 241.

> [I call You]: [A song of ascents.] Of D[avid.] O Lord [my heart is not proud]: [A song of ascents. O Lord,] remember [in David's favour]: [A song of ascents.] Of D[avid.] Look [how good and how pleasant]: [A song of ascents.] Now bless [the Lord]: Hallelujah.

As can be seen from this reconstruction, only the first and sometimes the second word after the incipit שיר המעלות (*shir ha-maʿalot*) is ever listed. Thus, only a little content is transported. Therefore, the fragment can only have served as a mnemonic anchor.

7.0. Conclusion

Several findings were deduced in this paper. First, it was determined that none of the writers of the lists could be identified. The handwriting of each list differs, so it can be concluded that the lists were made by various persons. One can at least say that the writers must have belonged to the circle of the Palestinian congregation, since they follow the rite of the land of Israel.

The context of the lists is also missing; the fragments are each present individually, although one of the lists could be reassembled from two fragments. All of the lists may have been independent of other writings before they were deposited in the Cairo Genizah; the lists were not, for example, part of a larger manuscript or booklet. In some cases they are found on recycled paper as a secondary use, or on paper that was subsequently used for a secondary use. This suggests that these lists were personal texts intended for personal use.

The examination of the material showed, in particular, that all the lists were in a very small format. Based on this, it can be assumed that they served as a kind of small memo to capture the order of the psalms. The purpose of the lists was, therefore, probably to serve as a kind of memory card for prayer.

Even though all the lists on the Songs of Ascents in the morning liturgy are united by their theme, they diverge in design and content. These differences are probably due to the individual preferences of the various scribes of the lists. Although their working procedures and approaches to the content differed, they all produced an abbreviated schema of the Songs of Ascents. These shortened representations helped the individuals in their particular situations to provide the best possible assistance in memorising the texts.

Next, the differences in the way the verses are cited and the extent of the citation should be noted. The citations sometimes follow the verse exactly; sometimes a shortening of the words is used; sometimes it is even indicated up to which place the psalm is quoted. Mostly, the last verse of the respective psalm is quoted for this purpose.

The form of list varies from scribe to scribe and reflects personal design preferences. One list has numbering before the psalm beginnings, while the others appear without numbering. Another list is characterised by a subdivision of the entries by long dashes (CUL T-S Misc. 10.184). Supporting the main text, some lists use various graphical aids in the creation of the lists. They use separators such as colons and dashes, whereas other lists use spacing between the entries (CUL T-S NS 218.41).

In terms of content, the arrangement of the elements of the Songs of Ascents lists is, on the one hand, predetermined by the order that these psalms already have in the Hebrew Bible. On the other hand, the list also reflects the order of liturgical practice. Each list may represent the knowledge of the person writing it. Nevertheless, there is the limitation that the scribe may reflect only the information that is necessary and important to him, for example, to support his memory. Other information that is self-evident to the person writing might be omitted.

REGULARITY AND VARIATION IN ISLAMIC CHAINS OF TRANSMISSION[1]

Maroussia Bednarkiewicz

One type of list in classical Arabic literature never ceases to attract considerable attention among scholars across a wide range of disciplines, from theology to legal studies, and from history to computer sciences. The list in question is called in Arabic an *isnād* (pl. *asānid*) and it records the names of each narrator, from one generation to the next, who narrated the narrative that follows the *isnād*. The narrative part—in Arabic, *matn* (pl. *mutūn*)—and the list—that is, the *isnād*—are the two constitutive elements of a *ḥadīth* (pl. *aḥādīth*), which can be translated in English by 'account', 'report', or 'narrative'. The *ḥadīth* literature usually designates the collection of famous accounts that purportedly preserve the words and deeds of Islam's prophet, Muḥammad, and his companions.

[1] I would like to thank the organisers and participants of the workshop 'Synopses and Lists' for inspiring discussions, as well as Ali Zaherinezhad and Álvaro Tejero Cantero for their comments on this paper. The research presented here is part of my current project funded by the Deutsche Forschungsgemeinschaft under Germany's Excellence Strategy (EXC number 2064/1, Project number 390727645).

 https://doi.org/10.11647/OBP.0375.09

The *isnād* or list of transmitters, also known as a chain of transmitters, traces the genealogy of the account to which it is attached and indicates its origins. It is mostly used as a tool to evaluate the authenticity of the narrative *matn*, and, as often happens with lists, *asānid* "are taken for granted and their content is seen as more interesting than the way in which they were put together."[2] In the computational analysis of text, the contrary occurs: regular structures and forms, such as lists, are often considered first for their forms, which allow a large quantity of textual data to be divided into smaller units following formal rules. These small units can then be processed by algorithms one at a time, like pixels in an image or vectors in a matrix.

Many computer scientists thought that, given a finite list of all the transmission terms and a list of the main characteristics of Arabic proper names, simple algorithms should be able to automatically recognise the *isnād* as a regular sequence of names and transmission terms. Their successive attempts suggest that the problem was more complex than initially thought. At first glance, the *isnād* does seem like a fairly regular list of narrators' names preceded by transmission terms, as shown in the following example, where the *isnād* runs until the asterisk and the transmission terms have been put in square brackets to mark the repetitive structure of the list: [transmission term(s)], proper name, [transmission term(s)], proper name, and so on.

---

[2] Bray, 'Lists and Memory', 214.

[حدثنا] يحيى بن يحيى [قال أخبرنا] عبيد الله بن إياد [عن] إياد [عن] البراء [قال قال] رسول الله صلى الله عليه وسلم [*] إذا سجدت فضع كفيك وارفع مرفقيك.

> Yaḥyá ibn Yaḥyá narrated to us, he said ʿUbayd Allāh ibn Iyād reported to us according to Iyād according to al-Barāʾ, he said the messenger of God may God bless him and grant him peace said [*] When you prostrate (in your prayer), place your palms on the ground and raise your elbows.[3]

Attentive readers will notice irregular patterns, which raise various questions: Why are the patronyms mentioned in some names and not in others? Why do the transmission terms vary? Why do we twice have two transmission verbs, and at the beginning only one, and twice a preposition in the middle? What do these variations mean? Why did the narrators or the scribes use different terms of transmission?

The *isnād* has long been "taken for granted" as a tool for the authentication of *aḥādīth*, and it is perceived functionally as a regular collection of names. As a list, on the other hand, the *isnād* pertains to a much older and more versatile textual tradition. This versatility starts with the dual effect of all literary lists, underlined by Lennart Lehmhaus in his contribution to this volume: lists bring order in their content, but they interrupt the narrative form of the text in which they appear. They create a structure and break the overall structure. The *isnād* fulfils the common list function of "ordering knowledge" (Lehmhaus) by arranging

[3] Muslim ibn al-Ḥajjāj, *Ṣaḥīḥ*, 251. All translations into English are my own.

the names in descending chronological order, starting from a student who received the account from his master who received it from his master and so on. This high concentration of names breaks the flow of the narration and disrupts the narrative structure.

But *asānid,* like many other lists, contain more information than names and transmission terms. Similar to the rabbinic lists, described by Lehmhaus, they participate in a discursive production of knowledge sourced in part from Muslims' cultural memory, as Herbert Berg has partially shown in a study about *isnād* in Qurʾān interpretations which we will introduce below. The producers and recipients of this knowledge are manifold: they are the students of a *ḥadīth* scholar who want to pass on their master's knowledge, the students of a legal scholar who seek righteous rulings to guide their life and their community, the exegetes who want to interpret the Qurʾān according to Muḥammad's teachings, the rulers in search of advice or religious supports regarding their reforms, the group of mystics trying to get closer to God; the enumeration can go on. The rich variety of producers and recipients influences the contents of the *isnād,* but what about its form? Are *asānid*'s forms as versatile as their content? And how does this versatility impact the computational analysis of *asānid*?

To better understand this variety of forms, I have adopted a twofold methodology, which consists in using a computer program to highlight the regularities and irregularities of *asānid* and then interpreting them in the broader context of lists in textual data, rather than specifically *asānid* in *aḥādīth.* A particular focus will be laid on refining our definition of an *isnād* and gaining new insights on the forms and patterns of *asānid*. I will start with a lengthy review of the scholarship on lists, on *asānid*, and on the computational analysis of classical Arabic texts, which serve as the framework for my approach. I will then briefly introduce the texts I gathered for this study and the computer program I used, before I turn to the various forms of *isnād* observed throughout the corpus and their potential interpretations.

1.0. The Origins of the *Isnād*

At the beginning of the twentieth century, a small debate took place between two orientalists: Josef Horovitz argued that the *isnād* in its primitive form was taken from the Jewish literary tradition, from which he cites a couple of chains of transmission with three transmitters, including women.[4] Horovitz sees these examples as the source of inspiration for the Islamic *isnād* that was then further developed by Muslim scholars and also contains female transmitters. To this, Friedrich Schwally answered that the Jewish chains of transmitters never played the role they did for Muslims, whose Arab ancestors were in any case using such authoritative lists of names in their pre-Islamic literature.[5] The presence of *isnād* in ancient Arabic poetry, according to Schwally, suggests a much older and 'foreign' (*fremd*) origin of the *isnād*, by which he probably means neither Arabic nor Jewish.

---

[4] Horovitz, 'Alter und Ursprung des Isnād'.

[5] Nöldeke, *Die Sammlung des Qorāns*, 128–29.

Horovitz countered these three points, conceding that Jewish chains of transmitters, like Islamic ones, could come from an altogether older tradition, but while the source of inspiration for the Jewish chains is unknown, they were undoubtedly the source of inspiration for the primitive form of the *isnād*.[6] According to Horovitz, the *isnād* evolved from the Jewish examples and not from the pre-Islamic literature, since in that tradition it occurs only in poetry and was never transferred to Arabic prose; the latter, he seems to suggest, is closer to the *ḥadīth* literature, where most *asānid* are found.

This whole discussion relied on a few examples that appear anecdotal and therefore rather unconvincing.[7] A comprehensive study of *asānid*, even within a single collection to start with, would have been and remains a prerequisite for understanding *isnād* and speculating on its origins. Ideally, one should also consider lists of names as bearers of authority in general terms within oral societies at large, such as the examples found among Buddhists or Inuits. Until this research is undertaken, the putative foreign origin of the *isnād* will remain a hypothesis.

2.0. Dating the Muslims' Adoption of the *Isnād*

The date of origin of the *isnād*—that is, the time it was first introduced by Muslim scholars—has also triggered debates, which usually point to an account narrated by the early Muslim scholar

---

[6] Horovitz, 'Noch einmal'.

[7] See the tentative criticism of Robson, 'Ibn Isḥāq's Use of the *Isnād*'.

and famous interpreter of dreams, Ibn Sīrīn (d. 110/728).[8] The account is rarely quoted in the Arabic literature, which is astonishing when we think of the great interest that Arabs and Muslims at large dedicated to stories of origins, known in Arabic as *awāʾil*.[9] Among the 2,582 authors present in the OpenITI corpus of Arabic literature, only 50 mention this *ḥadīth*.[10]

The version of the *ḥadīth* that is most often quoted comes from the introduction (in Arabic, *muqaddima*) to the *Ṣaḥīḥ* of Muslim ibn al-Ḥajjāj (d. 261/875).[11] This collection of *aḥādīth* was compiled in the first half of the third/mid-ninth century at the beginning of a great effort by *ḥadīth* scholars to prevent non-authentic *aḥādīth* from circulating. Collections of *aḥādīth* existed before then and concerns for authenticity were not new, yet Muslim ibn al-Ḥajjāj's *Ṣaḥīḥ* and the other so-called canonical *ḥadīth* collections mark a certain shift in *ḥadīth* sciences and Muslim cultural history, for these new collections eclipsed other collections and became the reference. Muslim ibn al-Ḥajjāj's 'Muqaddima' is an important writing to understand the context in which his *Ṣaḥīḥ* emerged. It is addressed to an unnamed person to whom Muslim justifies his methodology in the selection and dismissal of *aḥādīth*, and explains why he disagrees with other scholars or methods.

---

[8] See Fahd, 'Ibn Sīrīn'.

[9] See Rosenthal, 'Awāʾil'; Bernards, 'Awāʾil'.

[10] Nigst et al., 'OpenITI'.

[11] Muslim ibn al-Ḥajjāj, *Ṣaḥīḥ*, 2–23. See the English text and commentary in Juynboll, 'Muslim's Introduction to His Ṣaḥīḥ'.

The *isnād* clearly occupies a preponderant place in the debate, which is concerned with the authenticity of *ḥadīth*. It is in this context that Muslim mentions Ibn Sīrīn's account about the introduction of the *isnād*:

> حدثنا أبو جعفر محمد بن الصباح حدثنا إسماعيل بن زكريا عن عاصم الأحول عن بن سيرين قال لم يكونوا يسألون عن الإسناد فلما وقعت الفتنة قالوا سموا لنا رجالكم فينظر إلى أهل السنة فيؤخذ حديثهم وينظر إلى أهل البدع فلا يؤخذ حديثهم
>
> Abū Jaʿfar Muḥammad ibn al-Ṣabāḥ narrated to us [that] Ismāʿīl ibn Zakariyyā narrated to us according to ʿĀṣam al-Aḥwal according to Ibn Sīrīn [who] said that they did not use to enquire about the *isnād*, and after the time of the *fitna* they said [to them]: "Name to us your men" then they examined the *ahl al-sunna* and they adopted their *ḥadīth* and they examined the *ahl al-bidʿa* but did not adopt their *ḥadīth*.[12]

Before Muslim, it seems that only two scholars mentioned Ibn Sīrīn's account: Ibn Ḥanbal (d. 241/855), who cites it in his *ʿIlāl wa-l-maʿrifa*, and ʿAbd Allāh al-Dārimī (d. ca. 255/869), who quotes a slightly different version in his *Sunan*.[13]

This *ḥadīth* has recently been the object of debates about the date of the *fitna*. The word *fitna* can mean 'tribulation', 'temptation', 'trial', or 'civil war' and it is often found with an adjective, as in the term 'the second *fitna*' to describe the upheavals around

[12] Muslim ibn al-Ḥajjāj, *Ṣaḥīḥ*, 9.

[13] Ibn Ḥanbal, *Al-ʿilal wa-maʿarifah al-rijāl*, 2:559 (3640); al-Dārimī, *Musnad*, 396 (430). Al-Dārimī replaced *ahl al-sunna* and *ahl al-bidʿa* with *ṣāḥib sunna* and 'those who are not *ṣāḥib sunna*'.

the death of the ʿUmayyad caliph Muʿāwiya in 60/680 and the revolt of ʿAbd Allāh ibn al-Zubayr (d. ca. 72–73/691–92). Without a complement, the word is ambiguous, for all its signifiers are used in Arabic sources to describe different events, troubles, and conflicts. Scholars seem to agree that the *fitna* to which Ibn Sīrīn referred describes the aftermath of the assassination of an influential political figure, but they disagree on his identity: traditionally, it is interpreted as referring to the assassination of the third caliph ʿUthmān ibn ʿAffān in 36/656; but Joseph Schacht argued for a much later date, affirming that it should be understood as the time following the assassination of Walīd ibn Yazīd in 126/744; while Gauthier Juynboll pushed it back to the time of Ibn ʿAbd Allāh ibn al-Zubayr (d. ca. 72–73/691–92).[14] More recently, Pavel Pavlovitch examined Ibn Sīrīn's report and its various versions and dated the birth of the *isnād* to the revolt of al-Mukhtār b. Abī ʿUbayd al-Thaqafī in 66–67/685–87 in Kufa.[15]

Interestingly, the idea that the *fitna* in this *ḥadīth* could refer to a period rather than an event, as suggested by Hawting and before him by Gardet, has not been investigated further, nor the possibility that Ibn Sīrīn was not referring to the 'birth' of the *isnād* but rather to its use as an identity marker to distinguish between two different factions of Muslims.[16] Indeed, the verb used in the text suggests that people started enquiring (*yasʾalūn* 'they asked, enquired') about the *isnād*, not that they introduced

---

14 Schacht, *Origins of Muhammadan Jurisprudence*, 71ff.; Juynboll, 'Date of the Great *Fitna*', 158–59.

15 Pavlovitch, 'Origin of the *Isnād*'.

16 Hawting, 'Significance of the Slogan', 453; Gardet, 'Fitna'.

it. It seems that despite all the ink that has been spilled, there are still pages to be written on this matter. Perhaps less pixel-like studies with more comprehensive scope, like the present one, will be a useful ground to give to this debate a new impulse.

3.0. *Isnād* and 'Personal Connectedness'

Although Ibn Sīrīn's report might not be *stricto sensu* an *awāʾil*, its topic, the use of the *isnād* as an identity marker, seems to pertain to this vast interest in origins and to the efforts to maintain strong ties with the past. Indeed, one of the *isnād*'s primary functions is to establish the origin of a report through personal connections between all those who reported it and transmitted it to the present. This function was examined by William Graham, who has argued that Muslims' need for 'personal connectedness' to the past is characteristic of the Muslim tradition and expressed by the "*isnād* paradigm":[17] in the *isnād* are preserved personal or individual connections up to Muḥammad or his companions and it is through this 'human' channel that knowledge is transferred, authority is derived, and truth is established.[18] In this sense, the *isnād* is both a tradition, *traditum tradendum*, "which is transmitted from the past to the present" and the ritual, the *actus tradendi*,

---

[17] Graham, 'Traditionalism in Islam', 501.

[18] Graham, 'Traditionalism in Islam', 502 and 510–11. This need for personal connectedness is visible outside the *isnād* paradigm, for instance in the "discourse of place," described by Zayde Antrim, *Routes and Realms*, 72, in which a Muslim geographer or historian described lands preferring "information mediated by earlier authorities over his own observations" even if the description was no longer accurate.

that is repeated to perpetuate the tradition.[19] As a ritual, it participates in the short-term communicative memory, and as a tradition, it shapes the long-lasting cultural memory.[20]

In his analysis of the cultural memory preserved in *asānid* related to Ibn ʿAbbās's interpretation of the Qurʾān, Herbert Berg exemplifies how the *isnād* served to transfer the communicative memory of one generation to Muslim cultural memory at large. He does not consider, however, the role of Muslim cultural memory in the production of the *isnād* itself. Conflating Graham's and Berg's studies shows how *asānid* are successively and sometimes simultaneously the source, the product, and the vehicle of Muslim cultural memory. Through this triple function, the *isnād* has played an important role in the preservation of the chains of transmission after the canon.[21]

4.0. The Spiritual Connection in *Asānid*

With each generation, the distance to Muḥammad grew, and thus *asānid* became longer, mirroring the increasing time span between the living generation and the sacred past. This distance was perceived as a progressive deterioration, expressed in a widely circulated *ḥadīth* where Muḥammad announced that the

---

[19] Shils, *Tradition*, 11.

[20] See Assmann, *Das kulturelle Gedächtnis*, esp. 34, 52ff.; Assmann, *Religion and Cultural Memory*, esp. 3ff., 40ff.; Berg, 'The *Isnād*', 278. See also Berg's discussion of the *isnād* as ritual (pp. 268ff.).

[21] See the recent investigation by Garrett Davidson about how Muslim scholars preserved the *isnād* which was "central to their ethos as a scholarly culture and community"; Davidson, *Carrying on the Tradition*, 9ff.

"best people are [those of] my generation, then [those of] the one which follows it, then [those of] the one which follows it."[22]

To temper the inexorable decline of their generation's quality, *ḥadīth* scholars deemed personal connectedness insufficient and they sought "the isnād with the fewest intermediaries" to establish closer connection through "elevation (*ʿulūw*)."[23] Eerik Dickinson explains how "[e]levation turned ḥadīth into a special kind of relic" which was recited orally for "spiritual self-improvement" and no longer for the transmission of knowledge, since this was guaranteed by the canon.[24] Although the *isnād* had lost its primary role as guardian of knowledge, it was reinterpreted as "a singular blessing which God had bestowed on Muslims" to distinguish them from other communities.[25] The "reconceptualization of the function of hadith transmission" is further examined by Garrett Davidson, who shows how "imagining the chain of transmission in mystical terms infused it with further meanings"[26] and allowed *ḥadīth* scholars to save "this core element of their scholarly culture" from obsolescence.[27] The *isnād* not only changed function over time, it seems to have also played a different role outside the *ḥadīth* literature.

---

[22] al-Bukhārī, *Ṣaḥīḥ*, III (*Kitāb al-Riqāq*):1305–6 (6504–5).

[23] Dickinson, 'Ibn al-Ṣalāḥ al-Shahrazūrī', 481.

[24] Dickinson, 'Ibn al-Ṣalāḥ al-Shahrazūrī', 504.

[25] Dickinson, 'Ibn al-Ṣalāḥ al-Shahrazūrī', 489.

[26] Davidson, *Carrying on the Tradition*, 31.

[27] Davidson, *Carrying on the Tradition*, 9.

5.0. Literary Emancipation without *Isnād*

In the *adab* literature concerned with love, Monica Balda-Tillier discovered that the *isnād* appears only in treatises where the author adopts a moralising tone, and is omitted in texts with lighter, more practical and sensible aims, where the authors share their own experience rather than the opinions of past authority. Balda-Tillier quotes a treatise about love by the Cordoban scholar Ibn Ḥazm (d. 456/1054) where the author cites few *asānid* and shuns the well-known sayings of ancient Arabs, which have already been covered by others, because of his interest in new or contemporaneous forms of knowledge.[28] Thus some authors distinguished themselves and developed an identity of their own together with new forms of literary quotations. The cultural identity that Graham concluded was embedded in the *isnād* appears here negated, in that some authors turned away from the 'personal connectedness' to the past and created therewith new forms of identity. Although the present study will be restricted to the *ḥadīth* literature, Balda-Tillier's reflection is a serious encouragement for further research on a broader corpus to map the *isnād* and all its diversity across Arabic literature. To this end, computational tools, in particular the most advanced machine learning algorithms, will be great allies.

---

[28] Balda-Tillier, 'La prose amoureuse', 191.

6.0. Machine Learning and Text Analysis

In traditional programming, humans give to the algorithm input data and explicit rules, then the algorithm analyses the data according to the rules and outputs answers. An example of such a typical rule-based system is the algorithm that counts how many times a given word appears in a text or a simple search and replace. Often, however, we are unable to formalise representative rules. For example, if we want to count every time the prophet Muḥammad appears in a corpus, we need to account for all the different names and pronouns used to refer to him and distinguish them from the same names and pronouns used to refer to others with the same name. It would be difficult to distil rules for a machine to perform this task accurately because there are too many possibilities, similarities, and contexts. And if we want to analyse all the topics which are associated with the prophet Muḥammad in a *ḥadīth* corpus, it would require the crafting of very complex rules, to account for the variability, richness, and ambiguity of the textual expressions that qualify as a topic.

Such recognition and classification problems are the battlefields of machine learning algorithms, which do not receive rules, in contrast to traditional programming, but generate them. The machine learning algorithms 'learn' from the input data and output candidate rules to solve a given task, for instance finding when a pronoun refers to the prophet Muḥammad or clustering *ḥadīth* narratives according to prominent topics. Machine learning is not limited to textual inputs: given images of manuscripts together with their digital transcription, algorithms can learn how groups of pixels map to letters, for instance. After some training, they are able to automatically transcribe previously unseen manuscripts, and with more training examples, they become strikingly accurate.

Four steps are required to solve problems with machine learning: (1) problem definition; (2) data preparation; (3) algorithm selection and training; and (4) performance evaluation and results interpretation. All four steps benefit from interaction between domain specialists and computer scientists. For automated *isnād* detection, one would need to first define what qualifies as an *isnād*. Then a digitised corpus should be built that is both representative and balanced. Depending on the problem definition and the corpus, a set of algorithms would be selected and trained; the selection of the data and the algorithms would influence both the quality of the results and the expense of the training. Finally, the trained algorithm could be applied to unseen texts in order to automatically highlight all the *asānid*. The results would have to be assessed critically in view of the expectations and in order to improve the choices that were made.

Before I turn to the problem of *isnād* detection, I will introduce two recent studies by Lange et al. and Alkaoud et al. which have shaped my approach to this task and exemplify the fruitful complementarity between Islamic studies and computer sciences.

7.0. Machine Learning for Islamic Legal Texts

In 'Text Mining Islamic Law', Lange et al. explore this complementarity and highlight how the combination of different computational analyses can confirm or correct previous conventional studies based on smaller data sets and extrapolation.[29] They computationally analyse "a representative corpus of Islamic substantive law treatises (*furūʿ al-fiqh*) from the beginnings of Islamic jurisprudence in the 2nd/8th and 3rd/9th centuries to the 13th/19th century," comprising 55 unique titles spread homogeneously across time and Islamic legal schools.[30] This choice introduces of course a level of subjectivity, yet the analysed corpus contains far more than any corpora used so far for traditional text analysis. In this sense, it constitutes a different bias from those present in previous studies and therefore brings new perspectives along with the confirmation of existing conclusions.

In particular, the authors examine the use of the Qurʾān, the 'Qurʾān footprint', and the most prominent verses, Islamic legal deontology, and the dominant topics in their corpus, applying different computational methods.[31] They are able to correct past assumptions regarding the reliance on the Qurʾān by some legal schools and quantify how much each work relied on which verses. They also show different positions and their evolution regarding the permissible and the forbidden and exemplify how prayer and property dominate the concerns of the authors selected for their study. These results are encouraging; they bring into Islamic studies different bases, notably quantitative data, to better situate and understand single texts within a larger corpus.

---

[29] See the conclusion in Lange et al., 'Text Mining Islamic Law', 275–78.

[30] See Lange et al., 'Text Mining Islamic Law', 239ff., 278ff., for a detailed description of the corpus.

[31] Lange et al., 'Text Mining Islamic Law', 245ff. and 246n35.

Last but not least, this study highlights three crucial measures that should always guide any scholars working in digital Islamic studies (or digital humanities in general). First, the reproducibility of the results: all the texts, tools, and instructions used in any study must be rendered available for scholars to further test the conclusions drawn from the output data, for this is the sine qua non criterion of valid scientific analysis. Second, the corpus of texts ought to be curated by specialists who can guarantee its representativeness and its accuracy vis-à-vis the manuscripts. And finally, more tools, notably tools to detect text reuse, should be tested, in order to extract further information from the corpus, such as the *ḥadīth* 'footprint', for instance.[32] The present study adopted these measures as guidelines to shape its approach and the goals it should achieve.

8.0. Machine Learning for *Ḥadīth* Texts

While the *ḥadīth* footprint has not yet been explored, a large *ḥadīth* corpus of prophetic *aḥādīth*—that is, those that contain only reports about the prophet Muḥammad—has been the object of two recent studies using computational analyses. In 'Verifying Source Citations in the Hadith Literature', Syed et al. deploy statistical methods to find different kinds of errors in the *asānid* of their corpus. Contrary to Lange et al., their initial corpus is annotated; that is, all the different parts of the *ḥadīth* are marked distinctively, as are the names of the transmitters in the *asānid*, which are associated with biographical information. This allowed

[32] Lange et al., 'Text Mining Islamic Law', 277.

them to use simple rule-based algorithms to detect when errors had been introduced in an *isnād*, whether by a transmitter, a scribe, a copyist, or an editor, and to correct them automatically. In doing so they curated their corpus and improved its quality to enable more accurate analysis of its content in the future.

The same corpus was used in 'Learning to Identify Narrators in Classical Arabic Texts', where Alkaoud and Syed trained machine learning algorithms (BERT models and Transformers) to automate the recognition of *asānid*. They parsed 1,400 works and were able to mark all the transmitters across the largest corpus ever analysed in *ḥadīth* studies. Thus they open the possibility to further investigate all the *asānid* of their corpus, and with a little more effort, the *mutūn* attached to them, which remain to be extracted.

All the algorithms used by Lange et al. can also be applied to other corpora, and the outcomes of this automated analysis of prophetic *aḥādīth* should in turn stimulate further exploration of the *ḥadīth* footprint in the legal corpus of Lange et al. These seminal works in digital Islamic legal and *ḥadīth* studies open the door to answering questions about the most prominent and the rarest *ḥadīth* transmitters, their favourite topics, their idiosyncrasies in terms of language and vocabulary, their relations with each other, the networks of knowledge they form, and so on.

The standards established by these interdisciplinary teams of scholars serve as a framework for the present study, which follows in their footsteps and expands on an area they have left untouched. The corpus on which the studies for this paper were conducted encompasses texts that have not yet been scrutinised, namely prophetic and non-prophetic, legal and non-legal *aḥādīth*. The digital framework adopted here will serve to analyse the forms of *asānid* and substantiate or revise the conclusions of previous historical studies, which have been concerned mainly with the origins and functions of the *isnād*, as will be shown next.

9.0. A Subcorpus for a Limited Scope

For this study to fit in the scope of the present paper, it was limited to a selection from a large *ḥadīth* corpus (which contains more than two thousand volumes) and to the annotation of the *asānid* within this subcorpus. The texts were taken from works attributed to students of Mālik ibn Anas (d. 179/795), a famous jurist from Medina, whose teachings have purportedly been collected by his students and gathered in one of the earliest collections of thematically arranged *aḥādīth*, called the *Muwaṭṭaʾ* (in English, the 'well-trodden path') or spread across the students' personal *ḥadīth* collections. These students were ʿAlī ibn Ziyād al-Ṭarābulsī (d. 183/799), ʿAbd Allāh ibn Wahb al-Qurashī (d. 197/813), Muḥammad ibn al-Ḥasan al-Shaybānī (d. ca. 187/803), Yaḥyá ibn Yaḥyá al-Laythī (d. 234/848), and ʿAbd al-Razzāq al-Sanʿānī (d. 211/827).[33] Apart from ʿAbd al-Razzāq, each student is associated with a recension of the famous *Muwaṭṭaʾ*, which in the cases of Ibn Wahb and al-Shaybānī seems to be more a per-

---

[33] Mālik ibn Anas, *Muwaṭṭaʾ riwāya al-Shaybānī*; Mālik ibn Anas, *Muwaṭṭaʾ riwāya Ibn Ziyād*; Mālik ibn Anas, *Muwaṭṭaʾ riwāya Yaḥyá al-Laythī*; Ibn Wahb, *Muwaṭṭaʾ*; ʿAbd Al-Razzāq, *Al-Muṣannaf*.

sonal collection than an unfaithful recension of Mālik's teaching.[34] As for ʿAbd al-Razzāq's collection, his *Muṣannaf* ('sorted'; a name usually given to a collection of traditions sorted by topic) contains mainly materials from ʿAbd al-Razzāq's Yemeni master, Maʿmar ibn Rāshid (d.153/770), yet it includes *aḥādīth* from Mālik as well.

This subcorpus covers a constrained time span to guarantee a certain degree of relation between the alleged collectors of the accounts, despite the geographically diverse area, spreading from Andalusia, Libya, Tunisia, Egypt, and Yemen, all the way to Iraq and Syria. Most of these texts were likely written down by students of the scholars mentioned above. The *asānid* often start with the name of Mālik's student rather than Mālik directly, which seems to indicate that many of Mālik's accounts did not reach the scribe directly, but only through at least one intermediary transmitter. Nevertheless, the texts still belong to a limited period, that is, one or two generations after Mālik. The patterns and idiosyncrasies found among the *asānid* of this subcorpus serve to examine the traces that Mālik in general or his students and their scribes in particular left in their common or diverging uses of *isnād*.

10.0. *Isnād* Annotation

Patterns are difficult for humans to detect in large quantities of textual data. A computer program was therefore used to mark the *asānid* semi-manually with the help of recommenders, which

[34] See Ibn Wahb, *Leben und Werk*, 16, 43.

learn each time an *isnād* is marked and can then automatically recommend the next *asānid* to be marked.[35] The recommendations are manually validated or corrected, and the recommenders, which are partially based on machine learning algorithms, learn further and so improve their performance. This process is called 'annotation', as the texts are annotated prior to being analysed computationally.

Two different recommenders were used for the annotation: the String Matcher and the Multi-Token Sequence Classifier. The String Matcher finds exact matches: every time a new *isnād* is marked, the String Matcher registers it and automatically marks all the *asānid* which are identical. It gives a first impression of the most frequent *asānid* within a collection or across collections. It is also useful for reflecting on potential editing systems, whereby a certain type of *isnād* is systematically added to a *matn* for reasons yet to be discovered. The Multi-Token Sequence Classifier, on the other hand, automatically suggests fuzzy matches, which are *asānid* displaying a similar structure or sequence of words but with slightly different words or word orders. This recommender finds patterns in the form of the *isnād* and is particularly useful for identifying overall types of *isnād* according to their forms.

The two recommenders not only accelerate considerably the process of annotation, but also highlight overarching regularities and irregularities among *asānid* which have not previously been examined.

---

35 The program is called INCEpTION. See Klie et al., 'The INCEpTION Platform'; for the recommenders in particular, see p. 7.

11.0. Delineating the Contours of the *Isnād*

When the recommenders' suggestions are accurate, there is often a pattern present. Three main categories of *asānid* were found as a result in the annotated corpus: (1) the *muʿanʿan isnād*, which is a list of names introduced by the preposition *ʿan* (according to) and which contains no verbs; (2) the non-*muʿanʿan* or verbal *isnād*, which is a full sentence with verbs and without prepositions; and (3) the mixed *isnād*, with verbs and the preposition *ʿan*, this latter usually introducing the final names of the *isnād*.

The following example illustrates the two first types of *isnād*, the *muʿanʿan* and the non-*muʿanʿan isnād*.

مالك [عن] أبي نعيم وهب بن كيسان [أنه] سمع جابر بن عبد الله الأنصاري يقول رأيت أبا بكر الصديق أكل لحما ثم صلى ولم يتوضأ

> Mālik according to Wahb ibn Kīsān that he heard Jābir ibn ʿAbd Allāh al-Anṣārī say: I saw Abū Bakr al-Ṣiddīq eat meat, then he prayed and he had not performed the ablution.[36]

In this *ḥadīth*, extracted from Yaḥyá al-Laythī's recension of the *Muwaṭṭaʾ*, the scribe distinguishes the *isnād* and the *matn* with the particle *an* (*annah*^{u} 'that he'), the *muʿanʿan isnād* documents the transmission path, and the narrative part starts with the narration of Wahb ibn Kīsān. In this version, Jābir belongs to the *matn*: he is thus a protagonist of the narrative not a transmitter.

The same *ḥadīth* is found in the recension of al-Shaybānī with a verbal *isnād*, in which the verbs of transmission appear between square brackets:

---

[36] Mālik ibn Anas, *Muwaṭṭaʾ riwāya Yaḥyá al-Laythī*, 2:34.

[أخبرنا] مالك [حدثنا] وهب بن كيسان [قال سمعت] جابر بن عبد الله [يقول] رأيت أبا بكر الصديق أكل لحما ثم صلى ولم يتوضأ

Mālik reported to us, Wahb ibn Kīsān narrated to us, he said: I heard Jābir ibn ʿAbd Allāh say: I saw Abū Bakr al-Ṣiddīq eat meat, then he prayed and he had not performed the ablution.[37]

In al-Shaybānī's version, each of the three transmitters is preceded by one or two different verbs. Do each of these verbs indicate a different mode of transmission? If so, are there degrees of authority attached to each mode? Where does the *isnād* end and the *matn* start? Does the *matn* start with the first verb in the first person singular (*samaʿtu* 'I heard'), or the second one in the reported speech of Jābir (*raʾaytu* 'I saw')? Al-Laythī's *isnād* contains potentially less information but it gains in clarity by avoiding noise with all the different terminology, which does not seem to have been universally recognised and adopted. It also cannot be excluded that al-Shaybānī's *isnād* was deliberately enhanced with verbs to temper the caesura introduced by the list of names and to give it a more narrative character, either for the scribe's personal stylistic reason or because of regional and cultural writing traditions. The *muʿanʿan isnād*, on the other hand, because of its simplicity and its regularity, might be easier to remember, since the memory can focus on the names, and simply separate them with the same preposition. Finally, the *muʿanʿan isnād* breaks with the text to which it is attached (*matn*) and forms a distinct

[37] Mālik ibn Anas, *Muwaṭṭaʾ riwāya al-Shaybānī*, 38.

unit, similar to the hypertext described by Wallraff in this volume. It is usually not introduced by a verb except for rare exceptions, and it starts abruptly with the proper name of the first transmitter. Its unique link to the *matn* is through a particle that implies the missing verb and renders its absence more visible, as the literal translation underlines.

Since it contains only proper names separated by prepositions, the *muʿanʿan isnād* can be described as a list of transmitter names, and so might be associated with the broader genre of lists. This opens new perspectives to understand the effect, function, and purpose of this type of *isnād*. Julia Bray noticed that Muḥammad ibn Ḥabīb (d. 245/860) used lists in his *Muḥabbar* "to throw up a new order of data, relational as opposed to narrative or declarative."[38] This is the impression given by the *muʿanʿan isnād* and the metaphoric English translation 'chain of transmitters': each transmitter is a shackle attached to the next with the link of the preposition *ʿan*, all forming a chain that is related (relational) but not fused with the narrative. Like many other lists, the *muʿanʿan isnād* has "proven a highly efficient and effective device by which to reduce noise in the communication channel."[39] Indeed, this *isnād* only contains one type of information: the names of the transmitters who partook in the transmission. It does not inform the reader whether the transmission occurred orally or in writing, in a group (*akhbaranā* 'he reported to us') or in private (*akhbaranī* 'he reported to me'). When reading al-Laythī's *ḥadīth*,

---

[38] Bray, 'Lists and Memory', 222.

[39] Young, 'On Lists and Networks', 1.

the reader's attention is directed first to the names and then to the narrative, whereas in al-Shaybānī's version, the attention is dispersed since all the pieces of information are merged in one sentence.

In al-Laythī's *Muwaṭṭaʾ*, the *muʿanʿan isnād* is the most frequent type, and it is attached to reports mainly from Mālik and often with more than two transmitters in the *isnād*. It almost never includes al-Laythī's name, unlike the non-*muʿanʿan isnād*. There are three types of non-*muʿanʿan* or verbal *isnād* in al-Laythī's *Muwaṭṭaʾ*. First, there are those with a structure like *qāl*[a] *Yaḥyá qāl*[a] *Mālik* 'Yaḥyá said [that] Mālik said', which represents a third of the *asānid*. Second, there are ones that begin with something like *suʾil*[a] *Mālik* 'Mālik was asked'. Finally, some non-*muʿanʿan asānid* in this text use *Mālik annah*[u] *balaghah*[u] 'Mālik [said?] that it reached him'.

Each different type of *isnād* seems to systematically correspond with one particular type of transmission path. This suggests that the scribe was writing the *asānid* following some rules. With different *asānid*, he differentiated the reports coming from Mālik and those coming from Yaḥyá for example, or those where Mālik answers a direct question and those in which he narrates an indirect account. This implies that the *isnād* starting with 'Mālik' could have been reported by Yaḥyá al-Laythī, while those starting with 'Yaḥyá' come from his student.

There is one more indication in the *asānid* of this text that the scribe was probably copying from different notes taken at different times, potentially by various people. Towards the end of the text, one of the recommenders, the Multi-Token Sequence Classifier, made a mistake in the marking of the following *isnād*:

مالك عن أبي الرجال محمد بن عبد الرحمن بن حارثة بن النعمان [*] الأنصاري ثم من بني النجار عن أمه عمرة بنت عبد الرحمن أن رجلين استبا في زمن عمر بن الخطاب فقال أحدهما....

> Mālik according to Abī al-Rijāl Muḥammad ibn ʿAbd al-Raḥman ibn Ḥāritha ibn al-Nuʿmān [*] al-Anṣārī then from the Banī al-Najār according to his mother ʿAmrah bint ʿAbd al-Raḥman *that* two men quarrelled at the time of ʿUmar ibn al-Khaṭṭāb and one of them said....[40]

The recommender suggested the text up to the asterisk as an *isnād* with 95% accuracy and ignored the text from that point to the end of the extract. Twice before in the text, there had been an *isnād* with the same transmitters, except that the information in his name about his origins—the *nisba*—was not given: "Mālik according to Abī al-Rijāl Muḥammad ibn ʿAbd al-Raḥman ibn Ḥāritha according to his mother ʿAmrah bint ʿAbd al-Raḥman." The recommender's error seems therefore to have been induced by the indication of his origin, the *nisba*.[41] An explanation about a change of *nisba* had occurred only once before this *isnād* and only in the *matn*, in the case of ʿAbd Allāh ibn Zayd al-Anṣārī who is said to have acquired his *nisba* from the tribe of al-Ḥārith ibn al-Khazraj. Otherwise, the expression *min banī* 'from the sons/

---

[40] Mālik ibn Anas, *Muwaṭṭaʾ riwāya Yaḥyá al-Laythī*, 2:1211.

[41] The *nisba* is a part of an Arabic name that indicates the origin of the person, often in the form of an adjective. In this case, both *al-anṣārī* and *min banī najār* 'from the tribe of Najār' are *nisba*.

tribe of' is exclusively used to specify the origin of an undefined transmitter: "a man from the tribe of... said..." or "two men from the tribe of... asked the Prophet...." The text where the error occurred was therefore the first time that this specific expression appeared within an *isnād*, which explains why the recommenders did not recognise it as part of the transmission chain. The recommenders are sensitive to variations, and the more regular a text is, the more sensitive the recommenders become. This simple error from the recommender underlines therefore the high level of regularity in this collection and also the possible use of different notes or notes from different times in the composition of the final manuscript, leading to Muḥammad ibn ʿAbd al-Raḥman ibn Ḥāritha being mentioned twice with his old name and once with his new *nisba*.

Another sign of this collection's regularity is the systematic absence of verbs of transmission, such as *akhbaranā* or *ḥaddathanā*. This led Nabia Abbott to conclude, when she analysed papyri with a section attributed to this recension of the *Muwaṭṭaʾ*, that "[i]n the earliest stages of the development of the *isnād*... the use of *ʿan*... was generally accepted as equivalent to *ḥaddathanī*... and *akhbaranī*."[42] Whether she meant that the preposition and the verbs had the same degree of authority or that transmitters used the preposition and the verbs interchangeably is difficult to say. In any case, the previous observations made here indicate that the prepositions and the verbs might not have been

[42] Abbott, *Qur'anic Commentary and Tradition*, 121.

deemed equivalent. The absence of transmission verbs in al-Laythī's *Muwaṭṭaʾ* might actually indicate an indirect transmission through notes that al-Laythī's student gathered from his own sessions with al-Laythī and from al-Laythī's notes, which came from Mālik directly or more likely indirectly, considering the large time gap between the two scholars.[43] The clear distinctions between the four types of *asānid* in this text, together with their regularity, suggest that its scribe applied certain rules to classify the information he was transmitting according to its origin or source.

In ʿAbd al-Razzāq's *Muṣannaf*, the vast majority of *asānid* are also *muʿanʿan* (about 80 percent), in the form of "ʿAbd al-Razzāq according to... according to...," which is similar to al-Laythī's *muʿanʿan isnād*, starting directly with a name without any introductory verb or preposition. The mention of ʿAbd al-Razzāq's name indicates again that his student was most probably writing these accounts—or perhaps it involved several students, given the size of the collection (about 21,033 narratives compared to approximately 3,676 in al-Laythī's *Muwaṭṭaʾ*). Despite the overall regularity in the form of the *asānid*, ʿAbd al-Razzāq's *Muṣannaf* displays some irregularities; these cannot necessarily be attributed to the involvement of different people or sources, because, even if there was only a single scribe involved, homogeneity would be almost impossible to achieve in such a large quantity of text, which must have been transmitted over a

---

[43] Ahmed El Shamsy, 'The Ur-Muwaṭṭaʾ', 29, has recently argued that Mālik's students had access to "shared written source" from Mālik himself.

long period of time. There are also *asānid* of another type in ʿAbd al-Razzāq's *Muṣannaf*, a mix of *muʿanʿan* and non-*muʿanʿan* (type (3) above), which systematically start with *akhbaranā ʿAbd al-Razzāq... akhbaranā... ʿan... ʿan....* The two types of *asānid* often appear in clusters, and they are not intertwined indiscriminately: rather, they seem to form small subunits in the whole collection. More advanced machine learning algorithms will be able to analyse the topics and vocabulary associated with each different type and perhaps confirm our hypothesis that *aḥādīth* are here clustered by types as well as by topics.

By contrast, in al-Shaybānī's recension, most *asānid* are mixed. Ninety percent of the *asānid* start with *akhbaranā Mālik* 'Mālik narrated to us', and they mostly continue with another *akhbaranā* or *ḥaddathanā* followed by the preposition *ʿan*, similar to the second, minoritarian type of *isnād* found in ʿAbd al-Razzāq's *Muṣannaf*. We also find verbal *asānid* with *akhbaranā Mālik akhbaranā/ḥaddathanā... qāla...*, but there is not a single *muʿanʿan isnād*; the preposition *ʿan* appears only to introduce the last or the two last transmitters of a mixed *isnād*. The scribe also distinguishes between the accounts of Mālik, introduced with *akhbaranā Mālik*, and the related comments by Muḥammad al-Shaybānī, which are preceded by *qāl*[a] *Muḥammad*. There is again a visible system of information classification according to their sources, even though in this case it is slightly less elaborated and rigorous, since it introduces a simple binary distinction (as opposed to the four subtypes found in al-Laythī) and uses two different verbs, *akhbaranā* and *ḥaddathanā*, for a seemingly identical meaning.[44]

The small collection of Ibn Ziyād (159 narratives) contains mainly two types of *isnād*, *muʿanʿan* and verbal *asānid*, almost always with the name of Mālik either introduced by the verbs *qālᵃ* or *saʾalᵃ* (around 65 percent of examples), or preceded by the preposition *ʿan* (around 27 percent). The *asānid* are short and they often link two names only. A few mixed *asānid* break the regularity with strange combinations, such as *akhbaranā ʿan Mālik* or *qālᵃ ʿan Mālik*, but all in all, there is a recognisable organisation. It seems that Ibn Ziyād, who must be the transmitter and potentially the scribe, since his name is never mentioned, gathered in this collection mostly Mālik's sayings, teachings, and opinions together with some ancient narratives from the time of Muḥammad. Although the *asānid* reflect his own selection, their close resemblance to al-Laythī's short *asānid* suggests a potential style coming from Mālik's lectures or notes.

Finally, the least organised collections are those of ʿAbd Allāh ibn Wahb. In his *Muwaṭṭaʾ*, mixed *asānid* dominate. They start with an introductory verb similar to the ones found in al-Shaybānī's *Muwaṭṭaʾ*, yet the pronoun attached to the verb is not the first person plural *-nā*, but the first person singular *-nī*: *akhbaranī* and *ḥaddathanī*. These forms are uncommon in the other collections analysed here: while these forms are present in

---

[44] The third/ninth-century Egyptian scholar Abū Jaʿjar al-Ṭaḥāwī wrote a treatise arguing that the two verbs were identical in meaning, contrary to the assertions of other scholars; al-Ṭaḥāwī, *Al-Taswīya*.

al-Shaybānī's (6.6%) and ʿAbd al-Razzāq's collections (12%) in very small quantities, in al-Laythī's they only appear in the *matn*, never in the *isnād*. Thus Ibn Wahb distinguishes himself with the use of this first person singular pronoun in mixed *asānid*, regular in their form and content, for *akhbaranī* and *ḥaddathanī* are systematically followed by the preposition *ʿan*. Another distinguishing element in Ibn Wahb's collection is the absence of a short verbal *isnād* to introduce the teaching and opinions of Mālik.

12.0. Separating Transmission from Narration

There is one common element across the collections which marks the transition from the *isnād* to the *matn*: the particle *an* (أن). This particle does not appear in the *isnād*, except for some rare exceptions which are likely mistakes, and seems to be used to distinguish between transmission and narration. This distinction is particularly clear in the list form of the *muʿanʿan isnād* that stands out from the *matn* visually, acoustically, and semantically. By contrast, the verbal *isnād* is merged with the *matn* and suggests a more direct relation between the narrative and its transmitters. This form of *isnād* is often found to render Mālik's teachings and opinions in the form of *qāl*[a] *Mālik* 'Mālik said' or *suʾil*[a] *Mālik ʿan* 'Mālik was asked about'. It then contains one or two names (Mālik and Yaḥyá, for instance) and seems to indicate a more straightforward mode of knowledge transmission from master to student, contrary to the convoluted transmission from Muḥammad's time all the way up to the last transmitter, which represents four to five generations for the texts analysed in this paper. A compromise is reached in the mixed *isnād*, which usually starts with a verb and ends with the preposition *ʿan* and thus retains part of the differentiating effect produced by the *muʿanʿan isnād*, but adds a narrative character which tones down the clear-cut distinction between transmission and narration.

With time, the mixed *isnād* gained in popularity, and further annotation of later *ḥadīth* collections is necessary to help us understand why the simpler form of the *muʿanʿan isnād* was not retained. When Muslim ibn al-Ḥajjāj wrote his 'Muqaddima', the introduction to his great work, the *Ṣaḥīḥ*, he dedicated a long section to countering the criticism addressed against the *muʿanʿan isnād*. The *muʿanʿan isnād* was being targeted for its lack of clarity regarding the modes of transmission that it represented, compared to an expression such as "*samiʿtu aw akhbaranī*" ('I heard or he reported to me'), because the preposition does not state clearly that the two transmitters met.[45] Muslim ibn al-Ḥajjāj stresses that this criticism is a late invention that had never been applied by scholars before, and he follows with two lines of argument: first, one should focus on the transmitters not on the transmission terms; and second, by examining thoroughly the transmitters, one will most likely be able to assess which mode of transmission was used—for example, a son can use *ʿan* in his report from his father, and the transmission was surely through hearing (*samʿa*) or reporting (*akhbara*). In short, for Muslim ibn al-Ḥajjāj, the transmission terms could not be considered out of context to evaluate *ḥadīth* authenticity. One could add one more

[45] Muslim ibn al-Ḥajjāj, *Ṣaḥīḥ*, 19–20.

argument, namely that Mālik ibn Anas, for instance, seems to indicate indirect transmission through the use of the verb *balagha* and not with the *muʿanʿan isnād*. Furthermore, students of Mālik, such as al-Laythī and ʿAbd al-Razzāq, mostly used the *muʿanʿan isnād*.

The mistrust towards *muʿanʿan asānid* appears in this broader perspective to be a result of newly introduced criteria for *isnād* analysis from the time of Mālik ibn Anas and the two generations following him (the generations of al-Shaybānī's and al-Laythī's scribes). This change in the assessment of the *isnād* is reflected in the fact that most *asānid* from the canonical collections are mixed: they are *muʿanʿan* from the Prophet's time to around the start of the second/eighth century, and then become non-*muʿanʿan* with the more systematic use of verbs that indicate the mode of transmission. In these *asānid*, at least two different systems of reporting and organising transmission coexist and mark the two different historical periods to which they belong.

13.0. Conclusion and Outlook

The annotation of the different collections from Mālik's students highlights the great diversity of forms and contents in the *asānid* that were used during this limited period by a small group of scholars. The criticism against the *muʿanʿan isnād* tackled by Muslim ibn al-Ḥajjāj indicates further that this diversity of forms was accompanied by a diversity of understandings regarding the content of the *isnād*. Through radical changes of context and added levels of subjectivity, it became increasingly challenging for the contemporaries of Muslim ibn al-Ḥajjāj to perceive or interpret the *isnād* as their predecessors did. This applies all the more to today's historians, who stand even further away from the evolutive period of the *isnād* than Muslim ibn al-Ḥajjāj and his opponent.

The inexorable disadvantage of the elapsed time is alleviated by the advantage of the quantity of information at our disposal. Enlarging the scope of *isnād* studies with a list perspective and combining it with computational analysis is a way to exploit this advantage and enlarge the subjective lens through which we look at the past. With the analysis of a large number of *asānid* and the errors of automated recommenders, I have shown the importance of departing from assumptions and extrapolations and instead providing detailed observations of the object of study in order to delineate its contours accurately and account for its various forms and content. The knowledge thus acquired can now be used to build a representative corpus of texts for the automated recognition of the *isnād* in its diversity.

Of course, we are still lacking a large digitised corpus that directly reflects the manuscripts which are the ultimate source for textual analysis. We must therefore always keep in mind the possible editors' interventions at different levels. However, the number of scholarly curated corpora, like the one used in this study, is growing and the increasing interactions between manuscript studies and corpus linguistics is already improving the quality of these corpora. Likewise, collaborations between domain specialists and computer scientists are on the rise, leading to reduced computational expense and biases. Between the ambiguous, where domain specialists are most at ease, and the univocal, where computer scientists thrive, there is an interdisciplinary middle ground which helps them both challenge existing assumptions and expand the perspectives of previous scholarship. Lists bring together ambiguous texts in a univocal order, and offer therefore a perfect object of study to challenge and please all scholars.

CHAPTER LISTS IN GIANT AND BENEVENTAN BIBLES: SOME PRELIMINARY REMARKS

Marilena Maniaci

1.0. Chapter Lists and the History of the Latin Bible

Codices containing the full or partial text of the Latin Old and New Testaments offer a great many research suggestions to scholars interested in the study of synopses and lists. On the one side, both the length of the Bible and its manifold forms and usages encourage the development of practices aimed at organising and retrieving the sacred contents; on the other side, the manuscript Bible, destined by its nature to last, is without doubt the book in which the use and reuse of spaces not occupied by the sacred text occurs with the greatest frequency and in the widest variety.[1]

The typology of book lists includes the so-called *capitula*, or chapter lists,[2] introducing the single biblical books in the majority of Latin Bibles prior to the thirteenth century, the era in which

[1] See the introductory remarks in Maniaci, 'Written Evidence', 85–86.

[2] The term *capitula* should more precisely refer to the sections in which the text is divided, while the initial titles should be called *tituli*, but it is customary to refer to the titles as *capitula* as well. The sets of *capitula*

 https://doi.org/10.11647/OBP.0375.10

the Paris Bible made its appearance and brought with it a new chapter subdivision of the biblical text, condemning the old *capitula* to disappear.[3] The Latin *capitula*, which are different in structure and wording from the *kephalaia* attested in Greek manuscripts,[4] briefly summarise, chapter by chapter, the contents of each section of the biblical text, or reproduce the words of the section's initial sentence. The eminent historian of the Vulgate Samuel Berger traced their composition back to Cassiodorus,[5] but some of the various sequences or 'families' attested, which differ (even significantly) by extension and wording of the individual *tituli*, can be traced back to late antiquity.[6]

---

listed at the beginning of each biblical book should rather be called *tabulae capitulorum*.

3 On the Paris Bible, see, among others, the recent overviews by Light, 'Paris Bible'; Ruzzier, 'Miniaturization'; Ruzzier, *Entre Université et ordres mendiants*.

4 In most Greek Gospel manuscripts, Matthew has 68 chapters, Mark 48, Luke 83, and John 18 or 19. A list of the chapter numbers and titles (*titloi*) is often written at the beginning of each Gospel; the chapter numbers and names (*kephalaia*) are repeated (usually in red ink) on the top (or bottom) of the page where the chapter begins. The *titloi* are listed according to the 'majority text' by Soden, *Die Schriften*, 402–75; for the New Testament, the variants from several individual manuscript witnesses can be found in the apparatus to Swanson's series *New Testament Greek Manuscripts*; see also the forthcoming volume by Dirkse, *Sum of Things Spoken*.

5 Berger, *Histoire de la Vulgate*, 307.

6 On the history of the Bible text's divisions, see Bogaert, 'Les particularités editoriales'; Houghton, 'Chapter Divisions'.

In a hypothetical—and surely premature—attempt to categorise the different types of lists found in ancient and medieval manuscripts, *capitula* belong to the family of 'closed' lists, whose extension and structure is determined by that of the reference text and aim to make it more easily understandable. The fact that biblical books are usually divided into a number of sections corresponding to the number of chapters of the preceding list has led manuscript scholars to consider these lists as actual indexes of content. However, neither the sections inside the books nor the chapter lists are consistently numbered (numbers may also be present in some books and absent in others), and the subdivision proposed by the list does not always correspond exactly to that marked in the text through the use of numbers or other devices. In a single Bible, the *capitula* of individual books or series of books can also belong to different families, and their relationship with the textual tradition of the books they refer to awaits a closer examination. The existence of different sets of lists for the same book, the textual instability of the individual chapter titles (*tituli*) and of their succession even within the same set, and the not always linear relationship with the corresponding biblical text lead one to wonder about the functions of the chapters and the exact meaning of their extensive—but not universal—presence among the paratexts of the Latin Bible between antiquity and the end of the monastic era.

Capitula were more generally placed before the individual books—even if there are cases of chapters set before groups of books (such as Kings) or even cases in which, for a single book, each title was arranged within the text, at the beginning of the corresponding section. The most common layout involved the use of a smaller script, usually identical or similar to that of the following text. Each *titulus* could be introduced by a rubricated initial, and was transcribed on a new line (see fig. 1) or after the previous chapter on the same line (see fig. 2); the arrangement on two narrow columns transcribed one after the other, side by side, is also attested (see fig. 3), and chapter titles could occasionally be inserted within the text, at the beginning of each chapter (see fig. 4). The lists could be introduced and/or followed by a rubricated incipit and/or explicit of a rather standardised formulation, but with variations and errors that can betray—as I will try to show—the relationship between codices belonging to the same branch of tradition or written in the same environment.

Figure 1: Montecassino, Archivio dell’Abbazia, Casin. 759, p. 5

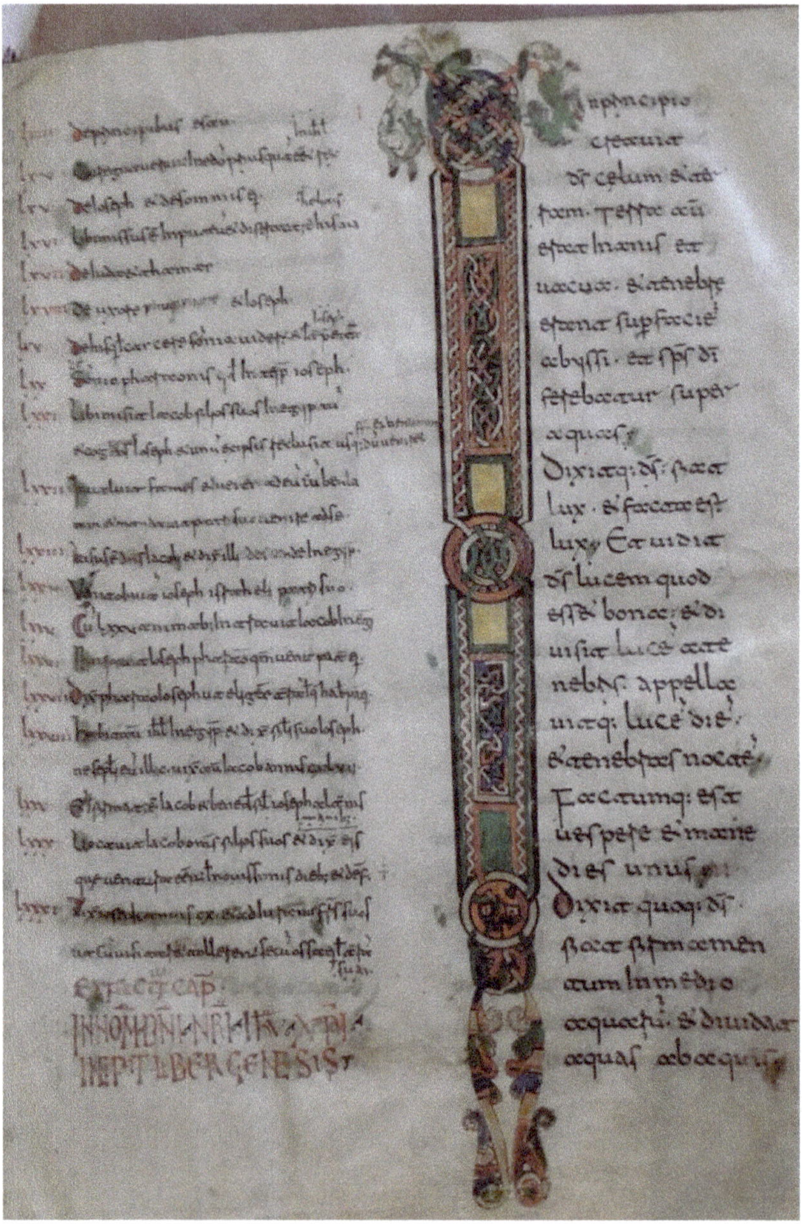

Figure 2: Montecassino, Archivio dell'Abbazia, Casin. 583, p. 51

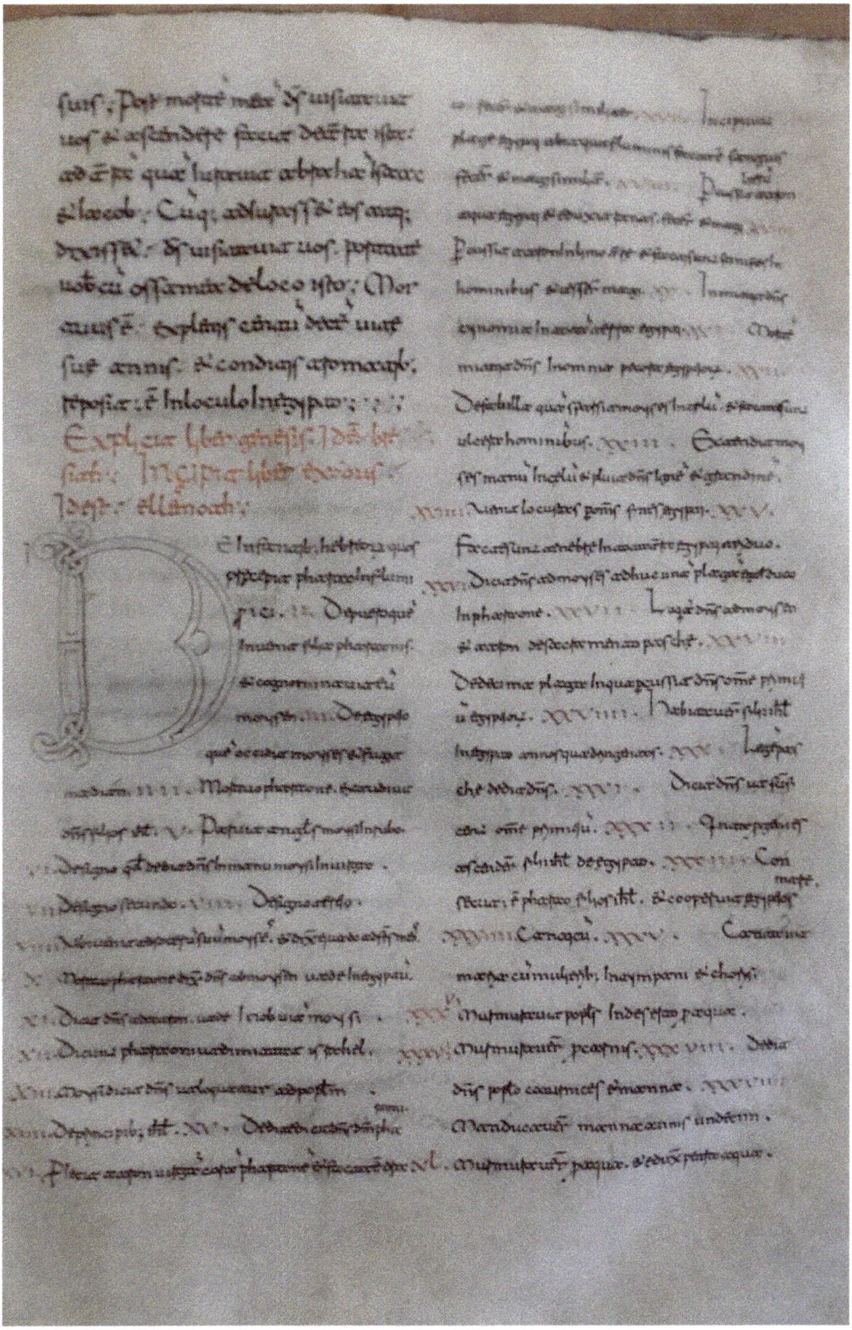

Figure 3: Montecassino, Archivio dell'Abbazia, Casin. 35, pp. 352v–353r

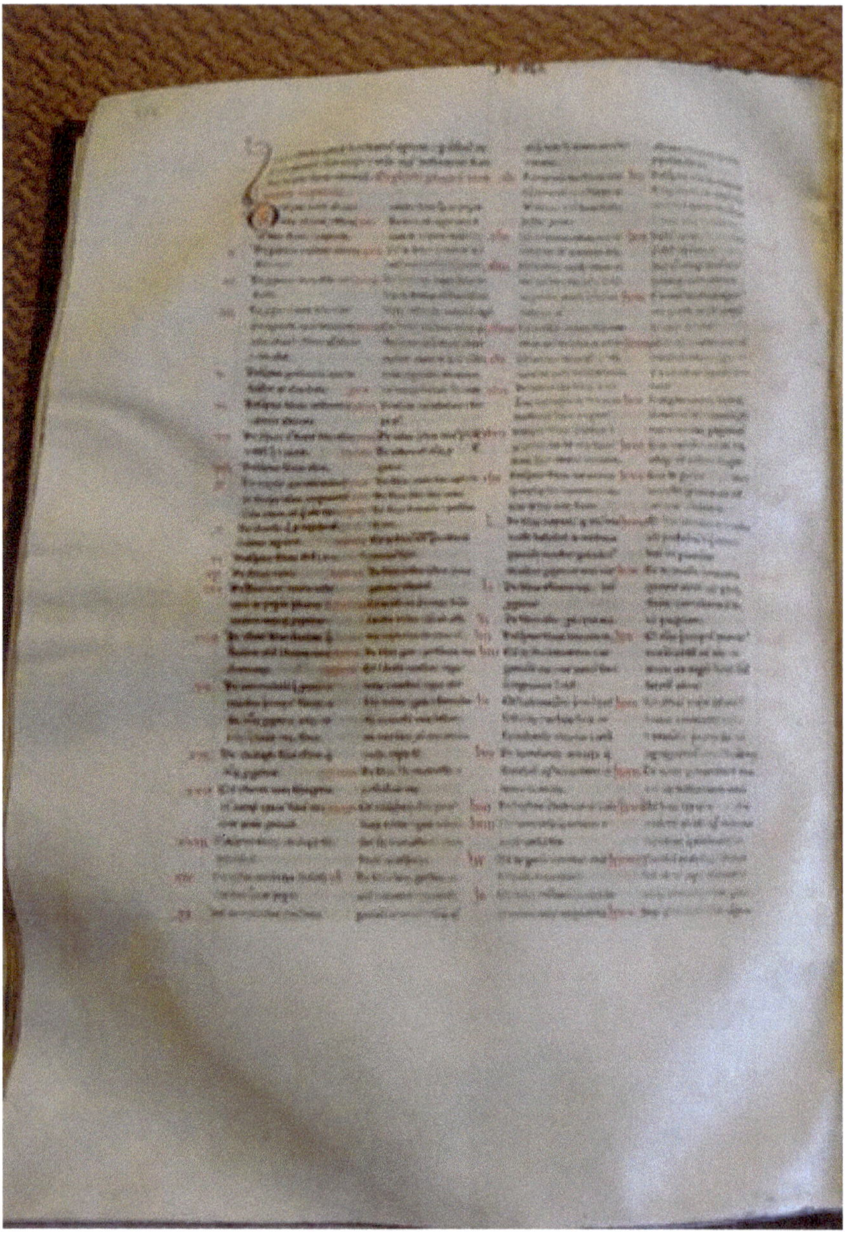

Figure 4: Montecassino, Archivio dell'Abbazia, Casin. 760, p. 90

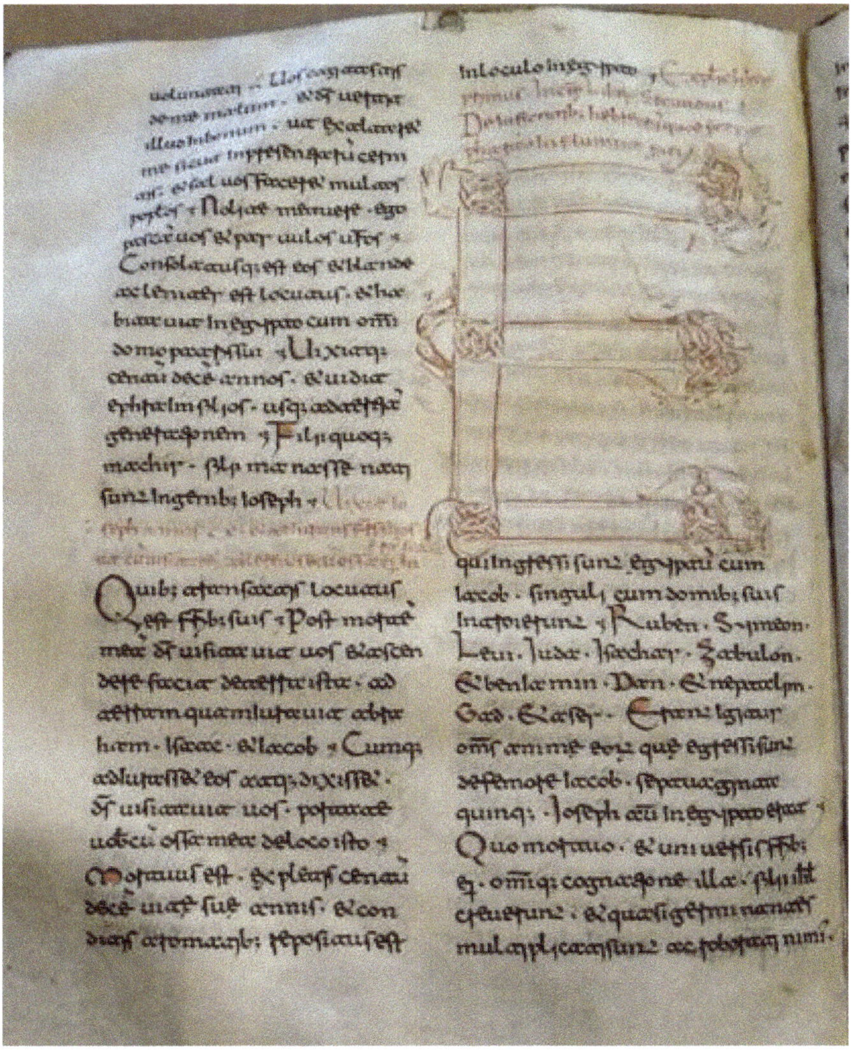

Since, in general, *capitula* as accessory texts were not subject to the revisions and corrections carried out on the main text, their wording is usually more conservative and therefore shows more clearly the continuity of local traditions, even if the preferences accorded to the different sets of lists in the various areas in which the biblical text circulated—which do not exclude the simultaneous presence of alternative solutions—remain to be explored.

Even if chapter lists were not the object of specific philological attention, it is reasonable to assume that, in their transcription, the scribe, in addition to making errors, jumps, and omissions favoured by the repetitiveness of the texts and the presence of recurrent formulations, felt himself authorised to operate with greater freedom than in the copying of the biblical text—although with limited margins of autonomy, which remain to be specified: as we will see, he or she could choose, for example, to merge two or more successive chapters, or on the contrary to split two long chapters into shorter units, assigning an individual number to each of them.

The essential reference for the study of the divisions of the biblical text is the repertoire of the Belgian Benedictine Donatien De Bruyne: as a member of the commission for the revision of the Vulgate founded at the beginning of the twentieth century by Pope Pius X, in 1914 he printed in semi-anonymous form the *Sommaires, divisions et rubriques de la Bible latine*. Sustained by the intuition that paratextual elements could facilitate the grouping of the manuscripts and therefore the emergence of textual families, De Bruyne's repertoire was conceived as a mere support to the edition of the biblical text and is therefore lacking details on the criteria applied for selecting the codices used as the basis for the preparation of: the chapter lists (*sommaires*), which are presented in parallel columns to facilitate their immediate comparison; the tables that summarise the different systems of capitulation of the text (*divisions*); and the lists of the sections of the Song of Songs and the Psalter used in the Liturgy of the Hours (*rubriques*). The recent republication of the *Sommaires* (as the *Summaries, Divisions and Rubrics of the Latin Bible*) by Brepols Publishers in 2014, is a very welcome initiative, although it does not fully help to clarify the work method of the Belgian scholar nor to identify the totality of his sources.

This preliminary contribution, which is a prelude to a wider study, aims to provide some examples of the potential interest of an in-depth analysis of the chapters, not only as a tool to highlight relationships between individual codices or operate groupings within specific strands of textual tradition, but also to deepen our knowledge of the practices of manufacture and transcription of the biblical text and of its accompanying paratexts. The objective is not to propose the mature or final results of research already at an advanced stage, but rather to share ideas and questions arising from a series of preliminary surveys, based on the non-exhaustive analysis of data and materials collected on the occasion of previous or ongoing research conducted by myself and other authors.

I will therefore focus on the discussion of two examples: one of them relates to the central Italian 'Atlantic' or 'Giant' Bibles of the Romanesque period, while the other concerns the tradition of the Bible in medieval Montecassino. It is interesting to observe that the Cassinese book collection also preserves one of the oldest Giant Bibles—Montecassino, Archivio dell'Abbazia,

Casinensis 515—which arrived soon after the mid-eleventh century from Rome or the Roman area: it would therefore be worth evaluating this codex, from the specific point of view of the *capitula*, in terms of its relationship with the local biblical tradition. Given the obvious impossibility of carrying out (at least at this first stage of the research) an overall examination of the *capitula* to all the Old and New Testament books, I have chosen to concentrate my attention on the Octateuch, whose chapters have not been the object of specific analyses since the pioneering work of Henri Quentin in 1922.[7] As for Montecassino, the research devoted by Elisabetta Unfer Verre to Casinensis 557, the first complete Bible set up in the abbey (and more generally in southern Italy), will allow me to briefly extend my gaze to other groups of biblical books.

2.0. Chapter Lists in Italian Giant Bibles

The first example I will deal with concerns the so-called Atlantic or Giant Bibles, which are the object of a research project started in 2000 at the University of Cassino with the organisation of a large manuscript exhibition, and continued in the following two decades with the analysis of single witnesses and with contributions aimed at deepening, in particular, the knowledge of the

---

[7] Quentin, *Mémoire*; with regard to Montecassino, I could also rely on the ongoing work by my colleague Roberta Casavecchia on the paratexts of the Beneventan Bibles kept in the abbey's library. At my suggestion, she recently conducted a thorough analysis of the *capitula* of the Book of Genesis, currently in press (Casavecchia, 'Bibbia e paratesti'), which takes into account the results of the present contribution.

techniques and contexts of manufacture, the writing, and the decoration of the Bibles.[8] Atlantic Bibles are codices of an imposing size and with a clearly recognisable—although far from perfectly uniform—codicological, graphic, and decorative physiognomy, that were produced in central Italy (and more precisely in Rome and the surrounding area) between the middle of the eleventh and the first decades of the twelfth century.[9] The manufacture of Atlantic Bibles—which is the result of an impressive effort of 'serial' production, probably due to the coordinated activity of several copy centres—has been plausibly interpreted as an instrument of political-religious propaganda in the context of the so-called Gregorian reform, initiated at the papal Curia around the middle of the eleventh century, with the aim of restoring the moral integrity and authority of the Roman Church.[10]

The in-depth analysis of a significant sample of individual codices has made it possible to bring to light the existence of an

---

[8] Maniaci and Orofino, *Le Bibbie atlantiche*; and the updated bibliographic survey by Maniaci and Orofino, 'Dieci anni'; for a general overview see also (from a not entirely coincident perspective) Condello, 'La Bibbia'.

[9] The production of the following decades, variously located in Tuscany, has an imitative character, with objectives and manufacturing methods which differ significantly from the original ones.

[10] Supino Martini, 'La scrittura delle Scritture', believes in the existence of a single scriptorium located in the papal residence of the Lateran Palace, an hypothesis that seems disproved by the textual and material variety of the extant Bibles; equally improbable seems the idea of a production by itinerant copyists that was proposed by Lila Yawn in 'Temporary Workshops' and other contributions.

intricate network of collaborations between artisans, scribes, and illuminators, facilitated by the adoption of working methods that included—according to a use already attested in the most ancient Greek and Latin pandects—a 'modular' subdivision of the biblical text into autonomous textual units (books or book sequences) corresponding to finite sequences of quires.[11] Unfortunately, the comparative approach has not been systematically extended so far to the text and paratexts of Atlantic Bibles, including their chapter lists.[12]

In order to attempt a first survey, a census of the Octateuch *capitula* in a sample of eight Atlantic Bibles was carried out, all approximately assigned to the second half of the eleventh and the early years of the twelfth century, selected based on the current presence of the Octateuch and the availability of complete and

---

[11] Maniaci, 'La struttura delle Bibbie atlantiche'. For the relationships between the modular articulation of the Bibles and the organisation of the work of scribes and illuminators, see Larocca, 'Le più antiche Bibbie atlantiche'; Orofino, 'Per un'iconografia comparata'.

[12] For some preliminary remarks on the text of the Atlantic Bibles, see Lobrichon, 'Riforma ecclesiastica'.

sufficiently legible digital reproductions.[13] Even at a still superficial level of analysis, table 1 offers material for some first, interesting remarks.[14]

Table 1: De Bruyne's chapter series for each of the eight Atlantic Bibles, together with the number of chapters actually present in each book, and the number given to the final chapter in each list

Genesis	Series	No. of chapters	Final chapter no.
Pal. lat. 3	Is (46)	46	46
Vat. lat. 4220	Is (46)	46	46
Sion 15	Is (46)	46	46
Vat. lat. 10405	Is (46)	46	46
Casin. 515	Is (46)	46	46
Barb. lat. 587	[D (63)]	62	unnumbered
Vat. lat. 12958	Is (46)	46	46
Laur. Plut. 15.10	Is (46)	46	46

[13] All the Bibles are described in Maniaci and Orofino, *Le Bibbie atlantiche*. Full reproductions (except for Casin. 515) are available at the following links: Vatican City, Biblioteca Apostolica Vaticana, Barb. lat. 587, https://digi.vatlib.it/view/MSS_Barb.lat.587; Pal. lat. 3, https://digi.vatlib.it/view/bav_pal_lat_3; Vat. lat. 4220, https://digi.vatlib.it/view/MSS_Vat.lat.4220; Vat. lat. 10405, https://digi.vatlib.it/view/MSS_Vat.lat.10405; Vat. lat. 12958, https://digi.vatlib.it/view/MSS_Vat.lat.12958; Sion, Chapter Library, MS 15, https://www.e-codices.unifr.ch/fr/searchresult/list/one/acs/0015; Florence, Biblioteca Medicea Laurenziana, Plut. 15.10, http://mss.bmlonline.it/s.aspx?Id=AWOMr0cjI1A4r7GxMYg_&c=Biblia.

[14] The sigla in tables 1, 2, and 5 correspond to the classification of the chapter series by De Bruyne, *Sommaires*, based on a choice of reference manuscripts that are not always identifiable and whose selection criteria were not made explicit by the Benedictine scholar and remain difficult to recognise.

Exodus	Series	No. of chapters	Final chapter no.
Pal. lat. 3	A (139)	152	102
Vat. lat. 4220	A (139)	158	156
Sion 15	A (139)	151	151
Vat. lat. 10405	A (139)	158	158
Casin. 515	A (139)	149	151
Barb. lat. 587	Is (21)	23	13 (23)
Vat. lat. 12958	Is (21)	24	24
Laur. Plut. 15.10	Is (21)	22	22
Leviticus	**Series**	**No. of chapters**	**Final chapter no.**
Pal. lat. 3	A (89)	88	88
Vat. lat. 4220	A (89)	88	88
Sion 15	A (89)	85	85
Vat. lat. 10405	A (89)	87	87
Casin. 515	Is (16)	16	16
Barb. lat. 587	Is (16)	16	16
Vat. lat. 12958	Is (16)	16	16
Laur. Plut. 15.10	Is (16)	15	15
Numbers	**Series**	**No. of chapters**	**Final chapter no.**
Pal. lat. 3	A (74)	74	74
Vat. lat. 4220	A (74)	74	74
Sion 15	A (74)	70	70
Vat. lat. 10405	A (74)	74	74
Casin. 515	Ps (50)	48	48
Barb. lat. 587	Ps (50)	50	50
Vat. lat. 12958	Ps (50)	50	50
Laur. Plut. 15.10	Ps (50)	50	49
Deuteronomy	**Series**	**No. of chapters**	**Final chapter no.**
Pal. lat. 3	A (155)	153	153
Vat. lat. 4220	A (155)	154	154
Sion 15	absent	—	—
Vat. lat. 10405	absent	—	—
Casin. 515	absent	—	—
Barb. lat. 587	absent	—	—
Vat. lat. 12958	absent	—	—
Laur. Plut. 15.10	absent	—	—

Joshua	**Series**	**No. of chapters**	**Final chapter no.**
Pal. lat. 3	A (33)	33	33
Vat. lat. 4220	A (33)	33	33
Sion 15	A (33)	34	34
Vat. lat. 10405	A (33)	33	33
Casin. 515	A (33)	34	34
Barb. lat. 587	A (33)	34	34
Vat. lat. 12958	A (33)	34	34
Laur. Plut. 15.10	A (33)	34	34
Judges	**Series**	**No. of chapters**	**Final chapter no.**
Pal. lat. 3	A (18)	17	17
Vat. lat. 4220	A (18)	20	20
Sion 15	A (18)	16	17
Vat. lat. 10405	A (18)	21	21
Casin. 515	A (18)	17	17
Barb. lat. 587	A (18)	20	20
Vat. lat. 12958	A (18)	18	17 (18 unnumbered)
Laur. Plut. 15.10	A (18)	18	18
Ruth	**Series**	**No. of chapters**	**Final chapter no.**
Pal. lat. 3	absent	—	—
Vat. lat. 4220	Tur	10	10
Sion 15	absent	—	—
Vat. lat. 10405	absent	—	—
Casin. 515	absent	—	—
Barb. lat. 587	absent	—	—
Vat. lat. 12958	absent	—	—
Laur. Plut. 15.10	absent	—	—

As shown in table 2, for the first nine biblical books, De Bruyne's census includes a number of chapter sets ranging from 3 to 11, defined on the basis of one or more 'reference manuscripts', identified through acronyms whose meaning is not always clear. In addition, the reason that the Octateuch series are divided into two groups is not made explicit by the Benedictine scholar.

Table 2: Summary of De Bruyne's series of chapters for each book of the Octateuch, showing the number of series he found, the sigla of the manuscripts on which he based his survey, and the number of chapters found in each of them

Book	**No. of series**	**Sigla and number of chapters**
Genesis	11 (6+5)	A (82), Fr (no numbering), B (157), D (63), X (34), C (38) / Afr [Afr^{sp}] (75), Y (31), Is (46), Is^{br} (46), W (61)
Exodus	9 (5+4)	A (139), Fr (no numbering), B (97), D (124), C (18) / Afr [Afr^{sp}] (80), Compl (81), Is (21), A^{r} (71)
Leviticus	9 (5+4)	A (89), Fr (no numbering), B (69), D (161), C (16) / Afr^{sp} (33), Compl (30), Is (16), Sg (21)
Numbers	11 (6+5)	A (74), Fr (no numbers), A^{add} (74), B (98), D (75), C (20) / Afr [Afr^{sp}] (61), Compl (29), Is (23), Ps (50), Sg (63)
Deuteronomy	10 (5+5)	A (155), Fr (no numbering), B (141), D (121), C (20) / Afr^{sp} (103), Compl (25), Is (18), Ps (34), Sg (45)
Joshua	8 (4+4)	A (33), Fr (no numbering), B (110), C (11) / Afr^{sp} (20), Compl (19), Is [Is^{1}, Is^{2}] (14), Ps (20)
Judges	8 (4+4)	A (18), Fr (no numbering), B [B^{r}] (60), C (9) / Afr^{sp} (32), Compl (30), Is [Is^{1}] (10), Ps (19)
Ruth	3 (3+0)	Tur (10), Fr (no numbering), L (14)

None of the Bibles considered in this first survey contains, for all the Octateuch books, a single set of chapters belonging to the same series. Altogether, four series of *capitula* are attested, A, Is, Ps, and Tur. The D series exhibited for Genesis in the so-called Santa Cecilia Bible (Barb. lat. 587) is a later restoration, and indeed the Barberini Bible appears among the witnesses on which De Bruyne's edition is based. The A series, which is the most represented in the Octateuchs, is the only one witnessed for the books of Joshua and the Judges; the book of Genesis, on the other hand, is always introduced by chapters belonging to the Is series. Chapters to Ruth are present only in Vat. lat. 4220 (mentioned by De Bruyne among the 'reference manuscripts' for the series Tur), while those to Deuteronomy are often omitted (in fact, they appear only in Pal. lat. 3 and Vat. lat. 4220, in both cases according to the A series).

The books of Exodus, Leviticus, and Numbers show the greatest variety of choices. Four of the codices under examination (Pal. lat 3, Vat. lat. 4220 and 10405, and the Bible held in Sion's Chapter Library) bear for all three books *capitula* of the A series; three manuscripts (Barb. lat. 587, Vat. lat. 12958, and Laur. Plut. 15.10) adopt for Exodus and Leviticus the Is series (in the case of Exodus, with the presence of three titles which are not in De Bruyne's list)[15] and for Numbers the Ps series; the Cassinese Bible 515 is close to this second group (but for Exodus it has chapters of the A series, like the four manuscripts of the first group).

Already at this first and quite elementary level of analysis, *capitula* confirm their usefulness for suggesting groupings and relationships between manuscripts, within a textual and book tradition which is only apparently homogeneous (far from the "véritable édition" postulated by Berger)[16] and for which the studies conducted in the last 20 years—by combining the analysis of

---

[15] Chapters after De Bruyne, *Sommaires*, n. 2: "ubi accepta uxore duos filios genuit et de visione in rubo"; after n. 8: "in consumatione decime plage"; after n. 9 (only in Vat. lat. 12958): "in marat et demanna in deserto in primum."

[16] Berger, *Histoire de la Vulgate*, 141–42.

structure, writing, and decoration—have instead contributed to identify the co-presence of distinct strands.

A closer look at the single witnesses of the *capitula* belonging, for each book, to the same series offers further elements of interest. In fact, the table shows how the number of *tituli* attested in each manuscript often diverges from that of the codices taken as a reference by De Bruyne. In contrast to more stable sequences (among which the Is series of Genesis stands out in particular), there is the case of the Exodus chapters, where there are always more items than in the reference series (due to the lists of the 10 plagues of Egypt and the 10 commandments always being assigned individual numbering);[17] in all the other cases, the shifts in the number of *tituli* range from four fewer than those printed in the *Sommaires* of De Bruyne (as in the A series to Leviticus in the Bible of Sion), to three more (as in the Is series to Exodus in Vat. lat. 12958).

The table also allows another observation, namely that the actual number of titles listed at the head of each book does not always correspond to the numbering given by the scribe (which in the Atlantic Bibles always appears in Roman numerals before the text). Taking Exodus as an example, an evident misalignment occurs in Pal. lat. 3, in which the last chapter appears as 102, due to a jump backwards from 62 to 11 between chapters 44 and 45 of De Bruyne's A series, at the transition from the recto to the verso of folio 21 (the scribe mistakenly follows the final number 10 of the first column of folio 21r, instead of the final number of

---

[17] De Bruyne, *Sommaires*, between chapters 16 and 17 and chapters 37 and 38.

the second column); in Barb. lat. 587 the last chapter of the Is series, represented in the codex by 23 titles, is numbered 13, due to a jump backwards from 20 to 11 between De Bruyne's chapters 18 and 19, which occurs, again, at the passage between the recto and the verso of folio 20.

These two examples, which could be easily multiplied, suffice to clarify that the comparison between the lists cannot limit itself to considering the initial and final titles and the numbering of the latter. For the same number and succession of *tituli*, the same series can end, in the manuscripts attesting it, with a different number (as it does in the case of Vat. lat. 4220 and 10405, again for the book of Exodus, due to the repetition of number 12 three times in Vat. lat. 4220).

On the other hand, series composed of the same number of titles and closed by the same ordinal number may present significant structural differences. This can result from various processes:

1. The splitting of one of De Bruyne's titles into two or even three distinct ones. This occurs in Vat. lat. 10405, Numbers, 33 + 34 and 35 + 36; and in Vat. lat. 4220, Judges, 10 + 11 + 12 (see fig. 5).
2. The merging of two of De Bruyne's titles into one. An example of this is Vat. lat. 10405, Numbers, 44 (= 42 + 43).
3. The omission of a title due to the scribe's distraction. This occurs in Sion, Numbers, 6, to cite just one of many examples.
4. The omission or duplication of numbers (of which some examples have already been mentioned) that occurs in a

very variable manner from manuscript to manuscript, and that in some cases may reveal unexpected relationships between witnesses or confirm those suggested by other clues (of a palaeographic, codicological, art historical, or philological nature).

Figure 5: Vatican City, Biblioteca Apostolica Vaticana, Vat. lat. 4220, f. 79r

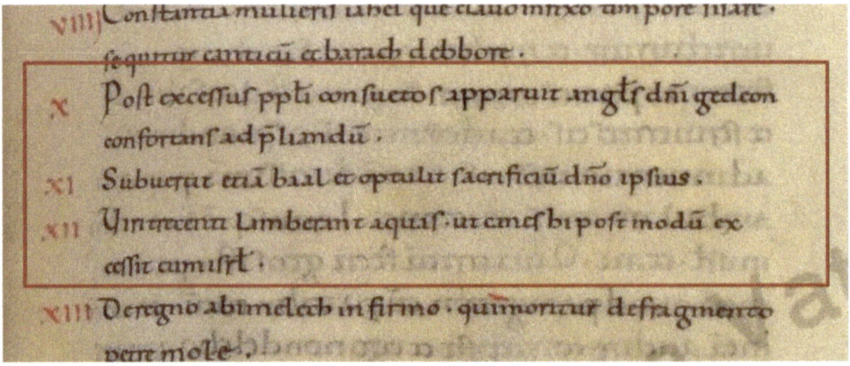

X. Post excessus populi consueto apparuit angelus domini gedeon confortans ad praeliandum. Subuertit etiam baal et obtulit sacrificium domino. Ipsius uiri trecenti lambierant aquas ut canes. Is postmodum excessit cum israel.

Given the impossibility of discussing all the anomalies found in the manuscripts, I will limit myself to some rather randomly chosen examples. Firstly, in some cases, the absence of individual chapters is common to all the manuscripts belonging to the same series. This can be seen, for example, with for the omission of the *titulus* 135 of the A series of the book of Exodus, which occurs in all the relevant codices (table 3).

Table 3: De Bruyne's numbering for the A series *tituli* in Exodus, and the corresponding numbers in each of the witnesses of this series

De Bruyne	Casin. 515	Pal. lat. 3	Sion 15	Vat. lat. 4220	Vat. lat. 10405
129	142	93	142	147	149
130	143	94	143	148	150
131	144	95	144	149	151
132	145	96	145	150	152
133	146	97	146	151	153
134	147	98	147	152	154
135	absent	absent	absent	absent	absent
136	148	99	148	153	155
137	149	100	149	154	156
138	150	101	150	155	157
139	151	102	151	156	158

Secondly and more frequently, deductions or additions with respect to the reference texts printed in De Bruyne appear to be variously distributed within the sequences. For example, the A series of Leviticus chapters in Pal. lat. 3 (fols 34v–35r) and Vat. lat. 4220 (fols 35v–36r) consists of 88 *tituli* and is closed in both cases by number 88. But while the scribe of the Palatine manuscript omits number 66 of De Bruyne's list (also absent in the Sion Bible), the Vatican codex omits number 62. As for the chapters to the book of Numbers, three of the four representatives of the A series have 74 *tituli*, with the last one numbered 74; but while in the cases of Pal. lat. 3 (fol. 44rv) and Vat. lat. 4220 (fol. 45rv), the sequence is identical to that printed in De Bruyne, in Vat. lat. 10405 (fol. 41rv), the final figure 74 results from the merging of two pairs of titles (44 = 42 + 43 De Bruyne and 64 = 63 + 64 De Bruyne) and from the splitting of two single titles into pairs (33 + 34 = 33 De Bruyne and 35 + 36 = 34 De Bruyne). Groupings and doublings also occur in other series. For example, the first *titulus* of Judges is split in two in five of the seven witnesses of the A series: Pal. lat. 3, fol. 78v; Casin. 515, p. 177; Barb. lat. 587, fol. 73v; Vat. lat. 12958, fol. 69r; Laur. Plut. 15.10, fol. 82r.[18]

Thirdly, in the only two codices bearing chapters to Deuteronomy—Pal. lat. 3 (fol. 54rv) and Vat. lat. 4220 (fols 58v–59v)—the difference in numbering between the two series is due to the omission of two titles (94 and 103) in the former and one (21) in the latter. This can be easily explained, in all cases, as a *saut du même au même*.

The coexistence of choices attributable to specific strands of tradition (which may differ from book to book), and to individual errors of copying, prevents the definition of clusters based solely on the distribution of the *capitula*, which cannot, moreover, be founded on a narrow and rather random selection of codices or on the analysis of the Octateuch alone, but needs to be correlated with the results of palaeographic, codicological, artistic, and text-critical analysis. Even from a first survey, however, the potential of a more detailed study of the *capitula* emerges quite evidently: a rather clear opposition appears between two groups (Pal. lat. 3, Vat. lat. 4220, Sion 15, and Vat. lat. 10405 on the one hand; Barb. lat. 587, Vat. lat. 12958, and Laur. Plut. 15.10 on the other), with Casin. 515 in an intermediate position; the second group is marked by a particularly close affinity between Vat. lat. 12958 (the so-called Pantheon Bible) and Barb. lat. 587 (the Santa Cecilia Bible), which are among the most richly illuminated witnesses of the Atlantic family. The relevance of these

[18] The first chapter is absent in Sion 15, fol. 73r.

groupings ought to be verified—in a further phase of the research—through the analysis of the palaeographic, decorative, and textual characteristics of the Bibles and of their possible relationships, as well as through an extension of the census proposed here to other important Atlantic witnesses of the most ancient period.[19]

3.0. Chapter Lists in the Bibles Kept at the Montecassino Abbey

For those wishing to analyse the evolution of the Bible as a book during the Middle Ages, Montecassino represents a unique situation, given the large number of testimonies still held *in loco*, distributed over the central Middle Ages and produced both in the abbey's scriptorium and the foremost regions of medieval Europe.[20] Such testimonies make it possible to follow the physical, textual, graphic, and decorative transformations undergone by the Bible, and also to document the role played by Montecassino, both as a centre with a strongly characterised local tradition and as a magnet for new cultural and technical trends developed elsewhere and embraced early on at the abbey, which added its own touches of originality.

---

[19] For the recurrence of the same scribes in several Atlantic Bibles, see Larocca, 'Le più antiche Bibbie atlantiche'; the same phenomenon is analysed, with reference to decorators and illuminators, by Orofino, 'Per un'iconografia comparata'. References to other contributions from the two authors may be found in Maniaci and Orofino, 'Dieci anni', 8n11, 8n14.

[20] Casavecchia et al., *La Bibbia a Montecassino*.

As already mentioned, the library of Montecassino preserves an Atlantic Bible, Casin. 515, which arrived in the abbey in an incomplete form—perhaps through the abbot reformer Desiderius—and was supplemented by typically Beneventan initials, not of the best quality (see figs. 6 and 7).[21] It serves here as a link to the second example, drawn from another recently ended project, dedicated to the cataloguing of all the manuscript of the Cassinese collection containing part or the totality of the biblical text (in a 'natural' sequence, with the exclusion of liturgical codices).[22] The descriptive protocol chosen for the Bibles adopts a 'syntactic' approach[23] and includes the census and the systematic identification of all the paratexts (prologues, titles, and chapters).

---

[21] On Casin. 515, see Dell'Omo, 'Il codice Casin. 515'; Maniaci and Orofino, 'Montecassino, Bibbia, riforma', 395–402, 405–7. These have different views concerning the role of Desiderius in the arrival of the Bible at Montecassino.

[22] Casavecchia et al., *La Bibbia a Montecassino*, contains the descriptions and bibliography of all the Cassinese Bibles mentioned in the following pages.

[23] On which see Andrist et al., *La syntaxe du codex*; a new (revised and expanded) edition in English is currently in preparation.

Figure 6: Montecassino, Archivio dell'Abbazia, Casin. 515, p. 426

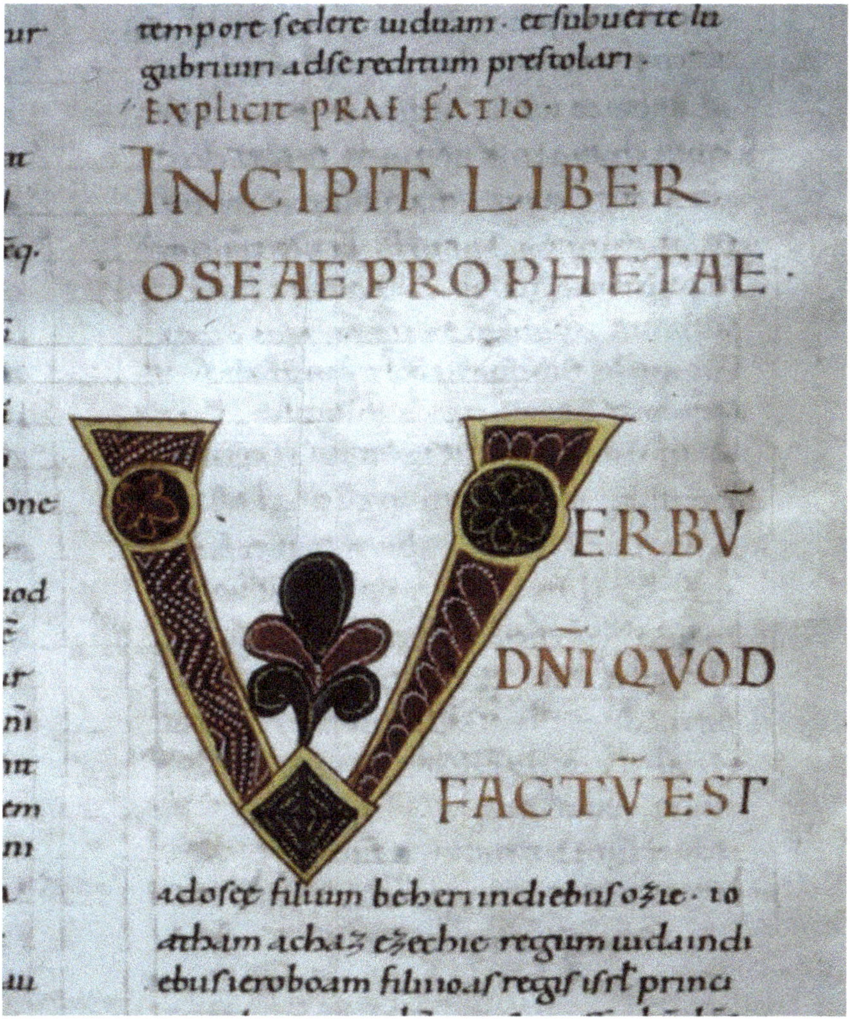

Figure 7: Montecassino, Archivio dell'Abbazia, Casin. 515, p. 515

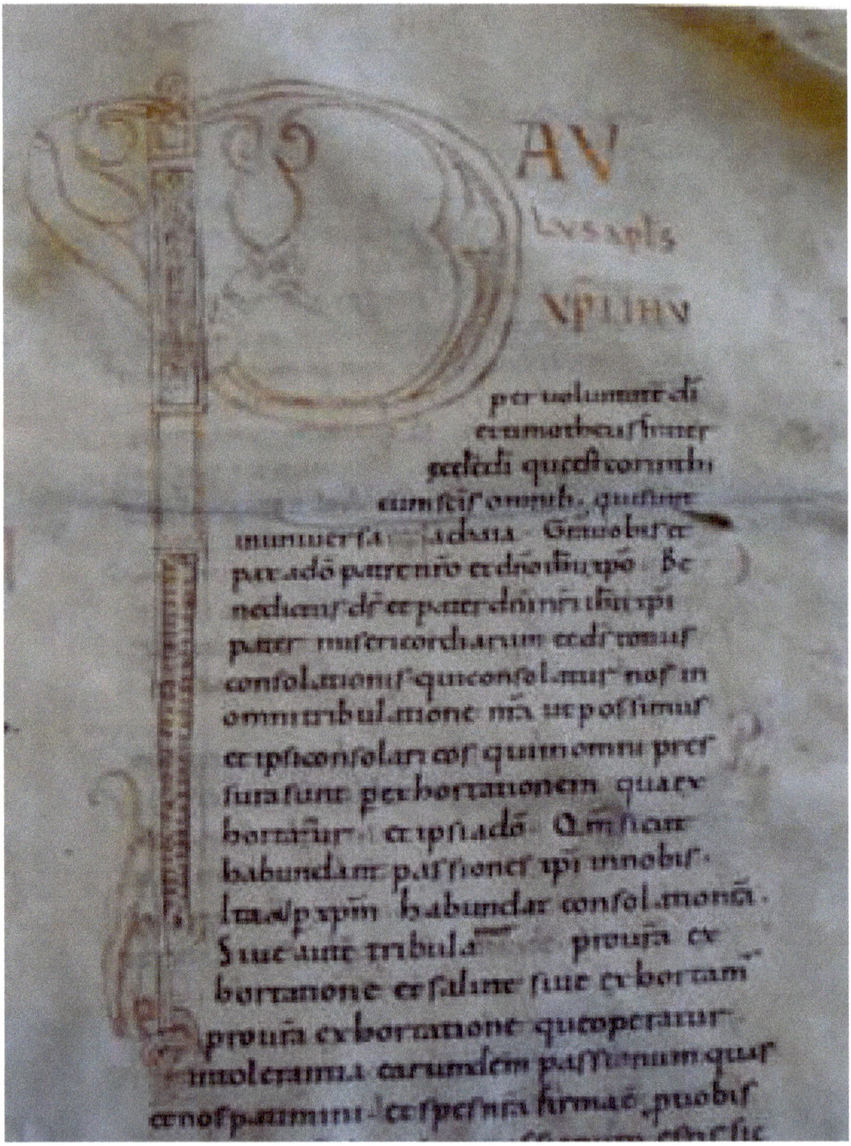

Among the slightly over a hundred biblical witnesses preserved at the abbey (including a series of fragments), 21 codices (corresponding to 27 production units) are written in Beneventan minuscule.[24] Despite the presence of an Atlantic Bible in Montecassino from shortly after the middle of the eleventh century, none of the biblical codices of local manufacture contains the complete sequence of the Old and New Testaments: the idea of the Bible as a pandect is in fact foreign to Longobard southern Italy, and Beneventan Bibles contain instead partial groupings of books, according to a division of the Bible into five parts (Octateuch; Prophets; Kings-Maccabees; Pauline Epistles; Acts, Catholic Epistles, Apocalypse) which reflects its use during the Divine Office through the liturgical year.[25]

Six of the biblical codices belonging to the Cassinese collection contain the Octateuch (in a more or less complete form), which was used for morning readings between Septuagesima and Lent (table 4).[26]

Table 4: Date and contents of Cassinese Octateuchs

Shelfmark	**Date**	**Contents**
520	second half of 11th century	Gen., Exod., Lev., Num., Deut., Josh., Judg., Ruth
531	early 11th century	Gen., Exod., Lev., Num., Deut., Josh., Judg. (mutilated)
565	first half of 12th century	Gen. || Exod., Lev., Num., Deut., Josh., Judg., Ruth
583	first half of 11th century	Gen. (acephalous), Exod., Lev., Num., Deut., Josh. (mutilated), Judg. (acephalous and mutilated)

24 Casavecchia et al., 'Montecassino e la Bibbia'.

25 Brown, 'I libri della Bibbia'.

26 The double vertical lines mark the modular units within the individual Bibles. See Maniaci, 'La struttura delle Bibbie atlantiche'. The dating of Casin. 583 refers to the first unit of the codex, containing the Octateuch.

759	early 11th century	Gen. || Exod., Lev., Num., Deut. || Josh., Judg., Ruth (mutilated)
760	early 11th century	Gen., Exod., Lev., Num., Deut., Josh., Judg., Ruth

In his fundamental study of the Octateuch text that appeared in 1922, Henri Quentin noted how the Cassinese group—supplemented by two complete later Bibles of local production, Casin. 557 and 35 (discussed further in the following section), and by two other manuscripts containing Genesis and Exodus (Casin. 534 and 557)—have well-marked characteristics, distinguished by the presence of rare or unique lessons.

A first examination of the *capitula* in this group of manuscripts—undertaken by Roberta Casavecchia[27] and currently being extended to other Cassinese Bibles—and a comparison with the *capitula* of the Atlantic Bible preserved in the abbey allows some interesting observations (table 5).

Table 5: De Bruyne's chapter series for each of the eight Cassinese Bibles, together with the number of chapters actualy present in each book, and the number given to the final chapter in each list

Genesis	Series	No. of chapters	Final chapter no.
Casin. 515	Is (46)	46	46
Casin. 520	A (82)	81	81
Casin. 531	A (82)	80	80
Casin. 565	A (82)	81	81 (added by later hand)
Casin. 583	acephalous	acephalous	acephalous
Casin. 759	A (82)	81	81
Casin. 557	A (82)	81	102
Casin. 35	A (82)	81	81

27 See Casavecchia et al., 'Montecassino e la Bibbia', 49–51; Casavecchia and Maniaci, 'Partial Bibles'; Casavecchia, 'Bibbia e paratesti'.

Exodus	**Series**	**No. of chapters**	**Final chapter no.**
Casin. 515	A (139)	149	151
Casin. 520	A (139)	158	156
Casin. 531	A (139)	156	156
Casin. 565	A (139)	156	unnumbered
Casin. 583	A (139)	157	157
Casin. 759	A (139)	157	157
Casin. 557	A (139)	157	165
Casin. 35	A (139)	156	155
Leviticus	**Series**	**No. of chapters**	**Final chapter no.**
Casin. 515	Is (16)	16	16
Casin. 520	A (89)	86	84
Casin. 531	A (89)	86	unnumbered
Casin. 565	A (89)	86	unnumbered
Casin. 583	A (89)	86	86
Casin. 759	A (89)	86	86
Casin. 557	A (89)	86	unnumbered
Casin. 35	A (89)	86	85
Numbers	**Series**	**No. of chapters**	**Final chapter no.**
Casin. 515	Ps (50)	48	48
Casin. 520	A (74)	73	71
Casin. 531	A (74)	73	73
Casin. 565	absent	absent	absent
Casin. 583	A (74)	73	73
Casin. 759	A (74)	73	73
Casin. 557	A (74)	73	unnumbered
Casin. 35	A (74)	73	73
Deuteronomy	**Series**	**No. of chapters**	**Final chapter no.**
Casin. 515	absent	absent	absent
Casin. 520	A (155)	21	21
Casin. 531	A (155)	21	21
Casin. 565	absent	absent	absent
Casin. 583	A (155)	21	21
Casin. 759	A (155)	21	21
Casin. 557	A (155)	21	unnumbered
Casin. 35	A (155)	21	21

Joshua	Series	No. of chapters	Final chapter no.
Casin. 515	A (33)	34	34
Casin. 520	A (33)	33	33
Casin. 531	A (33)	32	32
Casin. 565	absent	absent	absent
Casin. 583	A (33)	33	33
Casin. 759	A (33)	33	33
Casin. 557	absent	absent	absent
Casin. 35	A (33)	33	33
Judges	**Series**	**No. of chapters**	**Final chapter no.**
Casin. 515	A (18)	17	17
Casin. 520	A (18)	18	18
Casin. 531	A (18)	18	17
Casin. 565	absent	absent	absent
Casin. 583	mutilated	mutilated	mutilated
Casin. 759	A (18)	18	18
Casin. 557	absent	absent	absent
Casin. 35	A (18)	18	18
Ruth	**Series**	**No. of chapters**	**Final chapter no.**
Casin. 515	absent	absent	absent
Casin. 520	absent	absent	absent
Casin. 531	absent	absent	absent
Casin. 565	absent	absent	absent
Casin. 583	absent	absent	absent
Casin. 759	absent	absent	absent
Casin. 557	absent	absent	absent
Casin. 35	absent	absent	absent

As in the Atlantic Bible, the *tituli* normally appear at the top of the biblical book, almost always introduced by a rubricated initial and an initial title (and sometimes closed by a final one) and preceded by Roman numerals also transcribed in red ink. The chapters of some books are not numbered, specifically Leviticus in Casin. 531; Genesis, Exodus, and Leviticus in Casin. 534 (numbers in front of the Genesis chapters are added by a later hand); and Leviticus, Numbers, and Deuteronomius in Casin. 557. The table omits one manuscript, Casin. 760, in which—unlike in the other Bibles—the *tituli* are incorporated in the text in the form of rubrics.

A first noteworthy fact is that, unlike what happens in Atlantic Bibles, both the *capitula* of the Cassinese Octateuchs and those of the two later complete local Bibles in Carolingian minuscule all belong to the A series (but with specific common traits that distinguish them from those of the Atlantic Bibles).[28]

A second, striking, peculiarity concerns the sequence of the Deuteronomy chapters—omitted by most of the examined Atlantic Bibles—that in all Cassinese Octateuchs (including Casin. 760), as well as in the two local Bibles, systematically end at chapter 21; this is also found in Bibles of Spanish origin.[29]

Other elements common to the Cassinese group, which help to make it identifiable, concern the systematic omission, in all the witnesses of the Octateuch (but also in the two later local pandects) of the same *tituli* of the A series—number 34 of Genesis; numbers 33, 121, and 122 of Exodus; numbers 54, 63, and 89 of Leviticus; number 71 of Numbers—which are always present in the Atlantic Bibles; also common to the entire local tradition is the permutation of Genesis chapters 75 and 76 of De Bruyne's A series.

Minor divergences in the numbering of the chapters of Exodus, Leviticus, and Numbers occur in two codices, Casin. 759 and Casin. 520, which are certainly related from both textual and

---

[28] Unfer Verre, 'Una Bibbia di Montecassino', 1818–22.

[29] Quentin, *Mémoire*, 360.

art historical points of view.[30] Casin. 759 was in fact produced in the early years of the eleventh century in Capua (in the scriptorium founded by the Cassinese monks after they had fled the Saracen raid that destroyed Montecassino in 883) and probably served as a model for the manufacture of Casin. 520.

An even more evident relationship exists between Casin. 531, 583, and 759, three Octateuchs which can all be dated to the first decades of the eleventh century. Particularly significant is the position of the same initial title of Exodus, placed right before the *capitula* rather than at the opening of the biblical text, as well as the same ungrammatical version of the rubric introducing the list of chapters in Numbers ("Incipiunt capitula de liber [*sic*] Numeri": Casin. 531, p. 190; Casin. 583, p. 168; Casin. 759, p. 299).

Within this relatively compact group, Casin. 565, produced at the beginning of the twelfth century, stands out for the absence of the *capitula* to Numbers, Deuteronomy, Joshua, and Judges: the last two are also omitted by the later Casin. 557, which I will go on to discuss as the last of my three examples.

4.0. Chapter Lists in the First Southern Italian Complete Bible

About a century after the making of the Cassinese Atlantic Bible, the first complete Bible of southern Italian origin was produced

---

[30] Compared to Casin. 759, Casin. 520 doubles the figure 121 in the chapter numbering of Exodus (p. 137), omits the numbering of chapters 16 and 18 in Leviticus (p. 242), and doubles the figure 32 in the chapter numbering of Numbers (p. 314).

in the third quarter of the twelfth century in Montecassino: the so-called Ferro Bible (Casin. 557), named after its unknown main copyist who signed himself, in a way that was totally unusual in the Latin tradition, highlighting the word in the text that corresponds to his name by writing it in capital letters, sometimes touched with red ink. Ferro also signed another codex written at Montecassino, Casin. 264: this glossed Exodus bears a colophon containing the name of abbot Theodinus (1166–67), offering us a close reference point for the dating of the Bible. The small dimensions and the very tiny script qualify the Ferro Bible as a book not intended for liturgical use, but for study and consultation, which testify to early connections between the Montecassino cultural environment and that of the great abbeys and cathedrals where biblical exegesis found a strong revival in twelfth-century northern Europe.[31]

When the Ferro Bible was produced, Montecassino lacked a local tradition which could serve as a model (in terms of size, order of the books, layout, text, and paratexts). The Cassinese Bible therefore appears as an unprecedented experiment, straddling tradition and innovation: this is clearly demonstrated by the text, which is composed by combining several local antigraphs, but with significant novelties, such as the presence of Ezra-Nehemiah and Paralipomena (the latter never directly attested in Beneventan Bibles, although occasionally mentioned in

---

[31] On the Ferro Bible, see Unfer Verre, 'Un contributo'; Unfer Verre, 'Una Bibbia di Montecassino'; see also more recently Zambardi, 'Le Bibbie glossate', with a focus on a glossed Exodus also written by Ferro (Casin. 264).

the catalogues), of Baruch (also attested for the first time in the Ferro Bible), of the Epistle of Jeremiah, and of four versions of the Psalter (Hebrew, Gallican, *Vetus*, and Roman), for whose coexistence the Cassinese Bible constitutes an absolute unicum. Also noteworthy is the presence of prologues and other paratexts typical of Beneventan manuscripts, alongside others belonging to external traditions.

In the Ferro Bible, most of the books are still preceded by chapter lists (with the exception of Joshua, Judges, Ruth, 1–4 Kings, 2 Paralipomena, Ecclesiastes, Song of Songs, Ezra, Nehemiah, Daniel, and all the Prophets). For the Pentateuch, as we have seen, these are fully in line with the *capitula* attested in the group of Cassinese Octateuchs,[32] with which they share the absence of: chapter 34 of Genesis (see fig. 8); 33, 121, and 122 of Exodus; 54, 63, and 89 of Leviticus; 71 of Numbers; and the interruption to chapter 21 of Deuteronomy. As already mentioned, the absence of the chapters to Joshua and Judges and some peculiarities in the sequence of the *tituli* of Genesis (the omission of no. 34, also found in Casin. 759) point to a particularly close relationship between the Ferro Bible and the Octateuch Casin. 565, which can be assigned to the beginning of the twelfth century and is in turn connected to Casin. 760 through a misunderstanding of the decorator (*E[c]* instead of *H[aec]* at the beginning of Exodus).

[32] On the texts of the *capitula*, see Thiele, *Sapientia Salomonis*, 134–35; Thiele, *Sirach (Ecclesiasticus)*, 89–90.

Figure 8: Montecassino, Archivio dell'Abbazia, Casin. 557, p. 6

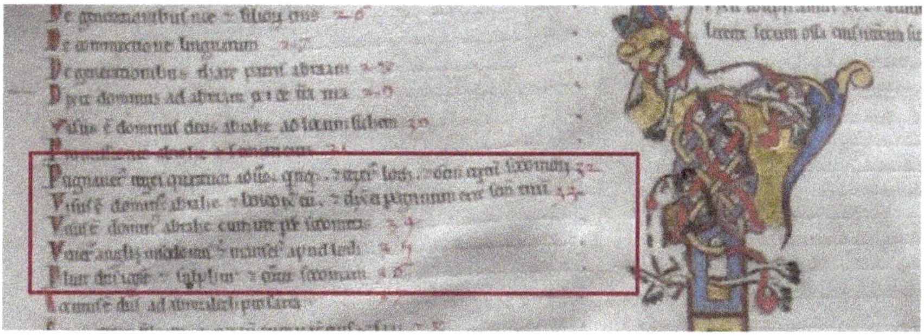

seminis ejus.

XXXII. Pugnauerunt reges quattuor adversus quinque et ceperunt loth et omnem equitatum sodomorum.

XXXIII. Uisus est dominus abrahae et benedixit eum et dixit ei : peregrinum erit semen tuum.

XXXIIII. Uisus est dominus abrahae et dedit ei signum circumcisionis et de isaac.

XXXV. Uisus est dominus abrahae cum iret perdere sodomitas.

XXXVI. Uenerunt (⁵ + duo) angeli in sodomis et manserunt apud loth.

A complete survey of the chapters, conducted by Elisabetta Unfer Verre, reveals the dependence of Casin. 557 on the Cassinese tradition for the other biblical books as well;[33] unlike what happens for the text and for the prologues, the text of the chapters is not subject to revisions and updating: this is probably a symptom of an early loss of interest in this type of text, destined to disappear with the diffusion of the model of the Parisian Bible.

[33] Unfer Verre, 'Una Bibbia di Montecassino', 1818–22.

The choices documented by the Bible named after Ferro, who is not only its main scribe but probably also its *concepteur*, completely ignore—not only for the texts and the order of the books, but also for the selection of the chapters—the model of the Atlantic Bibles, represented in Montecassino by Casin. 515, which was surely present in the abbey when the later pandect was transcribed.

A further century later, another locally made pandect, Casinensis 35, exhibits a biblical text that is still, for the most part, a typically Cassinese one, and a sequence of chapters laid out on two narrow columns placed side by side, which is still completely in line, for the Octateuch, with local customs (as is shown by the presence of the 'short' version of the *capitula* to Deuteronomy or by the absence of the same *tituli* omitted in the Cassinese Octateuchs).

5.0. Some Final Remarks

What can be inferred from this preliminary (and largely provisional) survey?

First of all, the potential of a systematic analysis of biblical chapters lists is clearly confirmed even by the few examples discussed here. For scholars interested in the tradition of the biblical text and its circulation in different periods and contexts, chapter lists represent on the one hand a particularly useful tool to highlight relationships between individual witnesses or groups of codices; on the other hand, they are also clues to cultural rather than editorial choices, perpetuated over time even after their rationale and their connection to the text had been forgotten (as evidenced by the misalignment between *capitula* and text partitions and the convergence of several strands of traditions in the same Bible). For book historians, the arrangement of the lists on the page, the use of visual and art historical devices to highlight the individual *tituli*, and the presence and hierarchy of initial and final titles (both of the biblical books and their accompanying texts) are all aspects that may allow us to better understand the work of artisans and copyists and the challenges involved in transcribing the 'Book among the books', in the multiplicity of its forms. In the specific perspective of paratextual studies, chapter lists obviously play a privileged role in the analysis of the interplay between the biblical books and the variety of their surrounding (organising, interpretive, navigational, accompanying, etc.) tools and materials.[34] Last but not least, chapter lists are texts of varying structure and length, which can—and should—also be analysed from the point of view of their contents (descriptions, quotes or paraphrases, summaries, etc.), literary choices, and quality.[35]

From a methodological and organisational point of view, the future development of this research needs to be set in the context of a broader project, whose formulation will have to take

---

[34] See the stimulating theoretical contribution by Andrist, 'Definition of Paratexts'.

[35] Chapter lists, and the interest in them, are of course not limited to the Bible. See, e.g., Colombi, 'Una prima ricognizione'; Colombi, 'Titoli e capitoli', with further bibliography and interesting methodological remarks.

into account the evidence that has emerged from this first survey, and the following facts in particular.

The study of Bible chapters is an immense work, which requires great patience. It cannot be limited to a single group of books, but should be extended to all attested series and to groups of witnesses which are representative of specific Bible types. This is true not only in the case of the Atlantic Bibles, but also—to mention another potentially interesting example—in the case of the so-called Turonian or Alcuin Bibles. For example, a quick survey conducted on Bern, Burgerbibliothek 3 revealed that the Octateuch only has A series chapters, exactly corresponding to the De Bruyne sequence.

The examination of the attested sequences cannot be limited to comparing simply the first and the last number of the series published in De Bruyne's *Sommaires*. Instead, it must include the systematic verification of the presence, absence, unification, duplication, and permutation of titles; the omission or duplication of numbers; and any other possible variations to the sequences.

The analysis of the sequences must be integrated with an analysis of their layout and of the visual and textual devices used (of a codicological, graphic, or decorative nature). This must be done to determine the identification, legibility, and functionality of the lists. There must also be a simultaneous examination of all the accompanying paratexts, such as the prologues and initial or final titles—these are mostly banal and repetitive, but can sometimes shed light on direct or indirect relationships between individual manuscripts or groups of codices.

The *tituli* transcribed at the head of a biblical book must be compared with the actual internal partitions within the book itself. As has been mentioned, these often do not correspond.

The study of the tradition of the chapters and the relationships between the witnesses cannot ignore the textual and philological analysis of the individual titles—the 'great absent' from this contribution. The relationship between the subdivision provided by the titles and the not necessarily compliant subdivision of the biblical text must also be verified.

The research on chapter lists should include the re-edition, in electronic format, of the fundamental repertoire by Donatien De Bruyne, based on a wider census of manuscripts and on their opportune and motivated selection.

BIBLIOGRAPHY

Abbott, Nabia. *Studies in Arabic Literary Papyri II: Qur'ānic Commentary and Tradition*. Chicago: University of Chicago Press, 1967.

ʿAbd al-Razzāq ibn Hammām al-Sanʿānī. *Al-Muṣannaf*. Edited by Ḥabīb al-Raḥman al-Aʿẓamī. Beirut: al-Majlis al-ʿIlmī, 1970.

Abū Rīda, Muḥammad ʿA., ed. *Rasāʾil al-Kindī al-falsafiyya*. 2 vols. Cairo: Dār al-Fikr al-ʿArabī, 1950–53.

Adamson, Peter. *The Arabic Plotinus: A Philosophical Study of the 'Theology of Aristotle'*. London: Duckworth, 2002.

———. 'Al-Kindī and the Muʿtazila: Divine Attributes, Creation and Freedom'. *Arabic Sciences and Philosophy* 13 (2003): 45–77.

Adamson, Peter, and Peter Pormann. *The Philosophical Works of al-Kindī*. Karachi: Oxford University Press, 2012.

Adelman, Rachel. *The Return of the Repressed: Pirqe de-Rabbi Eliezer and the Pseudepigrapha*. Leiden: Brill, 2009.

Adler, William. *Time Immemorial: Primordial History in Christian Chronography from Julius Africanus to George Syncellus*. Dumbarton Oaks Studies 26. Washington, DC: Dumbarton Oaks Research Library and Collection, 1989.

Ahmed, Asad Q. *The Religious Elite of the Early Islamic Ḥijāz: Five Prosopographical Case Studies*. Oxford: Unit for Prosopographical Research, University of Oxford, 2011.

al-Balādhurī. *Ansāb al-ashrāf*. Edited by M. Schloessinger. Jerusalem: Magnes, 1938.

al-Balādhurī. *Ansāb al-ashrāf*. Edited by Wilferd Madelung. Berlin: Klaus Schwarz Verlag, 2002.

Alber, Jan. 'Absurd Catalogues: The Functions of Lists in Postmodernist Fiction'. *Style* 50, no. 3 (2016): 342–58.

al-Bukhārī, *Ṣaḥīḥ*. Vaduz: Thesaurus Islamicus Foundation, 2000.

al-Dārimī, Abū Muḥammad ʿAbd Allāh b. ʿAbd al-Raḥmān. *Musnad*. Edited by Ḥusayn Salīm Asad al-Dārānī. Riyadh: Dār al-Mughnī, 2000.

Alexander, Philip S. 'The Rabbinic Lists of Forbidden Targumim'. *Journal of Jewish Studies* 27 (1976): 177–91.

al-Fārābī, Abū Naṣr. *On the Perfect State (Mabādiʾ ārāʾ ahl al-madīna al-fāḍila)*. Edited and translated by Richard Walzer. Oxford: Oxford University Press, 1985.

Alkaoud, Mohamed, and Mairaj Syed. 'Learning to Identify Narrators in Classical Arabic Texts'. *Procedia Computer Science* 189 (2021): 335–42. https://doi.org/10.1016/j.procs.2021.05.109.

al-Kindī. *Cinq épîtres*. Edited and translated by Daniel Gimaret. Paris: Éditions du CNRS, 1976.

Allard, Michel. 'L'Épître de Kindī sur les définitions'. *Bulletin d'études orientales* 25 (1972): 47–83.

Allony, Nehemya. *The Jewish Library in the Middle Ages: Book Lists from the Cairo Genizah*. Oriens Judaicus 1/3. Jerusalem: Ben-Zvi Institute for the Study of Jewish Communities in the East, Yad Izhak Ben-Zvi, & the Hebrew University of Jerusalem, 2006.

al-Ṭabarī, Muḥammad ibn Jarīr. *Annales quos scripsit Abu Djafar Mohammed ibn Djarir at-Tabari*. Vol. 1. Edited by M. J. de Goeje and J. Barth. Leiden: Brill, 1879.

———. *Taʾrīkh al-rusul wa al-mulūk*. Edited by M. J. de Goeje et al. Leiden: Brill, 1879–1901.

———. *The History of al-Ṭabarī*. 39 vols. Albany: State University of New York Press, 1989–98.

al-Ṭaḥāwī, Abū Jaʿfar Aḥmad. *Al-Taswīya bayn ḥaddathanā wa akhbarnā*. Edited by Samīr ibn Amīn al-Zahīrī. Riyadh: Muṭābiʿ al-Taqnīya, 1990.

Altmann, Alexander, and Samuel M. Stern. *Isaac Israeli: A Neoplatonic Philosopher of the Tenth Century*. Chicago: Chicago University Press, 2009. Originally published in 1958.

al-Yaʿqūbī, Ibn Wāḍiḥ. *Taʾrīkh*. Edited by M. Th. Houtsma. 2 vols. Leiden: Brill, 1883.

Amsler, Monika. *The Babylonian Talmud and Late Antique Book Culture*. Cambridge: Cambridge University Press, 2023.

Andersson, Tobias. *Early Sunni Historiography: A Study of the Tarikh of Khalifa b. Khayyat*. Leiden: Brill, 2019.

Andrist, Patrick. 'Towards a Definition of Paratexts and Paratextuality: The Case of Ancient Greek Manuscripts'. In *Bible as Notepad: Tracing Annotations and Annotation Practices in Late Antique and Medieval Biblical Manuscripts*, edited by Liv Ingeborg Lied and Marilena Maniaci, 130–49. Berlin: De Gruyter, 2018.

———. 'Au croisement des contenus et de la matière: Les structures des sept pandectes bibliques grecques du premier millénaire—Étude comparative sur les structures des contenus et de la matérialité des codex Vaticanus, Sinaiticus, Alexandrinus, Ephrem rescriptus, Basilianus, "Pariathoniensis" et de la Biblia Leonis'. *Scrineum Rivista* 17 (2020): 3–106.

Andrist, Patrick, Paul Canart, and Marilena Maniaci. *La syntaxe du codex: Essai de codicologie structurale*. Turnhout: Brepols, 2013 (new English version forthcoming).

Anheim, Étienne. *Le pouvoir des listes au Moyen Âge*. Paris: Éditions de la Sorbonne, 2020.

Anthony, Sean. 'Was Ibn Wāḍiḥ al-Yaʿqūbī a Shiʿite Historian? The State of the Question'. *Al-ʿUṣūr al-Wusṭā* 24 (2016): 15–41.

Antrim, Zayde. *Routes and Realms: The Power of Place in the Early Islamic World*. New York: Oxford University Press, 2013.

Arnaud, Daniel. *Recherches au pays d'Aštata: Emar*. Vol. 6/4, *Textes de la bibliothèque: Transcriptions et traductions*. Paris: Éditions Recherche sur les civilisations, 1987.

Asper, Markus. 'Katalog'. In *Historisches Wörterbuch der Rhetorik*, vol. 4, edited by Gert Ueding, 915–22. Tübingen: Niemeyer, 1998.

———. *Griechische Wissenschaftstexte: Formen, Funktionen, Differenzierungsgeschichten*. Stuttgart: Franz Steiner, 2007.

Assemani, Giuseppe S. *Bibliotheca Orientalis Clementino-Vaticana*. Vol. 3, Part 1. Rome: Typis Sacrae Congregationis de Propaganda Fide, 1725. https://archive.org/details/BOClementino1, accessed 6 November 2021.

Assmann, Jan. *Das Kulturelle Gedächtnis: Schrift, Erinnerung und politische Identität in frühen Hochkulturen*. Munich: C. H. Beck, 1992.

———. *Religion and Cultural Memory: Ten Studies*. Stanford: Stanford University Press, 2006.

Badger, George P. *The Nestorians and Their Rituals: With a Narrative of the Mission to Mesopotamia and Coordistan in 1842–44*. Vol. 2. London: Joseph Masters, 1852.

Baffioni, Carmela, and Ismail K. Poonawala. *Epistles of the Brethren of Purity: Sciences of the Soul and Intellect, Part 3—An Arabic Critical Edition and English Translation of Epistles 39–41*. Oxford: Oxford University Press & London: Institute of Ismaili Studies, 2017.

Balda-Tillier, Monica. 'La prose amoureuse arabo-islamique médiévale, de l'isnād traditionnel aux sources livresques'. *Journal of Arabic and Islamic Studies* 12 (2012): 186–214.

Barnes, Jonathan. 'The Platonic Lexicon of Timaeus the Sophist'. In *Mantissa: Essays in Ancient Philosophy IV*, edited by Maddalena Bonelli, 244–358. Oxford: Clarendon Press, 2015.

Barney, Stephen. 'Chaucer's Lists'. In *The Wisdom of Poetry: Essays in Early English Literature in Honor of Morton W. Bloomfield*, edited by Larry Dean Benson and Siegfried Wenzel, 189–223. Kalamazoo: Western Michigan University Press, 1982.

Barton, Roman Alexander, Julia Böckling, Sarah J. Link, and Anne Rüggemeier, eds. *Epistemic, Literary, and Visual Enumeration*. Freiburg: University of Freiburg Press, 2022.

Baumstark, Anton. *Geschichte der syrischen Literatur*. Bonn: A. Marcus und E. Webers Verlag, 1922.

Belknap, Robert E. *The List: The Uses and Pleasures of Cataloguing*. New Haven: Yale University Press, 2004.

Bellino, Francesca. 'History and Adab in the *Kitāb al-Maʿārif* of Ibn Qutayba'. *Quaderni di Study Arabi* 16 (2021): 61–97.

Bellver, José. 'MS London, British Library, Add. 7473'. *Ptolemaeus Arabus et Latinus: Manuscripts*, updated 27 November 2020. http://ptolemaeus.badw.de/ms/664, accessed 29 June 2021.

Belser, Julia W., and Lennart Lehmhaus. 'Disability in Rabbinic Judaism'. In *Disability in Antiquity*, edited by Christian Laes, 434–452. London: Routledge, 2017.

Ben Zvi, Ehud. 'The List of the Levitical Cities'. *Journal for the Study of the Old Testament* 54 (1992): 77–106.

Bensly, R. L., and W. E. Barnes. *The Fourth Book of Maccabees and Kindred Documents in Syriac First Edited on Manuscript Authority*. Cambridge: Cambridge University Press, 1895.

Berg, Herbert. 'The *Isnād* and the Production of Cultural Memory: Ibn ʿAbbās as a Case Study'. *Numen* 58 (2011): 259–83. https://doi.org/10.1163/156852711X562317.

Berger, Samuel. *Histoire de la Vulgate pendant les premiers siècles du moyen âge*. Paris: Hachette, 1893.

Berlin, Adele, ed. *The Jewish Study Bible*. Oxford: Oxford University Press, 2004.

Bernard, Daniel. 'Listing and Enlisting: The Rhetoric and Social Meaning of Tractate Avot'. Doctoral dissertation, Department of Religion, Concordia University, Montreal, 2008.

Bernards, Monique. 'Awāʾil'. In *Encyclopaedia of Islam, THREE*, edited by Kate Fleet, Gudrun Krämer, Denis Matringe, John Nawas, and Everett Rowson. Brill, 2014. https://doi.org/10.1163/1573-3912_ei3_COM_24255.

Bernheimer, Teresa. *The ʿAlids: The First Family of Islam*. Edinburgh: Edinburgh University Press, 2013.

Bernheimer, Teresa, and Tamima Bayhoum-Daou. 'Introduction'. In *Early Islamic History*, edited by Tamima Bayhoum-Daou and Teresa Bernheimer, 1:1–8. Critical Concepts in Islamic Studies. London: Routledge, 2013.

Beyer, Susanne, and Lothar Gorris. '"We like lists because we don't want to die": Interview with Umberto Eco.' *Der Spiegel*, 11 November 2009. https://www.spiegel.de/international/zeitgeist/spiegel-interview-with-umberto-eco-we-like-lists-because-we-don-t-want-to-die-a-659577.html, accessed 14 September 2023.

Biesterfeldt, Hinrich. 'Eine arabische Klassifikation der Wissenschaften aus dem 4./5. Jahrhundert H.'. *Studia graeco-arabica* 10 (2020): 261–70.

Böck, Barbara. *Die babylonisch-assyrische Morphoskopie*. Vienna: Institut für Orientalistik der Universität Wien, 2000.

Boddy, Kaira. *The Composition and Tradition of Erimhuš*. Leiden: Brill, 2021.

Bogaert, Pierre-Maurice, 'Les particularités editoriales des Bibles comme exégèse implicite ou proposée: Les sommaires ou capitula donatistes'. In *Lectures bibliques: Colloque du 11 novembre 1980*, 7–21. Brussels: Institutum Judaicum, 1982.

Borrut, Antoine. *Entre mémoir et pouvir: L'espace syrien sous les derniers Omeyyades et les premiers Abbassides (v. 72–193/692–809)*. Leiden: Brill, 2011.

———. 'Vanishing Syria: Periodization and Power in Early Islam', *Der Islam* 91, no. 1 (2014): 37–68.

Borrut, Antoine, and Paul Cobb, eds. *Umayyad Legacies: Medieval Memories from Syria to Spain*. Leiden: Brill, 2010.

Borst, Arno. *Der Turmbau von Babel: Geschichte der Meinungen über Ursprung und Vielfalt der Sprachen und Völker*. 4 vols. Hiersemann: Stuttgart, 1957–63.

Braga, Isabel M.R. Mendes Drumond. 'Os manuscritos árabes de Frei João de Sousa: Erudiçaõ e ensino em Portugal no século XVIII'. In *Documentos y manuscritos árabes de occidente musulmán medieval*, edited by Nuria Martínez de Castilla, 399–417. Madrid: Consejo Superior de Investigaciones Científicas, 2010.

Bray, Julia. 'Lists and Memory: Ibn Qutayba and Muḥammad b. Ḥabīb'. In *Culture and Memory in Medieval Islam: Essays in Honour of Wilferd Madelung*, edited by Farhad Daftary and Josef W. Meri, 210–31. London: I. B. Tauris, 2003.

Brock, Sebastian P. 'Aesop'. In *Gorgias Encyclopedic Dictionary of the Syriac Heritage: Electronic Edition*, edited by Sebastian P. Brock, Aaron M. Butts, George A. Kiraz, and Lucas Van Rompay. https://gedsh.bethmardutho.org/Aesop, accessed 20 December 2020.

———. 'Aḥiqar'. In *Gorgias Encyclopedic Dictionary of the Syriac Heritage: Electronic Edition*, edited by Sebastian P. Brock, Aaron M. Butts, George A. Kiraz, and Lucas Van Rompay. https://gedsh.bethmardutho.org/Ahiqar, accessed 10 December 2020.

———. 'Abraham and the Ravens: A Syriac Counterpart to Jubilees 11–12 and Its Implications'. *Journal for the Study of Judaism* 9 (1978): 135–52.

———. *A Brief Outline of Syriac Literature*, rev. ed. Moran Etho 9. Kottayam: St Ephrem Ecumenical Research Institute, 2008.

———. 'Eleazar, Shmuni and Her Seven Sons in Syriac Tradition'. In *La mémoire des persecutions: Autor des livres des Maccabées*, edited by M.-F. Baslez and O. Munnich, 329–36. Collection de la REJ 56. Paris: Peeters, 2014.

———. '"The Young Daniel": A Little Known Syriac Apocalyptic Text—Introduction and Translation'. In *Revealed Wisdom: Studies in Apocalyptic in Honour of Christopher Rowland*, edited by John Ashton, 267–85. Ancient Judaism and Early Christianity 88. Leiden: Brill, 2014.

Brock, Sebastian P., and James F. Coakley. 'Church of the East'. In *Gorgias Encyclopedic Dictionary of the Syriac Heritage: Electronic Edition*, edited by Sebastian P. Brock, George A. Kiraz, and Lucas Van Rompay. https://gedsh.bethmardutho.org/Church-of-the-East, accessed 4 November 2021.

Brock, Sebastian P., and Susan A. Harvey. *Holy Women of the Syrian Orient*. Berkeley: University of California Press, 1987.

Brooks, E. W. *Joseph and Asenath: The Confession and Prayer of Asenath Daughter of Pentephres the Priest*. London: Society for Promoting Christian Knowledge, 1918.

Brown, Virginia. 'I libri della Bibbia nell'Italia meridionale longobarda'. In *Forme e modelli della tradizione manoscritta della Bibbia*, edited by Paolo Cherubini, 281–308. Vatican City: Scuola Vaticana di Paleografia, Diplomatica e Archivistica, 2005.

Burchard, Christoph. *Untersuchungen zu Joseph und Aseneth*. Wissenschaftliche Untersuchungen zum Neuen Testament 8. Tübingen: Mohr Siebeck, 1965.

Burgess, Richard W., and Shaun Tougher. 'Eusebius of Caesarea'. In *The Encyclopedia of the Medieval Chronicle*, edited by G. Dunphy, 595–97. Leiden: Brill, 2010.

Buschhausen, Heide, and Helmut Buschhausen. *Codex Etschmiadzin: Vollständige Faksimile-Ausgabe von Codex 2374 des Matenadaran Mesrop Maštocʿ in Erevan*. Codices Selecti 105. 2 vols. Graz: Akademische Druck- und Verlagsanstalt, 2001.

Cancik-Kirschbaum, Eva. 'Writing, Language and Textuality: Conditions on the Transmission of Knowledge and the Emergence of Systematic Thought in the Ancient Near East'. In *Globalization of Knowledge and its Consequences*, edited by Jürgen Renn, 125–51. Berlin: Edition Open Access, 2012.

Carey, Sorcha. *Pliny's Catalogue of Culture: Art and Empire in the Natural History*. Oxford: Oxford University Press, 2003.

Casavecchia, Roberta. 'Bibbia e paratesti a Montecassino: i *capitula* al libro della Genesi'. *Scripta: An International Journal of Codicology and Palaeography* 16 (2023, forthcoming).

Casavecchia, Roberta, and Marilena Maniaci. 'Partial Bibles in Southern Italy: The Case of Montecassino'. In *Manuscrits bibliques médiévaux de la Tamise à l'Euphrate: Textes, paratextes, formes et usages*, edited by Patrick Andrist, Élodie Attia, and Marilena Maniaci, 83–102. Berlin: De Gruyter, 2023.

Casavecchia, Roberta, Giulia Orofino, and Marilena Maniaci. *La Bibbia a Montecassino / The Bible at Montecassino*. Turnhout: Brepols, 2021.

———. 'Montecassino e la Bibbia: Forme, contenuti, decorazione / Montecassino and the Bible: Forms, Contents and Decoration'. In Roberta Casavecchia, Giulia Orofino, and Marilena Maniaci, *La Bibbia a Montecassino / The Bible at Montecassino*, 12–69. Turnhout: Brepols, 2021.

Cavallo, Guglielmo. 'Libro e pubblico alla fine del mondo antico'. In *Libri, editori e pubblico nel mondo antico*, 2nd ed., edited by Guglielmo Cavallo, 81–132. Rome: Laterza, 1977.

Cavigneaux, Antoine. 'Une crux sargonica et les quatre vents'. *Orientalia* 76 (2007): 169–73.

Cavigneaux, Antoine, Hans G. Güterbock, Martha T. Roth, and Gertrud Farber. 1985, *The Series Erim-huš = anantu and An-ta-gál = šaqû*. Rome: Pontificium Institutum Biblicum, 1985.

Ceriani, Antonio Maria. *Monumenta Sacra et Profana*. Vol. 2. Milan: Bibliothecae Ambrosianae, 1863.

Charles, R. H. *The Ethiopic Version of the Hebrew Book of Jubilees*. Anecdota Oxoniensia. Oxford: Clarendon Press, 1895.

Charlesworth, James R. 'Introduction for the General Reader'. In *The Old Testament Pseudepigrapha*, edited by James R. Charlesworth, 1:xxi–xxxiv. New York: Doubleday, 1983–1985.

———. 'Foreword: The Fundamental Importance of an Expansive Collection of "Old Testament Pseudepigrapha"'. In *Old Testament Pseudepigrapha: More Noncanonical Scriptures*, vol. 1, edited by Richard Bauckham, James R. Davila, and Alexander Panayotov, xi–xvi. Grand Rapids, MI: Eerdmans, 2013.

Chartier, Roger. *The Order of Books*. Stanford: Stanford University Press, 1994.

Childers, Jeff W. '‘Abdisho‘ bar Brikha Ebedjesus (d. 1318)'. In *Gorgias Encyclopedic Dictionary of the Syriac Heritage: Electronic Edition*, edited by Sebastian P. Brock, Aaron M. Butts, George A. Kiraz, and Lucas Van Rompay. https://gedsh.bethmardutho.org/Abdisho-bar-Brikha, accessed 18 January 2021.

Civil, Miguel. 'The Mesopotamian Lexical Lists: Authors and Commentators'. In *Reconstruyendo el pasado remoto: Estudios sobre el P.O.A. en homenaje a Jorge R. Silva Castillo*, edited by G. del Olmo Lete and D. A. Barreyra Francaroli, 63–69. Sabadell: Editorial AUSA, 2009.

Civil, Miguel, Margaret W. Green, and Wilfred G. Lambert. *Ea A = nâqu, Aa A = nâqu, with their Forerunners and Related Texts*. Rome: Pontificium Institutum Biblicum, 1979.

Cohen, Mark R. *Poverty and Charity in the Jewish Community of Medieval Egypt*. Princeton, NJ: Princeton University Press, 2005.

———. *The Voice of the Poor in the Middle Ages: An Anthology of Documents From the Cairo Geniza*. Princeton, NJ: Princeton University Press, 2013.

Collins, Derek. *Magic in the Ancient Greek World*. Malden, MA: Blackwell, 2008.

Colombi, Emanuela. 'Una prima ricognizione sui *tituli* e i *capitula* nella trasmissione degli *Evangeliorum libri IIII* di Giovenco'.

In *Felici curiositate: Studies in Latin Literature and Textual Criticism from Antiquity to the Twentieth Century—In Honour of Rita Beyers*, edited by Guy Guldentops, Christian Laes, and Gert Partoens, 187–232. Turnhout: Brepols, 2017.

———. 'Titoli e capitoli nella trasmissione del *De Civitate Dei* di Agostino'. In *Diagnostica testuale: Le 'tabulae capitulorum'*, edited by Lucia Castaldi and Valeria Mattaloni, 61–106. Florence: SISMEL, 2019.

Condello, Emma. 'La Bibbia al tempo della riforma gregoriana: Le Bibbie atlantiche'. In *Forme e modelli della tradizione manoscritta della Bibbia*, edited by Paolo Cherubini, 347–72. Vatican City: Scuola Vaticana di Paleografia, Diplomatica e Archivistica, 2005.

Cooper, Alix. *Inventing the Indigenous: Local Knowledge and Natural History in Early Modern Europe*. Cambridge: Cambridge University Press, 2007.

Coxon, Peter W. 'The "List" Genre and Narrative Style in the Court Tales of Daniel'. *Journal for the Study of the Old Testament* 35 (1986): 95–121.

Crawford, Matthew R. 'Ammonius of Alexandria, Eusebius of Caesarea and the Origins of Gospels Scholarship'. *New Testament Studies* 61 (2015): 1–29.

———. *The Eusebian Canon Tables: Ordering Textual Knowledge in Late Antiquity*. Oxford: Oxford University Press, 2019.

Crawford, Matthew R., and Nicholas J. Zola, eds. *The Gospel of Tatian: Exploring the Nature and Text of the Diatessaron*. The Reception of Jesus in the First Three Centuries 3. London: Bloomsbury, 2019.

Daiber, Hans. 'Masāʾil wa-Adjwiba'. In *Encyclopaedia of Islam, Second Edition*, edited by P. Bearman, Th. Bianquis, C. E. Bosworth, E. van Donzel, and W. P. Heinrichs, vol. 6, cols 636–39. Leiden: Brill, 2012.

Daniel, Elton. 'Al-Yaʿqūbī and Shiʿism Reconsidered'. In *ʿAbbasid Studies: Occasional Papers of the School of ʿAbbasid Studies, Cambridge, 6–10 July 2002*, edited by James E. Montgomery, 209–31. Leuven: Peeters, 2004.

Davidson, Garrett. *Carrying on the Tradition: A Social and Intellectual History of Hadith Transmission across a Thousand Years*. Leiden: Brill, 2020.

Davidson, Herbert. 'Saadia's List of Theories of the Soul'. In *Jewish Medieval and Renaissance Studies*, edited by Alexander Altmann, 75–94. Cambridge, MA: Harvard University Press, 1967.

Debié, Muriel. 'Syriac Historiography and Identity Formation'. In *Religious Origins of Nations? The Christian Communities of the Middle East*, edited by Bas ter Haar Romeny, 93–114. Leiden: Brill, 2009.

De Bruyne, Donatien. *Sommaires, divisions et rubriques de la Bible latine*. Namur: Godenne, 1914.

———. *Summaries, Divisions and Rubrics of the Latin Bible*. Turnhout: Brepols, 2014.

de Lagarde, Paul. *Materialien zur Kritik und Geschichte des Pentateuchs*. Vol. 1. Leipzig: Treubner, 1867.

Dell'Omo, Mariano. 'Il codice Casin. 515, una Bibbia gigante in un secolo aureo: L'orizzonte culturale e ideologico di Montecassino negli anni dell'abate Desiderio (1058–1087)'. In

Les Bibles atlantiques: Le manuscrit biblique à l'époque de la réforme de l'église du XIe siècle, edited by Nadia Togni, 317–36. Florence: SISMEL & Edizioni del Galluzzo, 2016.

———. 'Montecassino, Archivio dell'abbazia, Casin. 515'. In *Le Bibbie atlantiche: Il libro delle Scritture tra monumentalità e rappresentazione*, edited by Marilena Maniaci and Giulia Orofino, 131–36. Milan: Centro Tibaldi, 2000.

Denis, Albert-Marie. *Introduction aux pseudépigraphes grecs d'Ancien Testament*. Studia in Veteris Testamenti Pseudepigrapha 1. Leiden: Brill, 1970.

de'Rossi, Azariah. *The Light of the Eyes*. Translated by Joanna Weinberg. Yale Judaica Series 31. New Haven: Yale University Press, 2001.

Deysel, Lesley C. F. 'King Lists and Genealogies in the Hebrew Bible and in Southern Africa'. *Old Testament Essays* 22, no. 3 (2009): 564–79.

Dickinson, Eerik. 'Ibn al-Ṣalāḥ al-Shahrazūrī and the Isnād'. *Journal of the American Oriental Society* 122, no. 3 (2002): 481–505.

Dirkse, Saskia. *The Sum of Things Spoken: A Study of the Gospel Kephalaia and their Tradition, with Critical Editions and Translations*. Berlin: De Gruyter, forthcoming.

DiTommaso, Lorenzo. *The Book of Daniel and the Apocryphal Daniel Literature*. Studia in Veteris Testamenti Pseudepigrapha 20. Leiden: Brill, 2005.

Doležalová, Lucie. 'The Potential and Limitations of Studying Lists'. Introduction in *The Charm of a List: From the Sumerians to Computerised Data Processing*, edited by Lucie

Doležalová, 1–8. Newcastle upon Tyne: Cambridge Scholars, 2009.

Dorival, Gilles. 'La forme littéraire des Hexaples d'Origène'. In *Origeniana Decima: Origen as Writer*, edited by Sylwia Kaczmarek and Henryk Pietras, 601–14. Leuven: Peeters, 2011.

Duval, R. *Lexicon syriacum auctore Hassano bar Bahlule: Voces syriacas græcasque cum glossis syriacis et arabicis complectens*. Vol. 2. Paris: Leroux, 1901.

Ecchellensis, Abraham. *Ope Domini Nostri Iesu Christi incipimus scribere tractum continentem catalogum tibrorum Chaldaeorum, tam ecclesisticorum, quam profanorum: Auctore Hebediesu Metropolita Sobensi*. Rome: Typis Sacrae Congregationis de Propaganda Fide, 1653. https://archive.org/details/bub_gb_5SbBq0O0rEIC/page/n5/mode/2up, accessed 6 November 2021.

Echterhölter, Anna. 'Jack Goody: Die Liste als Praktik'. In *Die Liste: Ordnungen von Dingen und Menschen in Ägypten*, edited by Susanne Deicher and Erik Maroko, 243–60. Berlin: Kadmos, 2015.

Eco, Umberto. *Die unendliche Liste*. Munich: Beck, 2009.

———. *Il vertigine della lista*. Milan: Bompiani, 2009. English translation: *The Infinity of Lists: From Homer to Joyce*. London: MacLehose, 2009. German translation: *Die unendliche Liste*. Munich: Hanser, 2009.

———. *The Infinity of Lists*. New York: Rizzoli, 2009.

El Shamsy, Ahmed. 'The Ur-Muwaṭṭaʾ and Its Recensions'. *Islamic Law and Society* 28, no. 4 (2021): 352–81. https://doi.org/10.1163/15685195-bja10011.

Endress, Gerhard, and Peter Adamson. 'Abū Yūsuf al-Kindī'. In *Philosophy in the Islamic World*, vol. 1, *8th–10th Centuries*, edited by Ulrich Rudolph, Rotraud Hansberger, and Peter Adamson, 143–220. Leiden: Brill, 2017.

Erasmus, Desiderius. *Novum testamentum omne, multo quam antehac diligentius ab Erasmo Roterodamo recognitum, emendatum ac translatum*. Basel: Frobenius, 1519.

Esmaeili, Mohammad Javad. 'The Sciences of the Ancients and Their Divisions: *Aqsām ʿulūm al-awāʾil*—A Text Attributed to Avicenna, an Edition with a Brief Introduction'. *Arabic Sciences and Philosophy* 31 (2021): 183–223.

Eutychius, Patriarch of Alexandria. *Annales*. Translated by Edward Pococke and edited by John Selden. Patrologia Graeca 111. Paris, 1863.

Fabricius, Johann A. *Codex pseudepigraphus Veteris Testamenti, collectus castigatus testimonisque, censuris & animadversionobus illustrates*. Hamburg: Felginer, 1713.

———. *Codicis pseudepigraphi Veteris Testamenti: Volumen alterum accedit Josephi veteris Christiani auctoria Hypomnesticon*. Hamburg: Felginer, 1722–23.

Fadhil, Anmar Abdulillah, and Enrique Jiménez. 'Literary Texts from the Sippar Library I: Two Babylonian Classics'. *Zeitschrift für Assyriologie* 109 (2019): 155–76.

———. 'Literary Texts from the Sippar Library III: A Syncretistic Hymn to Marduk'. *Zeitschrift für Assyriologie* 112 (2022): 229–74.

Fahd, Toufic. 'Ibn Sīrīn'. In *Encyclopaedia of Islam, Second Edition*, edited by P. Bearman, Th. Bianquis, C. E. Bosworth, E. van

Donzel, and W. P. Heinrichs. Brill, 2012. https://doi.org/10.1163/1573-3912_islam_SIM_3382.

Figanier, Joaquim. *Fr. João de Sousa: Mestre e intérprete da língua arábica*. Coimbra: Faculdade de Letras da Universidade de Coimbra, 1949.

Finkel, I. L. 'On an Izbu VII Commentary'. In *If a Man Builds a Joyful House: Assyriological Studies in Honor of Erle Verdun Leichty*, edited by Ann K. Guinan, Maria de J. Ellis, A. J. Ferrara, Sally M. Freedman, Matthew T. Rutz, Leonhard Sassmannshausen, Steve Tinney, and M. W. Waters, 139–48. Leiden: Brill, 2006.

Fleischer, Ezra. *Eretz-Israel Prayer and Prayer Rituals as Portrayed in the Genizah Documents* [in Hebrew]. Publications of the Perry Foundations in the Hebrew University of Jerusalem. Jerusalem: Magnes Press & Hebrew University, 1988.

Fonrobert, Charlotte E. 'The Semiotics of the Sexed Body in Early Halakhic Discourse'. In *How Should Rabbinic Literature Be Read in the Modern World?*, edited by Matthew A. Krauss, 79–104. Piscataway, NJ: Gorgias Press, 2006.

———. 'Regulating the Human Body: Rabbinic Legal Discourse and the Making of Jewish Gender'. In *Cambridge Companion to the Talmud and Rabbinic Literature*, edited by Charlotte Elisheva Fonrobert and Martin Jaffee, 270–94. Cambridge: Cambridge University Press, 2007.

Forness, Philip Michael. 'Narrating History through the Bible in Late Antiquity: A Reading Community for the Syriac Peshiṭta Old Testament in Milan (Ambrosian Library, B 21 Inf)'. *Le Muséon* 127, nos 1–2 (2014): 41–76.

———. 'The First Book of Maccabees in Syriac: Dating and Context'. *Aramaic Studies* 18, no. 1 (2020): 99–123.

Frahm, Eckart. *Babylonian and Assyrian Text Commentaries: Origins of Interpretation*. Münster: Ugarit, 2011.

Frame, Grant. *The Royal Inscriptions of Sargon II, King of Assyria (721–705 BC)*. University Park, PA: Eisenbrauns, 2021.

Frank, Tamar Z. 'Al-Kindī's *Book of Definitions*: Its Place in Arabic Definition Literature'. PhD thesis, Yale University, New Haven, 1975.

Freeman, David L. 'The Gittin "Book of Remedies"'. *Korot* 13 (1998): 151–64.

Frenkel, Miriam. 'Genizah Documents as Literary Products'. In *'From a Sacred Source': Genizah Studies in Honour of Stefan C. Reif*, edited by Ben Outhwaite and Siam Bhayro, 139–55. Cambridge Genizah Studies Series 1. Leiden: Brill, 2010.

———. 'Book Lists from the Cairo Genizah: A Window on the Production of Texts in the Middle Ages'. *Bulletin of the School of Oriental and African Studies* 80, no. 2 (2017): 233–52.

Friedrich, Michael, and Cosima Schwarke. 'Introduction: Manuscripts as Evolving Entities'. In *One-Volume Libraries: Composite and Multiple-Text-Manuscripts*, edited by Michael Friedrich and Cosima Schwarke, 1–26. Studies in Manuscript Cultures 9. Boston: Walter de Gruyter, 2016.

Gabriel, Gottfried. 'Literarische Form und nicht-propositionale Erkenntnis in der Philosophie'. In *Literarische Formen der Philosophie*, edited by Gottfried Gabriel and Christiane

Schildknecht, 1–25. Stuttgart: J.B. Metzlersche Verlagsbuchhandlung, 1990.

Gacek, Adam. *Arabic Manuscripts: A Vademecum for Readers*. Leiden: Brill.

Gallagher, Edmon L., and John D. Meade. *The Biblical Canon Lists from Early Christianity: Text and Analysis*. Oxford: Oxford University Press.

Gardet, Louis. 'Fitna'. In *Encyclopaedia of Islam, Second Edition*, edited by P. Bearman, Th. Bianquis, C. E. Bosworth, E. van Donzel, and W. P. Heinrichs. Brill, 2012. https://doi.org/10.1163/1573-3912_islam_SIM_2389.

Geller, Markham J., 'The Last Wedge'. *Zeitschrift für Assyriologie* 87 (1997): 43–95.

———. 'An Akkadian Vademecum in the Babylonian Talmud'. In *From Athens to Jerusalem: Medicine in Hellenized Jewish Lore and in Early Christian Literature*, edited by Samuel Kottek and Manfred Horst-Mannhoff, 13–32. Rotterdam: Erasmus, 2000.

———. *Akkadian Healing Therapies in the Babylonian Talmud*. Berlin: Max-Planck-Institut für Wissensgeschichte, 2004.

———. *Babylonian Medicine in the Talmud: Cuneiform Remnants in Late Antiquity*. Tübingen: Mohr Siebeck, forthcoming.

Geller, Markham J., Lennart Lehmhaus, Eva Kiesele, and Tanja Hidde. *Sourcebook of Medical Knowledge in Talmudic Texts (Mishnah, Tosefta, Yerushalmi, Bavli)*. Vol. 1, *The Medical Clusters*. Tübingen: Mohr Siebeck, 2024 (forthcoming).

Gelzer, Heinrich. *Sextus Julius Africanus und die byzantinische Chronographie*. Leipzig: Teubner, 1880–98.

Genty, Thomas. 'Les commentaires dans les textes cunéiformes assyro-babyloniens'. MA thesis, Université Lumière Lyon 2, 2010.

George, A. R. *The Babylonian Gilgamesh Epic: Introduction, Critical Edition and Cuneiform Texts*. Oxford: Oxford University Press, 2003.

Gero, Stephen. 'The Legend of the Fourth Son of Noah'. *The Harvard Theological Review* 73 (1980): 321–30.

Gilhus, Ingvild Sælid. 'Betydningen av religiøse lister: *Johannes' hemmelige bok* og oppramsingens kunst'. In *Religion i skrift: Mellom mystikk og materialitet*, edited by Ingvild Sælid Gilhus and Lisbeth Mikaelson, 46–61. Oslo: Universitetsforlaget, 2013.

Goitein, Shlomo D. *A Mediterranean Society: The Jewish Communities of the Arab World as Portrayed in the Documents of the Cairo Geniza*. 6 vols. Berkeley: University of California Press, 1963–1993.

———. 'Three Trousseaux of Jewish Brides from the Fatimid Period'. *Association for Jewish Studies Review* 2 (1977): 77–110.

Golani, Shira J. 'Three Oppressors and Four Saviors: The Three-Four Pattern and the List of Saviors in I Sam 12,9–11'. *Zeitschrift für die alttestamentliche Wissenschaft* 127 (2015): 294–303.

———. 'New Light and Some Reflections on the List of False Prophets (4Q339)'. *Revue de Qumran* 28, no. 2 (2016): 257–65.

Goldberg, Jessica L. 'Lists'. *Jewish History* 32, nos 2–4 (2019): 419–28.

Goody, Jack. *The Domestication of the Savage Mind.* Cambridge: Cambridge University Press, 1977.

———. 'What's in a List?'. In *The Domestication of the Savage Mind,* 74–111. Cambridge: Cambridge University Press, 1977.

Graf, Georg. *Geschichte der christlichen arabischen Literatur.* Vol. 2. Vatican: Biblioteca Apostolica Vaticana, 1947.

Grafton, Anthony, and Megan Williams. *Christianity and the Transformation of the Book: Origen, Eusebius and the Library of Caesarea.* Cambridge, MA: Harvard University Press, 2006.

Graham, William A. 'Traditionalism in Islam: An Essay in Interpretation'. *Journal of Interdisciplinary History* 23, no. 3 (1993): 495–522.

Grohmann, Adolf. 'Arabische Papyri aus der Sammlung der Universität Mailand'. In *Papiri della R. Università di Milano*, edited by Achille Vogliano, 241–69. Milan: U. Hoepli, 1937.

Guttmann, Jacob. *Die philosophischen Lehren des Isaak ben Salomon Israeli.* Münster: Aschendorffsche Verlagsbuchhandlung, 1911.

Haelewyck, Jean-Claude. 'Le canon de l'Ancien Testament dans la tradition syriaque (manuscrits bibliques, listes canoniques, auteurs)'. In *L'Ancien Testament en syriaques*, edited by Françoise Briquel Chatonnet et Philip Le Moigne, 141–72. Études Syriaques 5. Paris: Geuthner, 2008.

Hallo, William W. 'Midrash as Mnemonic: A New Approach to Rabbinic Exegesis'. *Hebrew Union College Annual* 74 (2003): 157–73.

Hanneken, Todd R. '8.5 The Book of Jubilees in Latin'. In *Textual History of the Bible*, edited by Armin Lange, vol. 2, *Deutero-canonical Scriptures*, edited by Frank Feder and Matthias Henze. Brill, 2019. http://doi.org/10.1163/2452-4107_thb_COM_0208050000.

Harkavy, Abraham. 'חדשים גם ישנים'. *haPisgah* 1 (1895): 58–59.

Hasse, Dag N. 'Three Double Translations from Arabic into Latin by Gerard of Cremona and Dominicus Gundisalvi'. In *Reading Proclus and the Book of Causes*, vol. 2, *Translations and Accumulations*, edited by Dragos Calma, 247–74. Leiden: Brill, 2021.

Hasse, Dag N., and Andreas Büttner. 'Notes on Anonymous Twelfth-Century Translations of Philosophical Texts from Arabic into Latin on the Iberian Peninsula'. In *The Arabic, Hebrew and Latin Reception of Avicenna's Physics and Cosmology*, edited by Dag N. Hasse and Amos Bertolacci, 313–69. Boston: Walter de Gruyter, 2018.

Hawting, G. R. 'The Significance of the Slogan *lā ḥukma illā lillāh* and the References to the *Ḥudūd* in the Tradition about the Fitna and the Murder of ʿUthmān'. *Bulletin of the School of Oriental and African Studies* 41, no. 3 (1978): 453–63.

Hein, Christel. *Definition und Einteilung der Philosophie: Von der spätantiken Einleitungsliteratur zur arabischen Enzyklopädie*. Frankfurt: Lang, 1985.

Hengel, Martin. *Die vier Evangelien und das eine Evangelium von Jesus Christus: Studien zu ihrer Sammlung und Entstehung*. Wissenschaftliche Untersuchungen zum Neuen Testament 224. Tübingen: Mohr Siebeck, 2008.

Hilgert, Markus. 'Von "Listenwissenschaft" und "epistemischen" Dingen: Konzeptuelle Annäherungen an altorientalische Wissenspraktiken'. *Journal for General Philosophy of Science* 40 (2009): 277–309.

Hilkens, Andy. *Anonymous Syriac Chronicle of 1234 and Its Sources*. Bibliothèque de Byzantion 18. Leuven: Peeters, 2018.

Himmelfarb, Martha. 'The Pseudepigrapha in Greek: Translation, Composition and the Diaspora'. In *The Old Testament Pseudepigrapha: Fifty Years of the Pseudepigrapha Section at the SBL*, edited by Matthias Henze and Liv Ingeborg Lied, 263–86. Atlanta: SBL Press, 2019.

Hoffmann, Friedhelm. 'Aufzählungen, Listen, Kataloge und Tabellen im alten Ägypten: Formale und inhaltliche Aspekte'. In *Die Liste: Ordnungen von Dingen und Menschen in Ägypten*, edited by Susanne Deicher and Erik Maroko, 87–124. Berlin: Kadmos, 2015.

Hogendijk, Jan P., and Fabian Käs. 'A Survey of Important Studies on Codex Ayasofya 4832'. In *Codex Ayasofya 4832*, edited by Fuat Sezgin, vii–xx. Frankfurt: Institute for the History of Arabic-Islamic Sciences at the Johann Wolfgang Goethe University, 2010.

Horovitz, Josef. 'Alter und Ursprung des Isnād'. *Der Islam* 8, nos 1–2 (1917): 39–47.

———. 'Noch einmal die Herkunft des Isnad'. *Der Islam* 11 (1921): 264–65.

Houghton, Hugh G. H. 'Chapter Divisions, Capitula Lists, and the Old Latin Versions of John'. *Revue Bénédictine* 121, no. 2 (2011): 316–56.

Howe, Nicholas. *The Old English Catalogue Poem*. Copenhagen: Rosenkildeand Bagger, 1985.

Hoyland, Robert. 'Arabic, Greek, and Syriac Historiography in the First Abbasid Century: An Inquiry into Inter-Cultural Traffic'. *ARAM* 3 (1991): 211–33.

Hrůša, Ivan. *Die akkadische Synonymenliste malku = šarru: Eine Textedition mit Übersetzung und Kommentar*. Münster: Ugarit, 2010.

Hullmeine, Paul. 'MS Istanbul, Süleymaniye Kütüphanesi, Ayasofya 4832'. *Ptolemaeus Arabus et Latinus: Manuscripts*, updated 13 November 2020. http://ptolemaeus.badw.de/ms/963, accessed 29 June 2021.

Hullmeine, Paul, and Peter Tarras. 'A New Manuscript Witness of the Kindian Definitions (MS Bursa, Hüseyin Çelebi Yazma Eser Kütüphansei, 1194)'. Unpublished manuscript, 2023.

Humphreys, Stephen. 'Taʾrīkh: II. Historical Writing. 1. In the Arab World'. In *Encyclopaedia of Islam, Second Edition*, edited by P. Bearman, Th. Bianquis, C. E. Bosworth, E. van Donzel, and W. P. Heinrichs. Brill, 2012. https://doi.org/10.1163/1573-3912_islam_COM_1184.

Hunger, Hermann. *Spätbabylonische Texte aux Uruk I*. Berlin: Gebr. Mann, 1976.

Ibn Ḥabīb, Muḥammad. *Kitāb al-Muḥabbar*. Edited by Ilse Lichtenstädter. Hyderabad: Jamʿiyāt Dāʾirat al-Maʿārif al-ʿUthmāniyya, 1942.

Ibn Ḥanbal, Aḥmad. *Al-ʿilal wa-maʿarifah al-rijāl*. Edited by Waṣī Allāh ibn Muḥammad Abbās. Riyadh: Dār al-Khānī, 2001.

Ibn Wahb, ʿAbd Allāh. *Leben und Werk: Al-Muwaṭṭaʾ. Kitāb al-Muḥāraba*. Edited and comments by Miklos Muranyi. Wiesbaden: Harrassowitz, 1992.

———. *Muwaṭṭaʾ al-imām ʿAbd Allāh ibn Wahb*. Edited by Ḥishām ibn Ismāʿīl al-Ṣaynī. Jeddah: Dār Ibn al-Jawziyya, 1999.

Ilan, Tal. 'Biblical Women's Names in the Apocryphal Traditions'. *Journal for the Study of the Pseudepigrapha* 11 (1993): 3–67.

Jacobus, Helen R. 'Calendars from Jewish Documents in the Judean Desert from the First Revolt to Bar Kokhba'. *Henoch* 35, no. 2 (2013): 273–89.

Jaffee, Martin S. 'Writing and Rabbinic Oral Tradition: On Mishnaic Narrative, Lists and Mnemonics'. *Journal of Jewish Thought and Philosophy* 4, no. 1 (1995): 123–46.

James, Montague R. *The Lost Apocrypha of the Old Testament: Collected, Translated and Discussed*. London: Society for Promoting Christian Knowledge, 1920.

Jiménez, Enrique. 'La imagen de los vientos en la literatura babilónica'. PhD dissertation, Universidad Complutense de Madrid, 2013.

———. 'Marginalia on the Cuneiform Commentaries Project. No. 1: A Proverb from the Series *Sidu*', *Nouvelles assyriologiques brèves et utilitaires* 2018, no. 2: 76–77.

———. *Middle and Neo-Babylonian Literary Texts in the Frau Professor Hilprecht Collection, Jena*. Wiesbaden: Harrassowitz, 2022.

Junge, Christian. 'Doing things with Lists: Enumeration in Arabic Prose'. *Journal of Arabic Literature* 50 (2019): 278–97.

Juynboll, G. H. A. 'The Date of the Great *Fitna*'. *Arabica* 20 (1973): 158–59.

———. 'Muslim's Introduction to His Ṣaḥīḥ: Translated and Annotated with an Excursus on the Chronology of *Fitna* and *Bidʿa*'. *Jerusalem Studies in Arabic and Islam* 5 (1984): 263–311.

Kaufhold, Hubert. 'Introduction: The Nomocanon of Metropolitan ʿAbdīšoʿ of Nisibis'. In *The Nomocanon of Metropolitan Abdisho of Nisibis: A Facsimile Edition of MS 64 from the Collection of the Church of the East in Thrissur*, edited by István Perczel, xi–xxiii. Piscataway, NJ: Gorgias Press, 2005.

———. 'Abraham Ecchellensis et le *Catalogue des livres* de ʿAbdīšoʿ bar Brīḵā'. In *Orientalisme, science et controverse: Abraham Ecchellensis (1605–1664)*, edited by Bernard Heyberger, 119–33. Turnhout: Brepols, 2010.

Keim, Katharina E. *Pirqei deRabbi Eliezer: Structure, Coherence, Intertextuality*. Leiden: Brill, 2017.

Kennedy-Day, Kiki. *Books of Definition in Islamic Philosophy: The Limits of Words*. London: RoutledgeCurzon, 2003.

Kessler, Gwynn. *Conceiving Israel: The Fetus in Rabbinic Narratives*. Philadelphia: University of Pennsylvania Press, 2009.

Khalīfa ibn Khayyāṭ. *Taʾrīkh Khalīfa ibn Khayyāṭ*. Edited by Akram al-ʿUmarī. Najaf: Maṭbaʿat al-ādāb, 1967.

———. *Ta'rīkh*. Edited by Suhayl Zakkār. Damascus, 1967–68.

———. *Ta'rīkh*. Edited by M. N. Fawwāz. Beirut, 1995.

Khan, Geoffrey. *Arabic Papyri: Selected Material from the Khalili Collection*. Oxford: Oxford University Press, 1992.

King, L. W. *Cuneiform Texts from Babylonian Tablets in the British Museum, Part XXIV*. London: British Museum, 1908.

Kirk, Athena. *Ancient Greek Lists: Catalogue and Inventory Across Genres*. Cambridge: Cambridge University Press, 2021.

Kister, M. J. 'The Battle of the Ḥarra: Some Socio-Economic Aspects'. In *Studies in Memory of Gaston Wiet*, edited by Myriam Rosen Ayalon, 33–49. Jerusalem: Institute of Asian and African Studies, Hebrew University of Jerusalem, 1977.

Klein-Franke, Felix. 'Al-Kindī's "On Definitions and Descriptions of Things"'. *Le Muséon* 95 (1982): 191–216.

Klie, Jan-Christoph, Michael Bugert, Beto Boullosa, Richard Eckart de Castilho, and Iryna Gurevych. 'The INCEpTION Platform: Machine-Assisted and Knowledge-Oriented Interactive Annotation'. In *Proceedings of System Demonstrations of the 27th International Conference on Computational Linguistics (COLING 2018)*, edited by Dongyan Zhao, 5–9. Association for Computational Linguistics, 2018. https://aclanthology.org/C18-2002.

Knopp, Gisbert. 'Sanctorum Nomina Seriatim: Die Anfänge der Allerheiligenlitanei und ihre Verbindung mit den "Laudes regiae"'. *Römische Quartalschrift* 65 (1970): 185–231.

Kottek, Samuel. 'Embryology in Talmudic and Midrashic Literature'. *Journal of the History of Biology* 14, no. 2 (1981): 299–315.

Kraft, Robert A. 'Daniel Outside the Traditional Jewish Canon: In the Footsteps of M. R. James'. http://ccat.sas.upenn.edu/rak/courses/735/Parabiblical/jamesdan.htm, accessed 6 November 2021.

———. 'Eve'. https://ccat.sas.upenn.edu/rak/courses/735/Parabiblical/jameseve.htm, accessed 20 January 2021.

———. 'Og and the Giants'. http://ccat.sas.upenn.edu/rak/courses/735/Parabiblical/jamesog.htm, accessed 20 January 2021.

———. '"Parabiblical Literature" in Early Judaism and Early Christianity'. http://ccat.sas.upenn.edu/rak/courses/735/Parabiblical/intro.htm, accessed 15 September 2020.

———. '"Parabiblical" Titles from Lists, with a Comprehensive List'. http://ccat.sas.upenn.edu/rak/courses/735/Parabiblical/lists.htm, accessed 15 September 2020.

———. 'Reviving, Refurbishing, and Repurposing the *Lost Apocrypha* of M. R. James'. http://ccat.sas.upenn.edu/rak/courses/735/Parabiblical/jameschr.htm, accessed 20 January 2021.

———. 'Updated version of Montague R. James's *The Lost Apocrypha of the Old Testament: Their Titles and Fragments Collected, Translated and Discussed* (1920)'. http://ccat.sas.upenn.edu/rak/publics/mrjames/jamesnew.htm, accessed 20 January 2021.

Kramer, Ross S. *When Aseneth Met Joseph: A Late Antique Tale of the Biblical Patriarch and His Egyptian Wife, Reconsidered.* New York: Oxford University Press, 1998.

Krause, Max. 'Stambuler Handschriften islamischer Mathematiker'. *Quellen und Studien zur Geschichte der Mathematik, Abt. B. Astronomie und Physik* 3 (1936): 437–532.

Laehn, Thomas R. *Pliny's Defense of Empire*. London: Routledge, 2013.

Lambert, W. G. 'The Historical Development of the Mesopotamian Pantheon'. In *Unity and Diversity: Essays in the History, Literature, and Religion of the Ancient Near East*, edited by Hans Goedicke and J. J. M. Roberts, 191–200. Baltimore: Johns Hopkins University Press, 1975.

———. 'Babylonien und Israel'. *Theologische Realenzyklopädie* 5 (1980), 67–79.

———. 'Ancient Mesopotamian Gods. Superstition, Philosophy, Theology'. *Revue de l'histoire des religions* 207 (1990): 115–130.

———. 'Notes on malku = šarru'. *Nouvelles assyriologiques brèves et utilitaires* 2011, no. 2: 36–37.

———. *Babylonian Creation Myths*. Winona Lake, IN: Eisenbrauns, 2013.

Lammer, Andreas. 'Defining Nature: From Aristotle to Philoponus to Avicenna'. In *Aristotle and the Arabic Tradition*, edited by Ahmed Alwishah and Josh Hayes, 121–42. Cambridge: Cambridge University Press, 2015.

———. *The Elements of Avicenna's Physics: Greek Sources and Arabic Innovations*. Berlin: Walter de Gruyter, 2018.

Landsberger, Benno. *The Series HAR-ra = hubullu: Tablet XV*. Rome: Pontificium Institutum Biblicum, 1967.

Lange, Christian, Maksim Abdul Latif, Yusuf Celik, Melle Lyklema, Dafne van Kuppevelt, and Janneke van der Zwaan. 'Text Mining Islamic Law'. *Islamic Law and Society* (2021): 234–81. https://doi.org/10.1163/15685195-bja10009.

Langer, Ruth. 'The Early Emergence of Jewish Daily Morning Psalms Recitation, *Pesuqe de-Zimra*'. In *The Psalms in Jewish Liturgy, Ritual and Community Formation from Antiquity to the Middle Ages: Biblical Texts in Dynamic, Pluralistic Contexts*, edited by Claudia Bergmann, Tessa Rajak, Benedikt Kranemann, and Rebecca Ullrich. Leiden: Brill, forthcoming.

Larocca, Noemi. 'Le più antiche Bibbie atlantiche: Un contributo paleografico'. *Scripta: An International Journal of Codicology and Paleography* 4 (2011): 49–77.

Larsen, Matthew D. C. *Gospels before the Book*. Oxford: Oxford University Press, 2019.

Lebram, J. C. H. 'Tobit'. In *The Old Testament in Syriac According to the Peshitta Version: Canticles or Odes; Prayer of Manasseh; Apocryphal Psalms; Psalms of Solomon; Tobit; 1 (3) Esdras*, edited by W. Baars, J. C. H. Lebram, and H. Schneider, 1–54. Leiden: Brill, 1972.

Lehmhaus, Lennart. 'Listenwissenschaft and the Encyclopedic Hermeneutics of Knowledge in Talmud and Midrash'. In *In the Wake of the Compendia: Infrastructural Contexts and the Licensing of Empiricism in Ancient and Medieval Mesopotamia*, edited by J. Cale Johnson, 59–101. Berlin: De Gruyter, 2015.

———. 'Beyond *Dreckapotheke*, Between Facts and Feces: Talmudic Recipes and Therapies in Context'. In *Collecting Recipes: Byzantine and Jewish Pharmacology in Dialogue*, edited by Lennart Lehmhaus and Matteo Martelli, 221–54. Berlin: De Gruyter, 2017.

———. '"Curiosity Cures the Reb": Studying Talmudic Medical Discourses in Context'. *Ancient Jew Review*, 11 October 2017. https://www.ancientjewreview.com/read/2017/10/2/curiosity-cures-the-reb-studying-talmudic-medical-discourses-in-context, accessed 19 November 2021.

———. '"Hidden Transcripts" in Late Midrash Made Visible: Hermeneutical and Literary Processes of Borrowing in a Multi-Cultural Context'. In *Exegetical Crossroads: Understanding Scripture in Judaism, Christianity and Islam in the Premodern Orient*, edited by Georges Tamer, Regina Grundmann, Assaad Elias Kattan, and Karl Pinggéra, 199–242. Berlin: De Gruyter, 2018.

———. 'Bodies of Texts, Bodies of Tradition: Medical Expertise and Knowledge of the Body among Rabbinic Jews in Late Antiquity'. In *Finding, Inheriting or Borrowing? Construction and Transfer of Knowledge about Man and Nature in Antiquity and the Middle Ages*, edited by Jochen Althoff, Dominik Berrens, and Tanja Pommerening, 123–66. Bielefeld: Transcript, 2019.

———. 'Making Moral Lists: The Creation and Teaching of Right Behavior in *Seder Eliyahu* and Rabbinic Traditions'. Unpublished manuscript, 2021.

———. 'Lore and Order: Enlisting Rabbinic Epistemology'. In *Forms of List-Making: Epistemic, Literary and Visual Enumeration*, edited by Roman Alexander Barton, Julia Böckling, Sarah Link, and Anne Rüggemeier, 53–80. New York: Palgrave Macmillan, 2022.

———. 'The Shoteh in Rabbinic Sources. Between Intellectual Disability or Mental Illness?' In *'Madness' in the Ancient World: Innate or Acquired?*, edited by Christian Laes and Irina Metzler, 189–228. Turnhout: Brepols, 2023.

Lepicard, Etienne. 'The Embryo in Ancient Rabbinic Literature: Between Religious Law and Didactic Narratives—An Interpretive Essay'. *History and Philosophy of the Life Sciences* 32, no. 1 (2010): 21–41.

Leube, Georg. *Kinda in der frühislamischen Geschichte: Eine prosopographische Studie auf der Basis der frühen und klassischen arabisch-islamischen Geschichtsschreibung*. Baden-Baden: Ergon, 2017.

———. 'Subversive Philology? Prosopography as a Relational and Corpus-Based Approach to Early Islamic History'. In *New Methods in the Study of Islam*, edited by Abbas Aghdassi and Aaron W. Hughes. Forthcoming.

Lev, Efraim. 'Drugs Held and Sold by Pharmacists of the Jewish Community of Medieval (11–14th centuries) Cairo According to Lists of "Materia Medica" Found at the Taylor-Schechter Genizah Collection, Cambridge'. *Journal of Ethnopharmacology* 110, no. 2 (2007): 275–93.

Lichtenstädter, Ilse. 'Muḥammad ibn Ḥabîb and His Kitâb al-Muḥabbar'. *Journal of the Royal Asiatic Society of Great Britain and Ireland* 1939, no. 1: 1–27.

Lied, Liv Ingeborg. 'Between "Text Witness" and "Text on the Page": Trajectories in the History of Editing the Epistle of Baruch'. In *Snapshots of Evolving Traditions: Jewish and Christian Manuscript Culture, Textual Fluidity, and New Philology*, edited by Liv Ingeborg Lied and Hugo Lundhaug, 272–96. Texte und Untersuchungen zur Geschichte der altchristlichen Literatur 175. Berlin: De Gruyter, 2017.

———. *Invisible Manuscripts: Textual Scholarship and the Survival of 2 Baruch*. Studien und Texte zu Antike und Christentum 128. Tübingen: Mohr Siebeck, 2021.

Light, Laura. 'The Thirteenth Century and the Paris Bible'. In *The New Cambridge History of the Bible*, vol. 2, *From 600 to 1450*, edited by Richard Marsden and E. Ann Matter, 380–90. Cambridge: Cambridge University Press, 2012.

Lipscomb, W. Lowndes. 'A Tradition from the Book of Jubilees in Armenian'. *Journal of Jewish Studies* 29, no. 2 (1978): 149–63. https://doi.org/10.18647/872/JJS-1978.

———. 'The Wives of the Patriarchs in the *Eklogē Historian*'. *Journal of Jewish Studies* 30, no. 1 (1979): 91. https://doi.org/10.18647/893/JJS-1979.

Lobrichon, Guy. 'Riforma ecclesiastica e testo della Bibbia'. In *Le Bibbie atlantiche: Il libro delle Scritture tra monumentalità e rappresentazione*, edited by Marilena Maniaci and Giulia Orofino, 15–26. Milan: Centro Tibaldi, 2000.

———. 'Le succès ambigu des Bibles "atlantiques": Triomphes et résistances dans l'Ouest européen, XIe–XIIe siècle'. In *Les Bibles atlantiques: Le manuscrit biblique à l'époque de la réforme de l'église du XIe siècle*, edited by Nadia Togni, 247–81. Florence: SISMEL & Edizioni del Galluzzo, 2016.

Machinist, Peter. 'On Self-Consciousness in Mesopotamia'. In *The Origins and Diversity of Axial Age Civilizations*, edited by S. N. Eisenstadt, 183–202, 511–18. Albany: SUNY Press, 1986.

Mai, Angelo. *Scriptorum veterum nova collection*. Vol. 10. Rome: Typis Collegii Urbani, 1838.

Mainberger, Sabine. *Die Kunst des Aufzählens: Elemente zu einer Poetik des Enumerativen*. Berlin: De Gruyter, 2003.

———. 'Ordnen/Aufzählen'. In *Literatur und materielle Kultur*, edited by Susanne Scholz and Ulrike Vedder, 91–98. Berlin: De Gruyter, 2018.

———. 'Musing about a Table of Contents: Some Theoretical Questions Concerning Lists and Catalogues'. In *Lists and Catalogues in Ancient Literature and Beyond: Towards a Poetics of Enumeration*, edited by Rebecca Laemmle, Cédric Scheidegger Laemmle, and Katharina Wesselmann, 19–34. Berlin: De Gruyter, 2021.

Mālik ibn Anas. *Muwaṭṭaʾ al-imām Mālik riwāya Muḥammad ibn al-Ḥasan al-Shaybānī*. Edited by ʿAbd al-Wahāb ʿAbd al-Laṭīf. Beirut: al-Maktaba al-ʿIlmiyya, 1979.

———. *Muwaṭṭaʾ al-imām Mālik riwāya Ibn Ziyād*. Edited by Muḥammad al-Shādhalī al-Nayfir. Beirut: Dār al-Gharib al-Islamiyya, 1980.

———. *Muwaṭṭaʾ riwāya Yaḥyá al-Laythī*. Edited by Muḥammad Musafá al-Aʿẓamī. Abu Dhabi: Muʾasasah Zāyd ibn Sulṭān, 2004.

Maniaci, Marilena. 'Written Evidence in the Italian Giant Bibles: Around and beyond the Sacred Text'. In *Bible as Notepad: Tracing Annotations and Annotation Practices in Late Antique and Medieval Biblical Manuscripts*, edited by Liv Ingeborg Lied and Marilena Maniaci, 85–100. Berlin: De Gruyter, 2018.

———. 'La struttura delle Bibbie atlantiche'. In *Le Bibbie atlantiche: Il libro delle Scritture tra monumentalità e rappresentazione*, edited by Marilena Maniaci and Giulia Orofino, 47–60. Milan: Centro Tibaldi, 2000. English version: 'The Structure of Atlantic Bibles' in *Trends in Statistical Codicology*, edited by Marilena Maniaci, 35–63, Berlin: De Gruyter, 2021.

Maniaci, Marilena, and Gulia Orofino. 'Montecassino, Bibbia, riforma'. In *La reliquia del sangue di Cristo: Mantova, l'Italia e l'Europa al tempo di Leone IX*, edited by Glauco Maria Cantarella and Arturo Calzona, 389–407. Mantova: Fondazione Centro Studi Leon Battista Alberti & Scripta Edizioni, 2012.

———. 'Dieci anni di studi sulle Bibbie atlantiche a Cassino'. In *Les Bibles atlantiques: Le manuscrit biblique à l'époque de la réforme de l'église du XIe siècle*, edited by Nadia Togni, 5–19. Florence: SISMEL & Edizioni del Galluzzo, 2016.

———, eds. *Le Bibbie atlantiche: Il libro delle Scritture tra monumentalità e rappresentazione*. Milan: Centro Tibaldi, 2000.

Mann, Jacob. 'Genizah Fragments of the Palestinian Order of Service'. *Hebrew Union College Annual* 2 (1925): 269–338.

Mazza, Roberta. 'Papyrology and Ethics'. Paper presented at the 28th International Congress of Papyrology, Barcelona, 5 August 2016.

McDonald, Lee Martin, and James A. Sanders, eds. *The Canon Debate*. Peabody, MA: Hendrickson, 2002.

McKenzie, Judith S., and Francis Watson. *The Garima Gospels: Early Illuminated Gospel Books from Ethiopia*. Oxford: Oxford University Press, 2016.

Melchert, Christopher. 'The Rightly Guided Caliphs: The Range of Views Preserved in *Ḥadīth*'. In *Political Quietism in Islam: Sunnī and Shīʿī Practice and Thought*, edited by Saud al-Sarhan, 63–80. London: I. B. Tauris, 2019.

Michalowski, Piotr. 'Negation as Description: The Metaphor of Everyday Life in Early Mesopotamian Literature'. *Aula Orientalis* 9 (1991): 131–36.

Migne, J.-P. *Dictionnaire des apocryphes, ou collection de tous les livres apocryphes*. Paris: J.-P. Migne & Ateliers Catholique, 1856.

Milic, Louis. *Stylists on Style*. New York: Scribner's, 1969.

Milik, J. T. 'Recherches sur la version grecque du livre des Jubilés'. *Revue biblique* 78, no. 4 (1971): 545–57.

Minov, Sergey. 'Syriac'. In *A Guide to Early Jewish Texts and Traditions in Christian Transmission*, edited by Alexander Kulik, Gabriele Boccaccini, Lorenzo DiTommaso, David Hamidovic, and Michael E. Stone, 95–137. Oxford: Oxford University Press, 2019.

———. 'A Syriac Tabula Gentium from the Early Abbasid Period: Dawid bar Pawlos on Genesis 10.' Христианский Восток [The Christian Orient] 9 (2021): 57–76.

Monger, Matthew P. '4Q216 and the State of Jubilees at Qumran'. *Revue de Qumran* 26 (2014): 595–612.

———. 'The Many Forms of Jubilees: A Reassessment of the Manuscript Evidence from Qumran and the Lines of Transmission of the Parts and Whole of Jubilees'. *Revue de Qumran* 30, no. 2 (2018): 191–211.

Mroczek, Eva. *The Literary Imagination in Jewish Antiquity*. New York: Oxford University Press, 2016.

Mulder, Tara. 'Ancient Medicine and Fetal Personhood'. *Eidolon*, 16 October 2015. https://eidolon.pub/ancient-medicine-and-the-straw-man-of-fetal-personhood-73eed36b945a, accessed 19 November 2021.

Müller-Wille, Staffan, and Isabelle Charmantier. 'Lists as Research Technologies'. *Isis* 103, no. 4 (2012): 743–52.

Muranyi, Miklos. 'Zur Entwicklung der *ʿilm al-riǧāl*-Literatur im 3. Jahrhundert d.H.'. *Zeitschrift der Deutschen Morgenländischen Gesellschaft* 142 (1992): 57–71.

Muslim ibn al-Ḥajjāj. *Ṣaḥīḥ*. Vaduz: Thesaurus Islamicus Foundation, 2000.

Na'aman, Nadav. 'Solomon's District List (1 Kings 4:7–19) and the Assyrian Province System in Palestine'. *Ugarit-Forschungen* 33 (2001): 419–36.

Nador, G. 'Some Numerical Categories in Ancient Rabbinic Literature: The Numbers Ten, Seven and Four'. *Acta Orientalia* 14 (1962): 301–15.

Nestle, Eberhard. 'Die Eusebianische Evangelien-Synopse'. *Neue kirchliche Zeitschrift* 19 (1908): 40–51, 93–114, 219–232.

Neusner, Jacob. 'The Mishna's Generative Mode of Thought: Listenwissenschaft and Analogical-Contrastive Reasoning'. *Journal of the American Oriental Society* 110, no. 2 (1990): 317–21.

Nigst, Lorenz, Maxim Romanov, Sarah Bowen Savant, Masoumeh Seydi, and Peter Verkinderen. 'OpenITI: a Machine-Readable Corpus of Islamicate Texts', version 2021.1.4. Zenodo. http://doi.org/10.5281/zenodo.4513723.

Noam, Vered. 'The Origin of the List of David's Songs in "David's Compositions"'. *Dead Sea Discoveries* 13, no. 2 (2006): 134–49.

Noegel, Scott B. 'Abraham's Ten Trials and Biblical Literary Convention'. *Jewish Bible Quarterly* 21 (2003): 73–83.

Nöldeke, Theodor. *Die Sammlung des Qorāns*. Part 2 of *Geschichte des Qorāns*. Edited by Friedrich Schwally. Leipzig: Dieterich, 1919.

Nordenfalk, Carl. *Die spätantiken Kanontafeln: Kunstgeschichtliche Studien über die eusebianische Evangelien-Konkordanz in den vier ersten Jahrhunderten ihrer Geschichte*. 2 vols. Göteborg: O. Isacsons, 1938.

———. 'The Beginnings of Book Decoration'. In *Beiträge für Georg Swarzenski zum 11. Januar 1951*, edited by Oswald Goetz, 9–20. Berlin: Gebr. Mann, 1951. Reprinted as pp. 1–8 of: Carl Nordenfalk. *Studies in the History of Book Illumination*. London: Pindar Press, 1992.

Noth, Albrecht. *Quellenkritische Studien zu Themen, Formen und Tendenzen frühislamischer Geschichtsüberlieferung*. Bonn: Orientalischen Seminars, 1970.

Nulman, Macy. *The Encyclopedia of Jewish Prayer: The Ashkenazic and Sephardic Rites*. Lanham: Jason Aronson, 1996.

O'Loughlin, Thomas. 'Harmonizing the Truth: Eusebius and the Problem of the Four Gospels'. *Traditio* 65 (2010): 1–29.

Oelsner, Joachim. 'Überlegungen zu den 'Graeco-Babyloniaca''. In *'He Has Opened Nisaba's House of Learning': Studies in Honor of Åke Waldemar Sjöberg on the Occasion of His 89th Birthday on August 1st, 2013*, edited by L. Sassmannshausen, 147–64. Leiden: Brill, 2014.

Olsson, Joshua T. '*Ḥudūd* in al-Kindī and Ibn Rabban al-Ṭabarī'. *Jerusalem Studies in Arabic and Islam* 41 (2014): 245–60.

Olszowy-Schlanger, Judith. 'Glossary of Difficult Words in the Babylonian Talmud (Seder Mo'ed) on a Rotulus'. In *Jewish Education from Antiquity to the Middle Ages: Studies in Honour of Philip S. Alexander*, edited by George J. Brooke and Renate Smithuis, 297–323. Ancient Judaism and Early Christianity 100. Leiden: Brill, 2017.

Oppenheim, A. Leo. 'Zur keilschriftlichen Omenliteratur'. *Orientalia* 5 (1936): 199–228.

Oppenheim, A. Leo, Erica Reiner, and Martha T. Roth. *The Assyrian Dictionary of the Oriental Institute of the University of Chicago*. Chicago: Oriental Institute, 1956–2011.

Orofino, Giulia. 'Per un'iconografia comparata delle Bibbie atlantiche'. In *Cicli e immagini bibliche nella miniatura: Atti del VI Congresso di Storia della miniatura (Urbino, 3–6 ottobre 2002)*, edited by Laura Alidori, 29–40. Florence: Centro Di, 2003. Also *Rivista di Storia della miniatura* 6–7 (2001–2): 29–40.

Pavlovitch, Pavel. 'The Origin of the *Isnād* and al-Mukhtār b. Abī ʿUbayd's Revolt in Kūfa (66–7/685–7)'. *Al-Qantara* 39 (2018): 17–48.

Perczel, István, ed. *The Nomocanon of Metropolitan Abdisho of Nisibis: A Facsimile Edition of MS 64 from the Collection of the Church of the East in Thrissur*. Piscataway, NJ: Gorgias Press, 2005.

Perles, J. *Beiträge zur Geschichte der hebraischen und aramäischen Studien*. Munich: T. Ackermann, 1884.

Philips, David. 'The Reception of Peshitta Chronicles: Some Elements for Investigation'. In *The Peshitta: Its Use in Literature and Liturgy—Papers Read at the Third Peshitta Symposium*, edited by Bas ter Haar Romeny, 259–95. Monographs of the Peshitta Institute 15. Leiden: Brill, 2006.

Phillips, Kim. 'A Shorthand Psalter: T-S A43.8'. *Fragment of the Month*, May 2020. Cambridge University Library. https://www.lib.cam.ac.uk/collections/departments/taylor-schechter-genizah-research-unit/fragment-month/fotm-2020/fragment-3, accessed 28 June 2021.

Polliack, Meira. 'Bible Translations and Word-Lists in the Cairo Genizah'. *Bulletin of the Israeli Academic Center in Cairo* 1997 (21): 31–34.

Pomata, Gianna. 'The Medical Case Narrative: Distant Reading of an Epistemic Genre'. *Literature and Medicine* 32, no. 1 (2014): 1–23.

Pommerening, Tanja. 'Bäume, Sträucher und Früchte in altägyptischen Listen: Eine Betrachtung zur Kategorisierung und Ordnung'. In *Die Liste: Ordnungen von Dingen und Menschen in Ägypten*, edited by Susanne Deicher and Erik Maroko, 125–66. Berlin: Kadmos, 2015.

Quack, Joachim Friedrich. 'Ägyptische Listen und ihre Expansion in Unterricht und Repräsentation'. In *Die Liste: Ordnungen von Dingen und Menschen in Ägypten*, edited by Susanne Deicher and Erik Maroko, 51–86. Berlin: Kadmos, 2015.

Quentin, Henri. *Mémoire sur l'établissement du texte de la Vulgate*. Vol. 1, *Octateuque*. Rome: Desclée & Paris: Gabalda, 1922.

Rashed, Roshdi, and Jean Jolivet. *Œuvres philosophiques & scientifiques d'al-Kindī*, vol. 2, *Métaphysique et cosmologie*. Leiden: Brill, 1998.

Raziel-Kretzmer, Vered. 'How Late was the Palestinian Rite Practiced in Egypt? New Evidence from the Cairo Genizah' [in Hebrew]. *Tarbiz* 85 (2018): 309–36.

———. 'The Palestinian Morning Service According to Prayerbook Fragments from the Cairo Genizah' [in Hebrew]. PhD dissertation, Ben-Gurion University, Beer Sheva, 2018.

Raziel-Kretzmer, Vered, and Jonathan Ben-Dov. 'The Qumran Psalter and the Medieval Palestinian *Tefillat ha-Shir*'. In *On Wings of Prayer: Sources of Jewish Worship—Essays in Honor of Professor Stefan C. Reif on the Occasion of his Seventy-Fifth Birthday*, edited by Nuria Calduch-Benages, Michael W. Duggan, and Dalia Marx, 299–316. Deuterocanonical and Cognate Literature Studies 44. Berlin: De Gruyter, 2019.

Redditt, Paul L. 'The Census List in Ezra 2 and Nehemiah 7: A Suggestion'. In *New Perspectives on Ezra-Nehemiah: History and Historiography, Text, Literature, and Interpretation*, edited by Isaac Kalimi, 223–40. Winona Lake, IN: Eisenbrauns, 2012.

Reed, Annette Y. 'Ancient Jewish Sciences and the Historiography of Judaism'. In *Ancient Jewish Sciences and the History of Knowledge in the Second Temple Period*, edited by Jonathan Ben-Dov and Seth L. Sanders, 195–254. New York: New York University Press, 2014.

———. 'Introduction to Forgetting'. Unpublished manuscript, 2021.

Reisman, David, and Amos Bertolacci. 'Thābit ibn Qurra's *Concise Exposition of Aristotle's Metaphysics*: Text, Translation, and Commentary'. In *Thābit ibn Qurra: Science and Philosophy in Ninth-Century Baghdad*, edited by Roshdi Rashed, 715–76. Berlin: Walter de Gruyter, 2009.

Ri, Su-Min. *La caverne des trésors: Les deux recensions syriaques*. Corpus Scriptorum Christianorum Orientalium 486. Leuven: Peeters, 1987.

Richardson, Brian. 'Modern Fiction, the Poetics of Lists, and the Boundaries of Narrative'. *Style* 50, no. 3 (2016): 327–41.

Rine, C. Rebecca. 'Canon Lists Are Not Just Lists'. *Journal of Biblical Literature* 139, no. 4 (2020): 809–31.

Ritter, Hellmut, and Martin Plessner. 'Schriften Jaʿqūb ibn Isḥāq al-Kindī's in Stambuler Bibliotheken'. *Archiv orientální* 6, no. 1 (1932): 363–72.

Robinson, Chase F. *Islamic Historiography*. Cambridge: Cambridge University Press, 2003.

———. *ʿAbd al-Malik*. Makers of the Muslim World. Oxford: Oneworld, 2007.

Robson, James. 'Ibn Isḥāq's Use of the *Isnād*'. *Bulletin of the John Rylands University Library of Manchester* 38, no. 2 (1956): 449–65.

Ron, Zvi. 'The Genealogical List in the Book of Ruth: A Symbolic Approach'. *Jewish Bible Quarterly* 38, no. 2 (2010): 85–92.

Rosenberg, Daniel, and Anthony Grafton. *Cartographies of Time*. New York: Princeton Architectural Press, 2010.

Rosenthal, Franz. *The History of Ṭabarī*. Vol. 1. Albany: State University of New York Press, 1989.

———. 'Awāʾil'. In *Encyclopaedia of Islam, Second Edition*, edited by P. Bearman, Th. Bianquis, C. E. Bosworth, E. van Donzel, and W. P. Heinrichs. Brill, 2012. https://doi.org/10.1163/1573-3912_islam_SIM_0863.

Rotter, Gernot. *Die Umayyaden und der zweite Bürgerkrieg (680–692)*. Wiesbaden: Franz Steiner Verlag, 1982.

Russell, James R. 'On an Armenian Word List from the Cairo Geniza'. *Iran & the Caucasus* 17, no. 2 (2013): 189–214.

Ruzzier, Chiara. *Entre Université et ordres mendiants: La production des bibles portatives latines au XIIIe siècle*. Berlin: De Gruyter, 2022.

———. 'The Miniaturization of Bible Manuscripts in the Thirteenth Century: A Comparative Study'. In *Form and Function in the Late Medieval Bible*, edited by Eyal Poleg and Laura

Light, 105–25. Leiden: Brill, 2013. Also in *Trends in Statistical Codicology*, edited by Marilena Maniaci, 65–86, Berlin: De Gruyter, 2021.

Savant, Sarah. *The New Muslims of Post-Conquest Iran*. Cambridge: Cambridge University Press, 2013.

Schacht, Joseph. *The Origins of Muhammadan Jurisprudence*. Oxford: Clarendon Press, 1979.

Schaffrick, Matthias, and Niels Werber. 'Einleitung: Die Liste, paradigmatisch'. *Zeitschrift für Literaturwissenschaft und Linguistik* 47, no. 3 (2017): 303–16.

Schmoldt, H. 'Die Schrift "Vom Jungen Daniel" und "Daniels Letzte Vision": Herausgabe und Interpretation zweier apokalyptischer Texte'. PhD dissertation, University of Hamburg, 1972.

Schofer, Jonathan W. 'Ethical Formation and Rabbinic Ethical Compilations'. In *The Cambridge Companion to The Talmud and Rabbinic Literature*, edited by Charlotte Elisheva Fonrobert and Martin Jaffee, 313–35. Cambridge: Cambridge University Press, 2007.

Scolnic, B. *Theme and Context in Biblical Lists*. Atlanta: University Press of America, 1995.

Sergi, Omer. 'The Alleged Judahite King List: Its Historical Setting and Possible Date'. *Semitica* 56 (2014): 233–47.

Şeşen, Ramazan. 'La description et la critique des manuscrits philosophiques arabo-islamiques'. In *Essays in Honour of Ekmeleddin İhsanoğlu*, vol. 1, *Societies, Cultures, Sciences: A Col-*

lection of Articles, edited by Mustafa Kaçar and Zeynep Durukal, 663–700, Istanbul: Research Centre for Islamic History, Art and Culture, 2006.

Sezgin, Fuat, ed. *Codex Ayasofya 4832: A Collection of Mathematical, Philosophical, Meteorological and Astronomical Treatises by Thābit ibn Qurra, Abū Yūsuf Yaʿqūb al-Kindī, Abū Ṣaqr al-Qabīṣī, Abū Sahl al-Kūhī, and Others*. Frankfurt: Institute for the History of Arabic-Islamic Sciences at the Johann Wolfgang Goethe University, 2010.

Sharpe, Richard. *Titulus: Identifying Medieval Latin Texts—An Evidence-Based Approach*. Turnhout: Brepols, 2003.

Shasha, Roy. 'The Forms and Functions of Lists in the Mishnah'. PhD thesis, University of Manchester, 2006. http://www.melilahjournal.org/p/2007.html, accessed 19 November 2021.

Shils, Edward. *Tradition*. Chicago: University of Chicago Press, 1981.

Shinnar, Shulamit. 'The Experiments of Cleopatra: Foreign, Gendered, and Empirical Knowledge in the Babylonian Talmud'. In *Defining Jewish Medicine: Transfer of Medical Knowledge in Premodern Jewish Cultures and Traditions*, edited by Lennart Lehmhaus, 215–44. Wiesbaden: Harrassowitz, 2021.

Shivtiel, Avihai. 'Judaeo-Romance and Judaeo-Arabic Word-List from the Genizah'. *British Journal of Middle Eastern Studies* 34, no. 1 (2007): 63–74.

Sidarus, Adel Y. 'Introduction: Arabic Studies in Portugal (1772–1962)'. In *Islão e arabismo na península ibérica: Actas do*

XI Congresso da União Europeia de Arabistas e Islamólogos (Évora–Faro–Silves, 29 set.–6 out. 1982), edited by Adel Y. Sidarus, 55–76. Évora: Universidade de Évora, 1986.

———. 'Un recueil de traités philosophiques et médicaux à Lisbonne'. *Zeitschrift für die Geschichte der Arabisch-Islamischen Wissenschaften* 6 (1990): 179–89.

Siegert, Folker. 'Minor Jewish Hellenistic Authors'. In *A Guide to Early Jewish Texts and Traditions in Christian Transmission*, edited by Alexander Kulik, Gabriele Boccaccini, Lorenzo DiTommaso, David Hamidovic, and Michael Stone, 344–46. Oxford: Oxford University Press, 2019.

Sijpesteijn, Petra. 'The Archival Mind in Early Islamic Egypt: Two Arabic Papyri'. In *From al-Andalus to Khorasan: Documents from the Medieval Islamic World*, edited by Petra Sijpesteijn, Lennart Sundelin, Sofía Torallas Tovar, and Amalia Zomeño, 165–86. Leiden: Brill, 2007.

———. 'Army Economics: An Early Papyrus Letter Related to ʿAṭaʾ Payments'. In *Histories of the Middle East: Studies in Middle Eastern Society, Economy and Law in Honor of A. L. Udovich*, edited by Roxani Eleni Margariti, Adam Sabra, and Petra Sijpesteijn, 245–67. Leiden: Brill, 2011.

Sokoloff, Michael. *A Dictionary of Jewish Babylonian Aramaic*. Baltimore: Johns Hopkins University Press, 2002.

Spittler, Janet. 'Is Vienna Hist. Gr. 63, Fol. 51v–55v a "Fragment"?' *Ancient Jew Review*, 6 May 2019. https://www.ancientjewreview.com/read/2019/4/30/is-vienna-hist-gr-63-fol-51v-55v-a-fragment, accessed 20 January 2021.

Spufford, Francis, ed. *The Chatto Book of Cabbages and Kings: Lists in Literature*. London: Chatto and Windus, 1989.

Stallmann, Marco. *Johann Jakob Griesbach (1745–1812): Protestantische Dogmatik im populartheologischen Diskurs des 18. Jahrhunderts*. Beiträge zur historischen Theologie 190. Tübingen: Mohr Siebeck, 2019.

Steinert, Ulrike. 'Catalogues, Texts and Specialists: Some Thoughts on the Assur Medical Catalogue, Mesopotamian Medical Texts and Healing Professions'. In *Sources of Evil: Studies in Mesopotamian Exorcistic Lore*, edited by Greta van Buylaere, Mikko Luukko, Daniel Schwemer, and Avigail Mertens-Wagschal, 158–200. Leiden: Brill, 2018.

———, ed. *Assyrian and Babylonian Scholarly Text Catalogues: Medicine, Magic and Divination*. Berlin: De Gruyter, 2018.

Stern, Sacha. *Calendar and Community: A History of the Jewish Calendar, 2nd Century bce to 10th Century ce*. Oxford: Clarendon, 2001.

Stern, Samuel M. 'Notes on al-Kindī's Treatise on Definitions'. *Journal of the Royal Asiatic Society of Great Britain and Ireland* 1959, no. 1/2: 32–43.

Stewart, Columba. *Yours, Mine, or Theirs? Historical Observations on the Use, Collection and Sharing of Manuscripts in Western Europe and the Christian Orient*. Analecta Gorgiana 126. Piscataway, NJ: Gorgias Press, 2009.

Stone, Michael E. *Armenian Apocrypha Relating to Adam and Eve*. Studia in Veteris Testamenti Pseudepigrapha 14. Leiden: Brill, 1996.

———. *Ancient Judaism: New Visions and Views*. Grand Rapids, MI: Eerdmans, 2011.

———. *Armenian Apocrypha Relating to Abraham*. Early Judaism and Its Literature 37. Atlanta: SBL, 2012.

———. *Armenian Apocrypha Relating to Angels and Biblical Heroes*. Early Judaism and Its Literature 45. Atlanta: SBL, 2016.

Streck, Michael P. 'Dattelpalme und Tamariske in Mesopotamien nach dem akkadischen Streitgespräch'. *Zeitschrift für Assyriologie* 94 (2004): 250–90.

Stroumsa, Guy G. 'Early Christianity: A Religion of the Book?' In *Homer, the Bible, and Beyond: Literary and Religious Canons in the Ancient World*, edited by Margalit Finkelberg and Guy G. Stroumsa, 153–73. Jerusalem Studies in Religion and Culture 2. Leiden: Brill, 2003.

Supino Martini, Paola. 'La scrittura delle Scritture (sec. XI–XII)'. *Scrittura e civiltà* 12 (1988): 101–18.

Swanson, Reuben J. *New Testament Greek Manuscripts: Variant Readings Arranged in Horizontal Lines against Codex Vaticanus*. Sheffield: Academic Press & Pasadena: William Carey International University Press, 1995–.

Syed, Mairaj, Danny Halawi, Behnam Sadeghi, and Nazmus Saquib. 'Verifying Source Citations in the Hadith Literature'. *Journal of Medieval Worlds* 1, no. 3 (2019): 5–20. https://doi.org/10.1525/jmw.2019.130002.

Tarras, Peter. 'The Textual Genesis of al-Kindī's *On Definitions*'. Unpublished manuscript, 2021.

Ta-Shma, Israel M. 'The "Open" Book in Medieval Hebrew Literature: Problems of Authorized Editions'. *Bulletin of the John*

Rylands University Library Manchester 75, no. 3 (1993): 17–24.

Tayyara, Abed el-Rahman. 'Ibn Ḥabīb's *Kitāb al-Muḥabbar* and Its Place in Early Islamic Historical Writing'. *Journal of Islamic Studies* 29, no. 3 (2018): 392–416.

Thiele, Walter, ed. *Sapientia Salomonis*. Vol. 11/1 of *Vetus Latina*. Freiburg: Herder, 1977–1985.

———, ed. *Sirach (Ecclesiasticus)*. Vol. 11/2 of *Vetus Latina*. Freiburg: Herder, 1987–2005.

Tisserant, Eugene. 'Fragments syriaques du Livre des Jubilés'. *Revue biblique* 30 (1921): 55–86, 206–32.

Toepel, Alexander. 'Yonton Revisited: A Case Study in the Reception of Hellenistic Science within Early Judaism'. *Harvard Theological Review* 99 (2006): 235–45.

———. 'The Cave of Treasures: A New Translation and Introduction'. In *Old Testament Pseudepigrapha: More Noncanonical Scriptures*, edited by Richard Bauckham, James R. Davila, and Alexander Panayotov, 531–84. Grand Rapids, MI: Eerdmans, 2013.

Towner, W. S. *The Rabbinic 'Enumeration of Scriptural Examples': A Study of a Rabbinic Pattern of Discourse with Special Reference to Mekhilta d'R. Ishmael*. Leiden: Brill, 1973.

Trobisch, David. *The First Edition of the New Testament*. New York: Oxford University Press, 2000.

Tsumura, David T. 'List and Narrative in I Samuel 6,17–18a in the Light of Ugaritic Economic Texts'. *Zeitschrift für die alttestamentliche Wissenschaft* 113, no. 3 (2001): 353–69.

Tzoref, Shani. '4Q252: Listenwissenschaft and Covenantal Patriarchal Blessings'. In *'Go Out and Study the Land' (Judges 18:2): Archaeological, Historical and Textual Studies in Honor of Hanan Eshel*, edited by Aren M. Maeir, Jodi Magness and Lawrence Schiffman, 335–57. Leiden: Brill, 2011.

Unfer Verre, Elisabetta. 'Un contributo alla storia della miniatura a Montecassino nel XII secolo: La Bibbia di Ferro'. *Rivista di storia della miniatura* 14 (2010): 32–43.

———. 'Una Bibbia di Montecassino del XII secolo: Continuità e innovazione'. In *Per Gabriella: Studi in ricordo di Gabriella Braga*, edited by Marco Palma and Cinzia Vismara, 4:1799–1831. Cassino: Università degli studi di Cassino, 2013.

Utley, Francis Lee. 'The One Hundred and Three Names of Noah's Wife'. *Speculum* 16, no. 4 (1941): 426–52.

Uusimäki, Elisa. 'Mapping Ideal Ways of Living: Virtue and Vice Lists in 1QS and 4Q286'. *Journal for the Study of the Pseudepigrapha* 30, no. 1 (2020): 35–45.

Vacca, Alison. *Non-Muslim Provinces under Early Islam: Islamic Rule and Iranian Legitimacy in Armenia and Caucasian Albania*. Cambridge: Cambridge University Press, 2017.

Van de Mieroop, Marc. *Philosophy before the Greeks: The Pursuit of Truth in Ancient Babylonia*. Princeton: Princeton University Press, 2016.

Van der Horst, Pieter W. 'Seven Months' Children in Jewish and Christian Literature from Antiquity'. *Ephemerides Theologicae Lovanienses* 54, no. 4 (1978): 346–60.

VanderKam, James C. *Jubilees: A Commentary on the Book of Jubilees, Chapters 1–50*. 2 vols. Hermeneia: A Critical and Historical Commentary on the Bible. Minneapolis, MN: Fortress Press, 2018.

Van Peursen, Wido. 'La diffusion des manuscrits bibliques conserves: Typologie, organisation, nombre et époques de copie'. In *L'Ancien Testament en syriaque*, edited by Françoise Briquel Chatonnet and Philip le Moigne, 193–214. Études syraiques 5. Paris: Geuthner, 2008.

Van Rompay, Lukas. 'Past and Present Perceptions of Syriac Literary Tradition'. *Hugoye* 3, no. 1 (2000): 71–104.

———. '1.1.3 The Syriac Canon'. In *Textual History of the Bible*, edited by Armin Lange, vol. 2, *Deuterocanonical Scriptures*, edited by Frank Feder and Matthias Henze. Brill, 2019.

———. 'Flavius Josephus' *Jewish War* in Syriac: Ms. Milan, Biblioteca Ambrosiana B 21 Inf. And Two Recently Studied Manuscripts from Deir al-Surian'. In *Gli studi di storiographia: Tradizione, memoria e modernitá*, edited by Alba Fedeli, Rosa B. Finazzi, Claudia Milani, Craig E. Morrison, and Paolo Nicelli, 433–49. Orientalia Ambrosiana 6. Milan: Veneranda Biblioteca Ambrosiana, 2019.

Varghese, P. K. 'Mar Oudisho Metropolitan of Suwa and his Literary Works'. *The Harp* 8–9 (1995–96): 355–63.

Veccia Vaglieri, Laura. 'Al-Ḥarra'. In *Encyclopaedia of Islam, Second Edition*, edited by P. Bearman, Th. Bianquis, C. E. Bosworth, E. van Donzel, and W. P. Heinrichs. Brill, 2012. https://doi.org/10.1163/1573-3912_islam_SIM_2742.

Veldhuis, Niek. 'Elementary Education at Nipur: The Lists of Trees and Wooden Objects'. PhD dissertation, Groningen, 1997.

———. 'TIN.TIR = Babylon, the Question of Canonization and the Production of Meaning'. *Journal of Cuneiform Studies* 50 (1998): 77–85.

———. *History of the Cuneiform Lexical Tradition*. Münster: Ugarit, 2014.

Veltri, Giuseppe. *Magie und Halakha: Ansätze zu einem empirischen Wissenschaftsbegriff im spätantiken und frühmittelalterlichen Judentum*. Tübingen: Mohr Siebeck, 1997.

Visi, Tamás. 'A Science of Lists? Medieval Jewish Philosophers as List-Makers'. In *The Charm of a List: From the Sumerians to Computerised Data Processing*, edited by Lucie Doležalová, 12–33. Newcastle upon Tyne: Cambridge Scholars, 2009.

Vollandt, Ronny. 'Glosses of Hebrew: Medieval Arabic'. In *Encyclopedia of Hebrew Language and Linguistics*, edited by Geoffrey Khan, 2:62–65. Leiden: Brill, 2013.

———. 'Ancient Jewish Historiography in Arabic Garb: *Sefer Josippon* between Southern Italy and Coptic Cairo'. *Zutot* 11, no. 1 (2014): 70–80.

Von Contzen, Eva. 'Lists in Literature from the Middle Ages to Postmodernism'. *Style* 50, no. 3 (2016): 342–58.

———. 'The Limits of Narration: Lists and Literary History'. *Style* 50, no. 3 (2016): 241–60.

———. 'Theorising Lists in Literature: Towards a Listology'. In *Lists and Catalogues in Ancient Literature and Beyond: Towards a Poetics of Enumeration*, edited by Rebecca Laemmle,

Cédric Scheidegger Laemmle, and Katharina Wesselmann, 35–55. Berlin: De Gruyter, 2021.

Von Soden, Hermann. *Die Schriften des neuen Testaments in ihrer ältesten erreichbaren Textgestalt hergestellt auf Grund ihrer Textgeschichte*, part 1. Berlin: Duncker, 1902.

Von Soden, Wolfram. 'Leistung und Grenze sumerischer und babylonischer Wissenschaft'. *Die Welt als Geschichte* 2 (1936): 411–64, 509–57.

Wallraff, Martin. *Kodex und Kanon: Das Buch im frühen Christentum*. Hans-Lietzmann-Vorlesungen 12. Berlin: De Gruyter, 2013.

———. 'The Canon Tables of the Psalms: An Unknown Work of Eusebius of Caesarea'. *Dumbarton Oaks Papers* 67 (2013): 1–14.

———. *Die Kanontafeln des Euseb von Kaisareia: Untersuchung und kritische Edition*. Manuscripta Biblica 1. Berlin: De Gruyter, 2021.

Weeks, Stuart, Simon Gathercole, and Loren Stuckenbruck. *The Book of Tobit: Texts from the Principal Ancient and Medieval Traditions*. Fontes et Subsidia ad Biblia pertinentes 3. Berlin: De Gruyter, 2004.

Wessel, Klaus. 'Kanontafeln'. *Reallexikon zur byzantinischen Kunst*, vol. 3, edited by Klaus Wessel and Marcell Restle, 927–68. Stuttgart: Hiersemann, 1978.

Westenholz, Aage. 'The Graeco-Babyloniaca Once Again'. *Zeitschrift für Assyriologie* 97 (2007): 262–313.

Whiston, William. *A Collection of Authentick Records Belonging to the Old and the New Testament*. London: Printed for the author, 1728.

Wintermute, O. S. 'Jubilees'. In *The Old Testament Pseudepigrapha*, vol. 2, edited by James Charlesworth, 35–142. New Haven: Yale University Press, 1985.

Witakowski, Witold. 'Mart(y) Shmuni, the Mother of the Maccabean Martyrs, in Syriac Tradition'. In *VI Symposium Syriacum, 1992*, edited by R. Lavenant, 153–68. Orientalia Christiana Analecta 247. Rome: Pontificio Istituto Orientale, 1994.

Wright, Jonathon. 'After Antiquity: Joseph and Aseneth in Manuscript Transmission—A Case Study for Engaging with What Came after the Original Version of Jewish Pseudepigrapha'. PhD dissertation, University of Oxford, 2018.

Wright, William. *Catalogue of Syriac Manuscripts in the British Museum Acquired Since the Year 1838*. Vol. 2. London: British Library, 1872.

———. *A Short History of Syriac Literature*, 2nd ed. London: A&C Black, 1894. Reprinted, Amsterdam: Philo Press, 1966.

Wünsche, August. 'Die Zahlensprüche im Talmud und Midrasch'. *Zeitschrift der Deutschen Morgenländischen Gesellschaft* 65 (1911): 57–100.

Wurtzel, Carl. *Khalifa ibn Khayyat's History on the Umayyad Dynasty (660–750)*. Prepared for publication by Robert Hoyland. Liverpool: Liverpool University Press, 2015.

Yawn, Lila. 'Temporary Workshops and Clustered Production of Italian Giant Bibles and Patristic Manuscripts'. In *Comment* *le Livre s'est fait livre: La fabrication des manuscrits bibliques (IVe–XVe siècles). Bilan, résultats, perspectives de recherche: Actes du colloque international organisé à Namur du 23 au 25 mai 2012*, edited by Chiara Ruzzier and Xavier Hermand, 87–109. Turnhout: Brepols, 2015.

Young, Liam Cole. 'On Lists and Networks: An Archeology of Form'. *Amodern* 2 (2013). https://amodern.net/article/on-lists-and-networks/, accessed 18 November 2021.

———. 'Un-Black Boxing the List: Knowledge, Materiality, and Form'. *Canadian Journal of Communication* 38 (2013): 497–516.

———. *List Cultures: Knowledge and Poetics from Mesopotamia to BuzzFeed*. Amsterdam: Amsterdam University Press, 2017.

Young, Robin Darling. 'The Anonymous Mēmrā on the Maccabees: Jewish Pseudepigraphon or Late Antique Festal Poem?' *Jews and Syriac Christians: Intersections across the First Millennium*, edited by Aaron Michael Butts and Simcha Gross, 321–35. Texts and Studies in Ancient Judaism 180. Tübingen: Mohr Siebeck, 2020.

Zambardi, Elvira. 'Le bibbie glossate conservate a Montecassino: ricerche in corso'. *Gazette du livre médiéval* 66 (2022): 142–51.

INDEX

A
Abdisho of Nisibis, 62–103
Ancient Near East, 26
antiquity, 2n3, 18, 142, 158, 195, 198, 284
apocrypha, 73, 73n31, 77n40, 78, 78n44, 79n48, 80
astrology, 31, 115, 118, 137
astronomy, 31, 115, 118, 137, 161

B
biography, 173

C
canon, 29, 29n17, 62–63, 69–70, 70n25, 74–76, 78n44, 83, 96–97, 97n100, 99, 101, 191, 195, 197–99, 199n9, 200–9, 211, 257–58
canonisation, 29, 29n17
catalogue, 23–24, 26, 29n20, 31, 33, 33n33, 34, 37–43, 45, 48–50, 52–53, 53n84, 54, 54n85, 55–59, 59n101, 60–61, 62n2, 63–67, 69n23, 70–71, 73–74, 80, 85, 89, 93, 95–102, 105n4, 181, 189, 192, 306, 316
Cave of Treasures, 142–44, 147–50, 157–59, 161–65, 167–69
Christianity, 29n17, 62–63, 70, 70n25, 71, 73, 77, 78n44, 81, 86–87, 91, 93–95, 123, 144, 148, 159, 171, 180, 186, 198–99, 201, 201n13, 202–4, 208, 213
chronography, 173, 175
cluster, 26, 36, 44, 49–50, 54–55, 58, 63n3, 72n30, 85, 100, 132, 275, 304
compilation, 3, 6, 32, 32n28, 42, 56, 106, 173
container, 24–26, 41, 43, 59
cultural inventory, 60
curriculum, 37, 40, 220

D
deictic, 30, 194, 205–6
divination, 3, 10, 15, 18

E
East Syriac, 65, 65n13, 74–75, 95n99, 97–98, 98n102, 99, 101–3, 163
editing, 128–29, 138, 267
embryology, 48n72, 49, 57
encyclopedia, 31, 44, 52, 110
epistemic genre, 23–61
epistemology, 38, 83
eschatology, 31
exegesis, 9, 21, 40, 58, 315

experiment, 42, 59, 315

G

genealogy, 3, 27, 34, 37, 94n94, 143, 145, 148, 148n26, 149, 163, 167, 179–180, 189, 248
geography, 27, 31, 38, 189
giant bibles, 291–92

H

ḥadīth, 175–76, 176n10, 247, 249–50, 252–55, 257–60, 263–66, 268, 270, 275, 278
Halakha, 57
Hebrew Bible, 25–26, 63, 63n3, 64, 66, 66n15, 67, 67n19, 69, 69n23, 70–76, 80, 81n57, 82, 84, 89, 91–92, 94–95, 95n99, 96–98, 98n104, 99, 99n105, 100, 145, 149, 203, 218n7, 235n44, 246
historiography, 31, 172–75, 177, 179, 181–83, 185, 187–89, 204
horizontal, 16, 34, 34n36, 35n37, 124, 127, 193–94, 207, 236
hymn, 7–8, 8n19, 21, 88n78, 217

I

illness, 36, 44, 44n65, 48n73, 55, 57, 59–60
information, 21–22, 24, 24n3, 27, 31, 37–38, 46n69, 54, 58, 63n3, 101, 114, 114n30, 132, 138, 143, 150, 157–58, 161, 163, 166, 170–71, 173, 176, 181, 192–93, 207, 217, 225, 240, 246, 250, 256, 256n18, 263, 269–72, 274–75, 280
inscription, 6, 7n15, 209, 211–13
instruction, 24, 28–29, 37, 39, 45, 48, 48n73, 50–52, 54, 58, 129, 195, 263
Islam, 28n14, 32, 32n28, 34n36, 44n65, 107, 134n62, 171–90, 247, 249, 251–53, 255, 256n18, 257, 259, 261–65, 267, 269, 271, 273, 275, 277, 279, 281
isnād, 176, 176n10, 247–81

J

Jubilees, 73n32, 83n61, 141n2, 142–47, 149–50, 153, 156–60, 162–64, 166–70
Judaism, 25–26, 29, 31, 34, 34n36, 38, 41, 45, 47, 62–63, 69, 72n30, 76, 76n39, 78–79, 81–82, 83n61, 89, 94, 99–100, 107n9, 142, 144, 171, 200, 202, 216, 220, 223, 251–52

L
late antiquity, 25, 61–62, 73, 91, 105, 143, 171, 283
library, 24, 40, 116, 119–20, 176, 192, 202, 292n7, 299, 306
list,
  administrative, 1, 1n2, 2n4, 27n11, 34, 41, 175, 178–79, 186–188, 219
  as content, 28, 28n13, 35, 38, 40, 55, 124, 127, 129, 168, 173–83, 222, 225, 227, 244–45, 248–50, 277, 280, 319
  as framework, 45, 49, 54, 173–74, 188–89
  bibliographical, 105
  chapter, 105, 221, 282–321
  definition, 106–140
  genealogical, 27n10, 148, 148n26, 149, 166, 173n5, 179
  heritage, 96, 98–99, 101, 103, 107
  lexicographical, 1, 136
  ordering, 26, 28n14, 39, 41, 97, 249
  philosophical, 104, 106–7, 109, 112–13, 131–32, 136–37
  shopping, 23, 34, 45, 192
  terminological, 106, 108, 121, 135
Listenwissenschaft, 5, 5n10, 26n8, 30n21, 40n54, 41
lost books, 62–63, 69, 76, 83, 99

M
manuscript, 8n19, 35, 65n14, 67, 67n19, 69n23, 77, 77n43, 78–79, 83, 85, 88, 91, 91n84, 92, 94n94, 95n99, 97n101, 100, 103, 106n8, 108, 109n11, 110–16, 118–27, 129, 129n54, 137–38, 141–42, 145, 145n11, 147–48, 150–52, 156, 156n34, 158, 160, 162, 166, 168, 171, 195, 198, 202, 202n14, 208–9, 211–12, 217–19, 226, 232, 244, 260–61, 263, 273, 280, 282–84, 290, 292, 295n14, 297–303, 306, 310, 312, 316, 320–321
mathematics, 106, 115, 118, 137
Maʿase Torah, 30, 32, 58
medicine, 31, 106, 115, 133
meteorology, 115, 118
Middle Ages, 26, 62, 73, 77, 91, 142–143, 158, 171, 215n1, 305
Midrash, 25, 29, 31n25, 58, 156n35, 158
Mishnah, 25n7, 30n21, 40n54, 44, 46–47, 86, 216
monotheism, 4, 5n9, 6, 22

Montecassino, 286–89, 291–92, 292n7, 305–9, 314–15, 317–18

N
narrative, 24–25, 33, 35, 43n63, 45, 48–49, 49n74, 55, 57–58, 58n98, 58n99, 71, 87–88, 88n78, 92, 94, 100, 143–44, 147–48, 148n26, 149, 163, 167, 174, 177, 181–82, 185, 188–90, 247–50, 260, 268–71, 274, 276–78
New Testament, 66, 71, 71n27, 89, 95, 98, 194n4, 199, 199n9, 202, 282, 283n4, 292, 309

P
paragraph marks, 125, 138
pharmaceutics, 44, 120
philosophy, 104, 104n2, 105n4, 106, 106n8, 112, 115, 117–18, 120–21, 132, 137
Pirqe de-Rabbi Eliezer, 36, 36n40
pregnancy, 48–49, 58, 60
prescription, 28, 33–34, 44–45, 48–49
prosopography, 173
punctuation, 124

R
recipe, 37, 43, 48–58, 220

S
salvation history, 28, 45
scribe, 2n4, 6–7, 20–21, 85, 88, 94, 101, 115–19, 126, 129, 137–38, 157, 162, 170–71, 179, 216n4, 218, 218n8, 219n9, 225, 231, 245–46, 249, 264, 266, 268–69, 271, 274–76, 279, 290, 294, 294n11, 300–1, 303, 305n19, 318
Seder Eliyahu, 29n19, 31
Shabbat, 27, 58, 216n4, 224, 227, 229, 233, 237, 240
structure, 23–24, 27n11, 34–35, 36n40, 38, 41, 45, 49–50, 50n78, 52–54, 59, 65n13, 70, 107–8, 113, 124–125, 127, 131, 134, 134n63, 137–38, 152, 181, 186, 188, 200, 211, 227, 248–50, 267, 271, 283–84, 300, 319
Sugya, 47
synopsis, 42, 79n48, 191–94, 196, 203, 206, 247n1, 282
syntax, 86, 127, 168

T
Talmud, 25, 36, 36n42, 44, 49, 53, 144, 158, 221, 223
taxonomy, 26, 29, 31, 42–44, 44n65, 60, 220
temporality, 45

textual, 23–25, 28, 50, 58, 83, 87, 106n8, 107, 107n9, 109–10, 114, 119, 125, 128–29, 137–38, 142, 150, 152, 156, 172n1, 174, 185, 189, 199, 204, 207, 211, 231, 248–50, 260, 266, 280, 284, 290–91, 293n10, 294, 299, 305, 313, 320–21
therapy, 48, 52, 55, 57
time, 7, 22, 31–33, 38, 45, 47–48, 55, 58, 60, 95, 98, 101, 109, 112, 115, 121, 123, 128, 133, 139, 147, 176–77, 180, 186, 188, 192–93, 200–3, 208, 212, 216–17, 236, 242, 248, 252, 254–55, 257–58, 260, 262, 266–67, 271–80, 301, 316, 318

V
vertical, 14, 14n31, 32, 32n30, 34–35, 35n37, 53n84, 124–25, 193–94, 206, 309n26

About the Team

Alessandra Tosi was the managing editor for this book and provided quality control.

Anne Burberry performed the copyediting of the book in Word. The fonts used in this volume are Charis SIL, SBL Hebrew, SBL Greek, Scheherazade New, Estrangelo Edessa, and Serto Antioch Bible.

Cameron Craig created all of the editions — paperback, hardback, and PDF. Conversion was performed with open source software freely available on our GitHub page at https://github.com/OpenBookPublishers.

Jeevanjot Kaur Nagpal designed the cover of this book. The cover was produced in InDesign using Fontin and Calibri fonts.

Cambridge Semitic Languages and Cultures

General Editor Geoffrey Khan

Cambridge Semitic Languages and Cultures

About the series

This series is published by Open Book Publishers in collaboration with the Faculty of Asian and Middle Eastern Studies of the University of Cambridge. The aim of the series is to publish in open-access form monographs in the field of Semitic languages and the cultures associated with speakers of Semitic languages. It is hoped that this will help disseminate research in this field to academic researchers around the world and also open up this research to the communities whose languages and cultures the volumes concern. This series includes philological and linguistic studies of Semitic languages and editions of Semitic texts. Titles in the series will cover all periods, traditions and methodological approaches to the field. The editorial board comprises Geoffrey Khan, Aaron Hornkohl, and Esther-Miriam Wagner.

This is the first Open Access book series in the field; it combines the high peer-review and editorial standards with the fair Open Access model offered by OBP. Open Access (that is, making texts free to read and reuse) helps spread research results and other educational materials to everyone everywhere, not just to those who can afford it or have access to well-endowed university libraries.

Copyrights stay where they belong, with the authors. Authors are encouraged to secure funding to offset the publication costs and thereby sustain the publishing model, but if no institutional funding is available, authors are not charged for publication. Any grant secured covers the actual costs of publishing and is not taken as profit. In short: we support publishing that respects the authors and serves the public interest.

This book was copyedited by Anne Burberry.

Other titles of the series

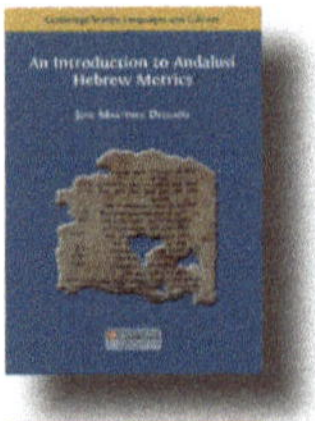

An Introduction to Andalusi Hebrew Metrics

José Martínez Delgado

doi.org/10.11647/OBP.0351

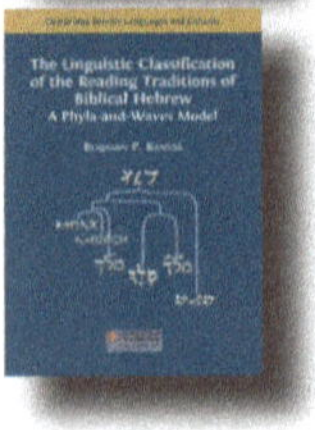

The Linguistic Classification of the Reading Traditions of Biblical Hebrew: A Phyla-and-Waves Model

Benjamin Paul Kantor

doi.org/10.11647/OBP.0210

UNIVERSITY OF CAMBRIDGE
Faculty of Asian and Middle Eastern Studies

More information and a complete list of books in this series can be found at:
https://www.openbookpublishers.com/series/2632-6914

www.ingramcontent.com/pod-product-compliance
Lightning Source LLC
Chambersburg PA
CBHW040332300426
44113CB00021B/2735
* 9 7 8 1 8 0 5 1 1 1 1 8 4 *